District Gazetteers of India Series 46

BENGAL DISTRICT GAZETTEERS

EASTERN BENGAL AND ASSAM

NOAKHALI

J. E. WEBSTER

52 VOLUMES

(VOL. 35th)

GYAN

Published by

Gyan Publishing House
5, Ansari Road
Daryaganj, New Delhi-110002
Phone: 011-47034999, 9811692060
E-mail: books@gyanbooks.com

Distribution Network
gyanbooks.com
India, USA, Canada, UK, Australia, France

ISBN: 978-93-6208-915-1 (Set) 52 Volumes
978-81-212-5909-5 (PB)

First Published, 1911

2nd Impression 2024

Printed at: Gyan Press, Delhi.

BENGAL DISTRICT GAZETTEERS (VOL. 35th)
Author:J. E. Webster

District Gazetteers of India Series 46

BENGAL DISTRICT GAZETTEERS

EASTERN BENGAL AND ASSAM

NOAKHALI

LIST OF VOLUMES

S. NO.	ISBN NO.	VOLUME	TITLE	AUTHOR	PRICE	PAGES
			ASSAM DISTRICT GAZETTEERS			
1	9788121285926	1st	Cachar	B. C. Allen	600	300
2	9788121285919	2nd	Sylhet	B. C. Allen	750	378
3	9788121285902	3rd	Goalpara	B. C. Allen	400	203
4	9788121285896	4th	Kamrup	B. C. Allen	675	344
5	9788121285889	5th	Darrang	B. C. Allen	725	364
6	9788121285872	6th	Nowgong	B. C. Allen	560	280
7	9788121285865	7th	Sibsagar	B. C. Allen	675	343
8	9788121285858	8th	Lakhimpur	B. C. Allen	690	347
9	9788121285841	9th	Naga Hills and Manipur	B. C. Allen	580	294
10	9788121285834	10th	The Khasi And Jaintia Hills, The Garo Hills And The Lushai Hills	B. C. Allen	675	363
11	9788121285827	11th	The Sadiya and Balipara Frontier Tract	B. C. Allen	375	190
			BENGAL DISTRICT GAZETTEERS			
12	9788121218672	1st	Angul	L. S. S. O'Malley	340	168
13	9788121259637	2nd	Bakarganj	J. C. JACK	970	194
14	9788121218696	3rd	Balasore	L. S. S. O'Malley	450	228
15	9788121259590	4th	Bankura	L. S. S. O'Malley	1000	199
16	9788121218375	5th	Bhagalpur	J. Byrne	390	194
17	9788121218290	6th	Birbhum	L. S. S. O'Malley	300	150
18	9788121259651	7th	Eastern Bengal and Assam - Bogra	J. N. Gupta	940	188
19	9788121218351	8th	Burdwan	J. C. K. Peterson	450	227
20	9788121259538	9th	Calcutta District Gazetteer - Statistics, 1901 - 02		340	68
21	9788121218313	10th	Champaran	L. S. S. O'Malley	410	205
22	9788121259613	11th	Eastern Bengal District Gazetters - Chittagong	L. S. S. O'Malley	1080	216
23	9788121259552	12th	Chota Nagpur Tributary		130	26
24	9788121259415	13th	The Cooch Behar Gazette: Statistics		1460	292
25	9788121218412	14th	Cuttack	L. S. S. O'Malley	490	248
26	9788121261357	15th	Eastern Bengal District Gazetteers Dacca	B. C. Allen	400	207
27	9788121218436	16th	Darbhanga	L. S. S. O'Malley	360	180
28	9789362089335	17th	Darjeeling	L. S. S. O'Malley	500	248
29	9788121259453	18th	Eastern Bengal District Gazetteers - Dinajpur	F. W. Strong	890	178
30	9788121259392	19th	Faridpur	L. S. S. O'Malley	700	140
31	9788121218474	20th	Gaya	L. S. S. O'Malley	540	270
32	9788121214032	21st	Bihar and Orissa District Gazetteer: Hazaribagh	E. Lister	715	234
33	9788121218337	22nd	Hooghly	L. S. S. O'Malley	680	340
34	9788121218191	23rd	Bengal District Gazetteer Howrah	L. S. S. O'Malley	390	199
35	9788121259293	24th	Eastern Bengal and Assam - Jalpaiguri	John F. Gruning	890	178
36	9788121259279	25th	Jessore	L. S. S. O'Malley	960	192
37	9788121259231	26th	Khulna	L. S. S. O'Malley	1100	220
38	9788121259217	27th	Malda	G. E. Lambourn	670	134
39	9788121267854	28th	Manbhum	H. Coupland	600	313
40	9788121218498	29th	Midnapore	L. S. S. O'Malley	500	252
41	9788121218597	30th	Monghyr	L. S. S. O'Malley	560	280
42	9788121259156	31st	Murshidabad	L. S. S. O'Malley	1250	250
43	9788121259576	32nd	Bengal District Gazetteers - Muzaffarpur	L. S. S. O'Malley	940	188
44	9788121259132	33rd	Mymensingh	F. A. Sachse	960	192
45	9788121259118	34th	Nadia	J. H. E. Garrett	1070	214
46	9788121259095	35th	Eastern Bengal and Assam - Noakhali	J. E. Webster	580	115
47	9788121218450	36th	Feudatory States of Orissa	L. E. B. Cobdenramsay	790	395
48	9788121259071	37th	Pabna	L. S. S. O'Malley	710	142
49	9788121218511	38th	Palamau	L. S. S. O'Malley	380	190
50	9788121218634	39th	Patna	L. S. S. O'Malley	500	250
51	9788121218535	40th	Puri	L. S. S. O'Malley	650	328
52	9788121218757	41st	Purnea	L. S. S. O'Malley	440	220
53	9788121258937	42nd	Rajshahi	L. S. S. O'Malley	1080	216
54	9788121256681	43rd	Bihar and Orissa District Gazetteers: Ranchi	M. G. Hallett	1350	278
55	9788121258913	44th	Eastern Bengal and assam - Rangpur	J. A. Vas	890	178
56	9788121218559	45th	Sambalpur	L. S. S. O'Malley	480	242
57	9788121214056	46th	Santal Parganas	L. S. S. O'Malley	940	308
58	9788121218610	47th	Saran	L. S. S. O'Malley	380	190
59	9788121218658	48th	Shahabad	L. S. S. O'Malley	380	190
60	9788121256704	49th	The Gazetteer of Sikhim	H. H. Risley	960	481
61	9788121218573	50th	Singhbhum, Saraikela And Kharsawan	L. S. S. O'Malley	560	280
62	9788121259439	51st	Eastern Bengal District Gazetteers - Tippera	J. E. Webster	730	146
63	9788121259033	52nd	24 Parganas	L. S. S. O'Malley	1420	284

S. NO.	ISBN NO.	VOLUME	TITLE	AUTHOR	PRICE	PAGES
			CENTRAL PROVINCES DISTRICT GAZETTEERS			
64	9789362081728	1st, Vol. A	Akola (Descriptive)	A. E. Nelson, C. Brown	870	436
65	9789362085481	2nd, Vol. A	Amraoti (Descriptive)	S. V. Fitzgerald, A. E. Nelson	1050	524
66	9789362089267	3rd,Vol. A	Balaghat (Descriptive)	R. V. RUSSELL	430	216
67	9789362083494	4th, Vol. A	Betul (Descriptive)	R. V. RUSSELL	610	306
68	9789362085146	5th, Vol. A	Bhandara (Descriptive)	R. V. RUSSELL	580	292
69	9789362088390	6th, Vol. A	Bilaspur (Descriptive)	R. V. RUSSELL	870	434
70	9789362086044	7th, Vol. A	Buldana (Descriptive)	A. E. Nelson	1090	543
71	9789362089014	8th, Vol. B	Chanda (Descriptive)	R. V. RUSSELL	470	234
72	9789362086938	9th	Chhattisgarch Feudatory State	E. A. De Brett	880	440
73	9789362082961	10th	Chhindwara (Descriptive)	R. V. RUSSELL	550	274
74	9789362089342	11th, Vol. A & B	Damoh (Descriptive and Statistical Tables 1891-1901)	R. V. RUSSELL	830	414
75	9789362081230	12th, Vol. A	Durg (Descriptive)	A. E. Nelson	460	232
76	9789362086037	13th, Vol. A	Hoshangabad (Descriptive)	R. V. RUSSELL	860	430
77	9789362086792	14th, Vol. A	Jubbulpore (Descriptive)	A. E. Nelson	950	474
78	9789362089663	15th, Vol. A & B	Mandla (Descriptive and Statistical Tables 1891-1901)	R. V. RUSSELL	370	186
79	9789362086419	16th, Vol. A	Nagpur (Descriptive)	R. V. RUSSELL	790	394
80	9789362080646	17th, Vol. A	Narsinghpur (Descriptive)	R. V. RUSSELL	510	257
81	9789362084835	18th, Vol. A	Nimar (Descriptive)	R. V. RUSSELL	600	299
82	9789362087737	19th, Vol. A	Raipur (Descriptive)	A. E. Nelson	790	396
83	9789362080264	20th, Vol. A	Saugor (Descriptive)	R. V. RUSSELL	570	285
84	9789362081117	21st, Vol. A	Seoni (Descriptive)	R. V. RUSSELL	460	232
85	9789362084965	22nd, Vol. A	Wardha (Descriptive)	R. V. RUSSELL	600	302
86	9789362083401	23rd, Vol. A	Yeotmal (Descriptive)	R. V. RUSSELL	550	277
87	9789362080325	24th, Vol. I, Pt. I	Gwalior (Text and Tables)	R. V. RUSSELL	980	489
88	9789362087133	24th, Vol. I, Pt. II	Gwalior (Maps)	R. V. RUSSELL	400	198
89	9789362086341	24th, Vol. I, Pt. III	Gwalior (Village List)	R. V. RUSSELL	810	406
90	9789362085467	24th, Vol. I, Pt. IV	Gwalior (Photos)	R. V. RUSSELL	1400	698
91	9789362087393	25th, Vol. II	Indore (Text and Tables)	C. E. Luard	1050	524
92	9789362084422	26th, Vol. III	Bhopal (Text and Tables)	C. E. Luard	540	272
93	9789362086815	27th, Vol. IV	Rewah (Text and Tables)	C. E. Luard	500	250
94	9789362087584	28th, Vol. V, Pt. A	Western States - Malwa (Text)	C. E. Luard	1520	762
95	9789362087300	29th, Vol. VI, Pt. A	Eastern States - Bundelkhand (Text)	C. E. Luard	930	463
96	9789362082169	30th, Vol. VI, Pt. B	Eastern States - Bundelkhand (Tables)	C. E. Luard	830	417
			GAZETTEER OF THE BOMBAY PRESIDENCY:			
97	9788121283441	1st, Part I	History of Gujarat	Ed.: James M. Campbell	3220	644
98	9788121285582	1st, Part II	History of the Konkan Dakhan and Southern Maratha Country	Ed.: James M. Campbell	4200	840
99	9788121285568	2nd	Gujarat, Surat and Broach	Ed.: James M. Campbell	2990	598
100	9788121285544	3rd	Kaira and Panch Mahals	Ed.: James M. Campbell	1690	339
101	9788121285520	4th	Ahmedabad	Ed.: James M. Campbell	1860	372
102	9788121285506	5th	Cutch, Palanpur, and Mahi Kantha	Ed.: James M. Campbell	2390	478
103	9788121285483	6th	Rewa Kantha, Narukot, Cambay, and Surat States	Ed.: James M. Campbell	1450	290
104	9788121285469	7th	Baroda	Ed.: James M. Campbell	3260	652
105	9788121285445	8th	Kathiawar	Ed.: James M. Campbell	3790	758
106	9788121285421	9th, Part I	Gujarat Population - Hindus	Ed.: James M. Campbell	3170	636
107	9788121285407	9th, Part II	Gujarat Population - Musalmans and Parsis	Ed.: James M. Campbell	1520	304
108	9788121285384	10th	Ratnagiri and Savantvadi	Ed.: James M. Campbell	2500	501
109	9788121285360	11th	Kolaba and Janjira	Ed.: James M. Campbell	2550	513
110	9788121285346	12th	Khandesh	Ed.: James M. Campbell	3190	638
111	9788121285322	13th Part I	Thana	Ed.: James M. Campbell	2050	413
112	9788121285308	13th Part II	Thana	Ed.: James M. Campbell	1770	357
113	9788121285285	14th	Thana - Places of Interest	Ed.: James M. Campbell	3290	659
114	9788121285261	15th Part I	Kanara	Ed.: James M. Campbell	2340	348
115	9788121285247	15th Part II	Kanara	Ed.: James M. Campbell	1740	348
116	9788121285223	16th	Nasik	Ed.: James M. Campbell	3490	698
117	9788121285209	17th	Ahmadnagar	Ed.: James M. Campbell	3860	772
118	9788121285186	18th Part I	Poona	Ed.: James M. Campbell	2930	586
119	9788121285162	18th Part II	Poona	Ed.: James M. Campbell	2680	537
120	9788121285148	18th Part III	Poona	Ed.: James M. Campbell	2500	503
121	9788121285124	19th	Satara	Ed.: James M. Campbell	3450	692
122	9788121285100	20th	Sholapur	Ed.: James M. Campbell	2730	547
123	9788121285087	21st	Gazetteer of the Bomaby Presidency: Belgaum	Ed.: James M. Campbell	2570	514
124	9788121285063	22nd	Dharwar	Ed.: James M. Campbell	4200	841
125	9788121285049	23rd	Gazetteer of the Bombay Presidency:Bijapur	Ed.: James M. Campbell	3550	712
126	9788121285025	24th	Kolhapur	Ed.: James M. Campbell	2250	450

S. NO.	ISBN NO.	VOLUME	TITLE	AUTHOR	PRICE	PAGES
127	9788121285001	25th	Botany	Ed.: James M. Campbell	2040	408
128	9788121284981	26th, Part I	Materials Towards a Statistical Account of the Town and Island of Bombay - History	Ed.: James M. Campbell	2500	504
129	9788121284967	26th, Part II	Materials Towards a Statistical Account of the Town and Island of Bombay - Trade and Fortifications	Ed.: James M. Campbell	2690	538
130	9788121284943	26th, Part III	Materials Towards a Statistical Account of the Town And Island of Bombay - Administration	Ed.: James M. Campbell	2450	702
131	9788121284929	27th	General Index	Ed.:R. E. Enthoven	2190	428

MADRAS DISTRICT GAZETTEERS

S. NO.	ISBN NO.	VOLUME	TITLE	AUTHOR	PRICE	PAGES
132	9788121258814	1st	Anantapur	W. Francis	1140	227
133	9788121258555	2nd	Malabar	C. A Innes & F. B Evans	3010	602
134	9788121258791	3rd	Bellary	W. Francis	1890	377
135	9788121258777	4th	Statistical Appendix For Chingleput		280	56
136	9788121258753	5th	Coimbatore	K. N. Krishnaswami Ayyar	3420	628
137	9788121232814	6th	Madras District Gazetteers District Gazetteer Cuddapah	C. F. Brackenbury	1120	285
138	9788121258715	7th	Statistical Appendix For Ganjam		370	73
139	9788121256766	8th, Vol. 1st	Godavari District Gazetteer	F. R. Hemingway	650	320
140	9788121256803	8th, Vol. 2nd	Godavari District Gazetteer	F. R. Hemingway	160	83
141	9788121258678	9th	Statistical Appendix For Kistna		640	127
142	9788121258654	10th	Statistical Appendix For Kurnool		270	54
143	9788121258616	11th	Madura	W. Francis	1900	379
144	9788121258579	12th	Statistical Appendix For Madura		740	148
145	9788121258630	13th	The Nilgiris	W. Francis	2190	437
146	9788121234276	14th	Madras District Gazetteers Gazetteer Of The Nellore District Brought Upto 1938		1150	386
147	9788121258517	15th	North Arcot		590	118
148	9788121258494	16th, Vol. 1, Part I	Salem	F. J. Richards	1710	343
149	9788121258593	16th, Vol. 1, Part II	Salem	F. J. Richards	1800	360
150	9788121258456	17th	South Arcot	W. Francis	2400	480
151	9788121258470	18th	Statistical Appendix For South Canara		400	80
152	9788121258432	19th, Vol. 1st & 2nd	Tanjore: Main Volume and Statistical Appendix		2070	401
153	9788121258395	20th	Tinnevelly	H. R. Pate	2740	547
154	9788121258418	21st	Statistical Appendix For Tinnevelly		320	64
155	9788121258371	22nd, 1st & 2nd	Trichinopoly: Main Volume and Statistical Appendix	F. R. Hemingway	2440	487
156	9788121241953	23rd	Vizagapatam District Gazetteer	W. Francis	760	385

PUNJAB DISTRICT GAZETTEERS

S. NO.	ISBN NO.	VOLUME	TITLE	AUTHOR	PRICE	PAGES
157	9788121255943	1st	Ambala District 1883-84		620	124
158	9788121255967	2nd	Amritsar		1180	236
159	9788121255981	3rd	Delhi		1300	260
160	9788121256001	4th	Ferozepore		950	188
161	9788121256025	5th	Faridkot		350	70
162	9788121256049	6th	Gujranwala 1893-94		1270	254
163	9788121256063	7th	Gujrat	C. E. Luard	1140	228
164	9788121256087	8th	Gurdaspur 1891-92		1260	252
165	9788121256100	9th	Gurgaon 1883-4		1020	203
166	9788121256124	10th	Hazara	H. D. Watson	2290	458
167	9788121256148	11th	Hissar district and Lohar State		1840	367
168	9788121256162	12th	Hoshiarpur		1420	283
169	9788121256186	13th	Jhang		1070	213
170	9788121256209	14th	Jhelam		1010	202
171	9788121256223	15th	Jalandhar District 1883-84		540	108
172	9788121256247	16th, Vol. XIV-A	Jullundur District, with maps and Kapurthala		1990	398
173	9788121256261	17th, Pt. I	Kangra (Proper)		1450	290
174	9788121256285	17th, Pt. II	Kangra (Kulu, Lahual, Spiti)		1800	357
175	9788121256308	18th	Karnal		1930	386
176	9788121256322	19th	Kohat		1540	307
177	9788121256346	20th	The Lahore District 1883-84		1220	244
178	9788121256384	21st	Ludhiana and Maler Kotla		1680	335
179	9788121256407	22nd	Lyallpur		735	147
180	9788121256421	23rd	Mianwali		1170	234
181	9788121256445	24th	Montgomery	P. J. Fagan	1590	318
182	9788121258364	25th	Multan (1901-02)	E. D. Maclagan	2400	480
183	9788121258708	26th	The Rohtak District 1883-84		980	196
184	9788121258746	27th, Vol. III A	Dujana State 1904		500	16
185	9788121256483	28th	Shahpur District		1780	356
186	9788121256506	29th	Simla District		800	159

S. NO.	ISBN NO.	VOLUME	TITLE	AUTHOR	PRICE	PAGES
187	9788121256520	30th	The Chamba State		2040	408
188	9788121256544	31st	The Chenab Colony 1904		1550	310
189	9788121256568	32nd	Kalsia State		270	53
190	9788121256582	33rd	Suket and Mandi		770	154
191	9788121256605	34th	Phulkian States, Patiala Jind And Nabha 1904		2070	414
192	9788121256643	35th	Simla Hill States		2220	443
193	9788121256667	36th	Sirmur		920	183
			RAJPUTANA DISTRICT GAZETTEERS			
194	9789362088994	1st, Vol. I-A & B	Ajmer-merwara (Text and Statistics Tables)	C. C. Watson	1230	246
195	9789362080882	2nd. Vol. II-A & B	Mewar Residency (Text and Statistics Tables)	K.D. Erskine	1700	339
196	9789362088444	3rd, Vol. III-A & B	The Western Rajputana States Residency And The Bikaner Agency	K.D. Erskine	3590	718
			UNITED PROVINCES OF AGRA AND OUDH DISTRICT GAZETTEERS			
197	9789362087560	Vol. I	Agra	H. R. Nevill	2260	452
198	9789362082466	Vol. II	Aligarh	H. R. Nevill	1300	260
199	9789362089779	Vol. III	Allahabad	H. R. Nevill	2050	409
200	9789362081346	Vol. IV	Almora	H. G. Walton	1670	333
201	9789362085658	Vol. V	Azamgarh	D. L. Drake Brockman	1750	349
202	9789362080547	Vol. VI	Bahraich	H. R. Nevill	1410	281
203	9789362085214	Vol. VII	Ballia	H. R. Nevill	1750	350
204	9789362084668	Vol. VIII	Banda	D. L. Drake Brockman	1750	349
205	9789362086518	Vol. IX	Bara Banki	H. R. Nevill	1720	344
206	9789362084101	Vol. X	Bareilly	H. R. Nevill	1640	327
207	9789362086631	Vol. XI	Basti	H. R. Nevill	1610	321
208	9789362083814	Vol. XII	Benares	H. R. Nevill	2290	458
209	9789362086105	Vol. XIII	Bijnor	H. R. Nevill	1820	363
210	9789362081674	Vol. XIV	Budaun	H. R. Nevill	1890	378
211	9789362086891	Vol. XV	Bulandshahr	H. R. Nevill	2100	419
212	9789362081520	Vol. XVI	Cawnpore	H. R. Nevill	2210	442
213	9789362088031	Vol. XVII	Dehra Dun	H. G. Walton	1710	342
214	9789362088710	Vol. XVIII	Etah	E. R. Neave	1600	320
215	9789362082992	Vol. XIX	Etawah	D. L. Drake Brockman	1390	277
216	9789362082220	Vol. XX	Farrukhabad	E. R. Neave	1620	324
217	9789362083869	Vol. XXI	Fatehpur	H. R. Nevill	1890	377
218	9789362085962	Vol. XXII	Fyzabad	H. R. Nevill	1700	339
219	9789362087997	Vol. XXIII	Garhwal	H. G. Walton	1270	254
220	9789362089892	Vol. XXIV	Ghazipur	H. R. Nevill	1600	320
221	9789362085436	Vol. XXV	Gonda	H. R. Nevill	1650	330
222	9789362080271	Vol. XXVI	Gorakhpur	H. R. Nevill	1890	378
223	9789362086129	Vol. XXVII	Hamirpur	D. L. Drake Brockman	1390	277
224	9789362087638	Vol. XXVIII	Hardoi	H. R. Nevill	1680	336
225	9789362081636	Vol. XXIX	Jalaun	D. L. Drake Brockman	1180	236
226	9789362084309	Vol. XXX	Jaunpur	H. R. Nevill	1750	350
227	9789362084187	Vol. XXXI	Jhansi	D. L. Drake Brockman	1960	391
228	9789362089168	Vol. XXXII	Kheri	H. R. Nevill	1650	330
229	9789362086778	Vol. XXXIII	Lucknow	H. R. Nevill	1760	352
230	9789362088635	Vol. XXXIV	Mainpuri	H. R. Nevill	1740	348
231	9789362080424	Vol. XXXV	Meerut	H. R. Nevill	2170	434
232	9789362081087	Vol. XXXVI	Mirzapur	D. L. Drake Brockman	2430	486
233	9789362085443	Vol. XXXVII	Moradabad	H. R. Nevill	1900	380
234	9789362082763	Vol. XXXVIII	Muttra	D. L. Drake Brockman	2140	428
235	9789362089915	Vol. XXXIX	Muzaffarnagar	H. R. Nevill	2260	451
236	9789362086143	Vol. XL	Naini Tal	H. R. Nevill	1890	377
237	9789362086761	Vol. XLI	Partabgarh	H. R. Nevill	1560	312
238	9789362081124	Vol. XLII	Pilibhit	H. R. Nevill	1570	314
239	9789362084453	Vol. XLIII	Rai Bareli	H. R. Nevill	1610	322
240	9789362088284	Vol. XLIV	Rampur	H. R. Nevill	1170	234
241	9789362083654	Vol. XLV	Saharanpur	H. R. Nevill	2190	438
242	9789362083142	Vol. XLVI	Shahjahanpur	H. R. Nevill	1510	302
243	9789362083623	Vol. XLVII	Sitapur	H. R. Nevill	1590	317
244	9789362089939	Vol. XLVIII	Sultanpur	H. R. Nevill	1330	266
245	9789362080851	Vol. XLIX	Unnao	H. R. Nevill	1530	305

EASTERN BENGAL AND ASSAM
DISTRICT GAZETTEERS.

NOAKHALI.

BY

J. E. WEBSTER,

INDIAN CIVIL SERVICE.

PRINTED AT THE PIONEER PRESS
ALLAHABAD

1911

PLAN OF CONTENTS.

CHAPTER.	PAGE.
I.—PHYSICAL ASPECTS	1
II.—HISTORY	14
III.—THE PEOPLE	31
IV.—PUBLIC HEALTH	43
V.—PRICES, RENTS, WAGES AND MEASURES ...	48
VI.—AGRICULTURE	53
VII.—NATURAL CALAMITIES	60
VIII.—MEANS OF COMMUNICATION	62
IX.—OCCUPATIONS, MANUFACTURES AND TRADES	67
X.—LAND REVENUE ADMINISTRATION ...	74
XI.—GENERAL ADMINISTRATION	88
XII.—LOCAL SELF-GOVERNMENT	96
XIII.—EDUCATION	98
XIV.—GAZETTEER	101
INDEX	107

TABLE OF CONTENTS.

CHAPTER I.

PHYSICAL ASPECTS.

Introductory—Origin of name—Boundaries—General configuration—Islands—Rivers—The Meghnā—Dākātiā—Bhawāniganj Khāl—Mahendra Khāl—Noākhāli Khāl—Feni River—Alluvion and Diluvion—Rennel 1780-90—Walters, 1819—Hooker, 1850—Revenue Survey—Hills—Marshes—Tanks—Geology—Botany—Fauna—Fish—Climate—Humidity—Rainfall—Temperature.

CHAPTER II.

HISTORY.

Ancient History—Hindu settlement—Tipperas—Muhammadans—Sandwip—Portuguese in Sandwip—Pirates of Chittagong—Dilāl Khān—Nawārā Mahāls—Slavery—Noākhāli under Mughal Government—Shāmsher Ghāzi—First British Settlements—Sandwip—Formation of the district of Noākhāli—Divisional Commissioners—Administration of justice—Law and order in early days—Difficulties of administration—Disturbances—Currency.

CHAPTER III

THE PEOPLE.

Census of 1872—Census of 1881—Census of 1891 and 1901—Migration—Density of population—Towns, villages and houses—Sex—Religion—Christians—Hindus—Caste—Brāhmans—Kāyasths—Sudras—Bārui—Sunri and Teli—Jugis—Kaibarttas—Namasudras—Bhuinmāli—Rise of castes—Muhammadans—Customs—Dress—Houses—Furniture—Food—Language.

CHAPTER IV.

PUBLIC HEALTH.

Births and deaths—Local variations—Seasonal variations—Principal diseases—Cholera—Other diseases—Infirmities—Small-pox and vaccination—Dispensaries—Water-supply.

CHAPTER V.

PRICES, RENTS, WAGES AND MEASURES.

Prices—Wages—Measures—Rent Rates—Indebtedness—Material condition.

CHAPTER VI.

AGRICULTURE.

Cultivation—Extension of cultivation—Manure—Effect of rainfall upon crops—Rice—Jute—Oilseeds—Spices and condiments—Vegetables—Sugarcane—Betelvine—Betel-nut—Coco-nut—Other fruit trees—Cattle.

CHAPTER VII.

NATURAL CALAMITIES.

Cyclones—Cyclone of 1876—Cyclones of 1893 and 1895—Earthquake.

CHAPTER VIII.

MEANS OF COMMUNICATION.

History—Roads—Expenditure—Trunk Road—Begamganj Road—Feni Road—Chittagong Road—Tāltoli Road—Bruce's Tank Road—Mr. Leake's Road—Rivers—Canals—Ferries—Railways—Rest-houses—Conveyances—Boats.

CHAPTER IX.

OCCUPATIONS, MANUFACTURES AND TRADES.

Salt—Fisheries—Fish—Weaving—Iron and steel work—Brass, copper and bell-metal—Mats and baskets—Imports and exports—Marts—Exhibitions.

CHAPTER X.

LAND REVENUE ADMINISTRATION.

Fiscal divisions—Early British settlements—Mughal administration—Valuation—Abwābs—Classification of lands—Land Revenue—Revenue of Sandwip—Sair revenue—Permanent settlement—Estates—Tāluks—Reclamation cases—Ryots—Transfers—Under-ryots—Revenue policy in 1821—Sub-infeudation—Government estates—Temporarily settled estates—Fishery estates—Revenue-free estates—Sale of estates—Public demands recovery—Land registration—Court of Wards—Kists—Zamindārs.

CHAPTER XI.

GENERAL ADMINISTRATION.

Staff—Sub-divisions—Thānās—Villages—Village servants—Police—Village police—Registration—Registration of Muhammadan marriages—Criminal justice—Crime—Civil justice—Jail—Finance—Income-tax—Excise—Stamps—Cesses—Arms Act—Postal and Telegraph—Statistics—Surveys.

CHAPTER XII.

LOCAL SELF-GOVERNMENT.

History—Municipalities—District Board—Income—Expenditure—Local Boards—Unions.

CHAPTER XIII.

EDUCATION.

History—Expenditure—Secondary education—Primary education—Madrasas—Educational standard—Female education—Management and inspection.

CHAPTER XIV.

GAZETTEER.

Ambarabād or Omarabād—Bābupur—Bhulua—Dāndrā—Feni—Jagdiā—Lakhipur—Rāipur—Sandwip—Sudhārām.

BIBLIOGRAPHY.

1. Statistical Account of Noākhāli by Sir William Hunter, 1876.
2. Rājmālā (Bengali) by Kailāsh Chandra Singh.
3. Report on the Survey and Settlement of Chakla Roshnābād by J. G. Cumming, 1899.
4. Noākhāli, Itihāsh by Piāri Mohan Sen (Bengali, not very reliable).
5. Mr. Duncan's Report on Sandwīp, 1778.
6. Mr. Walter's Report on Sandwīp, 1819.
7. Voyages of Cæsar Fredericke, Hakluyt's Voyages, Vol. V.
8. Recent Changes in the Ganges, James Ferguson. Journal of the Geographical Society of London, Vol. XIX, page 329.
9. Ancient India, R. C. Dutt.
10. The Portuguese in India, F. C. Danvers.
11. Bernier's Mughal Empire.
12. Stewart's History of Bengal.
13. Fifth Report on the Affairs of the East India Company.
14. Colebrooke's Supplement to the Bengal Regulations.
15. District Report on the Census of 1891.
16. Official Correspondence and Publications.

9. [illegible]
10. Tavernier's Travels in India by [illegible] Ball.

GAZETTEER

OF THE

NOAKHALI DISTRICT.

CHAPTER I.

PHYSICAL ASPECTS.

Introductory. The district of Noākhāli lies between 22° 10′ and 23° 17′ north latitude and between 90° 39′ and 91° 35′ east longitude. At the census of 1901 its area was 1,644 square miles and its population 1,141,728.

Origin of name. The district takes its name from that of the river, the Noākhāli Khāl (or new channel) on which the head-quarters station is built.

Boundaries. The district is bounded on the north by the district of Tippera and the Native State of Hill Tippera, on the east by Hill Tippera and the Chittagong district, from which the big Feni river separates it, on the south by the Bay of Bengal, and on the west by the main stream of the Meghnā. The western boundary is difficult to find or locate accurately owing to the constant changes in the channel of the Meghnā, but it has been defined by the notification of the 17th September 1891 as the main stream of the Meghnā river.

General configuration. The district consists of a strip of the mainland about 55 miles long from Jāliā Char on the Meghnā to the point at which the big Feni river first touches Noākhāli, and an average depth from north to south of 20 to 22 miles, with a long horn-like peninsula on the extreme north-east running up into Hill Tippera. This north-eastern portion is elevated, undulating, and intersected by numerous hill streams which find their way into the Feni river. West of this the country presents the aspect of a vast rice plain dotted over with numerous villages, where rich groves of areca-nut and coco-nut palms rising out from a dense undergrowth of Māndār trees and other shrubs, make every village look like a forest. A striking feature of the landscape is the multitude of tanks of every size while brick built mosques, white plastered, and exceedingly numerous, help to break the monotony of plain and grove.

Islands.

South of the mainland lie a large number of islands, of which the most notable are Sandwīp, measuring with its appurtenant islands Badu and Siddhi about 20 miles from north-west to south-east, and about 10 miles across, and Hātiā now nearly 25 miles from north to south and about 8 miles broad on an average. Between Hātiā and the mainland are a multitude of *chars* which are constantly changing their positions and boundaries.

The most important of these alluvial formations and their approximate extent are shown in the following list :—

Serial No.	Name of Estate.	Area in square miles.	
1	Char Ghuia Dhopa, Part I ...	·5	In the Bāmni river near the mouth of the Feni.
2	" " " Part II ...	·2	
3	" Kachāpiā	Not known	
4	" Fischi	Do.	
5	" Rām Narayan	1·2	
6	" Pir Baksh	6·4	Additions to the island of Sandwip.
7	" Badu Lakhi	22·5	
8	" Lance	·5	Additions to the island of Hātiā.
9	" King	11·2	
10	" Bharat Sen	4·8	
11	" Iswar Ray, Part I ...	25·7	
12	" " " Part II ...	2·6	
13	" Nilakhimay Kunjatoli ...	1·5	
14	" Nālchira	29·1	
15	" Amānullah	12·8	
16	" Mir Muhammad Ali, Part I...	21·6	
17	" Mir Muhammad Ali, Part II	Not yet surveyed.	
18	" Ghāzi	7·1	
19	" Alexander	17·1	
20	" Hasan Husain	1·3	
21	" Goshai	·9	
22	" Lakhi Afzal Fakir ...	·3	
23	" Sekandar Mudafat Dulagāzi	·3	
24	" Mehar	4·7	
25	" Niāmat	·7	
26	" Jabar	14·9	Islands in the Hātiā river.
27	" Jubilee	7·5	
28	" Jum Mādhale	·3	
29	" Bailey including Batu, Langoha and Sona.	11·9	
30	" Macpherson	Not yet surveyed.	
31	" Princess Alexandra ...	·6	
32	" Bedoma Private Estate ...	... ...	
33	" Poragacha Do. ...	... ...	
34	" Sita Do. ...	... ...	
35	" Behāri	15·7	Islands in the Meghnā separate from Hātiā.
36	" Lawrence	2·1	
37	" Bose	2·2	
38	" Bansi	14·2	Formations at the mouth of Dākātiā river.
39	" Mirzamārā	1·9	
40	" Udmārā	1 6	
41	" Abābil	2·1	

The *chars* of the oldest formation present much the same appearance as the mainland; there are villages consisting of little groups of houses surrounded by *māndār* trees and palms, with intervening stretches of rice-field. The newer *chars* are marked by the absence of trees, and consist generally of a uniform cultivated plain intersected with numerous *khāls*, with here and there bare patches where the soil is still unfit for cultivation. Yet younger formations are the banks barely above water, but covered with grass on which herds of buffaloes may be seen grazing; and youngest of all are the banks of mud and sand emerging from the river only when the tide is low, and still of no value but to the fishermen. All along among these *chars* and islands may be seen traces of constant change, upright or overhanging banks marking the places where the river is cutting away the dry land, and gently sloping banks those where new land is forming.

Rivers. On the west and south of the district and between the islands flows the Meghnā, and on the east the Feni sub-division is drained by the great and little Feni rivers. In the intervening country there are no rivers of any size and the drainage there depends on a few tidal channels or *khāls*, of which the principal are the Noākhāli Khāl, the Mahendra Khāl, and the Bhawāniganj Khāl.

The Meghnā. The Meghnā is the great river which in older days formed the uttermost limit of the wanderings of the Aryans. The story runs that when in their wanderings the Pāndavas reached its banks, Bhīm, the most adventurous of those heroes, was sent across to explore the country on the further side and on his return adressed his elder brother, Yudisthira, in such intemperate language that the latter turned his back forever on a land which could so pervert a man of gentle breeding; and thenceforward the country east of the Meghnā has been to orthodox Hindus *Pāndava barjita desh*, a land of utter barbarism Originally, the Meghnā seems* to have been only the estuary of the rivers of the Surmā Valley.

The Brahmaputra then flowed far to the west, and at some not very distant date, perhaps as the result of the great convulsion of nature to which the Madhupur jungle owes its upheaval, it turned eastward and met the Meghnā. Then began a great battle of the rivers, ending about the beginning of last century in the Brahmaputra turning back more or less to its former course and meeting the Ganges at Goalundo, whence the combined streams fall into the Meghnā near Chāndpur. At present the Meghnā carries to the sea the great bulk of the waters of the Brahmaputra and Ganges, as well as of the Sylhet rivers. It touches the Noākhāli district first a little way below Chāndpur at the corner of Char Abābil. Here it is about four miles wide. A few miles further down nearly opposite Lakhipur, it receives a portion of the waters of the Dākātiā river. A little further down

* Fergusson—Recent Changes in the Ganges, Journal of the Geological Society of London, Vol. XIX, p. 321.

again, about latitude 22° 48′, it divides on either side of Char Lawrence. The right channel, known henceforward as the Shāhbāzpur river, lies in the district of Bākarganj. The other channel passes on between the mainland of Noākhāli on its left and Chars Shibnāth, Bihāri, Bose, Sitā, and Alexander on the right. Shortly before reaching the southernmost point of the mainland, the river is again divided by the large new island of Char Jabar, the right or southern stream becoming the Hātiā river, which flows to the sea between the islands of Hātiā and Sandwīp, while the left or northern branch under the name of the Bāmni river flows on between Sandwīp and the mainland as far as the mouth of the Feni river, then turning south along the coast of Chittagong and again changing its name reaches the Bay of Bengal by the Sandwīp channel. Between the islands of north and south Hātiā there is another wide channel, known as the Kālaiyā, connecting the Hātiā with the Shāhbāzpur river. From Char Ababil to the mouth of the Feni is a distance of about 64 miles, and the Hātiā river is about 32 miles long. The width of the river varies from year to year, not very greatly in the upper reaches, where as the bank advances on the one side it recedes nearly as fast on the other, but showing great changes lower down as islands form and disappear. At present the distance between Hātiā and the mainland is nearly twenty miles (though the island of Char Jabar intervenes), the Bāmni river is more than ten miles wide, while Hātiā and Sandwīp are fully twenty miles apart. But in spite of its great size and the immense volume of water which it carries at all seasons of the year, the Meghnā is not very suitable for navigation. Even in the cold weather from November to February, when there is little fear of storm, the great rise and fall of the tide, which is as much as 18 feet at the springs, and the constantly shifting sandbanks, are serious obstacles to navigation, and after February the estuary is often rough and dangerous.

The most dreaded of all the channels is the Kālaiyā between north and south Hātiā, where the tides coming from either side meet and raise a particularly dangerous sea.

Sir Joseph Hooker in his "Himalayan Journals" lays stress on the great increase in the tidal range going from west to east along the head of the Bay of Bengal. On the west coast the tide rises twelve or thirteen feet, on the east from forty to fifty feet. Noākhāli occupies a central position, and Hooker found the rise of the tide at Hātiā to be only 14 feet, but much more at the mouth of the Feni. The range varies, of course, with the season, and depends also very much on the wind. 'The normal tide,' wrote Mr. Whinfield, Officiating Collector in 1870, 'comes up the easternmost channel by way of the Sandwīp and Bāmni rivers. It is called the Chittagong tide, and makes first. Another tidal wave called the *daula* sweeps round the south of the islands of Sandwīp and Hātiā, and being deflected by Bākarganj turns to the north through the Hātiā and Shāhbāzpur channels and meets the Chittagong tide off the south-west corner of the mainland. In all the *khāls*, or water-courses, running through Sandwīp and Hātiā from east to west, the tide flows in from both sides, but with most force from the east. At every full and new moon, especially at the time of the equinox, there is a bore, or tidal wave, for several successive days. This wave is highest at the mouth of the Feni river, and in the channel between Hātiā and the mainland, where the tides meet, and it runs up as far as Bhawāniganj. The worst bores occur with a southerly wind. The wave presents the appearance of a wall of water, sometimes twenty feet in height, with a velocity of fifteen miles an hour. The natives say that the maximum height on the east is eighty feet; but this is certainly an exaggeration as the banks are nowhere higher than forty feet above the level of low water.' The bore comes up at the first of the flood-tide with a roar which is heard miles off, and rushes with great force. This renders the navigation of the river extremely difficult, and accidents are constantly occurring. Owing to the shoals at the mouth of the Noākhāli Khāl, boats are obliged to anchor in mid-channel between Hātiā island and the mainland during the ebb, and are often caught by the bore before there is sufficient depth of water for them to ride in, in which case they are frequently driven on the shoals and capsized. Occasionally, at the period of the south-west gales in May and October, these waves roll inland for miles and overflow the smaller islands at the mouth of the Meghnā. In the cyclone of November 1867, Hātiā island was entirely submerged in this way, and sea-drift was found on the embankments in the interior of the island at a height of four feet above the level of the country. On this occasion the wave must, the Collector states, have been forty feet in height, and in the great cyclone of 1876 the waters were piled up to a depth of twelve feet on Sandwīp. The Meghnā is nowhere fordable at any season of the year, but many of the small rivers and creeks are nearly dry at ebb-tide.

The first tributary that the Meghnā receives after entering Noākhāli is the Dākātiā river, which rising in the hills and flowing eastwards through the Tippera district, finds its way to the Meghnā by several mouths, of which the southernmost passes Rāipur in Noākhāli. Formerly the Dākātiā was a most important channel for trade to the north and west, and though most of its waters now find their way to the sea through the Chāndpur channel in the Tippera district, the Rāipur mouth is still navigable for country boats at all seasons of the year, and Rāipur is still an important mart from which coco-nut, betel, plantains, and oranges are exported. The length of the river in the Noākhāli district is about 15 miles. *Dākātiā.*

Bhawāniganj Khāl.

The next tributary of importance is the Bhawāniganj Khāl, which, rising in the north of Lakhipur *thānā*, passes by Lakhipur and through Bhawāniganj to the great estuary. It is navigable for country boats throughout the year as far as Lakhipur, a distance of twelve miles, though in the dry season big boats can only get up at high tide.

Mahendra Khāl.

In Rennell's map the Mahendra Khāl, rising in the Tippera district and flowing southward past Nandonā to the Meghnā, north of Hātiā, appears as the principal internal river of the district, but in its upper reaches it is now much silted up and overgrown with weeds.

Noākhāli Khāl.

The Noākhāli Khāl, rising near Begamganj in the centre of the district flows past the town of Noākhāli and is navigable for a distance of 20 miles in the rainy season, but in the winter only at high tide.

Feni river.

The little Feni or Dākātiā river, rising in the hills of Tippera and passing through the plains close to Comilla, enters the Noākhāli district near Sikandarpur, and flows in a tortuous course through the western portion of the Feni sub-division for a distance of about 50 miles. It is navigable through its entire length during the cold weather, though much obstructed in parts by shallows and sandbanks. The big Feni river, rising in the hills, enters the district at its extreme eastern point, and from there to the sea forms the boundary between it and the district of Chittagong. About half way in its course along the boundary it receives on its right bank the waters of the Muhuri, a river which rises in the Tippera hills and entering the district at the north-eastern corner of the Chhāgalnaiyā *thānā* flows nearly due south through the east of the Feni sub-division, and is navigable for a distance of 51 miles. The Seloneāh river is a tributary of the Muhuri, and is navigable for a distance of 21 miles between it and the hills. It forms the boundary between Chhāgalnaiyā and Feni *thānās*. These eastern rivers are fed by streamlets running down from the hills, and after heavy rain are liable to overflow their banks and flood the surrounding country.

Besides these rivers, there are numerous small drainage cuts, not deserving the name of rivers, but which during the rains form a ready means of navigation from place to place and help to carry off the water when it begins to fall.

Alluvion and diluvion.

The country is of comparatively recent formation and the dividing line between land and water can hardly be said to be definitely fixed even now. To trace the changes in historical times would need a most minute and laborious examination of old records, but a comparison of Rennell's map of the estuary (circa 1780—90 A.D.), Mr. Walters map of 1819 A.D., the Revenue Survey maps (1862—67 A.D.), and the rough plans prepared for the use of the Settlement Department, supplemented by a few notes from the old correspondence, will give some idea of the magnitude of the movements that are even now going on. Of yet older times it must suffice to say that Sandwīp Hātiā and Bāmni are believed to have formed one island, or at least to have been divided by very narrow channels, and that they probably became inhabited before the mainland opposite.

To turn first to Rennell's map; it shows us the Meghnā flowing past Lakhipur, then an important factory of the East India Company, sweeping in a steady curve round the south-west of the district and passing some five miles south of the present station of Noākhāli, and then inclining slightly northward on to the mouth of the Feni where it flowed some two miles south of Companyganj. Rennell shows also the coast line of 1730, which he must have ascertained by enquiries on the spot. This line passed nearly through the present position of Noākhāli town and from there ran nearly east and west, showing that accretion during the fifty years had been chiefly in the centre of the district. Rennell, 1780—90.

In the upper reach of the Meghnā Rennell shows none of the *chars* that now exist, perhaps he did not attempt to give complete details. Hātiā appears as an undivided block of land some 15 miles from north to south, and 10 miles from east to west. Sandwīp is placed very much in the position it now occupies, but between it and the mainland is shown a large island called Bāmni. Alluvion and diluvion must have been going on very fast at that period, and in 1815 it was found necessary to appoint a special officer, Mr. Tucker, to enquire into the state of the *chars*. He prepared a map, but this is not to be found now and without it his report is difficult to follow. In his time a great part of the island of Bāmni had diluviated, and the bed of the river which had flowed between it and the mainland was silting up and on the way to become dry land. The river had also been cutting away land along the southern face of the district, and a new *char*, called Darvesh, was forming south of the town of Sudhārām.

In the year 1819, Mr. Walters found Bāmni still separated from the mainland by a narrow channel, the Machua Duna. With the new forming accretions its south-eastern point stretched below the latitude of Mirka Sarai (in Chittagong) and nearly down to Sitākund. Thence the coast of the mainland ran in a nearly straight line west-north-west, passing 9 miles from Noākhāli, where *char* Darvesh had joined the mainland, and on to *char* Bhuta (latitude 22° 50′). There a turn nearly due north took it past Lakhipur, where *char* Shāmsundar was forming at the mouth of the Dākātiā. Sandwīp was still a single island, 12 miles from the Chittagong coast, and 8 miles from Bāmni, measuring 14 miles from north to south, and 12 from east to west. Neither Badu nor Siddhi had become habitable, but banks are shown in his sketch forming to the north of the island. Hātiā was an island 16 miles by 20 lying 5 to 7 miles away from the mainland and 16 from Sandwīp. To the north Walters, 1819.

it was being washed away and new *chars* were forming to the south and west; indeed the river on the west was full of new islands, some gradually joining up with Hātiā, others being added to Dakhin Shāhbāzpur. Comparing his sketch with Rennell's map we may say that there had been great diluvion from the mouth of the Bhawāniganj Khāl along the south-western coast, and great accretion in the delta of the Feni rivers; while the irruption of the Ganges stream had quite changed the condition of Hātiā.

Hooker, 1850.

Sir Joseph Hooker who sailed down the Meghnā in the year 1850 found it moving gradually to the west, leaving much dry land on the Noākhāli side and forming islands opposite that coast, while it was encroaching on the Sundarbans and cutting away the islands in that direction. The mainland of Noākhāli was extending gradually seawards and had advanced 4 miles within 23 years. The elevation of the land was, in his opinion, caused by the overwhelming tides and south-west hurricanes in May and October, which carried the waters of the Meghnā and Feni back over the land in a series of tremendous waves that covered islands of many hundred acres and rolled three miles on to the mainland.

Siddhi was then in existence, for Hooker landed on it and sailed across from there to Hātiā, which he found to be moving bodily to the westward. He records that the surface was flat and about 4 feet above mean high water level, and that the tide rises about 14 feet up the bank and then retires for miles.

Revenue Survey.

Coming down to the time of the Revenue Survey we find that large *chars* had formed on the right of the mouth of the Dākātiā river, and that Lakhipur, shown by Rennell as on the banks of the Meghnā, was some three miles away. The shape of the coast line below Lakhipur had changed since 1820. The point of *char* Bhuta had been washed away, and the coast ran nearly south-east from the mouth of the Bhawāniganj Khāl to a point due south of Sudhārām, in about latitude 22° 41′, showing slight diluvion there also. West of this point along the Bāmni river the coast line is shown as convex, and the south-eastern point of Bāmni (now part of the mainland) is in latitude 22° 45′, some miles north of its position in 1819, indicating very extensive diluvion. From latitude 22° 45′ down to 22° 10′, an almost continuous series of *chars* divided the Hātiā from the Shāhbāzpur river. The most northerly of these, *char* Sāhibnāth and *char* Falcon, find no place in Rennell's map, but on the other hand Hātiā which in 1870 lay almost wholly north of latitude 22° 30′, seems to have receded southward, and had received *char* Nālchira covering nearly 200 square miles, on its south, and beyond this again *char* Mīr Muhammad Alī is shown forming in the Bay of Bengal. Passing on to Sandwīp the map shows to its north two new *chars*, Badu and Siddhi, making the total length of the island over 25 miles and its northern point in latitude 22° 42′; the Sandwīp channel has dwindled to nine miles, but in spite of the new *chars* the Bāmni river is still six miles across at its narrowest. Since then the *chars* in the Meghnā have been extending to the north, seriously impeding navigation. The most northerly of them is *char* Lawrence, just above Sibnāth *char* shown in the published maps. Coming down the river we find the several *chars* much grown and in slightly different position to those shown in the survey maps, and east of *char* Bose lies a big new island, *char* Jabar, with an area of nearly 15 square miles extending across the mouth of the Noākhāli Khāl. Hātiā is being cut away on the east, but is extending rapidly to the south, *char* Sen having formed beyond *char* Mīr Muhammad Alī. The wide channel shown in the maps between north and south Hātiā at one time nearly closed up but has again returned to its former dimensions. In the Hātiā river Tum *char* is being cut away, and *char* Macpherson, shown in the survey maps as just emerging from the water, after having grown into importance, is now once more diluviating. The northern portion of *char* Siddhi has gone, and land is being washed away on the west and accreting on the east of Sandwīp, while *char* Pir Bakhsh has added 5½ square miles to this island.

Coming back to the mainland, the bank at the mouth of the little Feni has been washed away, and that river once more finds its way into the Bāmni channel, some two miles below Companyganj. All along the southern coast of the mainland the river has been encroaching, it is now within some three miles of Noākhāli town, and advancing steadily. In these changes *char* Jabar seems to play an important part, dividing the waters of the Meghnā it throws one strong stream on to the coast of the mainland and another on to north Hātiā, and there is reason to fear that Noākhāli station is in danger of destruction unless something intervenes.

Hills. There are no hills in the Noākhāli district, though the country on the extreme east is elevated and undulating with spurs from the Tippera hills running out into it.

Marshes. The northern and central portions of the district are lower than the banks of the Meghnā. It is suggested in Hunter's Statistical Account of the district that these depressions may be due to the great earthquake of 1762, which is said to have engulfed a tract of the country round Lakhipur, 15 miles in extent. By that earthquake* a large tract of land was submerged, other parts were elevated, two volcanoes broke out, and the whole settlement of Chittagong was shattered. Even at Dacca the shock was so violent that the wave from the river swept off a large number of the inhabitants. It is not necessary, however, to seek for any such sudden convulsion of nature to account for the

* Fergusson's Delta of the Ganges, Journal of the Geological Society of London, Vol. XIX, page 329.

depression. It is a common feature of deltaic formation that the land nearest the streams rises more rapidly than that further away, and the presence of great masses of still water lying in the low lands tends to exaggerate the difference of level by holding back the river floods and compelling them to deposit their silt before over-running the inland tracts.

In 1875 the Collector of the district gave a list of 77 marshes, covering an area of more than 8 square miles. It is said, however, that at the present date nearly all these marshes have been drained and brought under cultivation, and no doubt their level will now rise steadily year by year until it approaches that of the land upon the banks of the river.

Tanks. Tanks form a striking feature of the district. In every village may be found numerous tanks, large and small. House sites in the low-lying country have to be raised above flood-level and for this purpose earth is dug and a tank formed. This accounts for the small pools that are to be seen adjoining almost every hamlet, but the larger tanks with wide sheets of water, of which there are many in the district, mostly owe their existence to the piety or desire for fame of some raja or landowner. In 1904-05, the number of tanks in the district was returned as 17,985, of which 12,671 were said to afford wholesome water.

Many of the tanks have high banks to keep out the brackish water from the estuary, and these being overgrown with palms and other trees add much to the picturesqueness of the scenery. There are no wells in the district and the rivers being tidal the people depend on these tanks for their water-supply.

Geology. The Tippera hills of which the spurs project into the east of the district are of upper tertiary formation and generally of a dull reddish colour. The rest of the district is alluvial, the soil consisting of an admixture of sand and clay in varying proportions. The soil along the southern face and in the islands is impregnated with salt, which at one time was the most important product of this part of the country.

Botany. The peculiar vegetation of the Sundarbans is represented but sparingly and plant life is confined generally to varieties belonging to the lower Gangetic plain.

The luxuriant growth of palms is the most characteristic feature of the vegetation. The *supāri* (*Areca catechu*) becomes more and more abundant towards the west of the district, and grows almost in forests along the Meghnā above Lakhipur. It is invariably accompanied by the *māndār* (*Erythrina indica*), a thorny tree that serves to shade the young betel-nut and grows thick round every village site. The coco-nut (*nārikel*) is also very common in the west of the district and on the islands, and the toddy palms (*Borassus flabelliformis*) or *tāl*, and the date-palm or *khejur*, are to be seen in most parts.

Mangoes grow freely, though the fruit is almost worthless, the almond tree (*bādām*) is unusually common, and all the ordinary shade and fruit-giving trees of Bengal, the banyan (*bat*), *pipal*, *nim* (*Azadirachta indica*), *gāb* (*Diospyros embryopteris*), *jām*, (*Eugenia jambolana*) or plum, tamarind, *bel* (*Aegle marmelos*), *jalpāi* (*Elæocarpus serratus*), etc., are found. There is no valuable indigenous timber except in Chhagalnāia *thānā*, where a few *chāplās* (*Artocarpus chaplasha*) and *gurjān* (*Dipterocarpus turbinatus*) grow. Generally all timber for boats or houses is imported, but the mahogany and teak trees planted along the roads have done well. There are several varieties of cane, and a good deal of bamboo. Thatching grass (*ulu* or *chhan*) is obtained from the mainland and islands.

Fauna.

The larger carnivora are now scarce, but tigers and leopards occasionally descend from the hills of the Tippera State on to the adjoining villages of the eastern border and carry off cattle and goats. Spotted deer and hog deer frequently commit depredations on the crops in the same locality. The only large wild animals belonging properly to the district are the wild buffalo and the wild pig. The wild buffalo is now found only in *char* Mīr Muhammad Alī in the extreme south of the Hātiā island, where they are so numerous as to be a trouble to the new settlers. Attempts have been made to capture them, but the work is attended with some danger and difficulty and the number captured has not been large. The old bulls are often extremely fierce, but the females and young bulls when caught can generally be tamed if they do not die within the first few days. They interbreed with the tame animals, and on the same *char* wild cattle are found, believed to be descended from domestic cattle which have been allowed to run wild. Wild pigs are found on the *char* in large numbers and in smaller numbers on the Meghnā *chars* in the Lakhipur *thānā* and in other parts of the district. Flocks of bar-headed geese appear occasionally on the Meghnā. Wild duck are scarce, but snipe are to be had during the cold weather in the Feni sub-division. Large flocks of curlew are to be seen, and tern, cranes, many species of fish eagle, hawks, herons, and other water-fowl. A list of the birds found in the district furnished by the Collector, Mr. Porch, will be found in the statistical account of the district by Sir W. Hunter, but it is probable that many of the varieties included are very scarce, and the list is too long to repeat here. Numbers of crocodiles are found in the Meghnā, and especially on the sand banks to the west of Hātiā. Occasionally they carry off cattle, but as the people of the district rarely bathe in the big rivers few human lives are lost.

Snakes are common in Sandwīp, and no less than five varieties of the cobra are recognised in the district, *viz.*, *phānak*, *khoiā phānak*, *bankā*, *dudhgā bāhār*, and *tilakya bāhār*. Other poisonous snakes are the *sankhini* (*Bungarus fasciatus*) and the *jinglā borā* and *urgaborā* (*Callophis macclellandii*). The *kuchaborā* (*Trimeresurens carinatus*) is less deadly. In 1908 it was reported that 50 persons and 85 head of cattle were killed by snakes. The figures are low in comparison with northern Bengal or the Dacca division. The monitor lizard, *gosāmp*, and the *girgit* or blood-sucker, are to be seen everywhere, and Mr. Porch when Collector mentioned three other species of lizard, of which one is said to attain a length of 12 feet.

Fish.

There are many species of sea and fresh water fish in the rivers, tanks, and creeks, and some account will be given later of those of economic value.* The genera best represented are the *siluridæ*, *cyprinidæ*, and *clupeadæ*, but there are many others. The saw-fish (*kharag*) is occasionally caught in the estuary.

Climate.

The district of Noākhāli is distinguished by the heaviness of its rain-fall, the evenness of its temperature, and the humidity of its atmosphere throughout the year. There are rainfall recording stations at Noākhāli, Feni, Harispur, Rāmganj, Chhāgalnāia, Hātiā, and Lakhipur, and the returns show a good deal of variation in the climate, the rainfall in the Feni sub-division and on the southern coast being decidedly heavier than in the north-west of the district.

Humidity.

Taking the district as a whole the percentage of saturation during the 12 months is 88, and only in April, when it is 82, does it fall below 85. From that time on the humidity increases steadily, reaching its maximum of 91 per cent in July and August, decreasing very slowly from then until March when it falls to 85 per cent.

Rainfall.

The normal rainfall for the twelve months is 112·22 inches, but of course there are great variations from one year to another. In 1902-03 more than 154½ inches of rain fell, while in 1908-09 there were just over 88 inches. In an ordinary year the rainy season may be said to begin in May, when it rains about one day in every three and the total fall is 10 inches. Sometimes however April is very wet, more than 15 inches fell in that month in 1902-03 and nearly 15 inches in 1893-04, while on the other hand in 1903-04 little more than 3 inches fell in the two months Apriland May. In any case in June the rains are established, and the fall in that month averages over 22 inches, increasing to 24 inches in either of the two succeeding months, and it rains practically two days out of three. Only once in eighteen years has less than 14 inches of rain been recorded in June, and that was in 1905-06, when there had been good rain in May, while the only year that shows serious deficiency during July and August is 1896-97, when only 13·3 inches fell in August, but that short fall was followed by good rain in September. In September the monsoon begins to slacken and the fall averages little more than 14 inches. Only 1895-96 shows less than 10 inches of rain in September. In October only 7½ inches of rain are to be expected and three days out of four should

---

* Page 70.

be fine, but the rainfall in this month shows considerable variations, less than an inch having fallen in 1896-97 and over 15 inches in 1893-94. In November the country is drying up, but one or two showers should give about an inch and a half. December and January are the driest months of the year and receive between them on an average less than an inch of rain. In February about an inch of rain should fall, and storms in March should give nearly 3 inches, but the rainfall at this season is quite uncertain, and there may be practically no rain or over 6 inches.

Temperature.

The normal mean temperature for the year is 77° Fahrenheit, mean maximum 84° and mean minimum 69°, the daily range averaging 15°. January is the coldest month, the mean temperature for the 24 hours being 65°, the mean maximum 77° and the minimum 53°. February brings a rise of about 3°, and March adds another 9° to the mean temperature. April brings in the real hot weather, though there is in this district no hot weather comparable with that of Hindustān, the mean temperature for the 24 hours rises to 82° with a maximum day temperature of 89° falling to 74° at night. May is the hottest month of the year, the day temperature being the same as in April, but the night warmer. In June the lowest temperature averages 77° and the maximum 87°. There is no change in the night temperatures during the three ensuing months, but the day temperature falls to 85° in July and August, rising again to 86° in September and October, but in the latter month the nights grow cooler, and in November, though the mean maximum is still 83°, the minimum has fallen to 64°. In December the mean for the 24 hours is 67° and the mean minimum is 55°.

To sum up, it may be said that the cold weather begins some time about the middle of November and lasts till the end of February. This is a pleasant time, neither too cold nor too hot, with clear skies and cool light breezes. March and April are hot, though not unpleasantly so, but from May onwards there come five months of warm, moist weather, with a daily range of temperature of less than 10 degrees, which is very trying and enervating, and would be more so, were it not for the sea-breeze which makes *pānkhās* almost superfluous. The prevailing wind is from the south-east from March till October and from the north-east from November till February.

CHAPTER II.

HISTORY

Ancient History.

Youngest among all the districts in the Ganges delta Noākhāli has really no ancient history. It is probably not more than 3,000 years since first it became fit for human habitation, certainly not half so long since the Aryans entered it, but there are no records to tell us who and what manner of men they were who first settled in it and reclaimed the jungles. Possibly they were the progenitors of the present Namasudras or Chandāls, a Lohitic or Mongoloid race, who according to Mr. O'Donnel* entered Bengal from the north-east before the Koches ; or they may be represented by the Jugis,* now the principal Hindu caste of the district, whose origin is obscure, though Dr. Buchanan thought they must have come from Western India with the Pāl Rājās. Whoever they were, the early settlers had no literature and left behind nothing to tell us how or when they first took up their abode among the swamps and islands of the Meghnā. Aryan mythology gives little help. The Rāmāyan contains a description of the route to be followed by the army sent eastward in search of Sitā as far as Java and across the milky sea. Beyond the country of the Angas were to be found the lands of silkworms and silver, and mountains and cities embosomed in the sea, and tribes with 'ears like cloth hanging to their lips' and those who lived on raw fish, and islanders with tufted hair and skins the colour of gold. But there is no mention of any land or tribe that can be identified with Noākhāli or its inhabitants.

Megasthenes writing of his experiences in the third century B.C. marks the Ganges as the eastern boundary of the country of the Gangaridae, and beyond that gives us only fabulous races. Opinion generally identifies Noākhāli and the country to its north and east with the mythological kingdom of Shukhma, one of the five formed by the division of Eastern India among the sons of Bāli. Of this country we know nothing except that Kālidās in his 'Raghubangsa' describes it as "a shore green with forests of palms," and the Mahābhārata records how Bhīm coming from Monghyr, after putting to flight the monarchs of Banga, Tāmralipta, and other neighbouring countries, defeated also the "King of Shukhma and the Mlechhas who dwelt by the seashore."

Hindu settlement.

According to local tradition the first Hindu settlement dates from the twelfth century, when Biswambhar Sūr, ninth son of Rājā Adi Sūr, king of Mithilā, returning through Noākhāli from a pilgrimage to Chandranāth in the Chittagong district saw in a

---

* Report on Census of Bengal, 1891, but the features of these people are not such as are associated with Mongoloid origin.

dream the goddess Bārāhi, who promised him the sovereignty of the country if he would worship her. Obeying the goddess' demand the prince built an altar to Bārāhi Devī, but the sky being overclouded he mistook the points of the compass and placed the goat with its head to the west when offering his sacrifice. When the rays of the sun shone out, he noticed his mistake and cried out in the vernacular "bhul huā" (it was wrong) and from this exclamation the district is said to have taken the name of Bhulua. To this day the Hindus of the greater part of the district point the heads of the sacrificed goat to the west. This occurrence is said to have taken place in the year 1203 A.D., when Bakhtyār Khiliji was conquering Gaur, and it is by no means improbable that at that time some of the Hindu princes may have been driven to take refuge east of the Meghnā. There are several versions of this tale and Dr. Wise doubted the accuracy of the date* but it is probably a fact that the early Rājās of Bhulua were Kāyasths from Western Bengal.

Adi Sūr is said to have been of Rājput extraction, but it is admitted that Biswambhar or his successor married into the Kāyasth caste and at present the *Sūrs* are a Kāyasth family. Tradition assigns Kalyānpur as the first capital of Biswambhar, but the author of the 'Rājmālā' suggests Amisāpārā as a more likely place, because this village contains a temple to Bārāhi Devī and a stone image of that goddess.

The fourth descendant from Biswambhar Sūr, Srirām Khān, is said to have established the village of Srirāmpur and built there a palace, the remains of which are still to be seen. It is certainly curious to find a Kāyasth rājā with the title Khān, but it was used by the 3rd, 4th and 5th rājās in the line of descent, the 6th resuming his ancestor's patronymic 'Rāy', while his sons adopted the title of 'Mānikya' used by the Rājās of Tippera. Sūr was also a title borne by the Muhammadan Governor of Bengal in the middle of the sixteenth century, Muhammad Khān Sūr *alias* Shamsuddīn. There are still some Sūrs living in Srirampur. The descendants of Biswambhar acknowledged the suzerainty of the Rājās of Tippera, and were reckoned by them as first among their vassals and accorded the privilege of placing the royal mark or *rāj tikā* on the forehead of the Rājā of Tippera at his coronation.

Tipperas.

These Tipperas appear to be a Lohitic tribe, who coming down through the valley of the Brahmaputra settled about 1,500 years ago in the plains of Sylhet and in the northern portion of the hills of Tippera. Gradually growing in strength and extending their dominions west, south, and east, the Tipperas became by the thirteenth century overlords of the whole country from the Meghnā to Manipur, and were constantly at war with the kings of Arakan on the one side and the Muhammadan Governors of Bengal on the other.

* J. A. S. B., Vol. XLIII, p. 203 "On the Bārah Bhuiyā of Bengal."

The most famous of the Rājās of Bhulua was Lakhman Mānikya, eighth in descent from Biswambhar, who brought into the district high-class Brahmans and settled them at Srirāmpur, Kilpārā, Chapali and Barābinagar, and was himself the author of two works in Sanskrit. He was one of the *Bārah Bhuiyas*, or twelve Lords of Bengal, and lived at the end of the sixteenth century, being a contemporary of Isā Khān of Khizrpur and of Kandarpa Nārāyan Rāy of Chandradwīp (Barisāl). Kandarpa Nārāyan died and was succeeded by his son Rāmchandra, whose youth was a subject of jest and ridicule to Lakhman Mānikya. Rumour spread the story till it reached the ears of Rāmchandra, who resolved to be revenged. Accordingly he crossed the Meghnā in his boats and invited Lakhman Mānikya to a feast, in the course of which armed men appeared and seized upon the guest who was carried off to prison in Chandradwīp and eventually put to death. Lakhman Mānikya was succeeded by his son, Balarām Rāy, who attempted to make himself independent of the Rājās of Tippera and refused to attend the coronation of Amar Mānikya in 1597 A.D. Consequently Amar Mānikya attacked Bhulua and compelled the Rājā to pay tribute.

Little is known of Balarām's successors; but in the year 1661 A.D. some Dutch sailors wrecked on the shore were hospitably entertained by a prince of Bhulua; and in 1728 we find Rājā Kīrtinārāyan recorded as zamīndār of *pargana* Bhulua.

Muhammadans.

It is difficult to say when the Muhammadans first entered the district of Noākhāli. In the year 1279 A.D. Muhammad Tughral aided Ratnaphā, afterwards known as Ratna Mānikya, to obtain the throne of Tippera, and it is probable that the earliest Muhammadan settlements in Noākhāli date from that time.

In the year 1347 Iliās Shāh *alias* Shamsuddīn, the Muhammadan Governor at Sonārgāon, attacked and defeated Rājā Pratāp Mānikya of Tippera and carried off a large booty in money and elephants, but obtained no permanent footing in the country. He also conquered Chittagong which appears to have remained in the possession of the Muhammadans for some time. When Ibn Batūta* visited it about the year 1350 A.D., Chittagong acknowledged the suzerainty of the Bengal governors, but after that it lapsed into the possession of the Arakanese and was taken from them in 1513 by the Rājā of Tippera.

Fakiruddīn Mubārak of Sonārgāon, the founder of the independent line of Muhammadan kings, about the year 1340 carried his banner to the north into Sylhet, to the east into Tippera and Noākhāli, and to the south into Chittagong. These Muhammadan raids seem to have been to a great exte due to a desire to obtain elephants, for which Tippera was famous, and to put a

* So says Babu Kailash Chandra Singh, but it seems more probable that the place which Ibn Batūta calls Sātkāwān or Sutirkāwān was Sātgāon (Chatgāon) on the Hooghly.

stop to them Rājā Dharma Mānikya who ruled in the first half of the fifteenth century attacked and took Sonārgāon, the Muhammadan capital. At the beginning of the sixteenth century there was a struggle between Tipperas, Muhammadans, and Arakanese for the possession of Chittagong. At first the former were successful. Husain Shāh, Governor of Bengal, then invaded Tippera. In two campaigns he was defeated by the Tipperas, who dammed the Gumti and flooded the country as the enemy approached, but making a third attempt Husain Shāh fortified a strong position at Kailār Garh and in the battle that followed was victorious, and thereafter assumed the title of conqueror of Kāmrup, Karnata and Jājnagar (Tippera). He does not appear to have retained a permanent hold on Noākhāli or Tippera, and must soon have lost Chittagong, which was taken by Rājā Deb Mānikya of Tippera from the Maghs in 1513 A.D., though it was not long before it was retaken by Sultan Nāsiruddīn. From this time onwards the Afghāns began to establish themselves on the east of the Meghnā.

In 1587 A.D., the country was overrun by the King of Arakan, and as late as 1610 A.D., we find the Arakanese aiding the pirate chief of Sandwīp to prevent the entry of the Mughals into Bhulua and invading the country by sea and land.

Sandwīp.

At this point it is necessary to turn to the history of the islands.

The centre of Sandwīp is believed to have been inhabited before the adjoining mainland, and Cesare Federico* the Venetian traveller who visited it about the year 1569 A.D., stated that the island was one of the most fertile places in the world, densely populated and well cultivated. He describes the inhabitants as Moors (Muhammadans) and found the island in possession of a Muhammadan governor, and it is known that in 1609 A.D., one Fateh Khān was governor of the island and had a strong Muhammadan garrison, besides a fleet of forty sail. According to the Portuguese historians Sandwīp had been before that a Portuguese possession and Fateh Khān had seized it on the death of its governor Manoel de Mattos and had murdered all the Christians on the island.

Portuguese in Sandwīp.

About the year 1605 one Sebastiao Gonzales Tibao, a Portuguese of obscure extraction, came to India, and two years later, having made a little money in the salt trade, carried a cargo to Dianga, a port in the kingdom of Arakan, and was there when the Portuguese residents were massacred by the king's orders.

Some few, including Gonzales, escaped in ten vessels and turned pirates, robbing in the ports of Arakan, and carrying their booty to Bhatkal on the Malabar coast, with whose ruler they were on friendly terms.

Fateh Khān sent his fleet against this set of robbers and found them off the island of Dakhin Shāhbazpur, but in the battle

---

* Voyage and travel of M. Caesar Fredericke: Hakluyt's Voyages.

which followed the Muhammadan fleet was entirely destroyed, and Fateh Khān himself was killed. After this the pirates elected Gonzales as their chief, and being joined by numbers of their countrymen determined to establish themselves in Sandwīp. Gonzales entered into a contract with the King of Bhatkal to give the latter half the revenues of Sandwīp in return for his assistance in taking it. The king sent some ships and 200 horsemen, and Gonzales having collected a fleet of forty sail manned by 400 Portuguese, attacked the island. The Muhammadans offered a vigorous defence and the issue was in doubt until the captain of a Spanish ship landed fifty men with whose aid the Portuguese captured the fort, and thereafter put to death more than a thousand of the Muhammadan garrison.

Once established in Sandwīp, Gonzales broke faith with the Rājā of Bhatkal and declined to give him the promised share of the revenues. Sandwīp was then an important centre of trade, and Gonzales erected a custom house and increasing rapidly in wealth and power found himself in command of 1,000 Portuguese, 2,000 well armed natives, 200 horse, and more than eighty vessels provided with good cannon. He married the sister of the King of Arakan, and entered into a treaty with that monarch for the defence of Sandwīp against the Mughals, who, says the historian, then contemplated the conquest of Bhulua.

The King of Arakan sent by land a force of some 90,000 men, mostly musketeers, and 700 elephants, and despatched by sea a fleet of 200 vessels, carrying 4,000 men, which was to join with Gonzales' fleet and be under his command. As usual Gonzales played false, and having taken the combined fleet into one of the island creeks, invited on board his vessel all the captains of the ships belonging to Arakan, had them murdered, and thereafter killed or enslaved the crews and returned to Sandwīp with all the ships. On land the forces of Arakan were defeated after a fierce struggle and the king escaped with only a few followers to the fort of Chittagong. As soon as he heard of the defeat of his ally Gonzales set out with his fleet, plundering and destroying the forts along the coast of Arakan, apparently to avenge the murder of the Portuguese at Dianga two years before. But he failed in an attack on the capital and the expedition bore no other fruit than the ruin of his reputation.

In the year 1616 Gonzales who had hitherto professed himself an independent sovereign, offered to become a tributary to Portugal and to pay a galleon load of rice yearly as tribute if the Viceroy of Goa would assist him in an attack on Arakan. Tempted by this offer and in the hope of obtaining the vast treasure supposed to belong to the King of Arakan, the Viceroy fitted out a fleet under Don Francisco, who sailed to Arakan, and was joined by Gonzales with fifty vessels well equipped. The combined fleets sailed up the river but were defeated by the Arakanese, supported by some Dutch vessels. Gonzales withdrew to Sandwīp, but not long afterwards the King of Arakan captured the island and put an end to the Portuguese dominion. Many of the Portuguese were transferred to Chittagong to serve as gunners and sailors against the growing power of the Muhammadans, and for the next half century the coasts of Bengal were ravaged by Portuguese and Magh pirates from Chittagong.

Pirates of Chittagong.

Many are the tales told of the fierceness and cruelty of these robbers, and how the whole countryside would tremble at the cry of 'the Magh! the Magh!' that told of their approach. Surprising the villagers in their homes or at their markets, they would carry off men, women and children, holding some to ransom, and keeping the rest as slaves, either to sell them to the Portuguese of Goa or Ceylon and other places, or forcibly converting them to Christianity to train them up as rowers in their own service. Bernier says that by their ravages large tracts were depopulated, and, though he may have overstated the case, there can be no doubt that the constant terror of attack must have driven away settlers from the coast even if the numbers killed and enslaved were not sufficient to make so great an impression.

Dilāl Khān

European writers speak of the pirates as Christians in the service of the Arakanese, but it appears that piracy at the mouth of the Meghnā was by no means confined to these people but was shared largely by the Muhammadans themselves. It was in the first half of the seventeenth century that Dilāl Khān, the famous bandit chief, arose. This man is said to have been the son of a woman who with her child was wrecked on the shore of Sandwīp. This child, left lying on the beach, was shielded from the sun's rays by a cobra. This fact, of course, marked him for a great destiny, and being brought up with the prospect before him he ultimately became the ruler of the island and a renowned robber. He is still the popular hero of Sandwīp and many strange tales are told of his powers, for like a second Robin Hood he plundered the wealthy and the stranger, and protected and was generous to his own people and the poor. He was an arbitrary ruler too, and had curious theories on the improvement of the race. The Hindu system of marriage within the caste he considered utterly pernicious, and he laid it down as a rule that the fair should wed with the fair irrespective of caste or even of creed; hence there is found to this day a strange medley of Hidnu and Muhammadan names, and the Hindus of the mainland, be they of high caste or of low, have no social intercourse with those of Sandwīp. Even in the genealogical table of the zamindārs we find a Kāyasth family connected by marriage with their Muhammadan neighbours.

Dilāl seems to have kept on good terms with both Mughals and Maghs for some years, and in 1639 exchanged presents with Shāh Shujā. At this time the Mughals had a garrison at Bhulua, and from the year 1620 onwards they had maintained an outpost at Noākhāli to guard the mouth of the *Khāl* there, but the Muhammadan soldiers were no match on the water for the pirates, who in their light galleys swept the whole coast, and often penetrated forty miles inland up the mouth and branches of the Meghnā. It was principally to relieve the country of this pest and to check the growing power and insolence of Arakan that Nawāb Shaista Khān, who was appointed Governor of Bengal in the year 1664, transferred his capital to Dacca. He fitted out a large fleet and equipped an army of 13,000 men; and, after strengthening the posts at Bhulua and Noākhāli, sent the fleet with 3,000 troops and some European gunners under the command of Husain Beg to clear the river of the pirates. Husain Beg took by storm the forts of Jagdia and Alamgīrnagar at the mouth of the river, which were in the possession of the King of Arakan. Dilāl Khān was ordered to assist in watching the river, and as he refused to do so, a detachment under Abul Husain landed in Sandwīp and besieged Dilāl in his fort. Dilāl fled to the jungles, where he collected a fresh force, and as at this time a party of Arakanese came to his assistance, Abul Husain withdrew to Noākhāli. Husain Beg then sailed to Sandwīp, and after some difficulty succeeded in expelling the Arakanese from their strong stockades and in capturing Dilāl, who with 92 members of his family was sent to Dacca where he ended his days in confinement.

Abdul Karim Khān was then appointed to the command of Sandwīp with a garrison of 1,000 men. Shaista Khān's ultimate objective at that time was Chittagong, but before attacking it he opened negotiations with the commandant of the Dutch Colony of Batavia and tried also by threats and cajolery to detach the Portuguese from the service of Arakan, offering them, if they would enter his service, more advantageous terms than they were receiving from their present chief and lands for the settlement of their families in Bengal, and warning them that if they adhered to the cause of Arakan he would, on the capture of Chittagong, put to death every one of them. Bernier says that the Nawāb adopted the expedient of getting the Portuguese in Bengal to transmit letters to their co-religionists in Chittagong containing promises of reward if they would come over to the Mughal side; and that these letters were intercepted and handed to the King of Arakan, who was thus made to believe that the Portuguese intended treachery.

In the Storia do Mogor another version of this tale is given, and it is said that Antonio de Rego of Hughly undertook for a bribe of Rs. 75,000 to procure the betrayal of Chittagong to the Mughal. Anyhow the Portuguese, who were already in trouble at Chittagong over the murder of a relative of the Rājā, deserted to the Nawāb, by whom they were graciously received and treated with better faith and generosity than they deserved.

The descendants of the Portuguese adventurers are still to be seen in Sandwīp and elsewhere in the district, but there is nothing in their features or complexion to distinguish them from the natives. From this time forward Sandwip was a Mughal dependency

Nawārā Mahāls.

For the protection of trade and to guard against the incursions of the Maghs and other foreign pirates, Shaista Khān organised a fleet of 768 armed boats stationed principally at Dacca. The whole cost of maintaining and manning the fleet, including the wages of 923 Firingi or Portuguese sailors, came to over eight lakhs of rupees, assessed on 112 *mahāls*, known as the Nawārā Mahāls, each of which was compelled to furnish a certain number of boats. It is not clear, however, that this fleet was actually maintained under Shaista Khān's successors, and it is certain that up to the time when Bengal came under the rule of the East India Company, life and property were not safe on the great rivers. In February 1717, says the East India Chronicle of 1758, the Maghs carried off from the most southern parts of Bengal 1,800 men, women, and children, and took them to the King of Arakan who chose all the handicraftsmen and about a fourth of the rest for himself and returned the rest to their capturers to be sold into slavery. So serious indeed were the depredations of the dacoits—"a race of outlaws," to quote Warren Hastings, "who live from father to son in a state of warfare against society, plundering and burning villages and murdering the inhabitants"—that the regulations of 1772 condemned every dacoit to death and his family to perpetual slavery; and in 1789 the construction of boats of the descriptions known as *luckās*, *jelkars*, and *paunchways* of certain dimensions was forbidden, except with the license of the Magistrate.

Slavery.

Nor did slavery cease until very much later. In a report on Sandwip, dated 22nd September 1879, Mr. Duncan gives the following account of slavery as it then existed in the island:—

"This unfortunate race of mankind bear in Sandwip a larger proportion to the other inhabitants than perhaps in any other district in the province, there being hardly a house-holder however otherwise indigent that has not at least one and the majority many in their families. This number also very soon increased by marriage to which they are encouraged by their masters, the custom of the country being such that on a free woman's marrying a male slave, she by that act reduces herself and family to be the perpetual slaves of her husband's master who also continuing ever after to retain him, her and their heirs in the same perpetual bondage, they soon became numerous. I have been assured that Abutorāb, the late rebel Chowdry, had more than fifteen hundred slaves, heads of families and whom he distributed in separate houses which he allotted them to live in. This multitude in Sandwip proceeds principally from the cheapness and plenty of grain it annually produces, which as often as there is any scarcity in the other Dacca districts attracts people to Sandwip, where on such occasions it has been common for many of them to sell themselves and their posterity for a bare maintenance. In a place where slavery is so prevalent, there will always be some cases of hardship, such as undue and most oppressive acquisitions by pretended purchase, children enticed away and deluded to sell themselves for the merest trifle before they arrive at years of discretion. On the whole, however, I only set free fifteen slaves and their families at liberty if they had any and got the matter compromised between four others and their masters, yet no part of my proceedings created more general apprehensions than my taking cognisance of this particular part of Sandwīvian grievances, because all the principal people were immediately interested; there being probably many of their slaves whom they acquired and hold in a manner that could hardly bear the test of regular trial; they therefore endeavoured, as I heard, to keep them at home, so that it was only a few perhaps who by accident making their escape gained access to complain to me, which must account for a much greater number not having been heard and redressed; since I uniformly set free all these on the Bill of Sale or Title Deed of whose purchase there was proven to be any defect arising from either the parties having been sold when young by persons not entitled by the custom of the country so to dispose of them, or from children's having been unduly decoyed away from the parents and made slaves or by selling themselves when very young."

And that slavery was not peculiar to Sandwīp appears from a letter written in the year 1790 regarding the prevalence of the practice of selling children, though this related to *parganas* which now form part of the Tippera district. There are no records to show how the practice was stamped out. Indeed the Company recognised slavery and ordered its officers to try cases regarding slaves according to the law of the land, and it was not until 1811 that the importation of slaves from foreign countries was prohibited, and not until 1832 that the sale of persons into slavery was made a crime, but there is no reason to suppose that it caused much misery, for it is recorded "that slaves are treated as the children of the families to which they belong."

Noākhāli under Mughal Government.

From the time of Shaista Khān onwards, Noākhāli and the islands were treated as part of the Mughal dependency, and though Tippera was not subjugated until the eighteenth century, it seems probable that Bhulua was severed from it long before.

In the reorganisation of the fiscal divisions of the Mughal empire made in the year 1722, both the mainland and the islands, as well as Sarkār Udaipur, comprising the estates of the Rājā of Tippera in the east of the district, were included in Chakla Jahāngīrnagar in the province or *Niābat* of Dacca.

Shamsher Ghāzi.

From the beginning of the sixteenth century the Rājās of Tippera appear to have had little to do with the affairs of Bhulua and their history belongs more properly to the adjoining district of Tippera, but the story of the rise and revolt of Shamsher Ghāzi may well be told here. Shamsher Ghāzi was the son of a poor Muhammadan of *pargana* Dakhinsik in Chakla Roshnābād, who being brought up with the sons of the local *tālukdār*, Nāsir Muhammad, and gifted with exceptional intelligence and strength, dared to aspire to the hand of the *tālukdār's* daughter. Naturally the *tālukdār* refused and would have punished Shamsher for his presumption, but the latter fled to the woods, and collecting there a number of followers attacked and killed Nāsir and his sons and took his daughter to wife. The Rājā sent soldiers against him, and Shamsher made his peace with the Vizier and obtained the zamīndāri of the *pargana* and afterwards took *pargana* Meherkul in farm. On the death of Bijay Mānikya there was a struggle between different claimants for the succession to the *rāj*, and Shamsher took advantage of this to refuse payment of rent. He defeated the soldiers sent against him and finally attacked the Rājā's capital of Udaypur with a force of 6,000 men and sacked it. From that day Udaypur has been abandoned, and is now overgrown with jungles. For a short time Shamsher Ghāzi was practically ruler of the plains, and was acknowledged even by few of the hillsmen. He appointed a manager to each *pargana* and gave lands to many of his relations and excavated tanks in many villages. Yet it is said he could not abandon his old robber-habits and would at times plunder the houses of the rich and distribute his booty among the poor. At length the heir designate Krishna Mānikya appealed to Mīr Kāsim, who recognised him as Rājā of Tippera, and sent a force against Shamsher, who was captured and carried off to prison in Murshidābād, and soon after was put to death.

First British settlements.

As early as 1756 A.D. the East India Company established factories for the weaving of cloth at Jagdia at the mouth of the Feni, but it was not until 1765 that the *dīwāni*, or authority over the revenues of Bengal, including the present district of Noākhāli, was conferred in perpetuity on the Company.

When the Company first took over the *dīwāni* of Bengal, they hesitated to stand forth themselves as direct collectors of the revenue, and up till 1769 left the administration in the hands of the native Naib or Deputy Dīwān at Murshidābād. In that year supervisors were appointed to enquire into the history of the province, its rental and revenue, the character and productiveness of its lands, its commerce, and the system of justice, and to make recommendations for its better management; and in 1772 the Board of Directors announced their intention of standing forth as *Dīwān* and by the agency of the Company's servants taking upon themselves the entire care and management of the revenues. In pursuance of this policy they divided the whole province into districts, appointing to the charge of each a European Collector aided by a native *Dīwān*. *Pargana* Sandwīp and its dependencies were under the Chief at Chittagong, who seems also to have exercised some authority over Tippera (comprising the present *thānā* Chhāgalnaia) though this was in the immediate charge of a Resident. The other islands at the mouth of the Meghnā were under Bākarganj and the rest of the mainland of Noākhāli was included in the Dacca district or province. Some time later Bhulua became a district and in the year 1787 A.D. there were a Collector and an Assistant Collector there. In that year, on the recommendation of Sir John Shore, the district was placed under the Collector of Mymansingh. This arrangement continued until the year 1790, when the whole of the mainland of Noākhāli was included in the district of Tippera then formed. The *pargana* of Bhulua, however, was in the immediate charge of Mr. Dandridge, who had been deputed there to partition the property. He seems to have been an assistant to the Collector of Tippera, but his position was ill-defined, and he interfered constantly in many matters that brought him into conflict with the salt agents and heads of the factories, and drew down upon him reprimands from higher authorities. This partition occupied Mr. Dandridge for three years, and at the end of that time the co-sharers refused to accept his award, and then Mr. Thompson was deputed to the district for a while. After that it seems to have come under the direct administration of the Collector of Tippera.

Sandwīp.

The pargana of Sandwīp had for a long time been held by several *chaudhuris*, who paid their respective quota of the revenue to an *ahdādār** who was a sort of contractor for the revenue and delegate of the Provincial Government. In the year 1763 the *ahdā* of Sandwīp was farmed by a society or partnership, which was registered in the name of one Bishun Charan Bose, though the directing member was really Gokul Ghosāl, who became the banyan of Mr. Verelst, the Governor of Bengal, and was the founder of the well-known Bhukailāsh family. The oppressive conduct of the *ahdādārs* led to a rebellion in 1767, which was quelled without difficulty by Captain Nollikins and a small force, and Gokul Ghosāl took advantage of this circumstance to obtain the confiscation of the property of some of the *chaudhuris* and to get it into his own hands.† Subsequently by threats and ill-treatment he forced others to sell their property until nearly the whole island had come into his possession. The complaints of the dispossessed *chaudhuris* finally came to the cognisance of the Dīwān, and in 1770 A.D. one of them was reinstated, and on the appointment of Collectors in 1772 A.D. the office of *ahdādār* was abolished. Gokul Ghosāl, however, and Bishun Charan Bose remained in possession of most of the island, and the former's position served for some time to prevent com-

* This means simply 'officer,' but is perhaps the same as *wahadādār*, a name given to the elected chiefs of the little village of Shella in the Khāsi hills.

† Paras. 130—133 of Mr. Duncan's report. It is a curious fact that Mr. Duncan was unable to find any authority for Captain Nollikins' action and it seems questionable whether there really was any rebellion.

plaints from reaching the ears of the authorities. At last in 1778 A.D. the Board of Revenue deputed Mr. Duncan to enquire into certain definite charges against the late *ahdādārs* and generally into the state of affairs in the island, and he submitted an interesting but very prolix report, which throws much light on the condition of the country and people. At the close of this enquiry Mr. Duncan urged that a European officer should be kept in charge of Sandwīp. The Governor did not accept this recommendation, but in 1790 a Mr. Booth had to be deputed as a Special Commissioner for the settlement of disputes, and a Mr. Rawlins was sent there to survey it about the same time; after that too it appears that special officers were sent there from time to time. In 1808 a Mr. Paton surveyed the islands and *chars*, in 1814 Mr. Tucker was deputed to enquire into a number of disputes over the salt lands and the alluvial formations in the Meghnā, and in 1817 serious disturbances led to Mr. Walter, Registrar of Chittagong, being deputed to the island. In his report submitted in the following year, Mr. Walter laid much stress on the inconvenience of the divided jurisdiction in the islands, some being under Chittagong, some under Tippera, and some under Bākarganj, and on the impossibility of proper supervision from stations so far away. From a letter of the 14th May 1811 it appears that "Bāmni and other *chars*" had then recently been transferred from Chittagong district to Tippera, but Sandwīp and Hātia continued to form part of the district of Chittagong until the year 1821.*

Formation of the district of Noākhāli.

In 1820 a Calaries Committee sat to investigate complaints of the inconvenience arising out of the position of the Salt Agent at Noākhāli, and recommended that he should be invested with certain executive powers.† Mr. Plowden, then Salt Agent, represented that any such encroachment on the province of the Collector must entail friction and that it would be better to form a new district and make him its Collector. In the upshot the Board concurred, and in 1821 Mr. Plowden was appointed in addition to his duties as Salt Agent to be Collector of Bhulua with jurisdiction over lands taken from the neighbouring districts, and comprising approximately the present mainland and islands of Noākhāli together with Dakhin Shāhbāzpur on the west of the Meghnā. In 1868 the district began to be known as Noākhāli. In 1869 Dakhin Shāhbāzpur was transferred to Bākarganj district. By a notification, dated 31st May 1875, the boundary between Tippera and Noākhāli was re-laid, 78 villages containing an area of 43 square miles going

* In 1786 the *Taraf* Bhawāni Charan Dās in *pargana* Sandwip was placed under the Collector of Bhulua, but this did not affect magisterial jurisdiction.

† The report is not forthcoming, but this much appears from the correspondence. Calary was the common term for a salt factory.

from Tippera to Noākhāli and 22 villages comprising nearly 13 square miles from Noākhāli to Tippera. In 1876 the Feni sub-division was formed, and *thānās* Chhāgalnaia of Tippera and Mirkāsarāi of Chittagong district were included in it; but the latter was re-transferred to Chittagong in 1878. The last revision of the boundaries was in 1881 when the Feni river was made the boundary between Noākhāli and Chittagong and four villages comprising an area of about four square miles were transferred to the former.

Divisional Commissioners.

In 1829 when Commissioners were first appointed to relieve the Board of Revenue and the Judges of some of their duties and the province was parcelled out among them, Noākhāli was assigned to the division of the Commissioner of Chittagong, and has remained so ever since.

Administration of justice.

In the year 1772 the East India Company established in each district two courts, the civil or *dīwāni* court over which the Collector presided aided by the native *dīwān* and other officers, and the *faujdāri* or criminal court presided over by the *kāzi* and *mufti* aided by two *maulavis*, who administered Muhammadan law. The Collector, however, supervised the proceedings of the criminal court, procured the attendance of witnesses, and executed its sentences. In 1775 the magisterial functions of the Collectors were transferred to native officers known as *faujdārs*. This system did not work well, and in 1781 A. D. the civil courts of the districts, other than Chittagong and a few others, were placed under separate judges who were invested with power to apprehend offenders and commit them for trial before the *daroga* of the nearest *faujdāri;* this being for Noākhāli mainland that at Mymensingh.

In 1787 the head of each district was invested with revenue, civil, and criminal powers, but three years later the system was again modified, and a Judge-Magistrate as well as a Collector was appointed to each district. As a civil court the Judge could try all suits arising within the district, subject to certain exceptions in favour of European British subjects, who were, however, required to agree to submit themselves to the jurisdiction of the local courts as a condition of being allowed to live more than ten miles from the Presidency. As Magistrate, the Judge could arrest offenders and try them for misdemeanours and minor crimes, the law being laid down by the Muhammadan law officers.

Thus in 1790 the Judge-Magistrate of Tippera exercised criminal and civil jurisdiction on the mainland, and the Chief of Chittagong in the islands, while serious criminal trials were conducted and appeals heard before the Court of Appeal and Circuit for the Dacca Division. As no Judge was appointed to the district of Bhulua on its formation in 1821, the jurisdiction in civil and criminal cases remained unaltered—Dakhin Shāhbāzpur being under the Judge of Barisāl; but the assistant to the Salt Agent was vested with the powers of a Joint Magistrate and placed in immediate charge of the police and criminal administration and seems to have acted to most intents as District Magistrate until in 1832, on the amalgamation of judicial and executive functions, the Collector became Magistrate. It is curious that the Joint Magistrate was called the "Joint Magistrate at Noākhāli" though the name of the district was Bhulua. In 1877 A. D. the district of Noākhāli was made a civil and sessions division and a separate Judge appointed.

Law and order in early days.

The following extract from Mr. Duncan's report on Sandwīp describes the system of administration of justice as it existed in that island before the East India Company took the responsibility:—

"The administration of justice was anciently conducted as to matters of meum and tuum under the authority of the Fauzdar, formerly resident in Sandwīp whence may be derived its late and (in some measure) current name of the Fauzdāry or Fauzedāry adālat. After the Government discontinued to maintain a fortress in Sandwīp and the consequent removal of the Fauzdār, justice was, it is said, carried on by the Daroga or officer appointed for that purpose; but, if not before, this Daroga is known to have from about the year 1760 acted entirely under the authority of the Naib Ahdādār who used on fixed days of the week to sit in the *adālat*, and attended by the Daroga, the Kānungo and the Zamīndār to settle causes which had been made ready for hearing by the Daroga and his assistants.

"The court took equally cognizance of all matters civil and criminal, its jurisdiction being only restrained as to matters of revenue, the cognizance of which rested with the Ahdādār in his separate capacity. The Zamīndārs affirm that their pargana was not included in the general Fauzdāri jurisdiction of the Province. In matters of debt this court retained the fourth of the sum litigated and exacted discretionary fines for theft, dacoity, fornication, assault and the like. Till the year 1171 (1764) it was customary to exact for the emolument of the Ahdādār an *Estāk** of $1\frac{1}{2}$ annas per diem from the parties together with 1 anna for the peon who had then in his charge; but this *Estak* being abolished, the peon fee was augmented to $1\frac{1}{2}$ anna which is now the current rate of the pargana.

"These articles composed a fund for defraying the charges of the court and its officers besides which 300 or 400 rupees had under the appellation of Fauzdāri been since 1170 settled as the Jamā or Government rental of this *mehal* and annexed to the taxes or general revenue of the pargana after the expenditure on which two accounts the residue was paid towards the Ahdādār's *Khansamany* or private account."

---

* Probably "Itlāk." This and all similar exactions were prohibited by the Regulations of the 15th August 1772.

Other abuses not unknown in Bengal at the present day appear to have been rife at that time. Frivolous and false complaints were a common weapon for the satisfaction of private grudges, so much so that while the Regulations of 1772 provided only a pecuniary penalty in such cases, in 1780 it was found necessary to empower the courts to award corporal punishment when the gravity of the offence required it. Another device, often resorted to by refractory *zamīndārs* to get rid of officers sent by the Collector to take possession of their estates, was to summon persons they wished to annoy to appear before the civil court, as witnesses in a case in which they had really no concern, thus giving them a needless journey to Dacca or Calcutta.

The report also brings out strongly the difficulties experienced by officers in those days in regulating their procedure. Forgery, we learn, was extremely common, and perjury the general rule. Hindus of good caste professed to be debarred from taking an oath, and apparently considered it by no means incumbent on them to speak the truth without it.

The technicalities of Muhammadan law seem also to have conduced to the failure of justice, for Mr. Duncan tells of a case in which a salt watcher was resisted in the execution of his duty, and on his attempting to carry out his object by force was killed. The case was clear, but the *maulavis* ruled that the circumstances did not bring the killing under any express head of the Muhammadan law, and the man was acquitted; though one learned officer appears to have suggested that the act might be punishable as a contempt of Government.

From 1772 onwards as experience was obtained rules were made to meet the difficulties and promote the ends of justice, and these were finally amplified and consolidated into Regulations IV and IX of 1793, which, while according recognition to the impropriety of administering oaths to certain classes of persons, made their evidence relevant, modified the application of Muhammadan law, and abolished mutilation as a punishment.*

Difficulties of administrations.

The correspondence of these early years is very incomplete, but such as it is serves to throw some light on the difficulties under which the administrators laboured. There were continual complaints of the refractory and turbulent character of the *zamīndārs* and *tālukdārs* of the district. *Pargana* Ambarābād in particular was a constant source of trouble. The *zamīndārs* having refused to engage for the *jamā* of Rs. 50,000 proposed, the Collector had been directed to take possession and collect the rents. He protested representing the impossibility of obtaining any reliable account of the assets or of realising rents from the tenure-holders. "The *talukdārs*," said he, "had in the first instance

* For a further account of the difficulties the reader is referred to Mr. Warren Hasting's letter of the 3rd August 1773 and other papers reprinted at page 114 of Colebrooke's Supplement to the Bengal Regulations. Space prevents a further account here of the growth of the present judicial system.

secreted their *patwāris* and falsified their accounts, inaependent of which they had delivered *pattas* to their *ryats* at an inferior rate to that of the village with the view of diminishing their assets during the period their land was held *khāss*." The Board, however, insisted, and *sazāwāls* were appointed and *amīns* deputed, but even so, the most rigorous measures failed at first. Two years later, however, the *pargana* was settled at a revenue of Rs. 95,631, nearly double that originally proposed, and the Board of Revenue wrote a characteristic letter to Sir John Shore emphasising the success of their postponement of the permanent settlement of the estate. In not a few instances the Collector's orders were treated with contempt and his peons beaten, and eventually he had to resort to the practice of borrowing the Judge's *chaprāsis*, who, apparently, commanded more respect. Some idea of the confusion then prevailing may be gathered from the fact that in 1793, *parganas* Bābupur, Dandra, Allahābād, Ambarābād and Jagdia, and part of Torah were held *khāss* for various reasons. One of the *zamīndārs* of Dandra and Allahābād was in prison on a multiplicity of charges, including murder and attempted rape; and many of his fellows seem to have been little better. Sandwīp was as bad, and as late as 1810 the Collector of Islāmābād (Chittagong) wrote to the Board before deputing an *amīn* there "as in a dispute of such a nature affrays of a serious nature frequently take place in this zillah."

Less is heard of these difficulties in the later correspondence, but the following extract from Mr. Plowden's letter of the 28th October 1821, regarding the formation of the district of Bhulua shows that there had not been much real improvement:—"Such is the turbulent and depraved character of the natives in the district in question that without the appointment of an active magisterial officer to aid my operations I must candidly state to your Board that I have not the most distant hope of carrying into effect one single object of my appointment. The local experience and information I possess has satisfied me that the populous inhabitants of the Chars have from the absence of all control, by the habitual resort to violence for the settlement of their dispute and adjustment of their grievances whether real or pretended, become a most lawless race of men, and that it is impossible to hope under such circumstances any advancement of success can attend my revenue proceedings unless I have the aid of a Joint Magistrate expressly appointed for the superintendence of the police jurisdiction of the same expanse of the country as that over which my revenue jurisdiction will extend. Indeed, not only the settlement of the Char lands, but the general state of the country calls for some measure of this kind. The very great distance, at least 80 miles of that part of the country in the neighbourhood of the Salt Agent's official residence and of the islands from the Sadar stations of the several

Magistrates, precludes all possibility of a vigilant and active superintendence of the police. The distress felt by the poorer class of people, the cruelties daily practised, and the murders and robberies that constantly take place, loudly call for that protection which the inhabitants of these districts are at present almost entirely denied. It is in my power to adduce instances to your Board of the most daring robberies, the most barbarous cruelties and the most atrocious murders that have recently occurred in this part of the country." Shortly before this was written a party containing two Europeans had been attacked, and one of them killed and another wounded, while two other Europeans wrecked on a *char* in the Meghnā had a narrow escape.

Disturbances.

After the outbreak in Sandwīp in the year 1767 which necessitated the despatch of troops to the island, the peace of the district was never disturbed by aggression from without. Even in November 1857 when the Mutiny was at its height and mutineers from Chittagong were marching through Hill Tippera, the Collector was able to report that his district was quiet and peaceful. On the 31st January 1860 a large body of Kukis from the mountain fastnesses at the back of the Tippera hills burst suddenly into the plains of Chhāgalnaia, which is now in the Noākhāli district but was then part of Tippera, murdered 185 British subjects and carried off about 100 captives. Troops and police were hurried to the spot, but the Kukis had only remained a day or two in the plains, retreating to the hills and jungles by the way they had come, and since then have given no trouble.

Currency.

The currency was a constant source of worry and confusion owing to the various denominations of rupees in circulation, and the early correspondence is full of references to this subject. In 1766 the Board of Directors endeavoured to establish the coinage upon a gold basis, but the experiment was abandoned before long. In 1788 we find the accounts kept in terms of both *sikka* and *dusmassa* rupees, and in 1790 the Collector complained that while the *zamīndārs* paid their revenue in *sikka* rupees, they made their *mufasal* collections in *Arcot* rupees.

The Regulations of October 1792 recognised 27 different varieties of rupees in circulation, all of which were to be accepted in payment of Government dues up till April 1794, after which only *sikka* rupees of the Company's coinage were to be legal tender. The *sikka* rupee was finally abolished in 1836 A.D. when the Company's rupee became the only legal tender. Copper coinage dates from 1781 when *faloos* and half and quarter *faloos* were coined, the *faloos* being equal to 80 *cowries* or one-sixty-fourth of a *sikka* rupee, and the largest copper coin, being the *madosie*, at 32 to the rupee.

CHAPTER III.

THE PEOPLE.

Census of 1872.

The first reliable census of the inhabitants was taken in 1872 and showed a population of 713,934, living in an area of 1,577 square miles. The general feeling among the people was strongly opposed to the census, and in one instance when the operations were about to begin, a large party of villagers assembled with sticks, assaulted the supervisor and threw him into a tank. The Assistant Superintendent of Police went to the supervisor's assistance and was himself mobbed, beaten and severely injured. It was said that the inhabitants of the district regarded the census simply as a stepping-stone to additional taxation, and, according to another version, the idea among many of them was that the 'General Saheb' wanted to see the women of a particular age and that they were to be sent to Calcutta for the purpose. No one knows who was meant by the General, but it shows how ignorant the people were and how little likely to give any help to the enumerators. Nevertheless, the Collector of the district expressed his belief in the general completeness and accuracy of the return and there seems no reason to doubt it; but even in 1891 there was a widespread idea among the people that the census was but a precursor of additional taxation.

Census of 1881.

In 1881, when the second census was taken, the population was found to have decreased by 2·14 per cent. The sole and sufficient reason was the terrible loss of life in the cyclone of 1876, in which over 36,000 persons are believed to have been drowned, while another 49,000 were swept away by the epidemic of cholera that ensued. Most of the deaths were in the *thānās* of Hātiā, Begamganj and Sandwīp, in which the numbers of inhabitants in 1881 were respectively 25·58, 15·54, and 16·72 per cent less than in 1872. In the rest of the *sadr* subdivision there was an increase, and that there was none in Feni and Chhāgalnaia seems to have been due to the absence of a good many men who had gone to collect forest produce in Hill Tippera.

Censuses of 1891 and 1901.

Since then the recovery of the district has been rapid and uninterrupted.

The prosperity of the decade preceding 1891 was practically unbroken, but in 1893 there was a cyclone, which did not cause directly much loss of life, but destroyed a great part of the ripening harvest, wrecked nearly half the betel-nut palms, drowned a large number of cattle, and was followed by an outbreak of cholera. The people had hardly recovered when a blight fell upon the betel-nut trees, which died by thousands, and the early cessation of the rains in 1896 damaged the harvest and occasioned a good deal of distress. Yet, in spite of these unfavourable conditions, there was not one year in which the recorded deaths numbered more than the births. The increase in the population between 1881 and 1891 was 23 per cent. In 1901 the population was 1,141,728, showing a further increase of 13·1 per cent, and the only local area which in either period failed to show a substantial advance is the Companyganj independent outpost (formerly known as Bāmni *thānā*), of which a great part has of recent years been washed away by the Bāmni river. Elsewhere the increase in the last decade has been least in Sudharām *thānā*, which has been losing land along its southern face, and in Chhāgalnaia which has 1,033 inhabitants to the square mile, a very high figure for a purely rural area, and has probably lost a good many emigrants to Hill Tippera.

The growth of the population in the western *thānās* is remarkable, most of all in the case of Rāmganj in the extreme north-west, which in the last three decades has shown advances of 27·25, 23·06, and 20·04 per cent, and had in 1901 no less than 1,023 inhabitants to the square mile. "The cause," said the Magistrate in 1891, "must be sought in the extraordinary fertility of the soil and the immunity of the district from scarcity caused by the vicissitudes of the season."

Mr. Gait, writing on the census of 1901, says: "These *thānās* escaped the cyclone of 1893, their climate is particularly good, and they adjoin the *thānās* in the Tippera district, where the greatest development in that rapidly-growing district has taken place."

On the other hand, they suffered severely from the blight that overwhelmed the betel-nut trees along the Meghnā, and have no very large area under jute. Looking to the map, it seems that there must have been a considerable addition to the cultivable area owing to the growth of *chars* and islands in the Meghnā and to the reclamation of marshes, and this may have led to some migration from other parts of the district.

Migration.

Immigration certainly has not contributed to the growth of the population.

In 1901 about 19,000 persons born outside the district were enumerated in Noākhāli, while 34,000 persons born in Noākhāli were found elsewhere, giving a preponderance of 15,000 on the side of the emigrants, while ten years before the difference was under 11,000. The immigration is almost entirely from the adjoining British districts, especially Dacca, Tippera and Chittagong; and the emigration is chiefly to Bākarganj (9,000), Tippera (12,000), and Hill Tippera (4,000). A good deal of the migration is probably temporary, the inhabitants of this part of the country carrying their produce to considerable distances by boat and also serving as boatmen or lascars. It is said, though, that there is a steady exodus to Hill Tippera, where land can be had cheap.

The nominal area of the district is 1,644 square miles, which gives an average of 694 inhabitants to the square mile; the greatest density of population being in Chhāgalnaia *thānā* (1,033 to the square mile), Rāmganj coming second with 1,023 to the square mile, while Sudharām has only 557 inhabitants, and Hātiā only 299 to the square mile. But there is some uncertainty as to the areas owing to the extent of alluvion and diluvion, and in 1891 the Magistrate could only account for the population of Chhāgalnaia on the supposition that the measurement was wrong. The low density in Hātiā is attributable to the fact that a good deal of land on this, as on other islands, is cultivated by men who come over from the mainland and do not bring their families. **Density of Population.**

The only municipal town in the district is Sudharām (Noākhāli), the head-quarters station, the population of which in the thirty years between 1872 and 1901 rose from 4,681 to 6,520. **Towns, villages and houses.**

The total number of villages according to the census of 1901 was 2,633, and the number of houses 209,147, giving an average of 79 houses to a village, and 5·46 persons, to a house. But the village and the house are more or less arbitrary divisions made for administrative convenience at the census.

In the census of 1901 the enumerators found females to outnumber males by about 4 per mille over the whole district, but there were considerable local variations; males being much in excess in Hātiā and Lakhipur, and females in Chhāgalnaia and Feni. **Sex.**

Looking to the much larger number of men who go to work in other districts (26,000 males against 7,000 females) and the nearly equal numbers of foreigners of either sex found in the district, it seems that males are really in excess, and the local variations may be ascribed to the absence of men from their homes

Of the total population 24·04 per cent. were at the census of 1901 returned as Hindu and 75·89 per cent as Muhammadan. In 1872 the proportion of Muhammadans was 74·66 per cent and that of Hindus 25·25, so that the Muhammadans have multiplied slightly faster than the Hindus. ***Religion.***

Islām is strongest in Sudharām *thānā*, where there were once Mughal outposts; while in Chhāgalnaia, belonging to the Hindu Rājās of Hill Tippera, more than a third of the inhabitants are Hindus. Generally the Muhammadans have more enterprise than their Hindu neighbours and are quicker to take up the reclamation of new alluvial formations, and therefore preponderate most on the islands and along the shore. An exception is Sandwip, where the large proportion of Hindus, 26 per cent, is attributable to the migration of many Hāliā Dās (Kaibartta) families thither owing to the washing away of the opposite coast by the Bāmni river. 662 Christians and 289 Buddhists were enumerated in the last census, but no Jews, Jains, or Animists. There were only 13 Brahmos.

Christians.

Of the 662 Christians 14 were of European and allied races and 490 were Eurasian. These latter belonged almost entirely to the Church of Rome and represent the descendants of the former Portuguese settlers. The history of the Portuguese pirates of Sandwīp who terrorised the coasts of Noākhāli throughout the seventeenth century has been given in Chapter II. Later on they inter-married with the women of the country, adopted native habits and superstitions, and that all trace of Christianity was not lost was due to the Elders, who were elected to baptise the children and celebrate marriages in the absence of a priest. This was their condition in 1844 when the first missionary, Jubiburn, arrived in Noākhāli. He stayed but a short while and on his departure the half-castes were left again to relapse into paganism, until the arrival of Father Verite of the American mission of the Holy Cross in 1852. His health gave way, but a fresh band of workers followed in his footsteps. They were caught in a storm in which two of their number were drowned and all their supplies lost; but the mission stayed on and is still working. The present congregation is returned as 751, scattered over 10 villages. Most of them are poor and are domestics or cultivators. They have given up intermarriage with non-Christians, and retain their old Portuguese names, though these have undergone great changes in every day speech, *e.g.*, Fernandez becomes Forān, Manual Manu, etc. The mission maintains two boys' schools and one girls' school at Noākhāli and one girls' school at Izbalia. It makes few converts.

In 1889 a lady missionary of the Queensland section of the Australian mission went to Noākhāli and worked there among the women, and lately a married missionary has taken up his residence in Noākhāli and branch missions have been opened at Feni and Chururia. At the latter place there is a flourishing school presided over by a lady missionary.

Brahma Samāj.

There are now two branches of the Brahma Samāj in the district, the Sādhāran Brahma Samāj, and the New Dispensation Church. Between them they have only twenty members, of whom but five are residents of the district.

Hindus.

As a rule the Brahmans and other high caste Hindus are Sāktas, worshippers of the active producing principle as manifested in one or other of the goddess wives of Siva (Durga, Kāli or Pārvati); while the lower castes are Baishnabs or followers of Chaitanya. These latter retain some aborginal rites and have adopted others from their Muhammadan and Magh neighbours; for instance, they offer cakes to the three lakhs of *pirs* and *satyapirs,* who in the vulgar tongue are disguised as Hindu godlings under the names of the "Trailakhya Narayan and Satyanarayan." The worship of Sitala (the cooler or healer) goddess of small-pox and chicken-pox, is very general and to raise funds for her *pūja* women, generally elderly women of low caste, adorned with vermilion and carrying a winnowing basket, a brass pot, and a little rice and fruit, go from door to door singing and begging, and having made a collection of rice and other offerings sell them and spend the proceeds on themselves and their goddess. In the rains, when snakes are plentiful, there is a *Nāg pūja* or serpent worship. In other parts of Bengal the serpent is worshipped in the name of Manasā Devi, a branch of the *manasā* plant being the symbol of the snake; but that is not so in Noākhāli. Saturn (*Sani*), the god who brings famine, plague, storms and earthquakes, has a great vogue, owing, it is clear, to the evidences of his power on this stormswept coast.

Vultures, *Sakuni*, are revered as messengers of Maghadeswari, a Magh deity. A she-goat or duck is sacrificed and a portion is roasted and with the skin and feathers is exposed in a bamboo basket. If no vultures are drawn to the offering, it is an omen of evil and more sumptuous offerings are vowed to propitiate the goddess. This worship prevails only in the outskirts of the district bordering on Hill Tippera and Chittagong.

Another peculiar festival observed by women has been brought here by the little colony of Dacca and Bikrampur people. On the day of the Sripanchami, sacred to Saraswati, the Hindu Minerva, the last day of the season (March to October) during which hilsa is proscribed to orthodox Hindus of Dacca, the women buy two fish and bury some scales under the post near the image of the goddess.

All the Hindu castes are divided into exogamous groups Cast
having no social relations with each other, *viz.*, those of Sandwip and those of the mainland. The cause of this is that Dilāl Khān's enforcement of marriage between pairs physically suited to one another is supposed to have ruined the caste of the Sandwip Hindus.

The better class Hindus of the mainland in their turn find themselves looked down upon by their fellow castemen of the other side of the Meghnā, because Noākhāli is an unclean land that was not visited by the Pāndavas in their exile.

The principal Hindu castes are the Brahman (21,000), Kāyastha (34,000), Sudra (13,000), Bārui (8,000), Kumhār (5,000), Sutradhar (4,500), Nāpit (16,000), Sunri (9,000), Teli (5,000), Jugi (47,000), Kaibartta (38,500), Namasudra (27,500), and Bhuinmāli (4,000).

There has been a great increase in the number of Brahmans Brahmans.
in the district during the last thirty years. In 1872 only 7,652 Brahmans were enumerated, in 1891 just under 12,000, and in 1901 the number had risen to nearly 15,000, of whom a little over 6,000 were Agradāni, Barna and Daibajna Brahmans ministering to Sudra and degraded castes, or acting as astrologers.

Considering that in all Bengal the increase in the number of Brahmans in two decades was under 4¼ per cent, these figures are remarkable.

Mr. O'Donnell in his report upon the census of 1891 advances a theory that the Brahmans of Eastern Bengal are of Mongoloid extraction, and nearer akin to the Chandāls of their own districts than to the Brahmans of Western India, but it is doubtful how far his remarks are applicable to the Brahmans of Noākhāli, who are said to be for the most part descendants of immigrants from western districts brought either by the Rajas of Tippera or by those of Bhulua with offers of Brahmottar grants.

Kāyasths. Thirty-four thousand Kayasthas were found enumerated in the district in 1901 as against over 45,000 ten years before. The reason for this difference seems to be that in 1891 all the Sudras, (which in Noākhāli is a caste name and includes the sub-divisions or subcastes of Ghulām Kāyastha, Sikdār and Bhandāri), returned themselves as Kāyasthas, whereas in the last census we find nearly 13,000 Sudras in the district.

In Noākhāli the Baidyas consider themselves superior to the Kāyasthas, but they cannot intermarry with Baidyas west of the Meghnā, and owing to their small number were compelled in some cases to take wives from among the Kāyasthas ,though they seldom gave their own daughters to the Kāyasthas in return. The Collector reports that such intermarriage has ceased completely. There are nearly 13,000 Kāyasthas in Chhāgalnaia *thānā*, and after that the largest number in any police circle is 5,300 in Rāmganj.

Sudras. From a little over 4,000 in 1872 the number of persons in the district describing themselves as Sudras has risen to nearly 13,000. The origin of this caste is obscure, but it is commonly supposed that they are descendants of slaves who served in the houses of Hindus of good caste. They hold a respectable position among the *Nabasākhs*, and follow generally the customs of the Kāyasthas, except that it is usually the bride and not the bridegroom who fetches a price (*pan*).

Kāyasthas have been known to take their wives from Sudra families, and to this day it is common enough for a Sudra of position to rise into the ranks of the Kāyasthas.

Bārui. The number of these returned in the census of 1901 was a little over 8,000, more than double what it was ten years before. In 1891 the Collector reported that Bārui was not a caste name in the district, but that some Sudras having taken to growing betel, and being thus united by occupation as well as ancestry had developed peculiar regulative caste arrangements among themselves. The great increase in their number shows that the process still continues.

Sunri and Teli. The Sunris and Telis of Noākhāli generally call themselves *Sāhā*. They are the great shopkeeping and trading caste of the district, and many of them are very well off.

Jugis. The Jugis, or Jogis as they prefer to be called, numbering nearly 47,000, are the principal race caste of Noākhāli. Their origin is obscure, but Dr. Buchanan thought it probable that they were either the priesthood of the country during the reign of the dynasty to which Gopi Chandra belonged, or Sudras dedicated to a religious life but degraded by the great reformer Sankarāchārya, and that they came with the Pal Rājās from Western India. They are weavers by profession, and regard the family of Dalāl Bazār in the Noākhāli district as the head of their race. In the middle of the seventeenth century Braja Ballav Ray of that family was *dalāl* or broker, and his brother appraiser, of the English factory of Char Pātā on the Meghnā, and the son of Braja Bullav was given the title of Rājā and a rent-free estate, which is still held by his descendants. The Jugis of Noākhāli belong generally to the Māsya group, who perform the Srāddha thirty days after death. They bury their dead instead of burning them, merely putting fire into the mouth of the corpse. They do not employ Brahmans, but have priests of their own, who are known as Mahātmas or Pandits, and sometimes as Goswāmis. Jugis usually call themselves Nāth, and the better classes of them describe themselves as Pandit-Nāth. At one time weaving in Noākhāli was in a bad way, and the Jugis, who rarely have cultivation of their own, were forced to work as day labourers, but in the last few years there has been some resuscitation of weaving and the Jugis seem to be doing well. They are a well educated and enterprising race and their numbers in Noākhāli have increased by about 24 per cent in 20 years, though in other parts of Bengal they seem to be dying out.

Kaibarttas. Next to the Jugis come the Kaibarttas, now over 38,000 and increasing rapidly. In the census of 1901 Kaibartta, Hāliā Das, and Jāliās, have been all classed together, though in 1891 only one section of the Jāliās were treated as Kaibarttas. About 11,000 Kaibarttas are now returned as belonging to the fishing or Jāliā section of the caste, but the figures must be received with caution, as there is naturally a tendency for the fishermen to enrol themselves in the more reputable class if they have any land. The Hāliā Dāses or cultivating section of the Kaibartta caste are now a rising race.

Namasudras. The Namasudras, or Chandāls, as they used to be called, are supposed to be the descendants of a tribe who entered Bengal from the north-east. The number enumerated in the district in 1901 was a little over 27,000, but this by no means represents the proportion of the population belonging to this race, for the greater part of the Muhammadans of the district are probably the descendants of converts from this caste. They are divided into four classes—*viz.*, (1) Bachhāri, who are cultivators, and also deal in *hoglā* leaves and mats; (2) Saralya, who are fishermen and carry palanquins; (3) Amarabādia, who are fishermen, but do not carry palanquins ; (4) Sandwīp, who live in Sandwīp and grow betel leaves. Each of these classes is endogamous in itself.

The cultivating Namasudras are rising in the social scale and in material prosperity. They are perhaps more industrious, persevering, and economical, but somewhat less intelligent than their Muhammadan fellow cultivators, rather obstinate and of an excitable temper.

Bhuinmāli.

These are the sweeper caste of Eastern Bengal, corresponding to the Hāris of Western Bengal, but consider themselves superior. Their women do not as a rule assist in scavenging, and they profess not to work for Chandāls. In Noākhāli they have two sub-castes, Barabhāgia and Chhotābhāgia ; the former are chiefly cultivators, musicians, and palanquin bearers, and having abandoned their race profession and abjured pork hold themselves aloof from their still degraded brethren.

Rise of castes.

Caste divisions are less rigid to the east of the Meghnā and it is said that well-to-do members of lower castes can obtain admission into one of higher rank ; not all at once, but by change of surname, association with members of the better caste, and judicious expenditure, recognition is obtained in course of time. Thus a successful Jugi, Saha, or Namasudra assumes a convenient title such as *Majumdār* or *Chaudhri*, and discarding the old forms of address weaves the new title into every conversation. His brothers become *Bara Majumdār*, *Chhotā Majumdār*, etc., and when the neighbours have become accustomed to the new name he boldly insists on its adoption, and what is at first overlooked and then tolerated meets by persistency and repetition with general acknowledgment

So the son of a Dhobi or a Namasudra may be found with the title of *Majumdār*, though as yet there is no record of their having been admitted into the ranks of the Kāyasthas or of their daughters having been accepted as brides by orthodox Hindus of the superior castes. Sudras, however, have been known to obtain admission to the ranks of the Kāyasthas, and Kāyasthas have become Baidyas.*

* It is perhaps not generally known that the Muhammadan Governors exercised a certain control over caste, and that this was in a measure claimed by the East India Company as their successors—*vide* the following extract from the proceedings of the President and Council dated the 16th August 1769 :—

"The peculiar punishment of forfeiting castes, to which the Hindus are liable, is often inflicted from private pique and personal resentment amongst themselves, and requires to be restrained to those occasions only where there may be a regular process, and clear proofs of the offence before the Brahmans, who are their natural judges. But when any man has naturally forfeited his caste, you are to observe that he cannot be restored to it, without the sanction of Government ; which was a political supremacy reserved to themselves by the Muhammadans, and which, as it publicly asserts the subordination of Hindus, who are so considerable a majority of subjects, ought not to be laid down ; though every indulgence and privilege of caste should be otherwise allowed them.

Out of the 866,290 Muhammadans in the district 860,580 returned themselves in 1901 as Shekhs; of the residue about 1,000 called themselves Pathāns and 1,300 Saiyads, the others include Nikari (fish dealers) 1,000, Nagarchi (drummers) 900, and Dai (midwives and castrators of cattle) 1,300. They are all Sunnis of the Hanafi sect. Among the Saiyads and Pathāns may be seen aquiline features and sinewy frames that proclaim unmistakably their foreign extraction, but it may safely be said that a vast majority of the Shekhs and lower sections of the community are descended from the aboriginal races of the district, some few also from Kāyastha converts. Indeed Pir Ambar Shāh in *pargana* Ambarābād and Pir Mīr Ahmed Khandkar in *pargana* Bābupur are credited even by Hindu historians with an immense number of conversions, and Muhammadans with surnames of Chanda, Pāl, and Dutt, are to be found in the district to this day. Formerly, it is said, the Muhammadans kept to many of their old Hindu customs, but about the middle of last century they came under the influence of a reforming priest, Maulavi Imāmuddīn, and are now, almost to a man, Farāzis. They abhor all innovations (*bida'at*) and the worship of saints (*shark*). Consequently they keep only the most orthodox of festivals and reverence no local shrine; even the worship of 'the three lakhs of pirs' is now confined to the Hindus. Muhammadans.

The birth of a child is an occasion for a feast to friends and relations, and the guests are expected to make small presents of from four annas to a rupee. Fifty to three hundred persons may be invited and Rs. 500 spent on such an occasion, but there is no music, dancing, or singing. *Customs.*

One curious custom in Noākhāli is that women who are yet not strictly secluded invariably carry an umbrella when they walk abroad, and it seems to offer as complete protection as a *barka.*

Hindu wedding ceremonies in Noākhāli are peculiar only in that they sometimes take place in the bridegroom's not the bride's house, the parents of the bridegroom bearing the whole expense. Remarriage used to be allowed among Namasudras, Dhobis, and other low castes, but is becoming more and more uncommon, as, in the effort to rise, the lower castes endeavour to assimilate their customs to those of the higher castes.

Muhammadan marriages are usually celebrated in the bride's house.

There is nothing in the dress of the Hindus of Noākhāli that differs from that found in others parts of Bengal. Formerly a rag round his waist was all that the peasant wore, but nowadays he has generally a decent *dhuti* of Manchester or country-made cotton, a cotton sheet (*chādar*) to wrap round his shoulders; and of late years woollen wests of English or German manufacture have become common. The Farāzi Muhammadans commonly wear a *lungi,* which is a cotton cloth, generally striped or in coloured *Dress.*

checks, wrapped round the loins but not passed between the legs, and a little muslin cap. Their shawls are often coloured, blue or pink. To wrap themselves in during the cold weather nights quilts stuffed with tree cotton (*dhusa*) are in general use and look very effective, while those who cannot afford this use a covering of old clothes and rags stitched together (*kantha*); and as a protection against sun and rain when working in the fields the peasants put on a large and strange kind of basket work or mat hat (*jongra*) shaped like a tortoise shell that shields the whole spine. Mat umbrellas, effective but clumsy, have been almost completely displaced by Manchester cotton umbrellas. The women wear *sāris*, a sheet about five yards long of white or coloured cotton. For ornaments a cultivator's wife will have lacquer bracelets (*lākh churi*), a silver necklace (*hāsuli*), and a gold nose ring (*nāth*). A locket (*ta'wiz*) will generally be added, and of course among the well-to-do classes there will be more ornaments, ear-rings perhaps, and anklets.

Houses. The substantial cultivator has usually four huts in his homestead, all facing on one courtyard, with one or two cattle-sheds and one or two houses for stores. Two of the huts would be set apart as sleeping rooms for the male and female members of the family; a third would be reserved for a cook-shed, and the fourth for the *baitakkhāna* or sitting room, in which visitors are received and where men sit and smoke in the evening. The huts are usually built on raised plinths plastered with clay and cow-dung. The walls are of hill bamboos interlaced and attached to wooden supports, roofs are of thatching grass (*ulu* or *chan*) laid on a bamboo framework. Those who can afford it, roof their houses with corrugated iron, and sometimes have the walls of the same material as a protection against incendiarism, which is not uncommon in this district.

In the east of the district the size of the homesteads is regulated strictly by convention, the common size being 7 *nals* by 10 *nals* (the *nal* being 12 feet), but other sizes are found, and an astrologer is consulted to determine the dimensions before a new homestead is marked out. Formerly even Muhammadans sought the advice of Hindu *achāryas* on this point, but at present they have recourse to their own *maulvis*.

Furniture. The furniture is of the simplest even in the houses of those who are comparatively well off. The poor sleep on mats (*chatai* or *pāti*) laid on the floor, but in more substantial houses the bedding is spread on a raised platform or bedstead of wood (*chauki*). The peasant generally squats and requires no chair, but a cane or bamboo stool and a plank bench will often be found. Muhammadans generally use earthenware plates and dishes, but these have not been adopted by the Hindus. A bellmetal plate (*thāl*), a brass water pot (*ghati*), a brass cup (*bāti*), a brass or whitemetal utensil with a spout like a teapot (*badna* or *gāru*), a few earthenware cooking pots and water pitchers, and an iron pan (*karai*), will be found in most houses. Muhammadans generally use copper vessels (*dekchi*) for cooking. Spoons, knives, pestles, baskets, etc., for cutting up and preparing the food complete the ordinary equipment.

Food. Rice is the staple food of the district. The cultivators have as a rule three meals in the day; at the midday and evening meals boiled rice forms the foundation, and with it are mixed pulses and vegetables, and fish, if this is to be had. In the morning a little of the rice left over from the previous night is taken cold, or perhaps a little parched rice (*chira*), or *muri*, which is rice boiled, dried, husked and blown up by cooking it on a pot of hot sand, or *khai*, another preparation of rice cooked in heated sand. A little jack or mango fruit may be added if in season, and the well-to-do have cakes of wheat flour.

Fowls and ducks are to be seen about the Muhammadan households, and are eaten on festive occasions, and goat's flesh is also a popular dish.

Language. It is a curious and interesting fact that the dialect of Bengali spoken in Sandwip differs from that in the rest of the district. The vernacular of Sandwīp resembles closely that of Dacca, and is classed by Dr. Grierson* in the Eastern Bengali group. The chief peculiarities of this dialect are as follows:—The inherent vowel is usually pronounced like 'o' in 'hot' but sometimes lengthened like the 'o' in 'boat.' An unaccented 'i' is almost invariably pronounced not in its own syllable but epenthetically in the preceding syllable. The aspirate whether standing by itself or in soft aspirated consonants is not sounded. The sibilants are all pronounced as 'sh', the sound of hard 's' being given to 'chh', while an initial 'ch' is pronounced as 'ts'. The consonant 'j' of standard Bengali becomes 'z'. The termination of the accusative dative is 'ere', and that of the instrumental locative is 'ẽ', or after a vowel 'tẽ'. Verbs form their infintives in 'to' or 'tām'. As special forms distinguishing it from the Dacca dialect may be noted the interpolation of 'gā' before the case terminations of the plural, the use of the verb 'dite' (to give) to form inceptive compounds as in *karan dila* (began to do), and the infinitive in 'tām'. There is also a tendency to drop the letter 'r'. In Hātiā and on the mainland of Noākhāli the dialect spoken is very similar to that of Chittagong and is placed by Dr. Grierson in the south-eastern group, though it contains several forms that belong rather to the eastern group. An initial aspirate is usually, and a medial one often, dropped. The initial 's' often becomes 'h' and 'p' and 'ph' are pronounced like 'f' or sometimes even as 'h', as 'holā' for 'polā' a son. 'S' when it does not become 'h' is pronounced as 'sh', and the sound of hard 's' is represented by 'chh'. 'T' and 'th' hard are often

---

* Linguistic Survey of India, Vol. V, page 247.

changed to 'd', thus 'chhotā' is pronounced '*sōdo*' and 'j' and 'jh' are pronounced like 'z' in zeal. Final 'a' in the past tenses of verbs is omitted as in *āchhil* (pronounced *āsil*) was, and final 'e' is often dropped. Short words with long 'a' in the first syllable sometimes insert 'i' or less frequently 'u', thus 'hāil,' for 'hāl,' a rudder. Single consonants between two vowels are often dropped, and 'm' in such a position is changed to *anunāsika*, thus 'chākar' is pronounced 'sãor' and *āmār* becomes *ār*. Curious grammatical forms are the termination in 'r' for first person present of the verb, *e.g.*, *mōriēr* (I die or am dying), *koriyer* (I do); the future in 'u' as *kamu* (I shall say); the infinitive in *tām*, more rarely in *to*, the second person singular in 't' as *āsŏt* (thou art); the use of *gā* to form the plural as in *tā-gā-re* (to them); and of *thun* for the ablative as in *hāt-re-thun* (from the market).

CHAPTER IV.

PUBLIC HEALTH.

In Hunter's statistical account of the district written about the year 1876 fever, diarrhœa, dysentery, rheumatism, and cutaneous affections were said to be endemic; cholera then rarely assumed an epidemic form though sporadic cases were met with in the cold season; and small-pox recurred annually, and inoculation against it was common. It was then reported that the jungle near Lakhipur and the tanks and marshes in Rāmganj *thānā* were particularly unhealthy. At present the general standard of health is wonderfully high considering the low level of the district and the habits of the people, who live in huts, generally on the bank of some weed-covered pool and so surrounded by trees that sunlight and air can hardly penetrate, and will bathe in that pool and drink its water even though some fine well-preserved tank exists a few hundred yards away.

Births and deaths. The number of deaths recorded in the years 1893—1902 amounted to 352,536, or 32·8 annually per thousand of the mean population for the decade, and for the next six years the number of deaths averaged 29·5 per mille per annum on the estimated mean population.* In 1888 the Civil Surgeon returned the average mortality at only 21·6 per 1,000, but it may safely be said that the reporting was defective. The number of births reported in the decade 1893—1902 was 475,366, showing an apparent increase in population of about 123,000 whereas the actual increase was 132,000, and that in spite of a preponderance of emigration over immigration. Calculated on the mean population for that decade the annual birth-rate was 44·2 per mille, and for the following eight years it averages a little less; we may take it that the population is increasing annually by about 1½ per cent, and must by 1908 have risen to nearly, if not quite, one and a quarter million. In 1908 the total number of deaths registered was 33,447 and that of births 53,581, giving an increase of over 20,000 persons, or more than 16 per thousand on an estimated population of 1,250,000. The year 1909 was exceptionally unhealthy; the deaths recorded being 42,996, or about 34 per mille of the population, against 52,448 births.

Local Variations. It is noticeable that the proportion of deaths among Muhammadans is much greater than among Hindus; the death rates among the former according to the returns of the Sanitary Com-

---

* The figures will not tally with those in Table VI of the district statistics in which the population has been taken wrongly at 1,221,728, a clerical mistake. Moreover I have thought it right in calculating percentages to allow for the growth of population, otherwise the figures must give a mistaken impression of an increasing death rate. The same remarks apply to the birth rates.

missioner for the years 1905—08 being from 2 to 5 per mille greater than among Hindus. Possibly however this is due to the ratios being falsified by the greater increase in the total Muhammadan population. Lakhipur, Rāmganj and Begamganj *thānās*, *i.e.*, the rich betel growing tract in the north-west of the district, have far lower death rates than Hātiā, Sandwip, Sudharām, or Companyganj (Bāmni). In the ten years ending 1902 the death rates in the former three *thānās* were less than two-thirds the rates in the other four. The most unhealthy division during that decade was Companyganj with an average annual death rate of 40·5 per mille; and Sudharām *thānā*, Hātiā, Sandwīp, and Chhāgalnāia all had death rates varying from 37 to 39 per mille. Since then there has been a good deal of change in the relative mortality. For the five years ending in 1909 Hātiā shows much the highest mortality, the death rates for the years 1907 and 1908 being 58 and 61 per thousand calculated on the population of 1901, and for the five years 48 per thousand on an average. The real percentage is lower, but it is impossible to estimate the present population of the islands. The Civil Surgeon attributes the high mortality partly to the large number of immigrants, who suffer from fever brought on by exposure and bad water, and partly to the ravages of cholera. Next to Hātiā comes Feni, which is liable to inundation and has a considerable immigrant population. The same applies to Chhāgalnāia which has about the same death rate as Companyganj. Birth rates vary less than the death rates, the annual number per thousand for the decade 1893—1902 ranging from 39 in Feni to 45 in Hātiā.

In 1908 the nominal birth rate in Lakhipur, calculated on the population of 1901, was over 53 per mille, and though allowance must be made for the increase in the adult population it is clear that the proportion of births was exceptional. On the whole birth rates are highest in Lakhipur, Rāmganj, Hātiā, and Bāmni *thānās*, and lowest in Chhāgalnāia, Sudharām and Feni. Sudharām town returns only 18⅔ births per thousand. An attempt was made at the time of the last census to establish some connection between birth rates and prices, but the conclusions were quite unconvincing.

Seasonal variations.

Statistics do not show very great variations from month to month and the distribution varies a good deal. Generally speaking the rainy months show the fewest deaths from fever, and the cold months, November to January, when the country is drying up, most; but the highest recorded fever mortality in any one month in the last five years, 3,722, was in May 1909 and the next highest in May 1905. Cholera is spread fairly evenly over the year; the greatest number of deaths in any month during the recent outbreaks being 1,373 in March 1907, but there were 963 and 759 deaths in November and December of that year, and 862 in August 1906.

Principal diseases.

Fever is, as everywhere in Bengal, the most general complaint. In Noākhāli it is mostly of the quotidian type and not very virulent ; and the district has not in the last century and a half suffered from any epidemic fevers such as have from time to time depopulated less fortunate parts of Bengal. For the first seven years of this century the deaths from fever decreased steadily. In 1908 fevers were stated to have caused 25,094 out of the 33,381 deaths reported, but it must be borne in mind that to the village chaukidar, who is the source of the information, fever is a convenient term covering all sorts of unrecognised diseases, and it is certain that many of the deaths put down to fever are not due to malaria. The Civil Surgeon is of opinion that lung diseases, pulmonary phthisis and pneumonia, are much more prevalent than the statistics show, and account for many of the deaths put down to fever.

Cholera.

Every year some deaths from cholera are reported, but it has rarely taken a serious hold. After the great cyclone of 1876 it raged in the islands and shores that had been swept by the storm wave, and there was a bad outbreak of it after the cyclone of 1893. Cholera seems to be more prevalent or better reported than formerly, for in the years 1885—87 the average number of deaths attributed to it each year was 674, while the average annual number of deaths from cholera in the years 1895—99 was 1,713, in the next quinquennium 2,511, and in the next four years 4,499. In 1904 it broke out all over the district, but chiefly in the west Next year it was worst in Sandwip, where over one per cent of the inhabitants died of it, and in 1906 there was a recrudescence of cholera over the whole district and 6,028 fatal cases were reported. In 1907 it was yet worse, especially in Hātiā where it caused over 2,000 deaths, but in 1908 the attack abated and the number of deaths fell to 1,561.

Other diseases.

Throughout the districts along the Meghnā the people suffer much from intestinal worms (*Ascaris lumbricoides*). This is not often a fatal complaint, but more than a third of the patients that attended the dispensaries in 1907 were treated for worms ; children are particularly subject to the invasions of this parasite. Ringworm and other diseases of the skin are exceedingly common and account for nearly another third of the patients at the dispensaries. In the markets men may be seen selling vermifuges and remedies for itch and ringworm in gaily coloured paper packets.

Dyspepsia, bowel complaints, and rheumatic affections are common, but not more so than in other districts.

Infirmities.

Leprosy is rare, affecting less than five persons in every 100,000, the lowest proportion in all Bengal. Blindness is on a par with other districts, the proportion of males being 79, and for females 57, in each 100,000. The figures for deaf-mutism, 82 males and 49 females in each 100,000, are high for Eastern

Bengal, but only 32 persons in each 100,000 were returned as insane. On the whole the district may be said not to be seriously affected by any infirmity.

Small-pox and vaccination.

Small-pox is endemic in the district, but has not taken an epidemic form in recent years. In the three years 1880 – 83, the deaths from small-pox were returned as 745 a year, or about 9 persons in every 10,000, but latterly the disease has become less common. There were 467 deaths from small-pox reported in 1901, but the average annual number for the decade ending 1902 was just under 100. Since then there have been rather more cases, or perhaps there has been better reporting, and for the ten years ending in 1908 the average annual number of deaths is about 4 in every 10,000 inhabitants, but in 1908 there were only 53 deaths. Small-pox occurs in every part of the district, but of late years the worst outbreaks have been in Companyganj, where 14 persons out of every 10,000 persons died of it in 1906, and in Sandwīp where nearly 1 in every 1,000 inhabitants died of it in 1907.

Vaccination is compulsory only in Sudharām town; elsewhere it is voluntary. In 1908-09 the establishment for vaccination under the control of the Civil Surgeon consisted of one Inspector, two Sub-Inspectors, one paid vaccinator, and 38 licensed vaccinators; the number of persons vaccinated was over 64,000, and the cost of the operations was Rs. 2,946. It is calculated that a third of the population is now protected by vaccination, but there is a good deal of opposition among the *farāzi* Muhammadans, and some difficulty in realising fees. The practice of in oculation has quite died out.

Dispensaries.

In 1892 there were only five dispensaries in the district and at these on an average 114 persons received treatment daily. Since then the number of dispensaries has grown steadily and in 1908 there were 14 public dispensaries attended daily by about 725 out-patients. Only two of the dispensaries have accommodation for in-patients, *viz.*, Noākhāli, in which the average daily number of in-patients in 1908 was 16·84, and Feni, in which the daily average number was 1·66 patients. Besides these there is a private dispensary at Subhapur, maintained by the Rājā of Hill Tippera. All the other dispensaries, except that at Dalāl Bāzār, which is supported entirely by Babu Surendra Kumar Ray, the local *zamīndār*, are managed by local committees and supported mainly by local fund contributions. Those at Noākhāli, Feni and Harishpur are in charge of Sub-Assistant Surgeons; the others are under qualified native doctors or compounders. The expenditure on these dispensaries in 1909 was Rs. 21,117 including nearly Rs. 5,000 on buildings, and their income Rs. 17,490 of which in round figures Rs. 3,000 came from Government, Rs. 10,000 from local funds, and Rs. 4,000 from subscriptions. The dispensaries are much appreciated, but many of the buildings are very poor,

Those at Begamganj and Bose's Hāt are being reconstructed at a cost of Rs. 1,200 each, and Rs. 12,000 are to be spent on a hospital at Feni. There are a good many native practitioners all over the district. Most of them are unqualified, but in Noākhāli town alone there are six qualified doctors, three Allopaths, and two Homœopaths, while one practises both systems.

Water-supply. For the supply of drinking water Noākhāli depends entirely upon the tanks that are to be found in large numbers in every village. Unfortunately, many of these have been much neglected and allowed to become overgrown with weed until the water is unfit for human consumption. For some time past endeavours have been made to improve the water-supply by excavating or re-excavating tanks where they are most wanted, and reserving them for drinking. To this end the District Board devotes, annually a certain portion of its income, contributing a third of the cost provided another third is contributed by the inhabitants, and when these conditions are fulfilled, Government pays the remaining third. In this way 37 tanks have been reserved, and although it is impossible to prevent their pollution without a larger expenditure on guards than the District Board can afford, yet it is said that these reserve tanks contain generally drinkable water and have proved of much benefit to the people.

CHAPTER V.

PRICES, RENTS, WAGES AND MEASURES.

Prices. Our first glimpse of prices in these parts is afforded by Cesare Federico, who, visiting Sandwīp about 1589, was astonished at the cheapness and abundance of provisions. He bought salted beeves at a little over three shillings each, hogs at half that price, and 'great fat hens' at a penny apiece, and was told he had been shamefully overcharged.

Shamsher Ghāzi, the notorious usurper, who in the beginning of the eighteenth century became for a while dictator of Tippera, fixed the prices at which commodities were to be sold in his dominion.

Clean rice, chillies and cotton were to be sold at 64 seers to the rupee, salt, peas and molasses at 32 seers to the rupee. No doubt these prices were low even for that period, but no other records of that time, or indeed till much later, are available. In 1763 the assessment of Sandwīp was made on the basis of 1¼ *kannua* of paddy to the rupee, but the weight of the *kannua* is an unsolved mystery. In 1866-67 when famine raged through the greater part of Bengal and prices reached an unprecedented height, common rice sold at Rs. 4-12-0 per maund, and the best at Rs. 7-4-0 per maund. In the years 1870—73 when prices had resumed their normal level, clean rice sold at from Re. 1-2-0 to Rs. 2-4-0 per maund according to the season and quality, and paddy at from 7 annas to Re. 1-4-0 per maund.

For the five years 1896—1900 the average price of common rice in Noākhāli was 14 seers per rupee, or Rs. 2-14-0 a maund, and it was slightly cheaper during the next five, but in 1906 there was a remarkable change, and only 8¼ seers of common rice were to be bought per rupee at Kālitārā Hāṭ, and 8½ seers at Feni. These high prices were maintained with slight fluctuations during the next two years, but now are falling fast, and the returns of January 1910 show common rice to be selling at 12 seers a rupee in Noākhāli and 15 seers in Feni. Fine rice may go up to double the price.

Salt is another article of which the prices have varied greatly. In 1766 the East India Company limited its retail price to Rs. 2 a maund, but in 1872-73 it was selling at Rs. 5 a maund and this was the price as late as 1897; after that it became slightly cheaper, and on the revision of the salt duties sold in 1905 at 13 seers to the rupee, and at present sells at 20 seers to the rupee.

Betel-nuts, a most important article of trade, sell at four seers, more or less, to the rupee. From a report of 1830 it appears that at that time the price was 2½ to 3 *kāhans* (16 to 19 seers) a rupee, and that this was less than half the price at the date of the permanent settlement. Betel-leaves fetch one to three annas a *bira*, containing from 96 to 112 leaves. A buffalo sells for about Rs. 45, a good bullock for Rs. 30, and a cow for Rs. 15.

Wages.

In 1852—58 earthwork on the roads was paid for at Re. 1 to Re. 1-8-0 per 1,000 cubic feet. The rates are now Rs. 3-8-0 and upwards. It appears from the Statistical Account that in the twenty years preceding 1876 wages had doubled, but since then there has been little change. The commonest labourer then got, and now gets, 4 annas a day; a man of some skill who can build a hut may get as much as 8 annas a day. Carpenters and masons get from 8 to 12 annas a day; a boatman will get Rs. 5 or Rs. 6 a month, besides two meals a day; and an agricultural labourer engaged for the season receives from Rs. 4 to Rs. 6 a month, or less, if he is given his food. These of course are average wages, and when the demand is great, higher rates prevail. Mr. Cumming states in his report of 1899 that the Noākhāli labourer, who goes north in the autumn and winter for the harvesting, is paid 4 annas and two meals a day, or from 7 to 8 annas without meals. The men who work on the *chars* at seed time and harvest are more highly paid getting as much as 12 annas* a day.

Measures.

Land is measured by the *kāni*, though this tends to be supplanted by the *bigha* of forty yards square which is the standard used in Government surveys. The *kāni* is the area in a rectangle 10 *nals* by 12 *nals*; but the *nal* (reed) varies in length. In 1790 Mr. Dandridge when engaged on the partition of Bhulua reported that the records of the Kanungos mentioned four different *nals*, *viz* :—

(1) the Ilāhi, or divine, containing 10 yards of 12 *musht*, or hands breadth, each ;

(2) the Shāhi, or royal, containing 10 yards of 11 hands;

(3) the Sikandari, or Alexandrian rod, containing 10 yards of 10 hands ;

(4) the *nal* of Mritanjay, containing 10 yards of 9 hands each.

There was no trace of the first two having been used here and the *zamīndārs* laid no claim to either.

The third was the measure claimed by the *zamīndārs* as the old established standard of the *pargana*. The last was the rod used in a general measurement of this district made before the year 1750, and the *zamīndārs* claimed the privilege of measuring the lands of their tenure-holders by it, while retaining for themselves the benefit of the Sikandari *nal*.

---

* Based on local information. In the last quinquenial report the wages of a coolie in Hātiā were given as 4 annas a day in addition to three meals.

The Board decided that the Mritanjay *nal* should be used, but a report made by the Collector in 1888 A.D. does not show the *kāni* so determined, which is equivalent to 2·65 acres, to be in use. The old *tāluks* of Bhulua are shown to be measured by the Sikandari *nal*, giving a *kāni* of 3·06 acres, while newer *tāluks* are measured with a *nal* of 16 cubits (*kāni*=1·58 acres), *haulas* with a *nal* of 15 cubits (*kāni*=1·39 acres) and *raiyati* lands with a *nal* of 14 cubits (*kāni*=1·21 acres). The *Amirābād tāluks* are measured with a *nal* of 18 cubits (*kāni*=2 acres).* For *haulas* the *nal* of 15 cubits, and for *raiyati* holdings that of 14 cubits are found in most *parganas*. Ambarābād has a huge *nal* of 40 cubits. Sandwīp has one of 48 cubits (*kāni*=14·28 acres), and tenures of some classes there are measured with a *nal* of 16 cubits, but each cubit is 20¾ inches. Mr. Duncan notes that the Sandwīp *nal* was regulated by the length of the arm of one of the *chaudhris*. In the southern division of Chakla Roshnābād there are only 30 square *nals* in the *kāni*, which is ·396 of an acre.

The divisions and multiples of the *kāni* are 20 *til*=1 *kāg*; 4 *kāg*=1 *kāuri*; 4 *kāuri*=1 *ganda*; 20 *gandas*=1 *kāni*; 16 *kānis* =1 *dron*.

Most articles are sold by the seer of 82⅜ tolās, but liquids such as milk sell by the standard seer of 80 tolās. The subdivisions and multiples of the seer are 4 *kancha*=1 *chatāk*; 4 *chatāk*=1 *poya*; 4 *poya*=1 *ser* (seer); 5 *ser*=1 *pasuri*; 8 *pasuri*=1 *man* (maund). The standard maund equals 82²⁄₇ pounds avoirdupois.

For time, the day is divided into eight watches (*prahar*), each of which contains 7½ *danda*. The *danda* is used also as a measure of distance, meaning the distance a man would walk in the time, or a mile and a bittock.

Betel-leaves are sold by the *birā*, containing 24 or 28 quartettes (*ganda*) of leaves.

Rent rates. In 1794 the average rate of rent paid by *tālukdārs* in Sandwīp, which was nominally four-fifths of that paid by the cultivator, was Rs. 2-9-0 an acre. By 1837 it had risen to Rs. 3-9-0. In *pargana* Bhulua about the year 1840 the rates of cultivators' holdings ranged from Rs. 2-4-0 to Rs. 4-8-0 an acre, and they rose by about 25 per cent in the next thirty years.

In the correspondence of the years 1860—64 there are numerous references to the rates, which are in almost all cases Rs. 4 or Rs. 5 a *kāni* (or from Rs. 2 to Rs. 4 an acre) for arable land, the measure varying rather than the rate. Homestead land fetched Rs. 7 a *kāni* or more.

In the permanent settlement of lands in Amirābād and Bedarābād made by the Courjon brothers in 1866 rates varied from

* In the Courjon estates (Amirābād and Bedarābād) the *kāni*, according to the sub-divisional officer, is equal to 4 bighas 16 cottas=1·6 acres.

Rs. 4 to Rs. 8 per *kāni* or about Rs. 2-8-8 to Rs. 5 an acre, and were about 20 per cent higher in the settlement of 1869.

In Chakla Roshnābād about 1896 Mr. Cumming found the all-round rate per acre on the holdings of occupancy ryots in the Noākhāli district to be Rs. 3-10-4 per acre, while the recognised rates varied from Re. 1-8-0 to Rs. 4 a *kāni*, or from Rs. 3-12-0 to Rs. 10 per acre.

Recent settlements on Government *chars* give rates of Rs. 2-4-0 to Rs. 2-13-0 an acre for cultivated land. Lower rates are fixed for land in the earlier stages of reclamation. In 1819 Mr. Walters found the tenants of Hātiā to pay no rent for the first eight years, and nowadays tenants begin by paying 6 annas an acre for *degi char* or *malanghi char* lands, the rates rising year by year to about Re. 1-8-0. For cultivable lands they pay at progressive rates rising from 12 annas to Rs. 2-4-0 or Rs. 2-8-0 an acre in five years.

In the settlement of Bāmni (1900—03) the average rents paid by settled *raiyats* were found to be Rs. 2-2-2 per acre, and that for tenure-holders Re. 1-7-2. Under-*raiyats*' rents averaged Rs. 6-15-0 per acre.

A note prepared in the Collector's office mentions a special enquiry made in the years 1896—97 which showed that the rates in the recognised central and southern *thānās* averaged Rs. 12-8-0 a *kāni*—say Rs. 10 an acre—and were slightly lower in the north and west. This note is not to be found, and these rates seem very high in comparison with other returns, even making allowance for the fact that they were only nominal rates, and that old tenants would pay much less.

Indebtedness.

The following account is taken from the Commissioner's Report for the years 1900—1905 :—

"From enquiry made by the Magistrate in two selected panchayati circles it was ascertained that in one circle out of 833 families, 218, or 24·7 per cent, are free from debt, and 102, or 11·5 per cent, are very poor. 107 familes, or 12·11 per cent, have contracted debts amounting to twice their annual income or more. In 29, or 27·1 per cent, of these cases the debts are due to the requirements of trade or the purchase of landed property, while in 57, or 53·3 per cent, the indebtedness is on account of expenditure on social ceremonies. In only 22 cases the debts are reported to be due to litigation. In the other circle out of 935 families, 268, or 28·6 per cent, are free from debts, while 152, or 16·3 per cent, are without any landed property. The debts incurred by 142 families, or 15·18 per cent, amount to twice their annual income or more. Out of these 142 cases, 54, or 38 per cent, have contracted debts for trade purposes or purchase of lands, and 45, or 31·7 per cent, for expenses on social ceremonies.

Taking the average of the two circles, it appears that 26·6 per cent of the families are free from debt and 13·9 per cent have no landed property, while 13·6 per cent are heavily involved, their debts amounting to double their annual income or more. But of these, 32·6 per cent have contracted their debts for the purpose of speculation, while 42·5 per cent. owe their indebtedness to expenditure on social ceremonies. These figures may be taken as representing with fair accuracy the state of things all over the district. It also appeared that the old supposition that extravagance in social ceremonies is the principal cause of poverty stands true, but that litigation contributes less to impoverishment than has generally been supposed."

Material condition.

In 1905 the Collector reported that scarcity was unknown in the district, and the pinch of poverty felt only by a small proportion of the population. The people, he said, were very backward and wanting in enterprise, and their standard of living, though rising slowly, was still lower than that of other parts of Bengal. They wear better clothing than formerly, use more oil in their cooking, and buy small articles of luxury, lamps, and various fancy goods and utensils. The amount in deposit in the savings banks grew steadily for a while, but in 1908-09 the withdrawals were nearly as heavy as the deposits, and it is said that the people are inclined to seek more profitable investments.

CHAPTER VI.

AGRICULTURE.

On the extreme east of the district the country is slightly undulating and intersected by numerous hill streams converging from the west, the north, and the east. The rest of the district is a level alluvial plain, lowest in the centre and rising slightly towards the banks of the Meghnā and the Feni rivers on either side. The soil is a rich alluvial deposit yearly inundated and fertilised by the overflow of the rivers, and with great capacity for retaining moisture. Salt deposits are not unknown, but they have done no serious damage, as owing to the heavy rainfall and the annual inundation crops can be raised in the rainy season on lands that show a saline efflorescence in the winter. Sir Joseph Hooker wrote in 1850 that though the soil at Noākhāli yielded an abundance of salt the water of the Meghnā was only brackish, and it was only the inrush of the tidal waves that did damage. Practically the whole country is cultivated, even the great swamps which occupied the low-lying portions 30 years ago having come under the plough. Irrigation is hardly a necessity, though at the foot of the Tippera hills streams are occasionally dammed up to form a reservoir of water against the hot and dry season.

Rice is the staple crop of the district and in 1908-09 was grown on 965,000 acres, or 76 per cent of the 1,263,900 acres cropped; other food-grains, chiefly pulses, occupied some 77,000 acres only. Oil-seeds are generally grown as a second crop, the most important kinds being linseed, of which the cultivation has increased from 15,000 to 22,000 acres in the present century. Gingelly and mustard are also grown pretty generally. The cultivation of jute extended rapidly during the first years of the century, and reached the maximum of 29,500 acres in the year 1908, but the fall in price has checked its popularity and in 1910, it was sown in only 29,000 acres. A very large area, 101,000 acres, is returned as under orchards and garden produce. To the visitor from other parts of Bengal nothing is more remarkable than the rapid increase in the number of areca-nut, coco-nut and other palms as he proceeds south from Comilla. In the south and west of the Noākhāli district almost every house is surrounded with a grove of betel-nut and coco-nut trees, and in some *parganas* the people depend largely on their produce.

Cultivation.

The soil of Noākhāli requires generally little preparation. The people use a light old-fashioned plough (*nangal*), with a beam (*is*) about 6 feet long, and a wooden share; the whole outfit costing Re. 1 to Re. 1-8. The harrow (*chāgam*), shaped like an ellipse with the ends cut off, is made of bamboo, and costs 5 to 7 annas; and a large rake with long bamboo teeth (*achra*) drawn by bullocks serves the purpose of an English horse hoe or scarifier. It costs Re. 1-4 to make. For digging the *kodāli* or *khanta* (crowbar) are used. Cows are used, as well as bullocks, for ploughing, and on the *chars* buffaloes are employed. Mr. Cumming estimates that three pairs of bullocks can plough an acre in six hours Thirty-five years ago the Collector reported that a pair of oxen would suffice for the cultivation of a 'plough' of land equal to five to six acres and that a pair of buffaloes could manage nearly twice that area.

Extension of cultivation.

In 1873-74 the Collector showed the cultivated area as over 75 per cent of the total area of the district. In 1902, after a special revision of the figures, 785,000 acres, or just under 75 per cent, were found to be cultivated, and in 1907-08 the proportion had risen to very nearly 85 per cent, leaving only 700 acres of fallow and under 36,000 of waste land available for cultivation. The estimates before 1902 must have been inaccurate, and there has been a very great extension of cultivation in recent years, so that little land now fit for the plough is allowed to lie fallow. But the constant formation of new, and diluvion of old, land makes it unsafe to accept the estimates of total area and consequently those of the margin available for extension of cultivation.

Manure.

Rice land requires and receives little manure, except that the last year's stubble is burnt and ploughed into the land in February or March. Jute needs manuring and the cultivator gives it as much cattle dung as he can afford and often some mud dug from the bottom of a tank or ditch. For betel-nut (*supāri*) and coco-nut, paddy husks are used as manure, and the leaves of the *māndār* trees. Betel-vines (*pān*) require rich feeding and are given oil-cake.

Effect of rainfall upon crops.

It is difficult to generalise as to the effect of the amount and distribution of rainfall on the harvest, as what is good for one crop may injure another. Light intermittent showers only are required in April and May, too much rain drowning and damaging the young jute and rice. The rain should be fairly heavy and continuous from the beginning of June till the middle of August, when intervals of fine weather are required for harvesting the *āus*. Too much rain in late August, September and October injured both autumn and winter rice in 1905-06, and in 1902 the fall of 97 inches of rain in the three months June, July, August did much harm. Late rain again interferes with the ploughing of land for the cold weather crops. These require some showers about Christmas, not too early or it may damage the mustard blossom, while showers in March are beneficial and enable the land to be got ready in time for early sowings.

Rice.

The Collector reports that no change has to be made in the account of the rice crop given in 1871. In Noākhāli, as elsewhere, the primary division is into *āus* and *āman*, each of which comprises two distinct classes and many varieties. The first class of *āus* paddy is sown broadcast on high lands in March and April and reaped in July and August; it includes *bālām sāil*, *sāthiā*, and seven other varieties. The second class is sown during the rainy season in June and July, and is reaped in October and November. It comprises four varieties, of which *rājāsāl*, much grown on *char* lands, is always transplanted and the others are sown broadcast.

The long stemmed varieties of *āman* rice, including *jāora* and five others, are sown in low and marshy land in March and April, transplanted in June and July, and reaped in November and December.

The short stemmed paddy, comprising *chaplās*, *rupsāil*, and 31 other kinds, is sown in July and August, transplanted later, and cut in November and December.

In the west of the district it is a common practice to sow autumn and winter rice together, the mixture being known as *bājāl*, each crop being reaped as it ripens.

Several Collectors have reported *boro* rice to be grown in Noākhāli, but the returns of the Agricultural Department do not show any, and the area planted with it must be insignificant.

In spite of a succession of bad or indifferent seasons the cultivation of rice, stimulated no doubt by the high prices, has been extending with astonishing rapidity. While the returns of the year 1901-02 show only 784,000 acres under this crop, those for 1908-09 give the area cropped with rice as 965,000 acres, of which 321,000 are under autumn rice; that is, the proportion of autumn to winter rice is very nearly as 1 is to 2, whereas for the whole province the proportion is as 1 is to 3; the difference is probably due to the classification of *rājāsāl*, which is grown very extensively on *char* lands, under autumn rice. It is very difficult to estimate the total quantity of rice produced, but according to the returns of the Agricultural Department the normal outturn is 9 maunds of clean rice per acre. The estimated outturn for the year 1908-09 was about 335,000 tons, and the average for the last five years was nearly 350,000 tons. The Collector estimates that in a year of average crop the rice produced is sufficient for the comsumption of the district for two years.

Mr. Cumming during the settlement of Chakla Roshnābād caused experiments to be made and found the outturn to be from 19 to 21 maunds of paddy per acre, or, say, from 13 to 14 maunds of clean rice. On this calculation the district should produce about 450,000 tons of clean rice annually.

Other food grains, covering 77,000 acres, consist chiefly of pulses, especially *mug* (*Phaseolus mungo*), *māskulai* (*Phaseolus radiatus*), and *khesāri* (*Lathyrus sativus*). These are generally sown after rice has been harvested from the land. *Arhar* (pigeon pea) is grown in the east of the district, chiefly as a hedge between fields.

Jute. In 1910 jute was grown on about 29,000 acres, producing some 12,000 tons of fibre. According to the returns there has been a very rapid advance in the cultivation of this plant during the present century, but there is reason to doubt the accuracy of the figures before 1908, when a special enquiry resulted in the return of nearly three times the area of the year preceding. The jute lands have to be ploughed four or five times or more and manured as heavily as the cultivator can afford. In February or March the seed is sown broadcast at the rate of 5½ to 7 seers to the acre; it is then ploughed and harrowed over. When the young plants appear, careful weeding is necessary. In July or August the cutting begins, and it takes 14 to 16 men to cut an acre in a day; the cut stalks are tied in bundles and steeped in water under a layer of grass and brushwood for from 10 to 20 days when they should be sufficiently rotted to enable the fibre to be separated by hand. Thirteen men can in a day strip the produce of an acre. The fibre is washed and tied up in bundles of about five seers and dried on bamboo frames; while the refuse is used for fuel.

Oilseeds. Oilseeds are very largely grown and the area devoted to them is increasing rapidly and is now about 45,000 acres. The most important of them is linseed (*tisi*) grown on some 22,000 acres and yielding from 2,000 to 3,000 tons of seed. It is sown in November on land from which rice or jute has been reaped and is harvested in February or March. Gingelly (*til*) is grown on about 14,000 acres, the area under it having nearly trebled in seven years. It is a high land crop, sown in March or April and reaped in May or June. The seed is used medicinally and taken in sweetmeats. Mustard is sown in October, generally on high lands on the river bank after an early crop of rice or jute, and reaped in October. The area under it is some 8,000 acres. There are three varieties, *rai* and the red and white *sarisha*.

Spices and condiments. About 15,000 acres grow condiments and spices, of which chillies (*marich*) are the most important. This is a most paying crop, but grown only in small patches. It is sown in a nursery about October. The seedlings must be kept under shade for a week and regularly watered, and when a month old are planted out about 9 inches apart in a field which has been ploughed seven or eight times, harrowed three or four times, and well manured. In June the plants are plucked, and yield from 2½ to 5 maunds, which may be worth from Rs. 12 to Rs. 50 as the price varies greatly. The plucking is always done by the widows of the village, who keep from a fourth to a sixth as the wages of their labour. Coriander (*dhaniya*), onions (*piyāj*), and garlic (*rasun*), grown at the same season are also included under this head; as also turmeric (*haldi*) which is sown in April and reaped in June. Some dyes, safflower (*kúsum*), etc., are grown in minute plots. Tobacco was once grown in quantities sufficient to affect the assessment, but now only a little for private use.

Vegetables. Radishes (*mula*) are perhaps the vegetable grown most largely. They are sown at the close of the rains and come into the market from the end of November to January. Cucumbers (*sasa*), pumpkin (*kadu*), *kumra* (*Cucurbita pepo*), a small bitter gourd, *baigun* or brinjal, and *ol* (*arum*) of several varieties, are also taken as vegetables.

Sugarcane. Sugarcane was once cultivated largely in Sandwīp; and there are still 600 acres under it in that island, and about the same area in *thānā* Chhāgalnaia and Lakhipur.

Betel-vine. Betel-vine (*pān*) is grown in many places in the district, but there is no record of the number of gardens or the area. It is grown on raised beds (*bhiti*) or on the bank of a tank, and wants a soil strong though sandy. The whole bed is enclosed in a frame of grass and reeds about 7 feet high close enough to protect the plants from the heat without excluding all light and air. The soil is carefully prepared and the seedlings planted out in it about October, and when they begin to grow the vines are trained up on sticks. In the rains new earth has to be added and the plant if well looked after should last for three years bearing continually. It is grown exclusively by Bāruis, and the increase in their number is evidence of the extension of the cultivation of the vine, though only 180 persons are shown in the census tables as occupied in growing it. There is no certainty as to the outturn, but it is a very profitable though very exhausting crop.

Betel-nut. Betel-nut or *supāri* (*Areca catechu*) is one of the staple products of the district. It is found everywhere but grows most thickly towards the Meghnā on the north-west where it forms dense groves extending for miles. The area devoted to this crop has not been ascertained accurately, but it represents a large portion of the 121,000 acres of orchard.*

In Noākhāli areca palms are planted in groves of *māndār* (*Erythrina indica*) which afford them protection from wind and sun and are supposed to improve the soil and to fertilise it with their leaves. The garden is prepared by planting branches of the *māndār* 12 to 15 feet apart each way, and in two to three years on high lands and four to six years on low lands the plantation is ready for the betel seedlings.† Betel-nuts are sown in nurseries in October or November, and two years later, sometimes three or four years, the seedlings are transplanted in July into high lands, or in February or April into low lands. In the first transplanting

* The figure 25,000 for the acreage under orchards given in the Statistical Table VII was based on a wrong classification.

† This account is based on an article by Sir George Watt, No. 8 in the Agricultural Ledger, for 1901.

the young palms are placed midway between the *māndār* trees and are thus 12 to 15 feet apart. But before these palms come into bearing, the *māndār* trees are cut down, all but a fringe round the groves, and their place taken by a second lot of areca palms, which in a fully planted grove thus stand about 6 or 7 feet apart.* Trees planted singly may come into bearing when only six or seven years of age, but in plantations they rarely fruit before the tenth or twelfth year, while the second lot of plants do not come into bearing for 20 years. The fruiting life of a tree is estimated at from 30 to 60 years, and its total life at from 60 to 100 years.

In 1896 the attention of Government was drawn to a plague that was devastating the plantations in Noākhāli and Bākarganj. A similar disease had appeared on previous occasions, but this outbreak started about the year 1892. Its attacks were confined to the cold weather and its symptoms were the withering of the leaves followed by the decay of the terminal bud and finally by the fall of the crown of leaves. Sir George Watt diagnosed the plague as *tyloses*, due to the want of sufficient moisture. The remedy was in his opinion more careful cultivation with better drainage and irrigation, more space between the trees, and leaving the *māndār* in the plantation. The disease however disappeared as mysteriously as it had come, and there is now none in the district. There are various estimates of the outturn of betel-nuts. In 1830 the Collector of Tippera reported that certain estates near the Noākhāli border had been settled on an estimate of the produce of the *supāri* trees, which was that a *kāni* contained 500 trees yielding 100 *kāhans* of nuts worth Rs. 80. The *kāhan* was 6 seers 6 chataks, but the *kāni* in that locality varied from about 1½ to 3 acres. In 1896 Mr. Nitya Gopal Mukherji of the Agricultural Department estimated the produce on the Mania estate at 8 to 15 maunds per *kāni*, say 5 to 9 maunds an acre, which is now worth from Rs. 50 to Rs. 100. It is sold in three states, *viz*:—

(1) *Khari* when after being plucked from the tree the fruit is steeped in water for a week, shelled, and the nut dried in the sun. In this state it is bought in in October-November by traders from Chittagong for the consumption of the Maghs. (2) Ātā, and (3) tāti.—These are more dried and prepared and are exported to western districts.

Coco-nut.

Coco-nut (*nārikel*) is grown extensively in the centre and west of the district and in Sandwīp and is often interspersed in the plantations of areca palm. The tree is raised from seed sown in high lands, generally on the banks of a tank or on the sides of the homestead, at the beginning of the rainy season and begins to bear fruit in its fifth year. Coco-nuts, both ripe and unripe, are consumed largely in the district, more by Hindus than by

* This is taken from Dr. Watt's report, but the Collector informs me that the trees in a grove are more often 1½ to 3 feet apart.

Muhammadans, and are exported by river to Chittagong and elsewhere. Coco-nut oil is prepared locally in small quantities, and *hukkas* are made from the shell, and the stem is used for beams and rafters.

Other fruit trees.

The toddy palm (*tāl*) is to be seen all through the *sadr* subdivision. It is not tapped for its juice, but the fruit is greatly appreciated; the thick reddish juice which it yields when ripe is used in sweetmeats, and the soft kernel (*phoprā*) of the mature nut is eaten also. The stem is used for posts and for small dugouts (*kunda*) that ply on inland *khāls*.

There are a good many date palms (*khajur*). The fruit does not ripen well, but the tree is tapped for the juice which is made into molasses. This is not a very important or profitable industry.

Mangoes are plentiful, but the fruit is among the worst in Bengal being infested with insects. Jack fruit does not do as well as in districts further from the sea. The plantains are fair and are exported in considerable quantities from Rāmganj and Raipur. Oranges and limes of excellent quantity grow in the north-west near Lakhipur, and as they ripen in October or November find a ready market. The tamarind, *papaya*, *badām* (Indian almond), *jalpai* (Indian olive), and several other fruits are also found in the district.

Cattle.

The cattle of the district are small but compare favourably enough with those of the rest of Eastern Bengal. Although there are few lands reserved for pasturage except *chars* not yet fit for the plough, the cattle get a certain amount of grazing on the roadsides and on the ridges which separate the fields, and appear on the whole to be fairly well fed.

No census of the cattle in the whole district has been made, but in tracts surveyed during the years 1892—1908 (about 192 square miles) the number of cattle found averaged just under 400 to the square mile. Of these, about one-twelfth were buffaloes, and a tenth calves, while among the rest five bulls or bullocks are found to every two cows.

Rinderpest is common in the district. In 1874—75 it was recorded that 20,522 head of cattle were attacked, and only 2,409 recovered; 2,542 cattle died in 1903; in 1908-09 the deaths reported were 1,095, of which 1,077 were due to rinderpest. Cases of anthrax also occur, and occasionally foot and mouth disease and hæmorrhagic septicæmia. There is a dispensary at Noākhāli in charge of a civil veterinary assistant. He treated 501 cases in the year 1908-09, and over 3,000 animals were inoculated by assistants deputed to the interior during the outbreak of rinderpest in that year. There are a good many goats in the villages—during the surveys about one was enumerated for every ten acres measured—and the Muhammadan peasantry keep a number of fowls and ducks.

CHAPTER VII.

NATURAL CALAMITIES.

Cyclones.

Thanks to the abundant and regular rainfall and the annual inundation of the rivers, the district is practically free from drought. The eastern portion between the great and little Feni rivers is liable to suffer from the overflow of the hill streams after heavy rain, but the water subsides rapidly and the damage caused is rarely very serious. But the islands and all the south of the mainland are exposed to the cyclones which sweep across the Bay of Bengal, driving the waters before them in great waves which sometimes overflow wide tracts of country, drowning men and cattle, destroying the crops, and often leaving behind them a residue of salt which interferes with cultivation for some time. In the year 1797 there was such a cyclone, described as the most destructive in the memory of men.

In 1822, and again in 1825 and 1848 much damage was done by floods. In November 1867 Hātiā island was entirely submerged by a storm wave, and sea-drift was found on the embankments in its interior four feet above the level of the country; but the destruction caused by the great cyclone of 31st October 1876 far surpassed that of any other of which record exists.

Cyclone of 1876.

For two days the sky had been threatening, drizzling rain falling at intervals, and clouds flying inland before an east wind. Late in the evening of the 31st the wind changed to the north and north-east, and blew with tremendous violence, uprooting some trees and breaking off others. In Noākhāli every mud or mat-walled building was levelled to the ground, and only one Deputy Collector's court remained standing. Those trees which stood against the storm were stripped of their leaves, and their branches broken and scattered. Early in the morning a tidal wave, at least six feet high, burst over Sandwip and Hātiā from the south-east, and was followed very shortly by another wave six feet higher from the south-west. The waves swept across the islands lifting roofs from the houses and whirling away the débris. On the outskirts of the island, where there were few trees and the people lived in detached houses, nearly all were drowned before they had time to escape. Further inland where the houses clustered together in villages surrounded by groves, many of the inhabitants were saved by being caught in the thorny branches of the *māndār*. About four in the morning the wave reached the mainland and swept over it for some miles from the shore; at 7 o'clock the water in the main streets of Noākhāli was still 3½ feet deep and running with a strong current, carrying along broken fragments of houses and shops. It was at first believed that 100,000 persons had been drowned in Noākhāli and the islands, but further examination showed these figures to be excessive, and the final estimate of the number of deaths from drowning was 36,324. But the pollution of tanks and water-courses both by salt water inundation and by the corpses of men and carcases of cattle left without burying or cremation brought on an epidemic of cholera, while another storm of wind and rain on the 23rd November, the "ghost," as the people called it, "of the cyclone," added much to the misery of the homeless people. Cholera accounted for over 49,000 deaths, and it is probably safe to put down the total number of lives lost in the cyclone and from its sequelæ at 100,000.

Cyclones of 1893 and 1895.

On the morning of the 27th October 1893 another cyclone burst on Noākhāli. The wind blew with great violence between 10 and 12 A.M., when there was an hour's lull, after which it blew again from the opposite quarter. There was no storm wave like that of 1876, but the waters banked up by the force of the wind rose gradually, overflowing the coast of Hātiā and the opposite mainland. The inundation subsided in about two hours, and as it took place in the daytime and the rise of the water was gradual, most people had time to save themselves, though a few who were in boats or in exposed *chars* were drowned; but nearly 5,000 cattle (mostly buffaloes) were lost, and the crops in the tracts of Bāmni and Sudhārām were seriously damaged by the brackish water. In Hātiā and further up the coast the water was fresh, and the damage to the crops estimated at not more than two annas to four annas. In the islands the damage done to houses was slight, but on the mainland three-quarters of those in the track of cyclone were blown down; all the thatched houses in the Noākhāli Collectorate and all the public buildings in Feni, except the inspection bungalow, were blown away, and about half the betel-nut trees and an even larger proportion of the *māndār* trees were destroyed. The cyclone was followed by an outbreak of cholera in the south-east of the district Again, in October 1895, a cyclone struck the district, causing a good deal of damage to the crops and trees, and drowning a large number of cattle on the *chars*. Those cyclones were followed by a plague among the *supāri* trees which is described elsewhere.

Earthquake.

The district lies outside the main earthquake zone and does not appear to have suffered much since the great earthquake of 1762, to which is popularly attributed the lowering of the level of the *bils* in Begamganj *thānā*. In 1897 the shock of the earthquake that did such great damage in the Surma Valley was sharply felt, but caused little injury.

CHAPTER VIII.

MEANS OF COMMUNICATION.

History.

In the eighteenth century there were few roads in the district, and such as existed were in very bad order.

Mr. Thomas Parr, Collector of Tippera, which then included the main land of Noākhāli, reported in 1794 that the roads leading to the southern parts were at all seasons of the year very bad, and that the only one passable in the rains extended but 10 miles from Comilla. There were indeed the remains of many old roads and embankments but so neglected that they had become impassable in the rainy season, and even in the dry season were obstructed by many unbridged gaps.

From Rennells's map and lists it appears that before 1790 A.D. roads were in existence, extending from Lakhipur on the Meghnā to Chāndpur, Comilla, Coliandi and Jagdia; while through the east of the district ran the Chittagong road, and one from Comilla to Khandal (*i.e.*, Chhāgalnāia). There were ferries over the Dākātiā and great and little Feni rivers; but many streams were unprovided with any means of crossing.

The military authorities at Chittagong were continually representing the inconvenience and danger caused by the absence of properly bridged roads, and Mr. Elliott, when Magistrate of the district, made great improvements, but in 1819 we find Colonel Sherwood reporting that the Chittagong-Dāūdkāndi road (the trunk road) was impassable in the rainy season and had been cut through in many places, and that even such bridges as existed were unfit to carry a gun-carriage; while the Jurerganj-Lakhīpur road had been reduced in parts to a width of only 4 or 5 feet.

Up to that time there seems to have been an impression that the *zamīndārs* were responsible for the maintenance of communications, but it was ascertained that no such duty was imposed on them by the agreements they had executed, and by a Resolution, dated the 20th November 1820, the Governor-General in Council formally absolved the land-owners from being called upon to furnish any aid or to incur any expenses for maintaining the roads, and at the same time a special officer was appointed to draw up a scheme and prepare estimates for the construction of the roads required.

Very little was done until the proceeds of the Ferry fund were placed at the disposal of the Magistrates. In 1855 when a programme of works was called for there were only three roads with an aggregate length of 70 miles passable for hackeries. The allotment of 1856-57 was Rs. 12,400 and in the next year only Rs. 5,000, and most of this was spent on bridges.

In 1872-73 it was reported that the land communications extended to 226 miles, that there were fifteen ferries and that the total extent of the waterway in the district was 340 miles.

Most of the principal roads now in existence had then been constructed, but they were sadly in want of bridges and some were in very bad repair. The northern half of the Begamganj-Laksām road had not been bridged. The old Lakhipur road, running eastward from the bank of the Meghnā to Begamganj and then on to the Chittagong road, had been much neglected, and was overgrown with jungle.

Roads.

The district is now remarkably well supplied with roads. The provincial trunk road from Dacca to Chittagong passes through the centre of the Feni sub-division and the District Board maintains 397 miles of main roads, and 255 miles of village roads, making a total of 652 miles, without taking into account the numerous small paths connecting hamlets with the public roads. The people generally show a good deal of enterprise in making such connections and there are few hamlets that have no pathway leading to the nearest road.

Expenditure.

The average annual expenditure on roads for the five years ending 1904-05 was Rs. 50,000 and in 1908-09 the District Board spent Rs. 79,000 on communications, of which Rs. 46,000 was on original works and the rest for maintenance. Many of the roads are on lands that have never been acquired, either because they were excluded from the *māl* lands of estates in the Permanent Settlement, or because they have been given by the proprietors for use as roads, without consideration. Much care has been taken in planting trees by the roadside, and the Board own about 4,000 mahogany trees besides numbers of *sissu*, almond, *jārul*, *mahwā* and mango. The "Silk Oak" is said to do particularly well, and there are fine rows of casuarina about the civil station. There are only 12 miles of metalled roadway, but the surface of the others is better than in most districts of Bengal, and in some places the traffic is maintained over unbridged rivers and water channels, by ferries. When the rain has been exceptionally heavy it is customary to cut, or allow the villagers to cut, channels through the roadway to let the water escape; but the damage is generally repaired before the cold weather is established. From the headquarters of the district good roads branch east to Feni and Chittagong, north through Begamganj to Comilla, and in a north-westerly direction to Lakhipur and the important markets on the Meghnā. Besides these, the old road running east and west through Begamganj passes through the whole length of the centre of the district, and the Feni sub-division has its own system of roads running generally north and south.

Trunk Road.

The first place must be assigned to the Dacca-Chittagong Trunk Road, of which a length of 14 miles lies in the Feni sub-division, which it nearly bisects passing through Feni station and Diwānganj. This road is maintained by the Local Government; it is not metalled except for a short length at Feni but is bridged throughout the sub-division, the Feni river on the border being crossed by a ferry.

Old Begamganj Road.

The road from the Meghnā through Lakhipur and Begamganj to the river Feni formerly extended to Chittagong, but the eastern part has been abandoned and to a great extent cultivated while the western end was washed away by the Meghnā which encroached near Lakhipur before it receded.

Feni Road.

Next ranks the Feni-Noākhāli road, 26 miles long with a crest of 18 feet on an average, bridged except at the 3rd and 22nd miles where there are ferries over the Noākhāli Khāl and the Little Feni river. Starting from the head-quarters station it goes in a north-easterly direction until it meets the Chittagong Trunk Road. A good bridged road leads on a distance of 16 miles to Pashurām, and from there Captain Leake's road leads to Chhāgalnāia and thence to the Great Feni. There are inspection bungalows at the 10th and 17th miles of the Feni road and at Pashurām and Chhāgalnāia.

Chittagong Road.

From the 6th mile of the Feni road the Chittagong road, 17 miles long, runs through the south of the district, past Companyganj, to Lālganj ferry on the big Feni. There is a wide ferry over the Little Feni, and between this and Sonāgāzi Chaprāsi's Hāt, where there is a rest-house, the road has been washed away.

Begamganj Road.

From Noākhāli the Begamganj road, 14 feet wide, runs along the west of the Khāl for nearly 9 miles to Begamganj, a place of importance in the centre of the district, where there is a bungalow. From there the road leads to Lāksām and so on to Comilla and Chāndpur, but there are five *khāls* crossed only by temporary bridges in the 8 miles that lie in Noākhāli.

Bhawāniganj Road.

From just outside the head-quarters station the Bhawāniganj road runs west by north to the Bhawāniganj *khāl* 18 miles away. It is bridged and has an inspection bungalow at the 10th mile; a continuation 5 miles long carries one on to Lakhipur, and from there the Dalāl Bazar road runs three miles to Dalāl Bazar, where it branches, one branch running north-west 6 miles to Rāipur on the Dākātiā and so to Chāndpur, and the other almost due north to Rāmganj, 10 miles. These roads are bridged and drained and there are bungalows at Lakhipur, Rāipur and Rāmganj.

Mr. Leake's Road.

About 20 miles, built about 1781 A.D., starts from *thānā* Chauddagrām in Tippera and runs in this district through Pashurām and Chhāgalnāia up to the side of the Great Feni river.

These are but the main arteries of the road system of the district, and there are also roads right through the islands of Sandwip and Hātiā, and many cross roads.

Rivers.

The Dākātiā, the Meghnā and its branches, the big and little Feni, with their tributaries, the Muhuri and Seloneāh as well as the Bhawānigarh Mohendra and Noākhāli *khāls* are all used for navigation, and between them afford some 430 miles of waterway.

Steamers run daily from the Noākhāli *khāl* to Hātiā and Sandwīp, completing the round in 12 to 18 hours according to the tide. For this service the India General Railway and Steam Navigation Company receive a monthly subsidy from the District Board. Another service runs four days a week between Noākhāli and Barisāl, touching at Hātiā, and three days in the week the Barisāl-Chittagong steamers call at the islands. There is also a steamer service between Bhawāniganj and Barisāl.

Canals. But in the rains the people depend chiefly upon the numerous narrow channels, *khāl* or *donā*, for communication and transport. Of these there are a great number, some natural, some artificial. The latter mostly have not been excavated expressly for the passage of boats, but are simply the trenches from which earth has been taken to raise the roadway above flood-level.

In 1893 the District Board took charge of the inland waterways and the latest returns now show 57 channels large and small with a total length of 547 miles, including 33 miles of the Muhuri river. Of these the more important are the Begamganj-Lakhīpur road side channel 22 miles long, the Mohendra *Khāl* 45 miles long from Naudona to the Meghnā (much overgrown with weeds near Naudona), the Begamganj-Seloneāh drain from Begamganj to the little Feni river and the Begamganj-Rāmganj drain 25 miles long. None of these are navigable except in the rains, and the last named can even then take only small boats, but all of them are much used.

Ferries. The ferries of the district are under the control of the District Board. There are now 46 over the principal rivers and channels and between the islands. Hātiā is served by two ferries, both starting from Lambakhāli in *thānā* Sudharām, and Sandwīp by a ferry that crosses to Siddhi from Bhānubibi. There are regular ferries connecting Chars Jabar and Jubilee with the mainland. The ferries over the big Feni are under Chittagong. The large ferries are served by *bālām* boats about 32 feet long by 7¼ feet wide and capable of taking from 60 to 80 passengers. The Tejania Nālchira ferry has two boats measuring 36 feet by 9 feet but licensed only for 40 passengers owing to the dangerous character of the crossing.

Railways. In 1896 the Assam-Bengal Railway from Chittagong to Lāksām passing through Feni, the eastern sub-division of the district, was opened for traffic, and in 1903 a branch line was constructed from Lāksām to Noākhāli station. This line brought the head-quarters of the district into communication with the port of Chāndpur, from which steamers run in all directions, while Feni is only 4½ hours' run from Chittagong. Both lines are used for passenger as well as goods traffic and have been of immense assistance to the people in disposing of their surplus produce.

9

Rest-houses. The District Board maintains 26 inspection bungalows and rest-houses along the principal roads of the district. Most of them are temporary structures with walls of matting and wooden-doors and containing two rooms. There is also a new circuit house at Noākhāli—occupied at present as the Collector's residence—and a *dāk* bungalow maintained by the District Board. At Feni there is a P. W. D. inspection bungalow.

Conveyances. Carts are now in general use throughout the district, and as soon as a new road is opened to traffic the people living near it will buy wheels and themselves put together rude carts in which they drive their bullocks. The wheels are made of a local wood (*karai*), which serves also for stools and other articles of furniture. Ponies are rare, and pack bullocks are not used. Fish and milk are carried in vessels or baskets slung from a bamboo (*bānk*) carried on the shoulder. Other articles are usually carried on the head. Those who cannot walk travel in carts or palanquins, or on a seat (*dhuli*) slung from a bamboo carried by two men.

Boats. But in the rainy season boats afford the principal means of transport for men and merchandise.

Muhammadan boatmen use generally the *kundā*, a heavy canoe made from the trunk of a large tree, and usually covered for a considerable part of its length by two or three strips of matting bent over to form a semi-circular roof. A smaller dug-out known as a *tengi* is used in the flooded fields for going to market or reaping crops. Another common boat is the *sharanga* built of planks fastened together and flat bottomed so as to draw as little water as possible, and sometimes enlarged with side planks and roofed with bamboo matting. It is propelled with short oars or paddles fastened near the bow, or is poled in shallow waters, or towed, and may be of any size from a little skiff for a single person to a big boat carrying 100 maunds and requiring three men to manage it. In the Meghnā a longer and more slender boat known as a *gāshi* boat is found, and in the estuary an altogether larger boat known as the *bālām*. The *bālām* is built from a solid bottom with planks fastened together with cane and caulked with false hemp or straw soaked with the juice of the *gāb* tree. These boats are made in Chittagong or Sandwīp, and carry 200—300 maunds and require a crew of from five to seven men. When not required, the fastenings are undone and the planks put away carefully. They have large square sails with which they go merrily before the wind, but cannot sail near the wind, and have to be poled and paddled, a most laborious process. Occasionally *kosh* boats from Dacca may be seen, and the Chittagong boatmen come in broad sterned *sāmpāns*. The best boats are made in Chittagong or Sandwīp with *jārul* or *chaplās* wood brought from the Chittagong hills, but light dug-outs are sometimes made locally from the stem of the toddy palm.

CHAPTER IX.

OCCUPATIONS, MANUFACTURES AND TRADES.

It is to be feared that Census Table 15, showing the occupations of the people of the district, is far from accurate, but some interesting facts may be gleaned from the study of it. We find that of every ten inhabitants three are workers, and support the remaining seven. More than 79 per cent of the population depend on agriculture; excluding dependants, there are some 6,000 rent-receivers, and 225,000 rent-payers, besides 8,000 agricultural labourers, and 5,000 herdsmen. Possibly we should add to these a large proportion of the 25,000 persons described as general labourers.

Next to agriculture, fishing is the most important industry of the district. Only 222 persons have described themselves as fishermen, but there are over 7,500 sellers of fish. It is notorious that fishing is a despised occupation, and it may safely be said that many of the fish-dealers are really fishermen, and that a good many of the agriculturists are employed largely in fishing, though less than a thousand have admitted that this is their subsidiary occupation. Some 9,000 persons, of whom nearly one-fourth are women, find occupation in spinning and weaving, and of these more than 2,000 hold land. There are 1,300 potters, of whom 500 are women, over 1,000 carpenters, and less than 500 masons. Boatmen and sailors number nearly 1,000, but there are only 56 cartmen, though carts are in general use. *Pālki* bearers number over 400, and it is well known that *pālkis* are much used by women and infirm persons. There are about 2,700 priests, and over 800 medical practitioners, of whom only two are said to have diplomas. Perhaps the most curious feature of the tables is the almost entire absence of certain professions. There are no pig-breeders and swine herds, and only two persons are shown as growers of fruits and vegetables. There are but 22 boat builders, which bears out the statement that nearly all boats are imported ready made from Chittagong. The district has to support 17,000 professional mendicants.

Salt.

The production of salt from the salt impregnated lands of the islands and the southern coast was in former times a most important industry. Mr. Duncan in his report on Sandwip states that down to the year 1728 salt was manufactured for the benefit of the *chaudhris*, and was then converted in the time of Murshid Kuli Khān into the private monopoly of the Naib of the Subah. In 1765 the East India Company granted the monopoly of the production of salt, betel-nut and tobacco, to the Trading Company, who were to pay a duty of 35 per cent of the value of the salt produced. Three years later the monopoly was withdrawn on the ground that the inland trade of the country should be confined to its native inhabitants. Then for a few years the manufacture was open to any one, but in 1772 it was resolved that salt should be manufactured by the Company, and that the calaries in each district should be let in farm for five years. In the five years ending in 1776 over 130,000 maunds of salt were produced annually on the lands of *pargana* Sandwīp. At that time the manufacture seems to have been in charge of Sir John Forbes, Agent at Chittagong. In 1780 the lands of Bhulua, Dakshin Shāhbāzpur, Sandwīp, Hātiā and Bāmni were constituted the Fifth Salt Division in charge of an Agent at Bhulua, and this arrangement seems to have continued for the next thirty years. In the year 1819 Mr. Walters found the average annual production of salt to be a lakh of maunds in Hātiā, rather more in Mankura, 20,000 maunds in Sandwīp, 21,000 in Bāmni, and 60,000 maunds in other islands in the Meghnā. Altogether the production was over three lakhs of maunds, and gave employment to upwards of 20,000 persons, but soon afterwards the salt lands in Bāmni were given up, and in 1826 it was recorded that they were becoming sweet. Sir William Hunter records that the manufacture was continued down to about 1862, but no correspondence on the subject of its abandonment is to be found.

Fisheries. In the course of the year 1909 an enquiry into the fisheries of the district was made by a Sub-Deputy Collector specially deputed for the purpose, and the account which follows is based mainly on his report. Along the west and south of the district flows the Meghnā, bearing at all seasons of the year a mighty volume of water past the rivers to the sea. It has many branches winding in and out through the islands, and the mainland itself is intersected in all directions by rivers and water channels, and in the interior there are still many *bils*, or shallow lakes more or less perennial, while for three or four months of the year the greater part of the district is submerged, and the fish swarm all over the rice-fields where they spawn and hatch out their fry. And yet the fisheries are not so valuable or so prolific as in many districts farther from the sea, and the supply of fish is not nearly equal to the demand. Several causes contribute to this state of affairs. In the first place, the deep sea fisheries are practically closed to the people, as they have no boats in which they dare venture out, and even the island channels at the mouth of the Meghnā, with their treacherous tides, are avoided except by the hardiest of the fishermen. Also the want of more rapid means of communication prevents fishermen from going far from their market except in the cold weather, and fish-curing, with or without salt, is unknown. Still the fisheries are of importance and according to the census returns more than 24,000 persons depend upon fishing or the selling of fish for their livelihood, and these figures take no account of the vast number of people who at the close of the rains, as the waters recede, catch fish for home consumption in their own fields and ditches with bamboo traps or dams and other simple contrivances. Among the fishing castes the Kaibarttas, Jele Kaibarttas as they are called to distinguish them from the Hāliā Kaibarttas or cultivators, who now prefer to call themselves Mahisya, come first in numbers and importance. Most of them have a little cultivation as well. The Namasudras also include many fishermen. The most venturesome of all the fishermen in the district are the Mālos or Jhālos, who live chiefly on the islands or on the coast of the mainland, but they are few in number, only 905 having been found in the census.

The methods of fishing and the instruments employed are many and varied. Of fixed engines the most familiar is the *bendi jāl*, consisting of a line of nets fastened across a tidal channel and leading to a basket trap of split bamboos; or a submerged sandbank may be surrounded with a bamboo or net enclosure, called *ber* or *chali*, which confines the fish as the tide recedes. Again, *bāndhs*, or plain screens of split bamboos, are to be seen fastened across nearly every water-course, often seriously obstructing the passage of boats. Of nets the commonest are the cast nets, or *jhānki*, made in various sizes and of various meshes, and the *behāl* or *dharma jāl*, two very similar nets, one triangular and the other quadrangular, fixed to a bamboo lever by means of which they are lowered into the water and raised again when a fish passes. Drag nets of different makes with or without pockets are worked with the help of boats, and sometimes the fishermen trawl a kind of net called *moi*, and in the shallows handnets not unlike those used on the English coasts for shrimping (*dharma jāl* or *jele jāl*) are employed. Besides these, there are several kinds of "gill" nets, known generally by the name of the fish for the capture of which they are adapted. Of purse nets a good example is the *suti jāl*, in the shape of a long funnel which is kept open by the stream. Down this funnel the fish drift and are entangled in the narrow end, from which they are taken from time to time by the fishermen. In shallow waters a cane basket shaped like a bell jar with an open neck (*polo*) is often used. It is plunged suddenly into the water and the fish found inside are taken out by hand through the opening at the top. Fish are also speared with the *konch* or *tentha* and are caught with a rod and line or with set lines. For the *koi* a fine split bamboo is used instead of a hook. The bamboo is bent, and its sharp ends are kept in position by means of the grass-hopper used as bait, and when a fish swallows this the points are released and spring apart piercing his gullet. As a rule the boats used for fishing are dugouts, (*kundā*, *dongā*, or *gāchh*) made from the trunks of palm, mango, sāl, chaplās, simul and other trees, hollowed out. The *sharanga* is a larger and more shapely boat requiring two men to work it, but is also fashioned from a scooped out trunk.

Fish.

The list of the varieties of fish caught in the district is too long to find place in this volume. The members of the carp tribe (Cyprinidæ), *ruhit* (Labeo ruhita), *katāl* (Catla Buchanani), *mrigāl* (Cyrrhiria mrigala), and *kalabāus* (Labeo calbasu) are plentiful and occupy the first place in popular estimation. Of other varieties the *chapila* (Clupea chapra), *phalai* (Notoptonis kapirat), *chital* (Notoptonis chitala), *pābda* (Callichrous paoda), *bachā* (Entropiichthys vacha), *bole* (Gobius giuris and Gobius kokins), *jaki* or *gani* (Ophiocephalus punctatus), *sol* (Ophiocephalus striatus), *jengra* (macrones of several kinds), *magur* (Clarious magur), *singi* (Saccobranchus fossilis) and *koi* (Anabas scandens or climbing perch) are thought to be good eating. The last three are in great demand as nourishing food for invalids. Of estuarine fish the most esteemed are the *rishya* or *topsi* (Polynemus paradiscus) commonly known as the mango fish, the *bhetki* or *korāl* (Lates calcarifar), the *bata* or *khoshrul* (Mugil corsula) and the *hilsa* (Clupeo ilisha), of which the first three are common. The *hilsa* is becoming scarce and it is said that those caught at the mouth of the Meghnā are not so good to eat as those from the higher reaches of the river. *Muralla, punti, kholisha* and *chela* are small fish and are found all over the district in great abundance, and though not so much relished as the choicer species, make up between them the major part of the fish consumed in the district. Prawns, crayfish (*ichha*), and crabs, are caught in numbers and always find a ready sale. It is impossible to state accurately the total weight or value of the annual catch, but the report puts it at about 300,000 maunds, or enough to allow each fish-eating member of the community an ounce a day. This is nothing like equal to the demand, and there is a general impression that the supply is diminishing, and this is accounted for chiefly by the contraction of the fishing grounds owing to the steady silting up of the water channels and to the reclamation of swamps. Nearly all the extensive marshes which existed thirty years ago in the centre of the district have been reclaimed and the formation of *char* Jabar between the larger islands and the mainland, and the increase of the banks in the Meghnā seems to have interfered with fishing in the estuary. The report suggests that the wholesale destruction of fry involved in the methods by which fish are caught is partly responsible. It would be difficult to regulate the methods of capture or to place any restriction on the size of fish caught, but the tanks found in every village might afford the means of replenishing the supply of at least the more valuable species. Carp are said not to breed in tanks, but the young thrive well when put in, and a good many private tanks are periodically restocked with fry, generally young carp brought from Chittagong, but the practice is not so universal as it ought to be, and unfortunately the tank is too often drained dry every year, which means of course the destruction of all the immature fish.

Weaving

In the year 1756 a cloth factory was established by the East India Company at Jagdia, near the mouth of the Feni river, and about the same time or soon afterwards other factories were started at Kalyāndi (Colinda), Lakhipur, and Charpātā, while the French also had a factory near Jagdia. In these factories cotton cloth, known as *bafta*, was manufactured. The indigenous cloth seems to have been inferior, for in a letter written by the Chittagong Council on the 16th February 1761 it is thus described *:— "The manufacture of this country is at present very indifferent, all piece-goods being of a thick woolly quality in no way durable, and short in length and breadth. This may be improved by making the combs of the looms closer, spinning the thread harder and more even, and striking them fuller." Cotton of poor quality was grown in the hills and also in Sandwīp, and in the early correspondence we find the Company much concerned in the means for improving it by the introduction of new seed or improved cultivation. Down to the year 1820 the industry appears to have flourished. Mr. Walters found many weavers in Bāmni and Sandwīp, and cotton was then grown in the islands, though the principal factory was at Lakhipur in the west of the district. After that, owing, it is said, to the competition of English piece-goods, the industry declined, and about 1828 the factories were closed. In 1876-77 it was reported that *dhutis*, *sāris*, *gamchas*, and other cotton cloths were made in small quantities for local use, but that the importation of cheap English piece-goods had reduced considerably the local manufactures. Of late years, however, there has been some revival. Besides the ordinary *sāris* and *dhutis* of coarse white cotton, checks and coloured cloths, both thick and thin, suitable for coats, shirts, etc., are woven. *Lungis* of superior quality in fast colours are being made in Noākhāli, and compete successfully with those imported from Holland and Burma. A species of coloured *sāri*, known as *jām sāri*, is now much in vogue among Muhammadan women, and is woven in the district, or imported from Mainamāti. It is said that about one thousand rupees worth of these *sāris* is sold on every *hāt* day at Chaumuhani †. The mosquito nets of Chaumuhani, white and coloured, have also a great reputation. Unfortunately, taking advantage of the increased demand for their goods, the weavers of Noākhāli have tried to impose upon the public cloths of inferior yarn, to the great injury of their trade. All local cloth is made with imported yarn, chiefly from the Bombay mills.

Iron and steel work.

From Mr. Jackson's Monograph on the iron and steel work of Bengal, it appears that he found 150 forges in Noākhāli

* Cotton's Revenue History of Chittagong, page 161.

† Survey of Industries and Resources of Eastern Bengal and Assam for 1907-08.

employing 600 persons. As a rule the work turned out is of the roughest, but at Dattapārā cutlery of fair quality is manufactured.*

Brass, copper and bellmetal.

The brass and bell-metal utensils made in the district are of inferior quality.

Mats and baskets.

Excellent baskets of many shapes and qualities are made from reed and cane, and in the east of the district very fine *pātis* or mats are prepared from a plant known as *mortāg* or *murtā*.

Imports and exports.

The external trade of the district is carried on by rail, steamer, country boats, and carts, and as statistics are available only for the first two of these, it is impossible to give any estimate of the total trade of the district. The chief imports are piece-goods, of which according to the published returns for the year 1908-09 about three-quarters are of European make, salt, kerosine oil, mustard oil, tobacco, sugar, brass and bell-metal articles, china and earthenware, and betel-leaves. Coal and coke also are imported in considerable quantities, and the latter is gradually coming into use for cooking, as fuel becomes more scarce. The chief export of the district is rice, most of which is carried to Calcutta by river. Next to this come betel-nuts, which are sent to Chittagong, Calcutta, and other districts, and from the markets in the north-west of the district considerable quantities of betel-nut paper (the inner skin of the sheaf covering the bunches of nuts) are sent to Burma where they are used to make wrappers for cheroots. This trade is in the hands of Burmese and a special enquiry made in 1908 showed that some 430 maunds of this substance, which sells at about two annas a seer had been exported from Sonaimura and Chaumuhani. Other articles exported are coco-nuts, linseed, chillies, onions, hides, fowls' eggs, raw cotton, and jute. The recorded exports of jute in 1908-09 were 212,477 maunds, a figure far in excess of that for any previous year.

Marts.

The chief marts and the principal objects of trade in the district are:—

(1) Rāipur on the Dākātiā: export of betel-nut, chillies, oranges, limes and plantains.

(2) Chaumuhani on the railway and only a mile from Begamganj *thānā*: jute, linseed, eggs, rice, oranges, and country cloth.

(3) Nadona in the north of the district connected with Noākhāli and Lāksām by road and waterways: rice and plantains.

(4) Lakhipur in the west of the district: a large business in molasses.

(5) Bhawāniganj in the south-east, connected by steamer with Barisāl: betel-nuts and *pān* as well as molasses and other articles; ranks next after Raipur and Chaumuhani.

* Survey of Industry and Resources of Eastern Bengal and Assam, 1907-08

(6) Sāntāsitā in Sudharām *thānā:* cattle, betel-nuts, coconuts, rice, chillies, etc.

(7) Chāprāsir Hāt on the *khāl* of that name: a large cattle market.

(8) Sonāgāzi in *thānā* Feni: timber, rice, linseed, and chillies.

(9) Pashurām in *thānā* Chhāgalnāia: fine mats and rice; famous for its *chirā.*

(10) Chāri Ānir Hāt, the principal mart of Sandwīp: coconuts.

In 1886 a considerable sum of money was raised, and a successful Agricultural and Industrial Exhibition was held in Sudharām. In 1904 again a sum of money raised for the purpose of a memorial to Queen Victoria was devoted to an exhibition, and this was continued for two years more until funds ran low. In March 1910 an agricultural exhibition was held in Sudharām and proved a success. *Exhibitions.*

CHAPTER X.

LAND REVENUE ADMINISTRATION.

Fiscal divisions.

There is no record of the system of revenue administration before Noākhāli came under Muhammadan influence, and not much information is to be had before the middle of the eighteenth century. Though Bhulua was included in the revenue assessment of Akbar's minister, Todar Mal, in the year 1582, it is obvious from what has been said already that the Mughal governors were not then in a position to collect revenue from it. During the next 150 years Bhulua, originally an undivided Hindu *rāj*, became completely Muhammadanised and was split up into a number of *parganas* or fiscal divisions.

The origin of some of these *parganas* is obscure, but in a few cases it is possible to trace their history. Jagdia, Dāndra, and Allahābād, were all at one time part of Bhulua, but after the defeat of the Arakanese in the year 1610 two generals, one Hindu and one Muhammadan, were appointed to guard the frontiers against invasion, and received grants of land, that given to the Hindu became in course of time *pargana* Jagdia, and the other being again divided formed the two *parganas* of Dāndra and Allahābād, which were treated as one estate. Kanchanpur is said to have been carved out of Bhulua and Singhergān by the Emperor Feroz Shāh and given to the Muhammadan *Pīr* Khandkar Mīr Ahmad; while Ambarābād, then covered with jungle, was granted by Muhammad Shāh to Amānulla and Sanāulla Khān of Delhi at the instance of *Pīr* Ambar Shāh.

In the revised revenue roll of Bengal for the year 1728 we find Bhulua divided into eleven *parganas* or estates, which with the islands of Sandwīp and its appurtenances formed part of Chakla Jahāngirnagar in the province of Dacca.

Each of these *parganas* was assigned to one or more persons, who under the designation of *zamīndār*, *chaudhri*, or *dīwān*, was responsible for the collection of the revenue and the payment of the assigned quota into the Nawab's Treasury, and also for the maintenance of law and order, while his accounts were kept by the *kānungo* of the *pargana* and a staff of village accountants (*patwāris*).

Early British settlements.

In course of time some changes were made in the boundaries of *parganas* and there are now 35 *parganas* recognised. In the thirty years preceding the grant of the *dīwāni* to the East India Company not much change was made in the arrangement of *parganas*, but the assessment was enormously increased, and as the Mughal hold on the country weakened, the whole system became more and more disorganised, so that in 1772 when the Directors decided to take the collections and the administration into their own hands, they had the greatest difficulty in obtaining correct information or accounts. They decided in the first place to farm out estates for five years to the highest bidders with the result that endless confusion was caused, and when fresh settlements were made in 1777 A.D. preference was given to the hereditary *zamīndārs*. The Regulations of the 10th February 1790 provided for a ten years' settlement of Bengal, but the application of this order to the districts of Tippera and Chittagong was postponed and yearly settlements continued to be made down till 1793, the year of the permanent settlement.

Mughal administration.

Of the early settlements on the mainland there is little record beyond what is to be found in published reports, but Mr. Duncan, to whose report reference has been made before, has left behind much valuable information as to Sandwīp. *Pargana* Sandwīp, which comprised the islands of Sandwīp, Hātia, Bāmni, and Shāgird-dihi, was in the year 1662, the *jāgir* of the Amir-ul-Omrah, and afterwards that of Nawāb Ibrahim Khān, and from the year 1713 that of Mir Jumla. When the management was first entrusted to an *ahdadār* does not appear; but there was one before the year 1753. The *pargana* was divided into three *tarafs* or shares known as the Niāmati, Musapur, and Rāmpur *tarafs*, the owners of which possessed some lands jointly and some separately. At first these divisions seem to have been unrecognised by the Mughal governors, and in 1716 when the islands were measured, the *āmin* divided the assessment in proportion to the land actually in possession of the co-sharers. The lands, both *maujūd* and *makhlūt* (original and added lands), were surveyed again in the years 1733 and 1743, and the proportions readjusted. The last measurement was made in 1763 when Bhawāni Charan was found in possession of 11 annas 4 *gandas* odd. In the meantime Bhawāni Charan had caused his name to be registered as *zamīndār* of an 11 annas 18 *gandas* 1 *kara* share, and the *kanungos*, to whom the point was referred, ruled that he could claim no abatement on the ground that he was actually in possession of less than his recorded share. They based the ruling on the ground that Sandwip was a *tahudi mahāl*, that is, one the revenue of which was fixed, and not a *hasb-ul-wusuli mahāl*, a class of estate in which the proprietor was liable to pay his whole collections less the proportion allowed him.

Valuation.

In the assessment of 1763 the lands were divided into full rated (*puradar*) and low rated (*kamdar*) lands. It was assumed that in every four *kānis* of first class cultivated land one produced 25 *kannuas** of grain, one 20, one 17½, and one 10, giving an average of 18⅛; one-fifth of this was deducted as the '*patta* privilege' of the *tālukdār*,† and half the residue or 7¼ *kannuas* (valued

* This measure is not defined.

† *Talukdar*, i.e., the holder of an intermediate tenure, *vide* page 79.

at 1¼ *kannuas* per rupee) was the measure of the rent to be paid by the *tālukdār* to the *zamīndār*. First class fallow lands were valued at five-eighths of the rate for cultivated land. Inferior cultivated lands and fallow lands were valued at half the rates for the best class.

Abwabs.

The assessment thus made constituted the *tashkisi jama*, but this was subsequently increased by several *abwābs, viz., mathaut*, an allowance to the *Nāib ahdadār* levied at 2 annas 17 *gandas* per rupee on the *tashkis* rent, *māshki* levied at 1 anna 7 *gandas* per rupee, and *dihi kharcha* (local expenses) also collected at 1 anna 7 *gandas* per rupee. The rates of collection of these *abwābs* varied in the different divisions, and they were not always shown in the accounts.

The *tālukdārs* complained bitterly of these additions to their rental, which amounted in 1787 to 5 annas 11 *gandas* per rupee on the *tashkis* revenue of the 12 annas estate; the *zamīndārs* agreed to reduce them to 4 annas, and this arrangement was allowed to continue pending a fresh measurement and assessment.

The regulations for the permanent settlement required all *abwābs* to be amalgamated with the rent, but many of these separate payments continued to be exacted. Even now in most estates the following will be found:—*punya*, a present, usually one rupee, to the landlord on the first day of the *zamindāri* year; *piyāda*, a small fee to a peon deputed specially to summon the tenant; *mārchā*, a fine on marriage of the ryot's son or daughter; *amlā*, a present to the servants of the estate; *salāmi*, a fee to the landlord on special occasions. These miscellaneous payments are often included in agreements taken from tenants, so that they may be recoverable at law.

Classification of lands.

The classification of the lands of Sandwīp is not easy to follow, but apparently the system was as follows:—The first division was into *taraf, maujūd*, and *makhlūt*, lands; the *chaudhuris* being accountable for the revenue of the first division, while by the custom of Sandwip the management of the other classes was in the hands of the *ahdadārs*.* The *taraf* lands seem to have been those separately possessed by different *chaudhuris*, the *maujūd* being the undivided assessed lands and the *makhlūt* additions to this area by reclamation and accretion. The lands (query *taraf* lands only) were again classified as *huzerea* (probably *huzuri*), *nij-tāluks*, and *khudkāsht*.† On the first class, which formed much the largest part and seems to have been let out in *tāluks*, the *zamīndārs* (*chaudhuris*) retained only the cess known as *māshki*, the *tālukdārs* paying the rest of their rent to the *ahdadār*. On the *nij-tāluks* they seem to have enjoyed the *tālukdār's* share (one-fifth of the produce), and on the *khudkāsht* they paid the nominal valuation but the *ahdadār* was expected

* Paras. 420, etc., of Mr. Duncan's report.

† Op cit., para. 443.

not to exact the full value of the produce or to enquire too closely into the profits. A similar arrangement appears to have prevailed in Bhulua which had been managed by *ahdadārs*. The correspondence of 1790 shows that the *makhlāt* lands of Bhuluā were undivided and were managed directly by Government; but the information obtainable is fragmentary.

The following table compares the past and present land revenue of the principal *parganas*; the early figures being based on Grant's View of the Revenues of Bengal. :— *Land revenue.*

Name of pargana.	Land Revenue in 1728 A.D.			Land revenue in 1765.	Present land revenue.	Remarks.
	Khālisa.	Jāgir.	Total.			
	Rs.	Rs.	Rs.	Rs.	Rs.	
Bhulua ...	14,271	26,891	41,162	1,35,982	1,23,929	In the year 1790 the revenue was Rs. 1,06,487.
Jagdia ...	...	16,984	16,984	17,734	28,705	
Dāndra and Illahābād.	2,348	5,138	7,486	48,638	18,768	These were long under *khās* management.
Bābupur ...	350	...	350	12,984	14,952	
Gopālpur Mirzanagar.	3,106	...	3,106	15,889	21,060	
Ambarābād ...	289	...	289	...	81,633	The land was covered with forest when first granted.
Shaistānagar ...	993	...	993	...	14,848	Ditto.
Kanchanpur ...	2,090	...	2,090	...	6,365	
Sandwip ...	54,696	...	54,696	1,08,470	1,52,105	

It is necessary to explain that the lands of all estates were divided into (1) *Khālisa*, (2) *Jāgir*; the revenue from the former being payable into the imperial treasury, and that from the latter appropriated to local expenditure, the large proportion of jāgir in Bhulua and its vicinity being for the support of the force necessary to protect the frontier against the Maghs and Tipperas.

It is doubtful whether the revenue shown for the year 1765 was collected, and certainly the enhancement made in the preceding 37 years got no further than the local officials. Fuller details regarding Sandwīp are to be had in Mr. Duncan's report, and may serve as an example of the course in other estates.

Revenue of Sandwip.

In the year 1662 the *māl* revenue, that is, the revenue from the land, was only Rs. 6,667. In 1713 nearly Rs. 4,000 were added in the guise of *lawāzimāt.* In 1728 a lump addition (*nazarāna*) of Rs. 4,000 was made, and other similar additions raised the *māl* revenue by 1751 A.D. to Rs. 22,793. In 1753 a new *ahdadār* was appointed, and payments to numerous officers and for police and other establishments increased the assessment by Rs. 14,000, but this seems to have been too much, for four years later another *ahdadār* was appointed and allowed a remission of Rs. 4,500. In 1763 Bishnu Charan Bose became *ahdadār* and gave an agreement to pay *dāsmāsha* rupees in place of the Arcot rupees that were the ordinary currency in the island, thus adding about 9 per cent. to his real payment. Large remissions were allowed in the next two years for inundation and *nājāy* (deficits) reducing the revenue at the time of the assumption of the Diwāni to Rs. 20,500. In 1772 the Committee of Revenue assessed the *pargana* at Rs. 77,974, of which Rs. 39,710 was subsequently determined to be the share of the *māl* revenue, and in 1777 the revenue was fixed at Rs. 50,584. The *jama wāsil bāki* enables us to compare this revenue with the actual receipts. In 1765 the gross rental was shown as Rs. 80,213, but of this Rs. 1,657 was postponed for the following year and the actual amount realised was Rs. 72,558, on which a *batta* or reduction for loss on light and base coins of Rs. 7,591 was allowed. The net realisations came to Rs. 65,000 Arcot rupees equivalent to about 59,000 *sikka*, so that the *zamindārs*, or rather the *ahdadārs*, retained in that year more than Rs. 38,000. In 1775 the collections from the land came to over Rs. 71,000 *sikka*, so that the enhanced revenue of the following year must have left the *zamindārs* with a substantial margin.

Sair revenue.

In the Mughal times *zamindārs* were allowed to levy tolls and landing dues, and enjoyed the profits of salt manufacture and markets. The total of this *sair* revenue of Sandwīp was in 1662 A.D. Rs. 23,864. Small additions, chiefly as *nazar* to new governors, were made from time to time down to 1751, when Rs. 5,615 was added for the Mahratta *chaut*, Rs. 1,100 for *khāsnavisi*, and Rs. 26,250 as a premium of 14 annas per rupee on a fictitious annual advance of Rs. 30,000 from the governor, thus bringing the total to Rs. 60,717. In 1763 the demand stood at Rs. 72,056, but of this Rs. 18,400 were subsequently remitted on account of losses. The assessment made in 1772 did not distinguish *māl* from *sair* revenue in the first instance, but when the Company decided to resume all *sair* collections as a preliminary to the decennial settlement, the share of the total to be remitted on this account was fixed at Rs. 38,264, though the accounts of the *pargana* do not show that a quarter of that sum was collected as *sair*.

Permanent settlement.

In the permanent settlement all distinction of *khālisa* and *jāgir* was abolished and lands of every description were made liable for the land revenue, which was fixed so as to leave the proprietor a net income, including profits from private lands, of 10 per cent. of the collections, but this proportion could be exceeded in the case of petty properties or for special reasons. In Noākhāli a good many estates were for some time on the Collector's hands and the revenue was fixed practically by a compromise.

The land revenue of Noākhāli amounted in 1842-43 to Rs. 5,31,775; in 1908-09 it was Rs. 7,24,678. The large increase is to be attributed to the assessment of new alluvial formations. The incidence per acre of cropped land is a little under 12 annas.

Estates.

All interests in land may be classified as either (1) estates, in which no interest intervenes between the proprietor and Government, (2) intermediate tenures, or (3) cultivators' holdings.

Estates are again sub-divided into revenue-paying and revenue-free, and the former of these classes into permanently settled, temporarily settled, and Government estates.

In 1908-09 there were 1,545 permanently settled estates with a land revenue of Rs. 4,51,658; 45 temporarily settled estates with a revenue of Rs. 52,859, and 245 Government estates with a demand of Rs. 2,12,947. Of these estates 128 represent whole and broken *parganas*. The policy of the decennial and permanent settlements required one *zamīndār* to be responsible for each estate, and every portion of a *pargana* in separate possession of one *zamīndār*, or a separate group of *zamīndārs*, became an estate; and after the permanent settlement provision was made for the partition of estates at the instance of any one of the proprietors.

Taluks.

In the eighteenth century a great part of Noākhāli was in the hands of intermediate tenure-holders. They were recognised in the assessments made by the Mughal administrators and were allowed a fifth of the gross estimated rental.

The Regulations for the decennial settlement provided for the separation of certain classes of *tāluks* (Ar. ta'aluk=dependant) or tenures from the parent estate, *viz.*, those that had existed before the estate, had been created by a superior authority, or had been conceded the privilege by the deed of creation (*vide* Regulations of 23rd November 1791), and the *tālukdārs* were encouraged though not compelled to seek such separation. Those who asked for and were found entitled to separation were admitted to engage at a revenue calculated to leave them an income of a tenth of the gross assets including the profits from their *Nānkar* lands. Such *tāluks* are known as *khārija tāluks;* they are permanently settled and differ only in their origin from the *zamindāri* estates. The number of estates so created in Noākhāli was returned as 2,181. There remained about 500 *tāluks* created before the permanent settlement which were not entitled to separation. They are called *petāo* (from the word *pet*=belly) and are the highest class of subordinate tenure. A *haulā* (Ar. *hawāla*= trust) is very similar to a *petāo tāluk* in its incidents, both being permanent, heritable, and divisible; but while there may be a *haulā* under a *tāluk* the order is never reversed. A *shikmi* tenure is similar in its incidents, but is subordinate to a *tāluk* or a *hāula*.

The term *hāula* appears to have been applied in the first instance to a commission granted to a man of energy and capital who undertook to bring newly formed land into cultivation, but in course of time it came into general use to designate a permanent hereditary tenure usually at fixed rates of rent. It is a term of great respectability, and many substantial cultivators call themselves *hāuladār* though they have no real title to the name. In early settlements it was customary to allow *hāuladārs* more favourable rates than were given to common cultivators, and they usually had the benefit of a deduction (*mutton*)* of from two and a half to ten per cent. from the measured area besides an allowance of $\frac{1}{32}$nd for the *ails* or ridges between the fields. This perhaps took the place of the different lengths of rod used in *zamindāri* estates for different classes of tenants. Many of these *tāluks* and *hāulas* are in fact *patni tāluks* subject to the provisions of Regulation VIII of 1819 and liable as such to be brought to sale by the Collector for default in payment of the rent, while the holders are bound to furnish security for their rent and good conduct, if so required. These permanent tenure-holders can devise similar rights to under-tenure-holders; thus under the patni may be found a *darpatni* and under that a *sepatni*. Below the *hāula* may be found a *nim hāula* or *osat hāula*, and below the *shikmi tāluk* a *darshikmi*.

Reclamation leases. *Jangalburi ābādkari tāluks* are found in Sandwip. They were granted at a progressive rent for the purpose of bringing waste lands under cultivation. The course of reclamation of *char* lands is usually as follows:—As soon as the new formation ceases to be overflowed by a normal tide, the landlord enters into a *gorkati* or grazing settlement with some contractor. When the grass and bush spring up roving herdsmen (Bāthaniā) come with their herds of cattle and bivouac on the *char* paying to the contractor a rent of so much a head for their cattle and a small fee for fuel. In course of time the land becomes fit for the plough, and formerly at this stage a *hāula* or *ābādkāri* lease would have been granted, but now a days it is usual to settle the land directly with ryots, who build temporary sheds and migrating there during the cultivating season with their plough and cattle begin to grow

---

* This was given also to *tālukdārs*. In early settlements it appears as a deduction from the area, in later ones as a deduction from the rate.

paddy. Later on as the land rises, they build permanent houses, dig large tanks to procure a supply of fresh water, and plant round them betel, cocoanut and date-palms, plantains, *māndār* and other trees. They dig drains, throwing up the earth to form pathways among their scattered homesteads, and thus they settle with their families. The whole district has been formed and settled in this way from one end to the other. Formerly tenants for such newly formed land were in great demand and obtained very favourable terms. Mr. Walters reported that in 1819 new settlers on the *chars* of Hātia paid no rent for eight years and thereafter low rates for several years more; even now they begin with low rates, paying in the first year only six annas an acre for *degichar* or *malanghi char** or lands still submerged at high tide. The rent is usually progressive, and higher rates also on a progressive scale are fixed after the land becomes culturable.

Though certain portions of the lands are cultivated by tenure-holders and petty proprietors with the aid of hired labourers, the great bulk of the cultivation is in the hands of hereditary cultivators, whose rents were regulated formerly by custom and now by the provisions of the Bengal Tenancy Act. At the time of the permanent settlement the ryots of Noākhāli rarely occupied the same land continuously for any length of time; they wandered from village to village, paying rent only for such lands as they actually cultivated. In Sandwīp, which had an earlier civilization, cultivation seems to have been less fluctuating. Mr. Duncan in his report of 1778 gives a translation of a typical ryoti lease, in which the lands are classified as ryoti, *kharsha*, and *barga*, and explains that the ryoti is that part of the tenure which the ryot is not at liberty to relinquish but must be answerable for the cultivation and revenue of it at the hazard of forfeiting his possession. The rent of the *kharsha* land was also payable in money but the tenant could relinquish the cultivation of it when he pleased. The *barga* was land for which a portion of the actual produce was deliverable as rent. *Ryots.*

Coming down to the nineteenth century we find a distinction drawn between *khudkāsht* or resident ryots, holding under *zamīndārs* or *tālukdārs*, and *jotdārs* cultivating under *hāuladārs*; more favourable terms being allowed to the former. The distinction is known no longer and the term *jotdār* means any cultivating tenant, ryot implying residence in the locality. In Chakla Bāmni (and probably elsewhere) a *jotdār* is a yearly tenant.

The relations of ryots with their landlords are now governed by the provisions of the Bengal Tenancy Act, and most of them have rights of occupancy. These rights are not transferable without the consent of the landlord, but in practice are sold at from *Transfers.*

* *Malanghi*=a salt maker. Such lands were used formerly for making salt.

Rs. 150 to Rs. 200 per *kāni*,* or roughly at from £12 to £16 an acre, and in many estates the transfer is recognised on payment of a fee, usually 25 per cent. of the purchase money. The Bhulua *zamīndārs*, however, refuse to recognise such purchasers and make it a rule to evict them. According to the registration returns the occupancy rights in some 500 acres of land were sold in 1909 at an average price of about £9-10-0 an acre. Hardly any ryots nowadays pay produce rents.

Under-ryots.

Under-ryots in Noākhāli have no occupancy rights, but it is recorded in the Settlement report of Chakla Bāmni that under-ryots' rights are sold, though *jotdāri* rights are not. Some of them pay produce rents and are regarded either as tenants or as labourers according to the circumstances of the case.

They are known as *osat-ryot*, and a further stage of sub-leasing is recognised in the *dar-osat-ryot*.

The distinction between tenure-holder, ryot, and under-ryot made by the Bengal Tenancy Act has given rise to difficulties in this district, where the holdings are often very large and the *jotdārs* arrogate to themselves the title of *hāuladār*. The Settlement Officer reports that in the settlements of Government *chars* made about 1876 the *hāuladārs* holding more than 100 *bighās* were treated as tenure-holders unless the whole area was in their own cultivating possession, and those holding less were classed as ryots unless the greater part was sublet—the under-tenants in either case being treated as *jotdārs* with occupancy rights. That a tenant can keep so much land in his own hands is due to the system of cultivation in the *chars*. The cultivators do not live there, but go for a short time in the spring and get the land ploughed and sown by hired labour—for which they pay very high—and then leave the rice plants alone until harvest time when they return with an army of hired reapers, cut, thresh, stack, and sell the paddy on the spot.

Revenue policy in 1821.

On the formation of the district the Board of Revenue set out their views and their policy in a letter of 46 paragraphs, which even now will repay perusal. The Board advised Mr. Plowden not to institute resumption proceedings in petty cases, and to alleviate hardship by allowing progressive revenue. One part of their instructions is particularly interesting as showing how the severity of the regulations was softened down in practice. The assessment of *mālikāna* was to be made on the principle of estimating the gross produce at 15 per cent. above the farming *jama* if the lands were let in farm, or at the net rent if *khās*, a moiety of which was to constitute the demands of Government, leaving as *mālikāna* to the proprietor the difference between that moiety and the *jama* at which the farmer had engaged. They give as an example the case of a property of which the

* Based on the Collector's report.

former revenue was Rs. 800, the gross assets were assumed to be Rs. 920, of which Government took Rs. 460, leaving Rs. 340 as *mālikanā* to the recusant proprietor. They urged the Collector to take steps for the survey of his charge, and said that they expected that he would with indefatigable industry and research discover the material records of the office of the former Collectorate at Bhulua; but this last injunction does not seem to have been complied with.

Sub-infeudation.

Tenures are exceedingly numerous in Noākhāli and sub-infeudation prevails to a deplorable extent. Exact statistics are not to be had without much labour, but the number of tenures assessed to cess is 167,305, greater than in any district of Eastern Bengal except Bākarganj and 2½ times as many as in the adjoining district of Tippera. Mr. Cumming's account of sub-infeudation in Chakla Roshnābād * may be taken as applicable to the district as a whole. He writes :—"In the area held by tenure-holders it may be generally asserted that the prevailing feature is not sub-infeudation, but sub-division. There is sub-infeudation, but not to the extent which exists in the neighbouring district of Bāckergunge or in the Sadar part of Noākhāli. One instance found was as follows:—proprietor, then a taluk, then a dar-taluk, then a patni, then a dar-patni and then the raiyat. Herein are four intermediaries between the cultivator and the Raj. The process of sub-division is the result partly of inheritance, especially amongst Muhammadans, and of transfers; but the sub-division is principally due to the system under which tenures were created without definite areas in a country in which and at a time when spontaneous increase of cultivated area was both possible and permissible. The result is an intermixture of tenures similar to that existing amongst the estates in Muzaffarpur and Chittagong. Anomalies of course are discovered when the record of rights is prepared. Several taluks are found to be holding some lands jointly, but the holders cannot say what the proportionate share of each taluk is. This is the chrysalis stage. Again, certain land is recorded as held jointly (ijmali) under several taluks and the shares are settled; but the holders of the taluks are receiving rents from the tenants out of proportion to the nominal shares. This is a further development, in which the weaker go to the wall. The last stage is when the area originally held jointly has been parcelled out by mutual arrangement, so that each taluk has the entire possession of the lands allotted to it (chinnit dakhal). The more inchoate the stage of growth of the tenure, the greater is the difficulty of record." The Sub-divisional Officer of Feni reports that in *pārgana* Amirābād alone there are 300 taluks, and in Bedarābād 800, and that the sub-infeudation and the intermixture of joint and several tenure is most complex. One peculiarity in the tenures of these *parganas* is that the owner of half the estate

* Paragraph 63, Report on the Settlement of Chakla Roshnabād.

let out his share in *tāluki* lease in 1866, while the same *tālukdārs* took fresh settlements three years later from the sixteen annas' proprietors preserving intact the former agreements. The forms of intermediate tenures are numerous. Under the landlords we find *pātni tāluks, kāimi tāluks, kāimi hāulās*, occupancy holdings and non-occupancy holdings; under the *pātni* tenures there are *dar-pātnis* and *se-pātnis* and beneath any one of these there may be in succession *tapas, shikmi tapas*, and *dar-shikmi tapas, kāimi jots* (ryots at fixed rates), and ordinary ryoti holdings. Beneath the *kāimi tāluk* come *dar-tāluks, shikmi tāluks* and *dar-shikmi tāluks*, and beneath any of these there may be *tapas, hāulas*, ryots at fixed rates, etc. Beneath the *hāulā* there may be a *nim hāulā*, and under that a *tapa*, and so on.

Government Estates.

After the Permanent Settlement Government acquired by purchase portions of estates sold to liquidate arrears of revenue, many new islands became its property under the law of alluvion, some invalid grants in Government estates were resumed, and a few properties escheated to Government. Most of these were farmed or let for short terms on *ābādkāri tālukdāri* tenures, the lessee undertaking to bring a certain area into cultivation during the term, and receiving 15 per cent. or more on the total collections. In 1861 the Board's decision to allow only annual leases provoked a protest from the Collector; but about the same time attempts were made to sell the Government estates, though the undeveloped condition of many made it hopeless to expect a full price. Ultimately 68 estates with an area of 80,443 acres have been sold for Rs. 4,12,512, subject to an annual revenue of Rs. 1,27,583. Others have been settled for varying periods, generally with neighbouring proprietors; and there remained in 1909 A.D. 245 estates with a gross revenue of Rs. 2,12,947 in the possession of Government. Of these 34 with a revenue of Rs. 58,638 are in *pargana* Sandwīp, seven with a revenue of Rs. 10,002 in Bhulua, and 68 with a revenue of Rs. 1,40,804 are in the islands of the Meghnā, *pargana* Zāzirah.* There are three administrative divisions in charge of a Deputy Collector at headquarters and of Sub-Deputy Collectors on Sandwīp and Hātiā, and ten tahsīl circles. The cost of management comes to 9 per cent. of the revenue demand, and the total outgoings on management and improvements are about Rs. 24,000 a year. In 1907-08 the number of certificates filed for the recovery of arrears of rent was 1,957, and only Rs. 7,587 were remitted. In the ten years ending in 1904-05 more than the total demand for the period was collected, but there have been large enhancements since then. For the years 1896—1901 the average demand was Rs. 1,12,000 a year and for the next five years Rs. 1,45,000 a year. The increase is due to the formation of new and improvement of older *chars*, which necessitate constant settlement and re-settlement.

---

* Zāzirah means alluvial formation.

Temporarily settled estates. There are 45 temporarily settled estates, paying a revenue of Rs. 52,859. They are scattered all over the district, but 14 with a revenue of Rs. 23,617 are in *pargana* Zāzirah.

Fishery estates. The right of fishing in the tidal rivers belongs to the public and no charge is made for it. There are only two petty *jalkar mahāls*, one in the Dākātiā *Dona*, and the other in the Rahmat Ali *khāl*.

Revenue-free estates. The Mughal Emperors from time to time granted lands free of revenue to holy men or to those who had done them service, and subordinate officials and even *zamīndārs* had made many such grants of the lands in their charge. In 1782 the 'Bāze Zāmin Daftār' was constituted to obtain a record of these grants, and Regulation XIX of 1793 defined the classes of grants that were to be recognised. All grants made before the year 1765 and in possession of the grantee were declared valid. Grants made between 1765 and 1790 were valid only if they had been made or confirmed by the Government, and grants of later date were declared null and void, whatever the length of possession. Government, however, claimed only the revenue to be derived from the resumption of grants of more than a hundred *bighās*, leaving the *zamīndārs* to apply for the resumption of smaller grants within their estates and to enjoy the profits. It was long before the investigation was completed, and ultimately 74 major grants were confirmed and became revenue-free estates, while the cess returns show 915 rent-free tenures within the ambits of estates.

The only revenue-free tenures in Noākhāli that call for special notice are the *khusbāsh lākhirāj* grants. This name was applied to the lands, originally 40 *drons*, occupied free of rent by the descendants of the garrison of 1,400 men sent to Bhulua in the seventeenth century to protect it from the incursions of the Maghs. In 1830 the tenures were resumed under the orders of the Board of Revenue, but in 1843 the persons in possession of 36 parcels of these lands were allowed to purchase the proprietary right free of revenue on payment of ten years' revenue.

Sale of estates. Following the practice of their predecessors the East India Company used at first to recover arrears of revenue from proprietors or farmers by confining the defaulter and sending officers (*sazāwal*) to collect the rents directly. The sale of the property itself was introduced by the regulations for the decennial settlement which allowed the Board of Revenue with the sanction of the Governor-General to sell a portion of the estate in default sufficient for the liquidation of the balance due. Regulation III of 1794 exempted landholders from imprisonment for failure to pay the land revenue, but this exemption was withdrawn by Regulation VII of 1799, and down to 1841 imprisonment of the landholder and sale of the whole or a portion of his property continued to be alternative or supplementary methods of realising arrears. The present law, Bengal Act XI of 1859, makes sale the only coercive measure and the whole property is liable to be sold for the most petty arrear unless any shares are protected by special registration, in which case they are to be sold only if the price fetched by the residue is less than the balance due. The number of such separate accounts registered was 851 in 1907-08.

It would be unprofitable to follow the long course of attachments and sales, but the result of them is that not a single *zamīndāri* estate remains in possession of the proprietors who held it when the district first came under British administration. It would not be fair to blame only the inelastic system for this : the records disclose a chronic state of quarrel and dispute among the *zamīndārs* that must of itself have proved the ruin of any estate.

Nowadays sales are infrequent; in 1901-05 though 337 estates and shares of estates became liable to sale only 24 were sold; and in the same period 85 tenures in Government estates were sold for arrears of rent. Revenue-paying estates fetch from 15 to 20 times the net profit.

Public demands recovery.

Arrears of public demands are recovered by means of certificates made under Bengal Act I of 1895 which have the force of a decree and are executed by attachment and sale of the defaulter's property.

In the ten years ending 1904-05 the average annual number of such certificates was just over 1,900 and in 1907-08 there were 3,122.

Land registration.

In 1907-08 there were 8,965 separate interests in estates recorded under Bengal Act VII of 1876. In the five years ending in 1905 the annual number of applications under the Act was nearly 600, and in 1907-08, 640 new interests were entered in the registers.

Kists.

The *kists* or instalments of rents vary in different estates. In Bhulua, Ambarābād, and some other estates the permanent tenures usually pay in ten instalments spread over the months of Baisākh to Māgh. Ryots usually pay in four instalments: in Bhulua, Ambarābād, and the 6 anna estate of Bābupur *pargana* these fall due in Āsārh, Áswin, Pous, and Chaitra. The Sub-divisional Officer of Feni reports that tenure-holders and ryots of the Courjon estates have to pay rent in 10 *kists*, and that at the end of the first month interest at one anna per rupee is due, at the end of the second *kist* two annas per rupee, and so on, until at the 10th *kist* a tenant in arrears has to pay double the original rent.*

Zamindars.

In the years that followed the Permanent Settlement all the big estates came to sale, and not one is now in possession of heirs of the original proprietors.

---

* This information was received too late for verification and coming from a reliable source has been entered; but I have never known such an arrangement.

The Administrator-General on behalf of Arun Chandra Singh and Satyendranāth Ghose of the Paikpārā family holds the great Bhulua estate, the six annas estate of Bābupur, nearly the whole of *pargana* Amirābād, and considerable properties in Sandwīp and the islands. The major portion of the old formations of Sandwīp, Hātiā, and Bāmni is shared by Mr. Delauney, Mrs. Massingham, and Shib Dulāl Tewāri—all foreigners. The largest estate in Omarābād belongs to Gobinda Chandra Singh and others of Murshidābād; Tappa Jaynagar belongs to a *zamīndār* of Muktagāchā. *Parganas* Bedarābād, Amirābād,* and Kādvā, formerly the property of the Rājā of Hill Tippera, were granted by him to Mr. Courjon and have passed into the possession of the heirs of Mahārājā Durga Charan Law. His Highness the Rājā of Hill Tippera owns $129\frac{1}{2}$ square miles of Chakla Roshnābād and a fourth of *pargana* Dāndrā. In fine, except the Dālāl Bazār *zamīndārs*, who are descended from the Banyan of Mr. Verelst, all the principal landowners are absentees.

---

* There are two Amirābāds.

CHAPTER XI.

GENERAL ADMINISTRATION.

Staff.

Noākhāli is a regulation district, that is to say, one in which the Bengal Regulations and all Acts applying to Bengal are in force unless expressly excluded. The head of the district is the Magistrate and Collector, who combines in one person magisterial, revenue and executive functions; as District Registrar he is the head of the local Registration Department, and as Chairman of the District Board has a general control over the communications, sanitation and primary education of the district. His superior staff for general administration consists of four Assistant or Deputy Magistrates, having also revenue powers, and a Sub-Deputy Collector, besides the staffs at Feni, Sandwīp and Hātia.

Sub-division.

Until the year 1876 the district was an undivided charge, but in that year *thānā* Chhāgalnāiya from Tippera and Mirkasarai from Chittagong were combined with *thānā* Feni to form the Feni sub-division; two years later Mirkasarai was retransferred to Chittagong. The sub-division is in charge of a Deputy Magistrate and Collector, who is immediately responsible for the administration of his charge, and though divorced from direct control of the specialised departments, such as Registration and Excise, is yet as the local representative of the district officer expected to keep an eye on them and bring to notice any defect.

Thanas.

The *thānā* was originally the seat of a *Faujdār*, but in its modern application means a police circle. These police circles were constituted originally under the provisions of the Regulations of 1793 and were supposed to have an area of 400 square miles. When the district was first formed there were included in it eight *thānās, viz.*, Sudharām, Begamganj, Lakhipur, Rāmganj, Amirgāon, Chāndia, Sandwīp, and Hātia, and since then there have been few changes.

The Dhanya Munya outpost of Chāndia was promoted later to be a *thānā*, and these two *thānās* were transferred to Bākarganj in 1869, while Chhāgalnāiya was added to Noākhāli in 1876.

Thānā Amirgāon was in the year 1875 removed to Farādnagar and was renamed Feni. A new *thānā* called Bāmni was opened in the south-east of the district, but in 1888 its name was changed to Companyganj, and it has been reduced to the status of an outpost under *thānā* Sudharām, so that at present there are eight *thānās* and one independent outpost in the district. Constituted purely for police purposes, the *thānā* has almost entirely superseded the *pargana* as a unit of revenue and general administration.

The village never existed as an integral unit of administration in this part of Bengal. The cultivators in early days were nomadic and had no village organisation such as is found in western India; consequently the survey officers found it difficult to define the village, and though the *mauza*, as the villages of the revenue survey are termed, is the unit for revenue purposes, it was found so inconvenient that it was not followed in the census of 1901, for which the whole district was divided into one town and 2,633 villages. At present the groups of villages, known as *chaukidāri* unions, have to a great extent taken the place of the village as a unit. Villages.

There were very few village servants in the district. A certain number of *patwāris* or accountants did exist, but they were really the servants of the *zamīndārs* and tenure-holders, and at the present day though many people bear the title of *patwāri*, it is rather an honorary distinction, implying some degree of education, than an indication of an office. *Village servants.*

Thirty years ago the village headmen, known as *mātabars* or *mahalladārs*, still enjoyed considerable dignity and power, but they have been almost entirely displaced by the *chaukidāri panchayets* described below.

The *chaudhuris* and other *zamīndārs* were under the Mughal administration responsible for the maintenance of peace and apprehension of offenders, but so far from doing their duty in this respect they seem to have been the chief supporters of dacoits. With the introduction of the farming system and the establishment of *faujdārs* they were relieved of this duty, but in 1782 a proclamation was issued by the Governor-General, ordering all *zamīndārs* "to erect *thānās*" in their respective jurisdictions. They were made liable to refund the value of any property stolen if they failed to recover it, and were warned that the penalty for complicity in robbery, murder or breach of the peace was death. *Police.*

The Regulations of the 7th December 1792 relieved them of their responsibilities. *Thānās* were then formed and placed in charge of *darogas* who had under them a few *barkandāzes* (thunderbolt throwers or musqueteers) and were paid from the proceeds of a tax levied on traders and shop-keepers, and encouraged to energy by rewards for the apprehension of offenders. This system continued with few modifications until the passing of Act V of 1861 by which the organisation of the police is now regulated.

It was better than nothing, but in 1818 we find Mr. Walters pointing out the defects of the system, defects that survive in part to this day. The *barkandāzes* were underpaid and inefficient, the charges were too big, the police had such a bad name that respectable men would not serve as *darogas*, and several of these officers were found guilty of complicity in serious crime. The petty exactions of the police and the delays and expenses of justice deterred the people from reporting the commission of offences; and above all he considered a river police absolutely essential to grapple with thefts and dacoity by gangs (*kāfila*) of professional thieves.

In 1860 the police force of Noākhāli consisted of 164 men and 37 officers. In 1908 there were a Superintendent, 3 Inspectors, 24 Sub-Inspectors, 36 head-constables, and 242 constables; or one policeman to every 3,707 inhabitants and every 5·3 square miles.

Of these a force of 25 men and 2 head-constables under a Sub-Inspector are kept and drilled at head-quarters as an armed reserve. For a long time this duty was performed by a company of the Chittagong Militia. Shortly before the Mutiny this company was disbanded; but in 1858 the Magistrate had enrolled a number of the old sepoys and others to form a guard 170 strong. The men were well paid getting Rs. 6 each, high wages in those days, but the correspondence does not show what became of them.

Village police.

That the Magistrates and police so entirely failed to maintain law and order in the early days of British administration may be ascribed in no small measure to the absence of a village watch or of any substitute for it. Mr. D. J. MacNeile, who made an enquiry into the village police of Bengal in 1866, failed to ascertain how or by whom the *chaukidārs* whom he found there were first appointed, but he was satisfied that there were none when Bhulua was separated from Tippera in 1821. It may be noted that in Sandwīp, and apparently near Noākhāli also, there were then living large numbers of ex-soldiers or descendants of ex-soldiers of the Mughal armies pensioned off with grants of land, but Mr. Walters found no *chaukīdārs* in 1819 and was so strongly impressed with the need of some such officers that he appointed *barkandāzes* at the principal *ghāts* as a provisional measure.

In 1840 the Collector reported that there were 1,760 village watchmen, who were appointed by the village headmen (*mātabars* or *mahalladārs*) and paid by collections from the villagers.

In 1876 the Bengal Chaukidāri Act was applied to the district, and the force organised as at present. Under this Act the villages are grouped together into "Unions," or *chaukidāri* villages, to each of which a managing committee of five persons, or *panchayet*, is appointed. The Magistrate fixes the number and pay of the *chaukidārs*, and the extent of each beat. The *panchayet* assess the villagers in proportion to their means, raising enough to meet the pay of the *chaukidārs*, and leave a small margin for contingencies. They have powers of distraint and are personally liable for the *chaukidārs'* pay if it falls into arrears. The tendency has been for the collecting member of the *panchayet* to get the whole power into his hands, and these collecting members have usurped almost all the dignity and functions of the former *mahalladārs* or village headmen. Of late years *dafadārs* or literate watchmen have been appointed to assist the *panchayet* and serve as a connecting link between them and the police. They are also responsible for looking up bad characters at night. In 1908 there were 198 unions with 198 *dafadārs* and 1,894 *chaukidars*, about 110 houses to each *chaukidār* according to the census. The *chaukidārs* get Rs. 5 a month, and the *dafadārs* Rs. 6, and their cost, including the 15 per cent. allowed for contingencies and the remuneration of the collecting *panchayet*, comes to Rs. 1,50,000. Most of the *chaukidārs* are recruited from the local Muhammadans.

Thirty-five *chaukidārs* were dismissed and 547 fined in 1908, and 134 got small rewards averaging Rs. 4. Under a system inaugurated in 1904 small additions to the monthly pay are provided from the *chaukidāri* reward fund for meritorious conduct; as more permanent marks of distinction brass chevrons are given.

Registration.

Under the Mughal rulers the local *kāzis* used to register deeds, but their registration was not always satisfactory, as will be seen from the following extract from Mr. Duncan's Report on Sandwīp.

The system of registration is described in the following terms:—

"There are two cazies or men who act under that quality in Sandwip, one for the 12 and another for the 4 anna division, receiving no allowance from Government and subsisting only by certain contingent fees and dues which they receive on attesting writings or performing other acts incident to their office in respect to marriages, etc. They are thence entirely dependent on the zemindar in whose part of the parganah they respectively reside, because his countenance and allowance is necessary to secure to them the regular receipt of their fees on sundry occasions."

By Regulation XXXVI of 1793 a registry of wills and deeds was established. The system was amended and amplified by various Acts, and finally by Act (III of 1877), which is (still) * in force. Under this Act 22 registration offices have been established in the district, and the number of deeds registered in 1908 was 73,716 of an aggregate value of Rs. 67,28,400. The deeds registered include over 15,000 deeds of sale or exchange, 23,000 mortgages, and 20,000 leases of which 5,200 were perpetual leases.

The Collector is also District Registrar and as such controls registration in the district subject to the direction of the Inspector-General. He is aided by a special Sub-Registrar who is in charge of registration at head-quarters, and also inspects rural offices. Since 1905 the Sub-Registrars have all been salaried and form a self-contained graded service; and the clerks and muharrirs on their establishment are now paid by Government. The receipts from registration in 1908 were Rs. 71,816 and the expenditure Rs. 52,458. The most important offices are Noākhāli, where a Joint Sub-Registrar is entertained to relieve the pressure, Lakhipur, Begamganj and Sandwīp.

* XVI of 1908 now.

Registration of Muhammadan marriages.

It appears that the Muhammadan Government levied a fee, known as *haldāri*, varying from Rs. 3 to Rs. 4-4 on all marriages, and in the case of a Muhammadan the ceremony had to be performed before the *kāzi* and *mufti*, who exacted further fees, and the expense of marriage under these conditions had proved a very serious encouragement to celibacy. The Regulations of 1772 abolished all these fees and prohibited *kāzis* from exacting any payment for officiating at a marriage except such as was offered voluntarily. Accordingly, though the appointments of *kāzis* in towns and *parganas* continued to be made by Government, these officers lost their position in the eyes of the people, and it became customary for marriages to be celebrated in the presence of any respectable Muhammadan, who chose to call himself *kāzi*. In 1864 the appointment of *kāzis* was discontinued, but the need of some system of registry of Muhammadan marriages became more and more apparent; the well-to-do indeed often executed marriage deeds, which were registered in the offices of the Registrars of Assurances, but the bulk of the people took no such precaution, and the courts found the greatest difficulty in dealing with questions of disputed marriage or legitimacy.

Bengal Act I of 1876 passed to remedy this evil provides for the appointment of Registrars of Muhammadan marriages, and Act XII of 1880 provides for the appointment of *kāzis*, though it imposes no obligation to have marriages performed by them. The Registrar is entitled to a fee of Re. 1 for registration, and to receive any gratuity that may be offered him. A *kāzi's* fees for officiating at any ceremony are regulated purely by agreement.

In 1907-08 there were 16 Registrars of Muhammadan marriages in Noākhāli, who registered upwards of 4,000 marriages and 1,000 divorces. All these Registrars have also been appointed to be *kāzis*, but there is no record of the number of ceremonies at which they have officiated in that capacity. The number of marriages registered is a very small fraction of the total, but in proportion to its size the system seems to have taken a greater hold on Noākhāli than on any other district.

Criminal justice.

The head of the judicial administration of the district is the District and Sessions Judge. As Sessions Judge he tries with the help of assessors all serious cases and hears appeals from all the first class Magistrates in the district. The District Magistrate tries but a few cases himself, but supervises the work of the other Magistrates, and hears appeals from those exercising second and third class powers.

In 1908 there were 9 subordinate stipendiary magistrates in the district besides a bench of Honorary Magistrates at Noākhāli and one Honorary Magistrate sitting singly.

Crime.

The crime in the district is comparatively light. As long ago as 1842 the Superintendent of Police (an Officer who corresponded to the present Inspector-General) commented on the absence of serious crime and expressed the opinion that there must be a good deal which was not reported, but his inference apparently was not justified, and Noākhāli has continued to maintain an enviable reputation for peacefulness among the districts of Eastern Bengal. For the five years 1900—04 the average number of cases cognisable and non-cognisable reported was 4,880, rather less than in the preceding quinquennium. In 1908, 5,590 cases came before the courts, but of these only 3,130 were accepted as true, and only 966 persons were convicted. The true cases included 15 riots, 10 murders or homicides, 16 cases of grievous hurt, 38 of serious mischief, chiefly cattle poisoning, 223 house-breaking, and 159 thefts. Cattle poisoning, arson, and the making or passing of false coin are peculiarly rife in this district. They are all difficult to detect, and the reported figures probably do not show the extent to which they prevail.

Civil justice.

For the administration of civil justice the District Judge is assisted by a staff of one subordinate judge and 10 munsiffs. In 1908 the total number of original suits instituted was 23,118, of which 7,830 were money suits, 12,631 rent suits and 2,657 title suits. Civil litigation is not increasing much, the largest number of suits in any year since 1893 having been in 1899. The average value of the subject-matter of the suits for each of the three years ending with 1908 was Rs. 15,06,000.

Jail.

There is a small jail at Noākhāli for the accommodation of 95 prisoners, though it is capable at a pinch of holding a good many more, and the average daily population in 1908 was 177 persons of all classes. It is a very healthy jail, and in spite of the overcrowding in 1908, the average proportion of sick in hospital was less than 1 in 30, and only one death occurred. The prisoners cost in that year Rs. 97-9-0 each to maintain, and the profits of their labour were estimated only at Rs. 15-8-0 per head.

Finance.

The total revenue raised in the district in 1824 was Rs. 5,18,000, and in 1850-51 it had risen to Rs. 11,54,000, of which Rs. 3,62,000 was derived from the manufacture of salt. Owing partly to the abandonment of this manufacture and partly to poor collections it had dropped in 1870-71 to Rs. 8,84,000. Since then the Income Tax and the Road and Public Works Cess have been imposed; Land Revenue has grown, owing chiefly to the assessment of new alluvial formations in the estuary; Stamps and Registration yield an ever increasing revenue; and in 1908 the receipts under the principal heads, including the moiety of the Road and Public Works Cess credited to Government, was Rs. 14,70,000. This does not include the village assessment for the *chaukidārs*, nor the rates and taxes credited to local bodies, which would bring the total up to over Rs. 18,00,000.

Income tax.

In 1902-03 the income tax yielded Rs. 23,000 paid by 1,136 assessees. From that year the lowest limit of assessable income was raised from Rs. 500 to Rs. 1,000 a year, but this measure while affording relief to a number of clerks and petty shokeepers, hardly affected the collections, which in 1908-9 amounted to Rs. 24,000 assessed on 600 persons.

Excise.

The people of Noākhāli, both Hindus and Muhammadans, are extremely temperate, and the excise revenue is far less than in any other plains district in the province. In 1908-09 it was only Rs. 24,772 against Rs. 17,691 in 1892-93. The increase is due almost entirely to the greater consumption of opium and hemp drugs.

There is but little consumption of spirits, which are distilled from molasses on the outstill system, and bring in about Rs. 6,000 a year.

The consumption of opium has doubled in the last 18 years, and in 1908-09 the duty and license fees on it amounted together to Rs. 7,183. Ganja is the most popular drug, and yields a revenue of about Rs. 10,600 a year.

Stamps.

The people of the district are highly litigious, ready to take the smallest dispute into court, and so distrustful of each other that the pettiest transactions are recorded in stamped agreements. Accordingly the revenue from stamps, both judicial and non-judicial, is expanding rapidly and amounted in 1908-09 to Rs. 5,40,398, of which Rs. 4,13,728 was derived from the sale of judicial stamps.

Cesses.

Bengal Act IX of 1880 empowered the Collector (to levy a road cess and a public works cess on the annual value of all immovable property in the district at a rate, not exceeding half an anna in the rupee for either cess, to be determined by the Road Cess Committee (now the District Board); the proceeds of the road cess to be paid to that Committee and that of the public works cess to be devoted to provincial public works and to subsidies to the district road fund.

These cesses are now levied at the maximum rate. The total demand in 1907-08 was Rs. 2,15,397 as against Rs. 1,37,278 in 1892-93. The rental of Noākhāli has increased enormously in the last thirty years, and large additions to the cess are obtained at every revaluation.

Arms Act.

The Indian Arms Act, 1878, is in force, and under its provisions licenses for 703 fire-arms, of which 17 were breech-loaders, were in force at the end of 1908. Nearly a fourth of the licenses were given for protection against wild animals, but none of the larger carnivora were shot in the district during the year, and only one man and four head of cattle were killed by tigers and leopards. No persons residing in the district were exempted from the provisions of the Act either as great *zamīndārs* or as a special personal distinction.

Postal and Telegraph Statistics.

In Noākhāli there are one head post office, 12 sub-offices, and 47 branch offices, and the number of letters received in 1909 was over 2,040,000. There has been a great expansion of post office work of late years. In 1861-62 the total number of letters and parcels received was under 39,000, and as late as 1899-1900 there were only 35 post offices in all. The value of the money-orders issued has risen from Rs. 12,04,000 in 1899-1900 to Rs. 17,16,000 in 1908-09, and that of money-orders received from Rs. 7,20,000 to Rs. 14,81,000 in the same years.

There are only two telegraph offices besides those at the railway stations.

Surveys.

Periodical measurements were made during the Mughal period and large portions of the district were surveyed and settled in the early days of British rule. Sandwīp and the connected islands were surveyed by a Mr. Rawlins in 1787 and in 1833 by Captain Hodges. The lands of *pargana* Bhulua were measured about the year 1790 by Mr. Dandridge and many other estates were at one time or another in the *khās* possession of Government and measured by its officers. But these early surveys were made with only a pole, usually ten cubits in length, carried by two men, and were necessarily inaccurate. The results were not embodied in any map, and in course of time most of the old papers were lost or worm-eaten. The revenue survey made by a professional party in the years 1864-65 shows the boundaries of villages and estates and the main topographical features of the country, and as regards the lands along the Meghnā, the results were corrected in the Diara Survey of the year 1881-82. In 1893-95, 129½ square miles of the Chāklā Roshnābād estate lying in Noākhāli were surveyed and settled and field-to-field maps and detailed lists of tenancies prepared. Similar cadastral surveys were made also for some 255 square miles, chiefly Government estates, during the years 1895—1905 and for another 158 square miles since then.

CHAPTER XII.

LOCAL SELF-GOVERNMENT.

History. The first experiment in Local Self-Government was the appointment in 1855 of a small committee to help the Magistrate in administering the Ferry Fund. Sir Frederick Halliday held that this gave no real assistance and only detracted from the Magistrate's responsibility* so the committee was abolished in 1857. Again in 1871 a Road Committee was established and was superseded from the 1st January 1875 by a Road Cess Committee which administered the proceeds of a cess levied at six pies in the rupee on the rental of the district.

Municipalities. The only Municipality in the district is that of Sudharām, the head-quarters station. This was constituted in July 1876, and has 12 Municipal Commissioners, of whom one holds office ex-officio, and three are nominated by the Local Government. In 1907-8 the total income, including the contribution from Government of Rs. 500, was only Rs. 12,049, of which Rs. 5,190 were raised by taxes on the houses and lands at the rate of 7½ per cent. on their annual value, Rs. 4,800 by conservancy rates, and the balance was made up of taxes on animals, vehicles, profession, and trades, and of profits on pounds, rents, and miscellaneous items. The expenditure for the same year was Rs. 12,498, of which about 11 per cent. was on administration, and more than half on conservancy. To lighting and roads the Municipality devoted a tenth of its expenditure. It contributed Rs. 646 to hospitals, and Rs. 228 to education. The Commissioners take an interest in their work, and considering the small amount of money at their disposal, the Municipality is well run.

District Board. The District Board of Noākhāli has 13 members, of whom four including the Chairman hold office ex-officio, three are nominated, and the rest elected by the Local Boards. The Board meet rather oftener than once a month, and the members are said to take a proper interest in their duties. Nearly all questions are considered in the first place by Standing Committees, on whom the bulk of the work falls.

Income. In 1908-9 the opening balance of the Board was nearly Rs. 84,000, and its receipts during the year were over Rs. 2,57,000. This is a very substantial increase, for its average income for the ten years ending in 1901-02 was only Rs. 1,46,000. The increase is due in part to the larger collections of road cess, but chiefly to the much larger contributions received from provincial revenues. The contributions from provincial revenues amounted in

* Minute of the 8th April 1857.

1908-09 to Rs. 75,000 of which about Rs. 50,000 were for expenditure on education, Rs. 22,000 for the improvement of communications, Rs. 1,000 for the improvement of water-supply, and Rs. 2,000 for special works.

Expenditure. The total expenditure in 1908-09 amounted to Rs. 2,40,000, out of which administration cost a little over Rs. 6,000. On education the Board spent Rs. 82,500, or 39 per cent. of its income; on communications it spent Rs. 79,000, of which about Rs. 46,000 were on original works, chiefly bridges, while it maintained five miles of metalled roads at an average cost of Rs. 280 per mile, and 390 miles of unmetalled road at an average cost of Rs. 166 per mile; this excludes 281 miles of village roads in charge of the Local Boards, on which only Rs. 48 per mile was expended.

There are 98 cattle pounds in the district under the charge of the Board. They are farmed out and yield a net profit of nearly Rs. 5,000 a year.

The ferries of the district are also in charge of the Board, and by an arrangement with the District Board of Chittagong half the profits of the Komira ferry are credited to Chittagong, and in return a half share of the sale proceeds of the Bāgkhāli, Sandwīp, and Lālganj ferries in Chittagong is paid to Noākhāli. The Board spent Rs. 19,600 on medical relief mostly in contributions to the dispensaries, which are managed by independent committees under its general control, and partly also in the direct relief of cholera by the deputation to the interior of medical officers to deal with outbreaks.

Local Boards. There are only two Local Boards in the district, the *Sadr* and the Feni Boards, the former having 11 and the latter 9 members, all of whom are nominated, except the Chairman, who holds office ex-officio. These Boards have very restricted powers and little to do beyond maintaining the village roads and tanks.

Unions. There are also four Union Committees at Feni, Lakhipur, Sandwīp and Hātia, each consisting of six members appointed by the Commissioner of the Division. They are entrusted with the maintenance of the village roads, the water-supply and the drainage, and are allowed to enjoy the income derived from the local funds, and may raise money by contributions or a local assessment. In 1908-09 their total income amounted to Rs. 2,640, of which Rs. 1,829 was contributed by the District Board. It is said that they worked fairly well, but in the previous year the Hātia Committee failed to take a proper interest in its duties, and had to be reconstituted.

CHAPTER XIII.

EDUCATION.

History.

In the year 1870-71 there were 26 Government and aided schools, in 9 of which English was taught, and the number of pupils was under 600. Sir George Campbell's educational reforms gave a great stimulus to the opening of schools, and in the year 1874-75 there were 187 Government and aided schools attended by upwards of 6,000 boys. In 1895-96 the number of schools attained its maximum of 2,775, and the returns of attendance showed nearly 58,000 pupils. At this time a change in the policy led to the disappearance of a good many bogus *pāthshālās* and in 1897-98 the number of schools was only 1,330 with less than 34,000 pupils. In 1908-09 the number of schools had risen to 1,518 with over 62,500 pupils on the rolls. Of these schools, 61 were secondary, 1,257 primary, 20 were special schools, and 180, of which 44 were advanced and the rest elementary, did not comply with any recognised standard.

Expenditure.

The expenditure on public instruction has risen steadily. In 1901-02 it was Rs. 1,12,000. In 1908-09 it was over Rs. 2,47,000. Of this sum Rs. 49,000 was contributed from provincial revenues, Rs. 77,000 from local funds, Rs. 1,00,000 from fees, and the balance from private sources. Classified otherwise, Rs. 64,000 were spent on secondary schools, Rs. 94,000 on primary schools, Rs. 8,000 on special schools, Rs. 59,000 on buildings and furniture, Rs. 17,000 on inspection, Rs. 2,500 on scholarships, and the balance chiefly on hostel charges.

Secondary education.

There are five High English Schools, of which one is maintained and three aided by Government, containing altogether over 1,300 pupils. There are also 55 English and Vernacular Middle Schools with some 5,700 pupils; of these 4 are managed by local authorities, and all the rest, except six, are aided.*

The cost of education comes to nearly Rs. 20 per pupil in the High Schools, and to rather over Rs. 6-4-0 in the Middle Schools, and the amount recovered from fees comes to Rs. 14 a head in the High Schools, and between Rs. 3-4-0 and Rs. 3-12-0 a head in the others.

Primary education.

There are 133 Upper Primary Schools with 8,500 pupils, and 1,124 Lower Primary Schools with 41,000 pupils, among which there are 307 Girls' Schools with 7,500 pupils. This comes to very nearly one primary school to every square mile or to every two villages.

The cost of education in the Upper Primary Schools comes to rather less than Rs. 3 per pupil, and the amount recovered

* Where no year is specified the figures are for 1908-09.

from fees to about Rs. 1-11-0 per pupil. In the lower primary standard boys cost a little under Rs. 2 each and two-thirds of this amount is recovered from fees; girls cost less than a rupee a head, but pay practically no fees.

Madrasas.

There are four aided *Madrasas* with some 500 pupils, but besides these there are 42 advanced schools with nearly 1,500 pupils, teaching Arabic or Persian according to their own standards, and 132 Elementary Schools in which 3,000 boys are taught the *Korān*. There are 14 Sanskrit *Tols*, besides two other schools in which Sanskrit is taught, but the total number of pupils is only 250.

Educational standard.

In 1881 about one male out of every eleven, and less than one woman in every 2,000 could read and write. In 1901-02 among the male population 21½ per cent. of the Hindus and 7 per cent. of the Muhammadans could read and write, while of women, one in every 110 Hindus and one in every 500 Muhammadans, were literate. The number of persons who could read and write English in 1901 was 2,270.

It is difficult to say whether there has really been much advance in education in the last 15 years. The number of schools shown in 1895-96 was 2,775 with nearly 58,000 pupils on the rolls. In 1898-99 there were only 33,500, and in 1907-08 there were 60,000 amounting according to the returns of the of the educational department to 35 per cent. of the population of the school-going age. The following year added about 2,500 to the number of students, but on the other hand the school-going population appears to have been calculated on the basis of the census of 1901, making no allowance for the rapid growth of population since then. It would be safe to say that the number of children of the school-going age must have increased by 10 per cent., and calculated on this basis the proportion of children at school in 1908-09 to those of school-going age is about 33 per cent. Of boys alone the number in 1908-09 was about 52,000 equivalent to 55 per cent. of those school-going age.

Female education

In 1899-1900 there were 63 girls' schools in the district with 1,138 pupils In 1908-09 there were one middle vernacular and 310 primary and elementary schools with upwards of 7,500 pupils, and another 3,000 were reading in boys' schools, making the total about 12 per cent. of the girls of school-going age. Two Model Girls' Schools have been established and 18 female teachers appointed.

The popular prejudice against the education of women is dying out fast, and the marriageable age of a girl in the respectable classes of Hindu society has risen perceptibly.

Management and inspection.

The management of primary and middle schools is entrusted to the District Board, and in towns to the Municipal Commissioners. High Schools are managed by School Committees subject to the control of the Educational Department. Such Committees exist also for Middle and occasionally for Upper Primary Schools, but in regard to these are rarely of much assistance. Unaided schools are of course free from Government control, except in so far as they have to conform with the orders of the University. Until the current year the Subordinate Inspecting Agency was under the local authorities, but has now been placed under the Educational Department. The sanctioned staff for Noākhāli consists of 3 Deputy Inspectors, 11 Sub-Inspectors, and 2 Assistant Sub-Inspectors, all under the orders of the Inspector of Schools for the Chittagong Division. The whole of this staff has not been appointed.

CHAPTER XIV.

GAZETTEER.

Ambarabad or Omarabad.—A *pargana* in the west of the district, lying west and north of Bhulua with an area of 124·4 square miles, containing 960 permanently settled estates with a total revenue of Rs. 81,633. It is said to have been carved out of the old *rāj* of Bhulua in the beginning of the eighteenth century when it was still an uninhabited waste. The story runs that a Persian *pīr* by name Ambar (or Omar) Shāh came to the district and lived there in his boat working miracles and making multitudes of converts by whom the wastes were gradually reclaimed. He gave his name to the *pargana*, and it was at his instance that the Emperor Muhammad Shāh settled it with two brothers of Dehli, Amānullah and Sanāullah Khān at the very low revenue of Rs. 289. It appears in the accounts of 1728 as Omarābād Noābād Bhulua at that revenue.

Gambling and extravagance soon brought the proprietors into difficulties and they crippled their resources further by giving away most of the *pargana* in *tāluks*. Down to 1791 they paid a revenue of Rs. 50,000, and the Board then ordered settlement to be made with the *tālukdārs*. The demand was fixed at Rs. 1,06,437 but the *tālukdārs* refused to accept this and the estate was held *khās* for some time. It was not until 1795 that the Board sanctioned the settlement of the *pargana* for a revenue of Rs. 95,631.

The *pargana* was divided at first into 1,406 estates of which 41 were in the possession of Government and 5 were unsettled. In the first quinquennial register these five became 188, and 380 others were bought in at sales for arrears of revenue; so that at the time of the formation of the district of Noākhāli Government was in possession of 605 estates with a nominal revenue of Rs. 41,683. Of these, however, 90 could not be identified and others had lapsed into jungle, and eventually they were all consolidated under two *tauzi* numbers and farmed out for Rs. 27,179. The farming settlements continued for many years, until in 1869 the property was settled with the late farmer's widow subject to a permanent revenue of Rs. 30,000 and a premium of Rs. 80,000. The estate is now in the possession of Gobinda Chandra Singh and others of Murshidabad.*

Babupur.—*Pargana* in Begamganj and Feni *thānās*, area 37·33 square miles, 35 estates, land revenue Rs. 14,952. Said to have been a part of Bhulua granted to Bābu Khān, a Brāhman

* Collector's letter dated the 3rd February 1863.

from Hīndustān, whose brothers' names survive in their houses Damad Khān bāti and Ārab Khān bāti. After Bābu Khān's death the *pargana* passed into the possession of a branch of the Sūr family, and in 1728 stood in the name of Uday Nārāyan Chaudhuri with a revenue of Rs. 350. In 1765 the revenue is shown as Rs. 12,984.

A feud among the owners, caused by the love affairs of one Rāj Chandra who wanted to marry a dancing girl, led to a great fight still celebrated in song as the 'Chaudhurir Larāi.' The estate was then divided and Government acquired successively at sales for arrears of revenue a one anna and a one anna eleven ganda share and settled them with other persons, while the greater part of the residue was bought by one Rādhākrishna Mazumdār, *diwān* of a former proprietor. His descendants were profligate and extravagant, and once more the estate came under the hammer. The six anna share went to the *zamīndārs* of Bhulua, and the rest to various persons.

A two anna share remained in the family down to 1865 when it was sold to satisfy the proprietor's debts and bought by Muhammad Kābil Miā for Rs. 10,920.

Bhulua.—The largest *pargana* in the district; area 245·5 square miles, divided into 185 estates at a total land revenue of Rs. 1,23,929. It represents the remnant of the dominions of the Sūr Rājās and in the revenue roll of 1728 A.D. stood in the name of Kirti Nārāyan with a revenue of Rs. 41,161; in 1789 A.D. the revenue was Rs. 99,469. In 1785 a four anna share was purchased by Ganga Gobinda Singh of Kāndi in the district of Murshidābād, the *Diwān* of Lord Hastings and founder of the Paikpārā family. He applied for partition, and Mr. Dandridge and afterwards a Mr. Meyer were deputed to effect it, but the parties objected to the award and in 1810 we find the twelve anna proprietors praying for the appointment of a common manager.* In 1833 the estate was brought to sale for arrears of revenue and bought by Dwarka Nāth Tagore, who sold it for about three lakhs of rupees to Rāni Katyāyani of the Paikpārā family, the ancestress of the present proprietors. The estate is now in the hands of the Administrator-General and is managed by a local Sub-Manager stationed at Noākhāli. Most of the property is let out in *pātni*.

Bhulua village a few miles west of Noākhāli on the Lakhipur road. Site of the Muhammadan fort established in the seventeenth century, and head-quarters of the district in the eighteenth

* *Vide* Collector's letters dated the 14th May 1790 and 19th March 1807. The purchaser is described as Ganga Nārāyan Chaudhri, and I am told that the purchase was made *benāmi* in this name. According to the Noākhāli Itihāsh the four anna share first purchased by Ganga Gobinda Singh was the part known as the Ashtahāzāri, which in the time of Rāni Shashimukhi, had passed out of the hands of the Sūr family and had been settled with her *diwān* Nara Nārāyan Rai.

century. It is not clear when it was abandoned, but in 1821 the Joint Magistrate was posted to Noākhāli, which seems to have been the head-quarters ever since.

Dandra.—*Pargana*, area 39·45 square miles. It is closely associated with Allahābād, area 8·17 square miles, and the two are divided into 36 estates with a land revenue of Rs. 22,340. These two formed the lands granted to a Muhammadan General for the protection of the frontier, and in 1728 stood in the name of Muhammad Arifat Chaudhuri with a revenue of Rs. 7,486. When it came under the Collector of Tippera in 1790 A.D. the *zamīndārs* were a most turbulent lot, and one of them before long was lodged in jail on charges of rape and murder, while the property was administered by the Collector. There were disputes as to the succession, and half was awarded to Muhammad Wāsik and Muhammad Amjad and the other half to Ilyās Khān. The main property was divided into five estates of Dāndrā and two in Allahābād. Three of the former, making up 8 annas 18 *gandas* of the *pargana*, were in possession of Government in 1861, a four anna share belonged to Muhammad Arshud and three annas odd to Afrunnissa. In 1864 Government sold its shares, four annas going to the Rājā of Hill Tippera and three annas to Faizunnissa Chaudhurani and others.

The other four anna share was bought by Manohar Ali Chaudhuri, and has since been sold again for arrears of revenue and bought by the Dālāl Bāzār *zamīndārs*. Chandra Nāth Chaudhuri of Senerkhil—*thānā* Feni—was the owner of a share of three annas odd. He is dead and his three sons and wife are now the joint proprietors.

Feni.—Sub-division in the east of the district; area 343 square miles; population 318,837. The sub-division was formed in 1876 and included at first *thānās* Feni, Chhāgalnāiya, and Mirkāsarai, but this last was retransferred in 1878 to Chittagong and part of Bāmni *thānā* was then made over to the sub-division. The central portion of the sub-division is low alluvial plain, similar to the rest of the district; the eastern portion, which abuts on Hill Tippera, is higher and sometimes undulating, with occasional mounds, *dipahs*, rising above the general level, and is liable to be flooded by the overflow of the hill streams. The Assam-Bengal Railway runs through the heart of the sub-division which is well supplied with roads and water communication. This sub-division is watered and drained by the big and little Feni rivers, the Muhuri and its tributaries the Silonia and Gotia, and by several sluggish canals or *khāls*.

The whole of *thānā* Chhāgalnāiya forms part of Chakla Roshnābād, an estate under the collectorate of Tippera belonging to His Highness the Rājā of Hill Tippera. Most of the neighbourhood of Feni station lies in *parganas* Amirābād and

Bedarābād, known as the Courjon estate but now the property of the Laws of Calcutta.

Feni.—Head-quarters of the sub-division of that name. There is no village of Feni, but in 1876 the head-quarters were established at Khyārā some two miles from the Feni river, which gave its name to the station. The site was found unsuitable and the town is now situated in *mauzas* Barāhipur, Shaivadebpur, Dādpur, Rampur, and Chāripur. It is on the Assam-Bengal Railway, 56 miles from the Chittagong terminus, the town is growing fast, and its roads and sanitation and that of the adjacent rural areas are managed by a Union Committee under the control of the Local Board. The principal buildings stand round the Rājāji's tank excavated by the District Board in 1890.

Jagdia.—*Pargana* between Bhulua and the Feni river. Area 67·37 square miles, 5 estates, land revenue Rs. 28,705. It was given as a *jāgīr*, valued in 1722 A.D. at Rs. 16,984, to Burā Khān, a Hindu appointed in the time of the Emperor Aurangzeb to guard the frontier. He is said to have given it to a Brāhman child, and in the decennial settlement it was divided into three estates, Brāhman, Dās and Kabirāj. There are now a large number of small proprietors who are represented by a common manager.

Lakhipur.—Site of a *thānā* of that name and of a sub-registry office, post office, and inspection bungalow. Connected by road with Sudharām (23 miles), Begamganj (19 miles), and Rāipur (10 miles). There was a cloth factory here established in 1756 and its ruins, known as Jackson's *kuti*, are still to be seen. It is an important mart, specially famous for its molasses, and has a population of over 5,000 souls. Its local affairs are managed by a Union under the *Sadr* Local Board.

Raipur.—At the mouth of the Dākātiā in the extreme north-east of the district on the Lakhipur-Chāndpur road. The most important mart in the district, with a large export of betel-nut, coco-nut, oranges, limes, and plantains. The office of the joint sub-registrar of Lakhipur is here, and there is an inspection bungalow.

Sandwip.—A large island in the Bay of Bengal separated from the mainland of Noākhāli by the Bāmni river. It was inhabited at a comparatively early date, and the Venetian traveller Cesare Federico who saw it in the year 1569 described it as one of the most fertile places in the world densely populated and well cultivated. It was then in the possession of the Muhammadans, and in the beginning of the seventeenth century passed into the hands of Portuguese adventurers. In 1662 it was under Mughal administration and formed with the adjoining islands of Hātia, Bāmni, and Shāgird-dihi, a single *pargana* divided into three estates or *tarafs*, each of which had lands in all the islands and a share of common lands. There were disturbances in the island in 1767 which were quelled by troops, the owner of a 4 annas 1 ganda 3 courie share, Abu Tarāp, being killed in the fighting and his interests confiscated and made over to one Gokul Ghoshāl, Diwān of the Nawāb and real Ahdadār of the islands, whose machinations and oppressions led to Mr. Duncan being deputed to hold an enquiry in 1778. This share was thereafter known as *tarāf* Bhawāni Charan, after a servant of Gokul Ghoshāl in whose name it was registered.* In 1786 this *tarāf* paid revenue in Bhulua, and the others in Chittagong. At the time of the permanent settlement a number of petty estates were formed by the separation of *tāluks* or the resumption of grants. Between 1797 and 1821 two *tarāfs*, 5 annas 0 ganda 2 couries and 2 annas 15 gandas were sold for arrears of revenue and bought by Prān Krishta Biswās, whose estate was in turn brought to sale on the 1st July 1824 and bought by Government. The other interests were sold up soon after, and by 1830 all the original estates of the *pargana* were in the possession of Government. By an order dated the 29th June 1830 Government cancelled the sale of *taraf* Bhawāni Charan and directed its return to the owners in satisfaction of a decree they had obtained; but there was delay in giving effect to the order and the lands were measured along with the rest of the estate. In 1841 they were made over to a receiver of the High Court, and the rest were settled for thirty years, those in Hātia, Sandwīp, and Bāmni being dealt with separately by three different officers. In these settlements new alluvial formations were included and several of the small petty estates consisting of *khārija tāluks* or resumed lands were amalgamated.

In 1890 the Government estates in Sandwīp, Bāmni, and Hātia were sold for Rs. 1,95,000, half being purchased by Mr. Courjon and half by Mr. Delauney and Shib Dulāl Tewāri jointly, the revenue for the three estates being fixed in perpetuity at Rs. 38,420. The present proprietors of these estates are the representatives of the purchasers, and those of Bhawāni Charan's estate are Mrs. Delauney and the heirs of Shib Dulāl Tewāri. It is worthy of note that the purchasers of the Government estates are not allowed to have any right to new accretions †.

Sudharam.—Sudharām on the west bank of the Noākhāli *khāl* about two miles from the sea is the head-quarters of the district. It is said that the Muhammadans had an outpost here in about the year 1620, but in Rennell's time, 1787, it was not important enough to be shown in his atlas. In 1821 it was chosen as the head-quarters of the Joint Magistrate appointed to the charge of the

* The twelve anna estate referred to in the old correspondence seems to have been made up of this share and of others of which Gokul Ghoshāl had possessed himself wrongly and which on Mr. Duncan's recommendation were restored to their former owners.

† This account is based on Mr. H. G. Cook's report of the 20th April 1882; and on the report of the settlement of Bāmni, 1903. Mr. Dampier's report of 1837 gives the fullest detail.

district of Bhulua. It was formerly known as Noākhāli, and took its present name from one Sudhārām Mazumdār, a wealthy merchant and benefactor, who excavated the large tank known by his name.

In 1876 it was constituted a Municipality, but the municipal revenue is only Rs. 12,000, and the population in 1901 was 6,520. It is really nothing but a rural bāzār with a few Government offices and residential buildings. It was completely wrecked by the cyclone of 1893, and the Government offices erected since then are fine substantial buildings. There is a neat little Town Hall with a stage, billiard room, and library attached to it, and a good Circuit House has been built lately. The drinking water is supplied from Sudharām's tank, a fine one but spoilt by the growth of weeds. The town is connected by railway with Lāksām, and steamers run from it to the islands and to Barisāl.

INDEX.

A

PAGE

Administration—General ... 88
,, —Land Revenue 74
Agriculture ... 53
Agricultural implements ... 53
Alluvion ... 6
Ambarābād ... 74, 101
Amirābād ... 83, 87
Arakanese ... 18
Area ... 1
Arms Act ... 94
Arts ... 71

B

Bābupur ... 77, 101
Bāmni—Island ... 7
,, —River ... 4
Bārah Bhuiyā ... 16
Bārui ... 36
Baskets ... 72
Betel-nut ... 57, 72
Betel-vine ... 57
Bhawāniganj Khāl ... 6
Bhuinmāli ... 38
Bhulua—Origin of name ... 15
,, —Pargana ... 102
Biswambhar Sūr ... 15
Boats ... 66
Botany ... 10
Boundary ... 1
Brāhmans ... 35
Brāhmo-Samāj ... 34

C

Canals ... 65
Carts ... 66
Castes ... 35
Cattle ... 59
Census ... 31
Cesses ... 94
Certificates ... 86
Chakla Roshnābād ... 87
Chandāl (See Namasudra).
Chaukidārs ... 90
Chaumohani ... 72
Cholera ... 45
Christians ... 34
Coco-nut ... 58
Communications ... 62
Configuration ... 1
Crops ... 53
Cultivation ... 53
Customs ... 39

D

PAGE

Dilal Khān ... 19
Diluvion ... 6
Dispensaries ... 46
District—name ... 1
,, —population ... 32
,, —area ... 1
,, —formation ... 25
District Board ... 96
Dress ... 39

E

Education ... 98
Estates—Government estates 84
,, —Number of ... 79
,, —Permanently settled... 79
,, —Temporarily settled... 85
Excise ... 94

F

Fauna ... 11
Feni—River ... 6
,, —Sub-division ... 103
,, —Town ... 104
Ferries ... 65
Fever ... 45
Fiscal divisions ... 74
Fish ... 12
Fishery ... 68
,, —Mahāls ... 85
Furniture ... 40

G

Game ... 11
Geology ... 10
Gonzales ... 17
Government Estates ... 84

H

Hātia (See also Sandwip) ... 2
Health ... 43
Hills ... 9
Houses ... 40

I

Islands ... 2
Income tax ... 93

J

Jagdia 2, 71, 104
Jugi ... 37
Jurisdiction ... 26
Justice ... 92
Jute ... 56

K

	PAGE
Kāyasth ...	36, 38
Khāls ...	6, 65
Khās Mahāls ...	84

L

Lakhipur ...	71, 104
Land—cultivated ...	54
Landlords and Tenants ...	79
Land Revenue—Administration.	74
„ —Amount ...	79
„ —Settlement ...	74 to 80
„ —of Sandwip ...	78
Language ...	41
Local Boards ...	97
Local Self-Government ...	96

M

Mahendra Khāl ...	6
Manufactures ...	71
Marriage ...	39
„ Registration ...	92
Marshes ...	9
Marts ...	72
Mats ...	72
Measures ...	49
Meghnā ...	3
Missions ...	34
Muhammadan—inhabitants ...	39
„ —invasions ...	16
Municipalities ...	96
Mythology ...	14

N

Namasudra ...	37
Nawārā Mahāls ...	21
Noākhāli—Khāl ...	6
Noākhāli—Origin of name ...	27
„ —Town *vide* Sudharam.	

O

Occupations ...	67
Oilseeds ...	56

P

Panchāyats ...	90
Parganas—See fiscal divisions.	
Physical conditions ...	1
Piracy ...	19
Police, Rural. ...	90
„ Stations ...	89

P—(*contd*).

	PAGE
Population ...	31
Portuguese in Sandwip ...	17
Pounds ...	97
Public demands recovery ...	86

R

Railway ...	65
Rāipur ...	104
Registration ...	91
Rest-houses ...	66
Resumption ...	85
Revenue of the district ...	93
(See also land revenue).	
Revenue-free lands ...	85
Rice ...	54
River communication ...	65
Rivers ...	3
Roads ...	62
Ryots ...	81

S

Salt ...	48, 67
Sandwip—Changes ...	7
„ —description ...	105
„ —History ...	17
„ —Revenue History ...	75
Schools ...	98
Shamsher Ghāzi ...	22
Slavery ...	21
Small pox ...	46
Stamps ...	94
Steamers ...	65
Sudharām ...	105
Sudras ...	36
Surveys ...	95

T

Tāluks ...	79
Tanks ...	10
Tenures ...	80
Thānās ...	88
Tipperas ...	15
Towns ...	33
Trade ...	72

U

Unions ...	97

V

Villages ...	33
Vital Statistics ...	43

W

Water supply ...	10, 43
Weaving. ...	71

Printed at the Pioneer Press, by Geo. Sim, No. 1438.—12-6-11.

DISTRICT GAZETTEERS OF INDIA {IN 245 BINDINGS}

ASSAM DISTRICT GAZETTEERS

11 VOLUMES

ISBN: 9788121285933 (PB Set)
Price: 6500/

BENGAL DISTRICT GAZETTEERS

52 VOLUMES

ISBN: 9789362089151 (PB Set)
Price: 35000/

GAZETTEER OF THE BOMBAY PRESIDENCY

27 VOLUMES
(IN 35 BINDINGS)

ISBN: 9788121285605 (PB Set)
Price: 90000/

CENTRAL PROVINCES DISTRICT GAZETTEERS

30 VOLUMES
(IN 33 BINDINGS)

ISBN: 9789362085399 (PB Set)
Price: 23000/

MADRAS DISTRICT GAZETTEERS

23 VOLUMES
(IN 25 BINDINGS)

ISBN: 9789362085627 (PB Set)
Price: 32000/

PUNJAB DISTRICT GAZETTEERS

36 VOLUMES
(IN 37 BINDINGS)

ISBN: 9789362084033 (PB Set)
Price: 46000/

RAJPUTANA DISTRICT GAZETTEERS

3 VOLUMES

ISBN: 9789362084781 (PB Set)
Price: 6000/

District
Gazetteers of India
{In 245 Bindings}
(Rs. 530000/- Hardcover)
(Rs. 370000/- Softcover)
Crown Size

UNITED PROVINCES OF AGRA AND OUDH DISTRICT GAZETTEERS

49 VOLUMES

ISBN: 9789362082183 (PB Set)
Price: 86404/

District Gazetteers of India Series 54

BENGAL DISTRICT GAZETTEERS

RANCHI

District Gazetteers of India Series 54

BENGAL DISTRICT GAZETTEERS

RANCHI

M. G. HALLETT

52 VOLUMES

(VOL. 43th)

GYAN

Published by

Gyan Publishing House
5, Ansari Road
Daryaganj, New Delhi-110002
Phone: 011-47034999, 9811692060
E-mail: books@gyanbooks.com

Distribution Network
gyanbooks.com
India, USA, Canada, UK, Australia, France

ISBN: 978-93-6208-448-4 (Set) 52 Volumes
978-81-212-5667-4 (HB)

First Published, 1917

2nd Impression 2024

Printed at: Gyan Press, Delhi.

BENGAL DISTRICT GAZETTEERS (VOL. 43th)
Author: M. G. Hallett

LIST OF VOLUMES

S. NO.	ISBN NO.	VOL.	TITLE	AUTHOR	PRICE	PAGES
			ASSAM DISTRICT GAZETTEERS			
1	9788121286046	1st	Cachar	B. C. Allen	1200	300
2	9788121286039	2nd	Sylhet	B. C. Allen	1500	378
3	9788121286022	3rd	Goalpara	B. C. Allen	800	203
4	9788121286015	4th	Kamrup	B. C. Allen	1370	344
5	9788121286008	5th	Darrang	B. C. Allen	1450	364
6	9788121285995	6th	Nowgong	B. C. Allen	1120	280
7	9788121285988	7th	Sibsagar	B. C. Allen	1370	343
8	9788121285971	8th	Lakhimpur	B. C. Allen	1380	347
9	9788121285964	9th	Naga Hills and Manipur	B. C. Allen	1170	294
10	9788121285957	10th	The Khasi And Jaintia Hills, The Garo Hills And The Lushai Hills	B. C. Allen	1350	363
11	9788121285940	11th	The Sadiya and Balipara Frontier Tract	B. C. Allen	760	190
			BENGAL DISTRICT GAZETTEERS			
12	9788121218665	1st	Angul	L. S. S. O'Malley	500	168
13	9788121259644	2nd	Bakarganj	J. C. JACK	1350	194
14	9788121218689	3rd	Balasore	L. S. S. O'Malley	675	228
15	9788121259606	4th	Bankura	L. S. S. O'Malley	1390	199
16	9788121218368	5th	Bhagalpur	J. Byrne	580	194
17	9788121218283	6th	Birbhum	L. S. S. O'Malley	450	150
18	9788121259668	7th	Eastern Bengal and Assam - Bogra	J. N. Gupta	1320	188
19	9788121218344	8th	Burdwan	J. C. K. Peterson	680	227
20	9788121259545	9th	Calcutta District Gazetteer - Statistics, 1901 - 02		480	68
21	9788121218306	10th	Champaran	L. S. S. O'Malley	610	205
22	9788121259620	11th	Eastern Bengal District Gazetters - Chittagong	L. S. S. O'Malley	1500	216
23	9788121259569	12th	Chota Nagpur Tributary		180	26
24	9788121259422	13th	The Cooch Behar Gazette: Statistics		2040	292
25	9788121218405	14th	Cuttack	L. S. S. O'Malley	740	248
26	9788121261364	15th	Eastern Bengal District Gazetteers Dacca	B. C. Allen	800	207
27	9788121218429	16th	Darbhanga	L. S. S. O'Malley	540	180
28	9788121204965	17th	Darjeeling	L. S. S. O'Malley	500	248
29	9788121259460	18th	Eastern Bengal District Gazetteers - Dinajpur	F. W. Strong	1250	178
30	9788121259408	19th	Faridpur	L. S. S. O'Malley	980	140
31	9788121218467	20th	Gaya	L. S. S. O'Malley	810	270
32	9788121214025	21st	Bihar and Orissa District Gazetteer: Hazaribagh	E. Lister	950	234
33	9788121218320	22nd	Hooghly	L. S. S. O'Malley	1020	340
34	9788121218184	23rd	Bengal District Gazetteer Howrah	L. S. S. O'Malley	590	199
35	9788121259309	24th	Eastern Bengal and Assam - Jalpaiguri	John F. Gruning	1250	178
36	9788121259286	25th	Jessore	L. S. S. O'Malley	1340	192
37	9788121259248	26th	Khulna	L. S. S. O'Malley	1540	220
38	9788121259224	27th	Malda	G. E. Lambourn	940	134
39	9788121297912	28th	Manbhum	H. Coupland	1250	313
40	9788121218481	29th	Midnapore	L. S. S. O'Malley	750	252
41	9788121218580	30th	Monghyr	L. S. S. O'Malley	840	280
42	9788121259163	31st	Murshidabad	L. S. S. O'Malley	1750	250
43	9788121259583	32nd	Bengal District Gazetteers - Muzaffarpur	L. S. S. O'Malley	1300	188
44	9788121259149	33rd	Mymensingh	F. A. Sachse	1340	192
45	9788121259125	34th	Nadia	J. H. E. Garrett	1500	214
46	9788121259101	35th	Eastern Bengal and Assam - Noakhali	J. E. Webster	800	115
47	9788121218443	36th	Feudatory States of Orissa	L. E. B. Cobdenramsay	1180	395
48	9788121259088	37th	Pabna	L. S. S. O'Malley	990	142
49	9788121218504	38th	Palamau	L. S. S. O'Malley	570	190
50	9788121218627	39th	Patna	L. S. S. O'Malley	750	250
51	9788121218528	40th	Puri	L. S. S. O'Malley	980	328
52	9788121218740	41st	Purnea	L. S. S. O'Malley	660	220
53	9788121258944	42nd	Rajshahi	L. S. S. O'Malley	1500	216
54	9788121256674	43rd	Bihar and Orissa District Gazetteers: Ranchi	M. G. Hallett	1950	278
55	9788121258920	44th	Eastern Bengal and assam - Rangpur	J. A. Vas	1250	178
56	9788121218542	45th	Sambalpur	L. S. S. O'Malley	730	242
57	9788121214049	46th	Santal Parganas	L. S. S. O'Malley	1250	308
58	9788121218603	47th	Saran	L. S. S. O'Malley	570	190
59	9788121218641	48th	Shahabad	L. S. S. O'Malley	570	190
60	9788121256698	49th	The Gazetteer of Sikhim	H. H. Risley	2280	481
61	9788121218566	50th	Singhbhum, Saraikela And Kharsawan	L. S. S. O'Malley	840	280
62	9788121259446	51st	Eastern Bengal District Gazetteers - Tippera	J. E. Webster	1020	146
63	9788121259040	52nd	24 Parganas	L. S. S. O'Malley	1990	284

S. NO.	ISBN NO.	VOL.	TITLE	AUTHOR	PRICE	PAGES
			CENTRAL PROVINCES DISTRICT GAZETTEERS			
64	9789362085474	1st, Vol. A	Akola (Descriptive)	A. E. Nelson, C. Brown	1740	436
65	9789362087232	2nd, Vol. A	Amraoti (Descriptive)	S. V. Fitzgerald, A. E. Nelson	2100	524
66	9789362085191	3rd,Vol. A	Balaghat (Descriptive)	R. V. RUSSELL	860	216
67	9789362085986	4th, Vol. A	Betul (Descriptive)	R. V. RUSSELL	1220	306
68	9789362082039	5th, Vol. A	Bhandara (Descriptive)	R. V. RUSSELL	1170	292
69	9789362087713	6th, Vol. A	Bilaspur (Descriptive)	R. V. RUSSELL	1740	434
70	9789362084255	7th, Vol. A	Buldana (Descriptive)	A. E. Nelson	2170	543
71	9789362082107	8th, Vol. B	Chanda (Descriptive)	R. V. RUSSELL	940	234
72	9789362084576	9th	Chhattisgarch Feudatory State	E. A. De Brett	1760	440
73	9789362084873	10th	Chhindwara (Descriptive)	R. V. RUSSELL	1100	274
74	9789362086426	11th, Vol. A & B	Damoh (Descriptive and Statistical Tables 1891-1901)	R. V. RUSSELL	1660	414
75	9789362080240	12th, Vol. A	Durg (Descriptive)	A. E. Nelson	930	232
76	9789362080448	13th, Vol. A	Hoshangabad (Descriptive)	R. V. RUSSELL	1720	430
77	9789362080028	14th, Vol. A	Jubbulpore (Descriptive)	A. E. Nelson	1900	474
78	9789362088079	15th, Vol. A & B	Mandla (Descriptive and Statistical Tables 1891-1901)	R. V. RUSSELL	740	186
79	9789362086693	16th, Vol. A	Nagpur (Descriptive)	R. V. RUSSELL	1580	394
80	9789362085221	17th, Vol. A	Narsinghpur (Descriptive)	R. V. RUSSELL	1030	257
81	9789362086501	18th, Vol. A	Nimar (Descriptive)	R. V. RUSSELL	1200	299
82	9789362082145	19th, Vol. A	Raipur (Descriptive)	A. E. Nelson	1580	396
83	9789362085948	20th, Vol. A	Saugor (Descriptive)	R. V. RUSSELL	1140	285
84	9789362080318	21st, Vol. A	Seoni (Descriptive)	R. V. RUSSELL	930	232
85	9789362089625	22nd, Vol. A	Wardha (Descriptive)	R. V. RUSSELL	1210	302
86	9789362088468	23rd, Vol. A	Yeotmal (Descriptive)	R. V. RUSSELL	1110	277
87	9789362083500	24th, Vol. I, Pt. I	Gwalior (Text and Tables)	R. V. RUSSELL	1960	489
88	9789362081667	24th, Vol. I, Pt. II	Gwalior (Maps)	R. V. RUSSELL	790	198
89	9789362087478	24th, Vol. I, Pt. III	Gwalior (Village List)	R. V. RUSSELL	1620	406
90	9789362089731	24th, Vol. I, Pt. IV	Gwalior (Photos)	R. V. RUSSELL	2790	698
91	9789362088956	25th, Vol. II	Indore (Text and Tables)	C. E. Luard	2100	524
92	9789362088543	26th, Vol. III	Bhopal (Text and Tables)	C. E. Luard	1090	272
93	9789362082732	27th, Vol. IV	Rewah (Text and Tables)	C. E. Luard	1000	250
94	9789362087065	28th, Vol. V, Pt. A	Western States - Malwa (Text)	C. E. Luard	3050	762
95	9789362080707	29th, Vol. VI, Pt. A	Eastern States - Bundelkhand (Text)	C. E. Luard	1850	463
96	9789362086273	30th, Vol. VI, Pt. B	Eastern States - Bundelkhand (Tables)	C. E. Luard	1670	417
			GAZETTEER OF THE BOMBAY PRESIDENCY			
97	9788121283458	1st, Part I	History of Gujarat	Ed.: James M. Campbell	4500	644
98	9788121285599	1st, Part II	History of the Konkan Dakhan and Southern Maratha Country	Ed.: James M. Campbell	5870	840
99	9788121285575	2nd	Gujarat, Surat and Broach	Ed.: James M. Campbell	4150	598
100	9788121285551	3rd	Kaira and Panch Mahals	Ed.: James M. Campbell	2370	339
101	9788121285537	4th	Ahmedabad	Ed.: James M. Campbell	2600	372
102	9788121285513	5th	Cutch, Palanpur, and Mahi Kantha	Ed.: James M. Campbell	3330	478
103	9788121285490	6th	Rewa Kantha, Narukot, Cambay, and Surat States	Ed.: James M. Campbell	2030	290
104	9788121285476	7th	Baroda	Ed.: James M. Campbell	4550	652
105	9788121285452	8th	Kathiawar	Ed.: James M. Campbell	5300	758
106	9788121285438	9th, Part I	Gujarat Population - Hindus	Ed.: James M. Campbell	4450	636
107	9788121285414	9th, Part II	Gujarat Population - Musalmans and Parsis	Ed.: James M. Campbell	2120	304
108	9788121285391	10th	Ratnagiri and Savantvadi	Ed.: James M. Campbell	3500	501
109	9788121285377	11th	Kolaba and Janjira	Ed.: James M. Campbell	3550	513
110	9788121285353	12th	Khandesh	Ed.: James M. Campbell	4450	638
111	9788121285339	13th Part I	Thana	Ed.: James M. Campbell	2880	413
112	9788121285315	13th Part II	Thana	Ed.: James M. Campbell	2490	357
113	9788121285292	14th	Thana - Places of Interest	Ed.: James M. Campbell	4600	659
114	9788121285278	15th Part I	Kanara	Ed.: James M. Campbell	3250	468
115	9788121285254	15th Part II	Kanara	Ed.: James M. Campbell	2440	468
116	9788121285230	16th	Nasik	Ed.: James M. Campbell	4880	698
117	9788121285216	17th	Ahmadnagar	Ed.: James M. Campbell	5400	772
118	9788121285193	18th Part I	Poona	Ed.: James M. Campbell	4100	586
119	9788121285179	18th Part II	Poona	Ed.: James M. Campbell	3750	537
120	9788121285155	18th Part III	Poona	Ed.: James M. Campbell	3500	503
121	9788121285131	19th	Satara	Ed.: James M. Campbell	4840	692
122	9788121285117	20th	Sholapur	Ed.: James M. Campbell	3820	547
123	9788121285094	21st	Gazetteer of the Bomaby Presidency: Belgaum	Ed.: James M. Campbell	3590	514
124	9788121285070	22nd	Dharwar	Ed.: James M. Campbell	5880	841
125	9788121285056	23rd	Gazetteer of the Bombay Presidency:Bijapur	Ed.: James M. Campbell	4980	712
126	9788121285032	24th	Kolhapur	Ed.: James M. Campbell	3150	450
127	9788121285018	25th	Botany	Ed.: James M. Campbell	2850	408

S. NO.	ISBN NO.	VOL.	TITLE	AUTHOR	PRICE	PAGES
128	9788121284998	26th, Part I	Materials Towards a Statistical Account of the Town and Island of Bombay - History	Ed.: James M. Campbell	3525	504
129	9788121284974	26th, Part II	Materials Towards a Statistical Account of the Town and Island of Bombay - Trade and Fortifications	Ed.: James M. Campbell	3750	538
130	9788121284950	26th, Part III	Materials Towards a Statistical Account of the Town And Island of Bombay - Administration	Ed.: James M. Campbell	4840	702
131	9788121284936	27th	General Index	Ed.: R. E. Enthoven	2990	428
			MADRAS DISTRICT GAZETTEERS			
132	9788121258821	1st	Anantapur	W. Francis	1590	227
133	9788121258562	2nd	Malabar	C. A Innes & F. B Evans	4210	602
134	9788121258807	3rd	Bellary	W. Francis	2640	377
135	9788121258784	4th	Statistical Appendix For Chingleput		390	56
136	9788121258760	5th	Coimbatore	K. N. Krishnaswami Ayyar	4790	628
137	9788121232821	6th	Madras District Gazetteers District Gazetteer Cuddapah	C. F. Brackenbury	1950	285
138	9788121258722	7th	Statistical Appendix For Ganjam		510	73
139	9788121256759	8th, Vol. 1st	Godavari District Gazetteer	F. R. Hemingway	1280	320
140	9788121256797	8th, Vol. 2nd	Godavari District Gazetteer	F. R. Hemingway	340	83
141	9788121258685	9th	Statistical Appendix For Kistna		890	127
142	9788121258661	10th	Statistical Appendix For Kurnool		380	54
143	9788121258623	11th	Madura	W. Francis	2650	379
144	9788121258586	12th	Statistical Appendix For Madura		1040	148
145	9788121258647	13th	The Nilgiris	W. Francis	3060	437
146	9788121234283	14th	Madras District Gazetteers Gazetteer Of The Nellore District Brought Upto 1938			2110
386						
147	9788121258524	15th	North Arcot		830	118
148	9788121258500	16th, Vol. 1, Part I	Salem	F. J. Richards	2400	343
149	9788121258609	16th, Vol. 1, Part II	Salem	F. J. Richards	2520	360
150	9788121258463	17th	South Arcot	W. Francis	3360	480
151	9788121258487	18th	Statistical Appendix For South Canara		560	80
152	9788121258449	19th, Vol. 1st & 2nd	Tanjore: Main Volume and Statistical Appendix		2900	401
153	9788121258401	20th	Tinnevelly	H. R. Pate	3830	547
154	9788121258425	21st	Statistical Appendix For Tinnevelly		450	64
155	9788121258388	22nd, 1st & 2nd	Trichinopoly: Main Volume and Statistical Appendix	F. R. Hemingway	3410	487
156	9788121241960	23rd	Vizagapatam District Gazetteer	W. Francis	1520	385
			PUNJAB DISTRICT GAZETTEERS			
157	9788121255936	1st	Ambala District 1883-84		870	124
158	9788121255950	2nd	Amritsar		1650	236
159	9788121255974	3rd	Delhi		1820	260
160	9788121255998	4th	Ferozepore		1320	188
161	9788121256018	5th	Faridkot		490	70
162	9788121256032	6th	Gujranwala 1893-94		1780	254
163	9788121256056	7th	Gujrat	C. E. Luard	1590	228
164	9788121256070	8th	Gurdaspur 1891-92		1764	252
165	9788121256094	9th	Gurgaon 1883-4		1420	203
166	9788121256117	10th	Hazara	H. D. Watson	3200	458
167	9788121256131	11th	Hissar district and Lohar State		2570	367
168	9788121256155	12th	Hoshiarpur		1980	283
169	9788121256179	13th	Jhang		1490	213
170	9788121256193	14th	Jhelam		1410	202
171	9788121256216	15th	Jalandhar District 1883-84		750	108
172	9788121256230	16th, Vol. XIV-A	Jullundur District, with maps and Kapurthala		2786	398
173	9788121256254	17th, Pt. I	Kangra (Proper)		2030	290
174	9788121256278	17th, Pt. II	Kangra (Kulu, Lahual, Spiti)		2500	357
175	9788121256292	18th	Karnal		2700	386
176	9788121256315	19th	Kohat		2150	307
177	9788121256339	20th	The Lahore District 1883-84		1710	244
178	9788121256377	21st	Ludhiana and Maler Kotla		2350	335
179	9788121256391	22nd	Lyallpur		1029	147
180	9788121256414	23rd	Mianwali		1640	234
181	9788121256438	24th	Montgomery	P. J. Fagan	2230	318
182	9788121258357	25th	Multan (1901-02)	E. D. Maclagan	3360	480
183	9788121258692	26th	The Rohtak District 1883-84		1370	196
184	9788121258739	27th, Vol. III A	Dujana State 1904		600	16
185	9788121256476	28th	Shahpur District		2490	356
186	9788121256490	29th	Simla District		1110	159
187	9788121256513	30th	The Chamba State		2860	408

S. NO.	ISBN NO.	VOL.	TITLE	AUTHOR	PRICE	PAGES
188	9788121256537	31st	The Chenab Colony 1904		2170	310
189	9788121256551	32nd	Kalsia State		370	53
190	9788121256575	33rd	Suket and Mandi		1080	154
191	9788121256599	34th	Phulkian States, Patiala Jind And Nabha 1904		2898	414
192	9788121256636	35th	Simla Hill States		3100	443
193	9788121256650	36th	Sirmur		1280	183
			RAJPUTANA DISTRICT GAZETTEERS			
194	9789362089847	1st, Vol. I-A & B	Ajmer-merwara (Text and Statistics Tables)	C. C. Watson	1720	246
195	9789362088895	2nd. Vol. II-A & B	Mewar Residency (Text and Statistics Tables)	K.D. Erskine	2370	339
196	9789362087935	3rd, Vol. III-A & B	The Western Rajputana States Residency And The Bikaner Agency	K.D. Erskine	5000	718
			UNITED PROVINCES OF AGRA AND OUDH DISTRICT GAZETTEERS			
197	9789362080523	Vol. I	Agra	H. R. Nevill	3160	452
198	9789362084149	Vol. II	Aligarh	H. R. Nevill	1820	260
199	9789362081452	Vol. III	Allahabad	H. R. Nevill	2860	409
200	9789362085917	Vol. IV	Almora	H. G. Walton	2330	333
201	9789362089717	Vol. V	Azamgarh	D. L. Drake Brockman	2440	349
202	9789362089069	Vol. VI	Bahraich	H. R. Nevill	1970	281
203	9789362089670	Vol. VII	Ballia	H. R. Nevill	2450	350
204	9789362080974	Vol. VIII	Banda	D. L. Drake Brockman	2440	349
205	9789362082657	Vol. IX	Bara Banki	H. R. Nevill	2410	344
206	9789362089588	Vol. X	Bareilly	H. R. Nevill	2290	327
207	9789362088772	Vol. XI	Basti	H. R. Nevill	2250	321
208	9789362086556	Vol. XII	Benares	H. R. Nevill	3210	458
209	9789362089762	Vol. XIII	Bijnor	H. R. Nevill	2540	363
210	9789362087522	Vol. XIV	Budaun	H. R. Nevill	2650	378
211	9789362085665	Vol. XV	Bulandshahr	H. R. Nevill	2930	419
212	9789362080899	Vol. XVI	Cawnpore	H. R. Nevill	3090	442
213	9789362082237	Vol. XVII	Dehra Dun	H. G. Walton	2390	342
214	9789362089489	Vol. XVIII	Etah	E. R. Neave	2240	320
215	9789362086983	Vol. XIX	Etawah	D. L. Drake Brockman	1940	277
216	9789362081650	Vol. XX	Farrukhabad	E. R. Neave	2270	324
217	9789362083326	Vol. XXI	Fatehpur	H. R. Nevill	2640	377
218	9789362081018	Vol. XXII	Fyzabad	H. R. Nevill	2370	339
219	9789362086907	Vol. XXIII	Garhwal	H. G. Walton	1780	254
220	9789362085092	Vol. XXIV	Ghazipur	H. R. Nevill	2240	320
221	9789362083272	Vol. XXV	Gonda	H. R. Nevill	2310	330
222	9789362088185	Vol. XXVI	Gorakhpur	H. R. Nevill	2650	378
223	9789362082756	Vol. XXVII	Hamirpur	D. L. Drake Brockman	1940	277
224	9789362081780	Vol. XXVIII	Hardoi	H. R. Nevill	2350	336
225	9789362085641	Vol. XXIX	Jalaun	D. L. Drake Brockman	1650	236
226	9789362080998	Vol. XXX	Jaunpur	H. R. Nevill	2450	350
227	9789362088123	Vol. XXXI	Jhansi	D. L. Drake Brockman	2740	391
228	9789362081568	Vol. XXXII	Kheri	H. R. Nevill	2310	330
229	9789362088161	Vol. XXXIII	Lucknow	H. R. Nevill	2460	352
230	9789362081155	Vol. XXXIV	Mainpuri	H. R. Nevill	2440	348
231	9789362086839	Vol. XXXV	Meerut	H. R. Nevill	3040	434
232	9789362080400	Vol. XXXVI	Mirzapur	D. L. Drake Brockman	3400	486
233	9789362088666	Vol. XXXVII	Moradabad	H. R. Nevill	2660	380
234	9789362082213	Vol. XXXVIII	Muttra	D. L. Drake Brockman	3000	428
235	9789362083555	Vol. XXXIX	Muzaffarnagar	H. R. Nevill	3160	451
236	9789362080820	Vol. XL	Naini Tal	H. R. Nevill	2640	377
237	9789362087799	Vol. XLI	Partabgarh	H. R. Nevill	2180	312
238	9789362082022	Vol. XLII	Pilibhit	H. R. Nevill	2200	314
239	9789362085337	Vol. XLIII	Rai Bareli	H. R. Nevill	2250	322
240	9789362088901	Vol. XLIV	Rampur	H. R. Nevill	1640	234
241	9789362082664	Vol. XLV	Saharanpur	H. R. Nevill	3070	438
242	9789362088406	Vol. XLVI	Shahjahanpur	H. R. Nevill	2110	302
243	9789362089823	Vol. XLVII	Sitapur	H. R. Nevill	2220	317
244	9789362083913	Vol. XLVIII	Sultanpur	H. R. Nevill	1860	266
245	9789362081544	Vol. XLIX	Unnao	H. R. Nevill	2140	305

BIHAR AND ORISSA DISTRICT GAZETTEERS

RANCHI.

Agents for the Sale of Books published by the Bihar and Orissa Government.

Agents in India :

(1) Messrs. Thacker, Spink & Co., Calcutta.

(2) Messrs. W. Newman & Co., Calcutta.

(3) Messrs. K. Lahiri & Co., College Street, Calcutta.

(4) Messrs. A. M. and J. Ferguson, Ceylon.

(5) Messrs. R. Cambray & Co., 6 and 8-2, Hastings Street, Calcutta.

(6) Messrs. Thompson & Co., Madras.

(7) Messrs. D. B. Taraporevala Sons & Co., 103, Meadow Street, Fort, Post Box No. 18, Bombay.

(8) Messrs. M. C. Sircar & Sons, 75, Harrison Road, Calcutta.

(9) Proprietor of the Newal Kishore Press, Lucknow.

(10) Messrs. M. N. Burman & Co., Bankipore.

(11) Babu Ram Dayal Agarwala, 184, Katra Road, Allahabad.

(12) Standard Literature Co., Ld., 13/1, Old Court House Street, Calcutta.

(13) Manager of the Indian School Supply Depôt, 309, Bow Bazar Street, Calcutta.

(14) Messrs. Butterworth & Co., Ld., 6, Hastings Street, Calcutta.

Agents in England :

(1) Messrs. Constable & Co., 10, Orange Street, London, W.

(2) Messrs. Kegan, Paul, Trench, Trubner & Co., 68-74, Carter Lane, London, E. C., and 25, Museum Street, London, W.C.

(3) Mr. B. Quaritch, 11, Grafton Street, New Bond Street, London, W.

(4) Messrs. P. S. King & Son, 2 and 4, Great Smith Street, Westminster, London, S. W.

(5) Mr. B. H. Blackwell, 50-51, Broad Street, Oxford.

(6) Messrs. Deighton Bell & Co., Trinity Street, Cambridge.

(7) Messrs. Henry S. King & Co., 65, Cornhill, London, E.C.

(8) Messrs. Grindlay & Co., 54, Parliament Street, London, S.W.

(9) Messrs. W. Thacker & Co., 2, Creed Lane, Ludgate Hill, London, E. C.

(10) Messrs. Luzac & Co., 46, Great Russell Street, London, W.C.

(11) Messrs. Oliver and Boyd, Tweeddale Court, Edinburgh.

(12) Messrs. E. Ponsonby, Ltd., 116, Grafton Street, Dublin.

Agents on the Continent :

(1) M. Ernest Leroux, 28, Rue Bonaparte, Paris.

(2) Martinus Nijhoff, The Hague, Holland.

BIHAR AND ORISSA DISTRICT GAZETTEERS

RANCHI

BY

M. G. HALLETT

INDIAN CIVIL SERVICE

PATNA:

SUPERINTENDENT, GOVERNMENT PRINTING, BIHAR AND ORISSA

1917

PLAN OF CONTENTS.

Chapter.		Pages
I.	Physical Aspects	1—19
II.	History	20—54
III.	The People	55—101
IV.	Public Health	102—110
V.	Agriculture	111—120
VI.	Forests	121—133
VII.	Natural Calamities	134—141
VIII.	Rents, Wages, Prices. Material condition of the people	142—168
IX.	Occupations, Manufactures and Trade.	169—174
X.	Means of Communication	175—182
XI.	Land Revenue Administration	183—201
XII.	General Administration	202—213
XIII.	Local Self-Government	214—218
XIV.	Education	219—223
XV.	Missions	224—240
XVI.	Gazetteer	241—261

TABLE OF CONTENTS

CHAPTER I.

PHYSICAL ASPECTS.

GENERAL DESCRIPTION—Changes in name and area—Scenery and Configuration—HILLS—RIVER SYSTEM—The Subarnarekhā—The South Koel—The Sānkh—The North Koel—Waterfalls—Lakes—GEOLOGY—BOTANY—Character of the Forest—Economic Uses—FAUNA—Ungulata—Game Birds—Reptiles—Fish—CLIMATE—Temperature and Humidity—Rainfall. 1—19

CHAPTER II.

HISTORY.

EARLY HISTORY—Settlement of the Mundās and Orāons—Organization of the Mundās—Election of a Feudal Chief—MUHAMMADAN RULE—Introduction of Hindu Settlers—BRITISH RULE—Military Collectorship of Rāmgarh—Administration of the Rājā—Disturbances of 1807 and 1808—Introduction of Police—THE INSURRECTION OF THE KOLS. 1831-37—Causes of the insurrection—Administrative reforms—Civil and Criminal Courts—Improvement in the Police administration—Failure of the system of Zamindārī Police—Defects of the administration—Further Reforms—Arrival of the Christian Missionaries—THE MUTINY—Spread of Christianity—Register of *Bhūinhārī* lands—Agitation of the Sardārs—Disturbances of 1889—The Birsā rising of 1895—Birsā's second rising—Lessons of the Birsā rising—Settlement operations, 1902—1910. 20—54

CHAPTER III.

THE PEOPLE.

CENSUS—Density and growth of population—Emigration—Towns and Villages—LANGUAGES—Nagpuriā—Mundāri—Turi—Asuri—Khariā—Kūrūkh—TRIBES AND CASTES—ABORIGINAL TRIBES—MUNDAS—Name—Appearance—Dress and Character—Tribal Organization—Marriage Customs—ORAONS—Name, Early history—Appearance and Characteristics—Dress—Organization—Panchāyats—Marriage Ceremonies—KHARIAS—Appearance and Character—Origin—Organization—Marriage customs—Religion—Funeral customs—ASURS—TURIS—BIRHORS—NAGESIAS—KORWAS—RAUTIAS—Organization—Marriage Customs—Religion—BHOGTAS—BINJHIAS—BHUIYAS—JHORAS—GONDS—GHASIS—GORAITS—LOHARS—MAHLIS—PANS and CHIK BARAIKS—RELIGION OF THE INHABITANTS—BIRSAITES—RELIGION OF THE MUNDAS—Ancestor worship—Other deities—Asur Legend—Hinduism among Mundās—RELIGION OF THE ORAONS—Ancestor worship—Exorcism and Witchcraft—FESTIVALS OF THE ORAONS AND MUNDAS. 55—101

CHAPTER IV.

PUBLIC HEALTH.

VITAL STATISTICS—PRINCIPAL DISEASES—Fever—Cholera—Small-pox—Plague—Bowel-complaints—Tuberculous diseases—Rabies—Other diseases—INFIRMITIES—LUNATIC ASYLUMS—HOSPITALS AND DISPENSARIES—Aided and private institutions—VACCINATION—SANITATION. 102—110

CHAPTER V.

AGRICULTURE.

CLASSES OF LAND—Soil—Rainfall—Cultivation of Rice—Bhadoi Crops—Tobacco—Market gardening—Fruit Trees—Tea—Silk—Lac—CATTLE—Veterinary Dispensary—District Agricultural Association. 111—120

CHAPTER VI.

FORESTS.

EXTENT OF FORESTS—Causes of deforestation—Effects of deforestation—Rights of Landlords and Tenants—Settlement Record of Jungle Rights—Proposals for the protection of forests—Reafforestation. 121—133

CHAPTER VII.

NATURAL CALAMITIES.

FAMINE—Causes of famine—Early famines—Famine of 1897—Famine of 1900—Famine of 1908. 134—141

CHAPTER VIII.

RENTS, WAGES, PRICES—MATERIAL CONDITION OF THE PEOPLE.

ORIGIN OF RENTS—Mundāri Khuntkatti tenancies—Breakdown of the Khuntkatti system—Bhūinhāri tenancies—Cultivating tenancies—Prædial conditions—*Rakumāts*—*Begāri*—Cash rents—System of Land Measurement—Gradual enhancements of rents—Incidence of rent—Produce rents—Rent of trees—WAGES—Wages of skilled labour—Monthly wages—*Dhangrai*—*Pasri*—PRICES—MATERIAL CONDITION OF THE PEOPLE—Indebtedness—Restriction on the Transfer of Lands—Co-operative Societies. 142—168

CHAPTER IX.

OCCUPATIONS, MANUFACTURES AND TRADE.

Census Statistics—INDUSTRIES—Cotton Weaving—Ironware and Cutlery—Gold-washing—Other industries—TRADE—Weights and Measures. 169—174

CHAPTER X.

MEANS OF COMMUNICATION.

DEVELOPMENT OF MEANS OF COMMUNICATION—Vehicles—ROADS—District Board roads—Aboriculture—WATER COMMUNICATIONS—RAILWAY COMMUNICATIONS—Imports and Exports—Passenger Traffic—POSTAL COMMUNICATIONS. 175—182

CHAPTER XI.

LAND REVENUE ADMINISTRATION.

THE CHOTA NAGPUR ESTATE—Origin of the Estate—Tribute payable to the Muhammadans—Payment of Revenue to the British Administration—Mode of collecting the Revenue—*Sayer* and Excise Duties—SUBORDINATE TENURES—Tenures of dependent Rajas—Service *jāgīrs*—Maintenance tenures—Incidents of service and maintenance tenures—Other tenures—Landlord's privileged lands—Exemption of estates from sale for arrears of debts—Encumbered Estates Act—GOVERNMENT ESTATES—Barkagarh—Patia—Silam—TENANCY LEGISLATION—Act II (B. C.) of 1869—Act I (B. C.) of 1879—Proposed amendment of Act I of 1879—Act IV (B. C.) of 1879—Act V of 1903—Act VI (B. C.) of 1908—SURVEYS AND SETTLEMENTS. 183—201

CHAPTER XII.

GENERAL ADMINISTRATION.

ADMINISTRATIVE STAFF—REVENUE—Land Revenue—Excise—Drugs—Stamps—Income Tax—Cesses—Registration—ADMINISTRATION OF JUSTICE—Criminal Justice—Civil Justice—POLICE—Ghatwāls and Ghatwāli cess—CRIME. 202—213

CHAPTER XIII.

LOCAL SELF-GOVERNMENT.

DISTRICT BOARD—Income—Expenditure—MUNICIPALITIES—Rānchi—Lohardagā 214—218

CHAPTER XIV.

EDUCATION.

PROGRESS OF EDUCATION—Secondary Education—Primary Education—Training Schools—Technical and Industrial Schools—Female education—Special Schools —Expenditure—Inspection—NEWSPAPERS. 219—223

CHAPTER XV.

MISSIONS.

Progress of Christianity—Foundation of Gossner's Mission—Mutiny of 1857—Progress, 1857-1867—Division of the Lutheran Mission—The Lutheran Mission —Progress—1870-1880, 1880-1913—Schools—Hospitals—The S. P. G. Mission—Bishopric of Chota Nagpur—Present day— Schools —Hospitals —The Roman Catholic Mission—Statistics—History—Staff—Schools—Industrial Schools—Co-operative Societies. 224—240

CHAPTER XVI.

GAZETTEER.

BARWE—BIRU—BUNDU—CHOKAHATU—CHUTIA—DOISA—DORANDA—GUMLA—GUMLA SUB-DIVISION—JAGARNATHPUR—KHUNTI—KHUNTI SUB-DIVISION—LOHARDAGA—MURHU—NAGPHENI—PALKOT—THE PATS—RANCHI—RANCHI SUB-DIVISION—SIMDEGA—SONAPET—SUTIAMBE—TAMAR—TILMI. 241—261

GAZETTEER

OF THE

RANCHI DISTRICT.

CHAPTER I.

PHYSICAL ASPECTS.

THE district of Rānchi, which forms the west-central portion of the Chota Nāgpur Division, is situated between 22° 21′ and 23° 43′ north latitude and between 84° 0′ and 85° 54′ east longitude. It extends over 7103·55 square miles and is the largest district in the Province. The population as ascertained by the census of 1911 is 1,387,516. It is bounded on the north by the districts of Palāmau and Hazāribāgh; on the east by the district of Mānbhum, the northern half of the boundary coinciding with the Subarnarekhā river; on the south by the district of Singbhūm, and by the Tributary State of Gāngpur; and on the west by the Tributary States of Surgujā and Jashpur and by the district of Palāmau. Rānchi, the chief town, is situated in 23° 23′ north latitude and 85° 20′ east longitude at a height of 2,128 feet above sea-level, and is the administrative headquarters of the district and of the Chotā Nāgpur Division. It is also at present the temporary capital of the Province of Bihar and Orissa. GENERAL DESCRIPTION.

In ancient times the tract which corresponds to the district of Rānchi and the neighbouring parganas was in the undisturbed possession of the Mundā and Orāon races and was known to the Aryans as Jhārkand or the "forest tract". In historical times, when the aboriginal village communities had come under the subjection of the chiefs of the Nāgbansi family, it formed part Changes in name and area.

of the Subah of Bihar and is mentioned in the Ain-i-Akbari as the realm of the Rājā of Kokrah, a name which still survives as the name of the most important pargana of the district. The region was also known to the Mughals as Nāgpur or Coira Orissa. The name Nāgpur probably dates back to the 15th or 16th century and is said in Hamilton's Gazetteer of Hindustan (1815) to indicate that the territory contained diamonds. It was by this name that the district was known to the early British administrators when it was ceded to them in 1765, and in covenants granted to the Rājā settlement was given of the Nāgpur pargana. The name Chutia or Chuta Nāgpur is found in Rennel's map (1792) and in Hamilton's Gazetteer (1815) and the latter explains the name by saying that "the district is distinguished by the term Chuta (little) to distinguish it from the other Nāgpur possessed by the Bhonslah Marāthā family," but this interpretation is almost certainly incorrect and the name is probably derived from Chutiā, a village close to Rānchi, which is reputed to be the original home of the Nāgbansi chiefs.

During the early period of British rule the country, with other adjoining territories, of a total area of 12,004 square miles, was placed under the charge of the Magistrate of Rāmgarh in the Hazāribāgh district, but the control from Rāmgarh which was situated outside the Rānchi plateau proved ineffective, and in 1833 the present district, with the adjacent parganas of Palāmau and Dhalbhūm, was formed into a separate Province known as the South-west Frontier Agency. The headquarters of the principal Assistant of the Agent to the Governor-General, who administered the area, were at first at Lohardagā but were removed in 1843 to Kishunpur, a village which forms part of the present town of Rānchi. On the abolition of the South-west Frontier Agency in 1854, Chotā Nāgpur became a non regulation Province under a Commissioner, and the district, which was still called by the name of the former headquarters of Lohardagā, consisted at that time of two subdivisions, pargana Palāmau forming the Palāmau subdivision and the present district with pargana Tori forming the Sadar subdivision. In 1892 Palāmau and Tori, with three parganas which had been transferred from Gaya to Lohardagā in 1871, were formed into the district of Palāmau, and from that date the area of the district has remained unaltered. The name of the district was changed in 1899 from Lohardagā to Rānchi, the name of a small village comprised in the headquarters station.

Configuration and Scenery.

The district of Rānchi consists of three plateaux. The first and highest plateau is in the north-west of the district and comprises roughly the area included in thanas Chainpur and Bishunpur and the western part of thana Lohardagā. It is shut off from the rest of the district by the line of jungle-covered hills which runs from the west of Pālkot and Gumlā to the boundary of the district north-west of Lohardagā, and forms such a striking feature of the landscape from the subdivisional headquarters at Gumlā. From the distance these hills give the impression of a magnificent natural wall stretching from north to south in an unbroken line, but a near view shows them to consist of rocky spurs of various heights with deep valleys radiating from the central mass. The average height of this area exceeds 2,500 feet above the sea-level, and the only level portions are the valleys of the Sankh and the North Koel, the former flowing in a southerly direction through the broad cultivated plain of Bhitar Barwe (Chainpur thana) and the latter rising in the hills between Kurumgarh and Jori and flowing through the narrow valley of Bahar Barwe (Bishunpur thana) towards Palāmau. A distinctive feature of this tract, and in particular of the north-western corner, are the level cultivated hill-tops locally called *pāts*. Of these the largest and best known are Rājāderā or Bānspahār in the north of Chainpur thana, and Onegara to the north-west of Lohardagā. In the latter table-land is the highest hill of the district, Sāru Pahār, which rises to a height of 3,615 feet above sea-level. The country is sparsely populated and the forests which have suffered little from the axes of the aboriginals are still of con siderable value.

The second and central plateau includes the eastern portion of the Gumlā subdivision, the whole of the head quarters subdivision, and the western part of the Khunti subdivision. The average level is about 2,000 feet ; the country is undulating, intersected with numerous streams and rivers, and studded with low rocky hills and isolated peaks of igneous origin, generally of gneissic formation. These hills form a conspicuous feature of the landscape in any portion of the plateau. They rise abrupt and black, their summits sometimes bare and dome-like, sometimes rugged and irregular. The highest portion of the central plateau is a ridge eight to ten miles south-west of Rānchi, which contains the sources of the chief rivers of the district, the Sabarnarekhā and the South Koel. Between the hills the land is for the most part under cultivation, the uplands producing crops of the hardier rice and millet, while in the lowlands, which are banked up and terraced to retain the water, good crops of fine rice are obtained. The plateau was formerly covered with forests, but the forests have gradually receded more and more before the axes of the inhabitants and commercial exploitation, and the region east of the meridian of Pālkot fully deserves the name given to it by the inhabitants of *Tānr Rāj* or "land of cultivated upland", in contradistinction to the *Ban Rāj* or "land of jungle", the name given to the western parganas and the Feudatory States. In the south-western thanas there is still a large expanse of forest, and from the summit of a hill the country appears covered with a waving sheet of low forest with little or no sign of human habitation, but a nearer view shows numerous small villages, each with their plots of cultivated *tānr* round the homesteads and the terraced *don* tucked away in the narrow beds of the streams. The fringes of the plateau are mountainous, and the traveller ascends by tortuous hill passes known as *ghāts*. Along the north boundary, from Silli on the east to Bairagi on the west, a tract of mountain and jungle extends almost without a break and divides off the district from Hazāribāgh and Palāmau. The high road from Rānchi to Hazāribāgh finds its way through these hills and, winding down from Chutupalu on the border of the district to the Dāmodar river at Rāmgarh, descends 700 feet in three miles. The scenery is extremely beautiful and in clear weather, from the top of the *ghāt*, a magnificent view is obtained of the steep wooded slopes of the hills and over the plains of Hazāribāgh to Parasnāth in the far distance. The *ghāt* by which both road and railway ascend from Purūlia presents equally beautiful views, though the hill-slopes are not so steep and the distant view is not so extensive.

The third plateau consists of the extreme southern and eastern portions of the district and in few places exceeds a height of 1,000 feet above sea-level. This region is known as the Five

Parganas and is well watered by the tributaries of the Subarnarekhā. A lofty range of hills divides the main portion of this plateau from the secluded valley of Sonapet in the south-eastern corner of the district.

The general lines of the hills have been described in the preceding paragraphs. The loftiest summits in the range of hills in the extreme west, which stretches south from Birpokhar (3,621 feet above sea-level) within the Palāmau border, are Oria (3,498 feet), Bardag (3,216 feet), Udni (3,419 feet), Hutār (3,209 feet) and the Koiāpat in Barwe (3,107 feet). To the north and north-west of Lohardagā are Salgipāt (3,511 feet), Dudhia (3,571 feet), Bulbul (3,351 feet) and Jalakdia, on the Palāmau border. In the range which stretches south from Dudhia and Bulbul is Sāru Pāhar (3,615 feet), the highest point in the district. Bluff isolated hills form conspicuous land marks in the central plateau; the most remarkable are Marang Buru (2,434 feet), the sacred hill of the Mundās, ten miles south of Rānchi, Bariātu (2,607 feet), four miles north of Rānchi, and the curious pyramid-shaped Rānchi hill (2,423 feet) crowned with a Hindu temple. In the hills which fringe the north-eastern side of the central plateau the highest points are Pāina (2,700 feet) and Kutam (2,462 feet), to the east and north-east of Rānchi, respectively. In the south-east where the plateau falls away to Singhbhūm, the range shutting off the Sonapet valley rises at one point to a height of nearly 3,000 feet. In the intricate hills of Biru the highest peaks are Bhāonr Pahār (2,492 feet) and the isolated peak of Alu Pahār in the valley of the Sankh (2,172 feet). HILLS.

The chief rivers of the district have their source either in the long ridge of high country which runs, at an elevation of nearly 2,500 feet, from south-east to north-west 8 to 10 miles south-west of Rānchi, or in the hills which shut off the Barwe plateau. The former contains the source of the Subarnarekhā and the South Koel, and in the latter rise the Sankh and the North Koel. RIVER SYSTEM.

The streams which unite to form the Subarnarekhā rise in the country 10 miles west and south-west of Rānchi town, between the villages of Nāgri and Hatia, and the river pursues a winding course to the east till it descends from the plateau by the falls of Hundrughāgh at the point where the three districts of Hazāribāgh, Rānchi and Mānbhūm meet; it then turns south and forms the The Subarnarekhā.

boundary between the two latter districts for a distance of 35 miles; turning east again, it traverses Singhbhūm, Māyūrbhanj and Midnapore, and flows into the Bay of Bengal after a course of 296 miles. The Subarnarekhā has three chief tributaries, the Kokro, the Kānchī and the Kārkarī, which, flowing in an easterly direction, drain the Khunti subdivision. The name Subarnarekhā means "the thread of gold" and the sands of the river and of some of its tributaries are auriferous.

The South Koel.

The South Koel rises on the northern slopes of the same ridge as the Subarnarekhā and flows in a north-westerly direction, almost parallel to the Lohardagā-Rānchi road; it turns south at a point 8 miles north-east of Lohardagā and follows a southerly and south-easterly course till it passes into Singhbhūm in the south of Bano thana. In Singhbhūm it again changes its course westward till it unites with the Sankh in Gāngpur, after an independent course of 185 miles. The two rivers united form the Brāhmani which flows through the district of Cuttack into the Bay of Bengal. The chief tributaries of the Koel are the Kāro, the Chata and the Bonai, which drain the western portion of the Khunti subdivision, and the Parās which drains Sisai thana. The name "Koel" is a common one for river in Chotā Nāgpur; its meaning is uncertain.

The Sankh.

The Sankh rises in the north-west of the district, flows in a northerly direction through the centre of the Rājāderā plateau, and then turns abruptly south and descends to the plains of Barwe by a beautiful waterfall known as Sadnīghāgh. After crossing the plains of Barwe in a south-westerly direction, it flows almost due south, forming for some distance the boundary between Rānchi and Jashpur, then passing through the hills which separate Barwe from Biru it flows in a westerly direction and, passing into Gāngpur near the village of Samserā in the extreme south of the district, unites with the Koel. Its chief affluents are the Palamanda and Bompai rivers which drain Biru. Tradition says that diamonds are found in the Sankh. Ptolemy states that diamonds were found in Kokkomaji, a region which probably included Chotā Nāgpur, and the reference in Muhammadan writings and the possession of diamonds by the local chiefs go to substantiate the tradition that the river did yield a number of more or less valuable gems.

A spot, 10 miles north of Kochedegā, near the Peruāghāgh, is locally reported to have contained diamonds and is still known as the *dangadhi dab*, or *hira dab*, the "diamond pool".

The North Koel, though rising within a very short distance of the Sankh, flows northward through the narrow valley of Bishunpur into Palāmau, where, after a course of 186 miles, it joins the Son under the plateau of Rohtās. The North Koel.

These four rivers, fed by numerous small streams from the hills near which they pass, effectively drain the whole district, and are sufficient to carry off even the heaviest rainfall. No part of the district is liable to flood. The South Koel alone has a drainage area of 3,600 square miles and the Sankh and Subarnarekhā of 1,100 square miles each within the district. For the greater part of the year they are easily fordable, but in the rains they frequently come down in violent and sudden freshets which for a few hours, or it may be for days, render them impassable even for the primitive *dongas* which, formed of hollowed-out trunks of trees, serve as ferries.

A description of the river system of the Rānchi district would be incomplete without mention of the waterfalls, any of which would in a western country be regarded as worthy of a visit even from a distance. Of these the most picturesque is the Hundrughāgh, 24 miles east-north-east of the town of Rānchi, where the Subarnarekhā descends from the edge of the plateau over a cliff with a sheer drop of 320 feet. In the rains, when the river is in flood, the falls present a most impressive spectacle, as the waters, red with the soil through which they flow, fall thundering over the cliff in a cloud of spray. From the top of the falls there is magnificent view of the river winding through a narrow gorge in the forest-clad hills to the plains of Hazāribāgh. The Dāsomghāgh (22 miles south-east of Rānchi near Taimāra) is formed by the Kānchi river falling over a ledge of rock in a sheer descent of 114 feet, amid rocky and sylvan scenery. There are also two Peruāghāghs in the Gumlā subdivison, one in Basiā thana and the other in Kochedegā thana, so named because wild pigeons in hundreds nest in the crevices of the rocks. The Sadnīghāgh by which the Sankh river drops from the Rājāderā plateau into the plains of Barwe is also extremely beautiful. Waterfalls.

Lakes.

Lakes are conspicuous by their absence, the explanation being that the granite which forms the chief geological feature of the district is soft and soon worn away. Artificial lakes and tanks have been formed at some places by erecting embankments across the beds of rivers. The largest of these are the Rānchi Lake in the centre of the town, the tank near the Mahārājā's palace at Rātu, and that near Toto in Gumlā thana.

GEOLOGY.

Excluding from consideration materials of such recent age as alluvium and soil, the geological formations observed in the Rānchi district are the Lower Gondwāna and the Archæan. The Karanpurā and South Karanpurā coal-fields, which lie almost entirely in the Hazāribāgh district to the north, encroach on the northern boundary of the district, and in these occur outcrops of the Panchet and Raniganj iron-stone shales and the Barakhar and Talcher divisions of the Gondwāna rocks.* With this exception, the whole of the district is occupied by ancient crystalline rocks-schists, quartzites, epidiorites, gneisses, and granites of Archæan age. They may be grouped into two divisions, one of which, comprising the schists and quartzites, with the epidiorites known as the Dalmā trap, was formerly termed submetamorphic, and is now considered to correspond to the Dhārwārs of South India. The gneisses and granites may be conveniently grouped together to form the other division of Archæan rocks.

The geology of the district has not in most parts been worked out in detail, but enough is known to show that almost the whole of it is occupied by gneisses and granites. In the south-east corner of the district, north of the Dhārwār boundary, these rocks comprise fine quartzitic gneisses, alternating with felspathic and ordinary granitic gneisses; a few bands of hornblendic gneiss also occur but trap is rare, if it is not altogether wanting. Elsewhere, on the Kāro river, the existence of coarse granitic and porphyritic gneisses has been recorded. It is probable that the gneisses and granites mentioned are typical of the whole area, but it is not unlikely that a close search would reveal the existence of occasional small areas or bands of schists in the gneiss and granite areas. The Dhārwār rocks occupy practically the whole southern fringe of the district, being really the northern

* An account of them and of their associated coal will be found in the Memoirs of the Geological Survey of India, Volume VII, pages 285—342.

edge of a large and roughly elliptical area of Dhārwārs, occupying by far the larger portions of Gāngpur and Singhbhūm and the south-east corner of Mānbhūm. They are separated from the gneiss-granite area to the north by a well-marked boundary fault, delineated by runs of pseudomorphic quartz and of red hematite, often giving rise to small hills. The fault has been traced for over 100 miles in an easterly direction from near Jati and Bandgāon to near Bhelaidiha in Bankura district. The Dhārwārs of this part of India consist mainly of quartzites, mica-quartz-schists, mica-schists, chlorite-schists, hornblendic schists, and their less metamorphosed phyllitic forms, and to a smaller extent, of staurolite-schists, alusite-schists, garnet-schists, kyanite-schists, and tourmaline-schists, the whole much traversed by epidioritic dykes; and any of these rocks might be found in the exposures in the Rānchi district. In addition, there is a great range of hills culminating in the peak of Dalmā in Mānbhūm, whence the name Dalmā trap is derived. To the south of Tamār, owing to a northward bend, this range of epidiorite hills, which constitutes a considerable part of the boundary between Rānchi and Singhbhūm, lies wholly in the Rānchi district, and the district boundary runs south of it so as to include the upper portion of the valley of the Sona Nadi, long famous as a source of alluvial gold. The valley of the Sona Nadi is occupied by schistose rocks of Dhārwār age.

Probably on account of the large area covered by gravels and gneisses, the district is, so far as is known, singularly barren of valuable minerals. The auriferous quartz veins which traverse the Dhārwār schists were the object of the disastrous gold boom of 1889-90, and there are gold-bearing sands in the Kānchi and other rivers, but an investigation by the Geological Survey tended to show that no occurrence is at present known of either vein or alluvial gold worthy of exploitation on European lines.* Specimens of galena have been obtained in the Subarnarekhā near Silli, and doubtless, when the two Karanpura coal-fields come to be worked, some of the coal production may come from this district.

BOTANY.

The greater portion of the district was at one time covered with dense forests. At the present day the central and eastern

* The gold-bearing rocks of Chotā Nāgpur have been described by S. M. Maclaren in *Records, Geological Survey of India*, Volume XXXI, Part II.

plateaux are for the most part denuded of forests, and only small scrub jungle, with few big trees, is found on the hills, while patches of jungle, known as *patra*, still remain dotted among the cultivated lands and are the only traces of the forest which once covered the whole of this area. In the west and north-west of the district there are still large areas of unbroken forest, but even in these parts cultivation is rapidly being extended at the expense of the forest and the large trees are being cut out and sold for commercial purposes. A more detailed description of the forests of the district is given in a later Chapter.

Character of the Forest.

The Rānchi district is the centre of the second, or South Gangetic, tract in which *sāl* (Shorea robusta) is gregarious. The best *sāl* forests are invariably found in the valleys, where in good soil straight trees, 100 to 120 feet in height, with a girth of ten to fifteen feet, used to be found; in the hills and on the slopes of the *ghāts*, the trees are short and stunted, and on the driest southern slopes *sāl* is supplanted by other trees of the so-called "Mixed Forest" type. In the valleys, especially in sheltered situations, the principal companions of *sāl* are the *Asan* (Terminalia tomentosa), *Gambhar* (Gmelina arboria), *Kend* (Diospyros tomentosa or melanoxylon, ebony) and *Simal* (Bombax malabaricum, the cotton tree). The *Mahuā* (Bassia latifolia) is common throughout Chotā Nāgpur, but in the forests is chiefly confined to the hills. *Tun* (Cedrela Toona) and *Sisu* (Dalbergia Sissoo), both valuable timber-yielding trees, are not native of Chotā Nāgpur, but are frequently planted. *Hara* (Terminalia chebula), *Karam* (Adina cardifolia), *Kusum* (Schleichera trijuga), *Paisar* (Pterocarpus Marsupium) are also important species of trees. In the inferior *sāl* forests in the hills are found *Dhaura* (Anogeissus latifolia), *Piar* (Buchania latifolia), *Sidha* (Lagerstrœmia parviflora), *Khair* (Acacia catechu), *Amaltas* (Cassia fistula) and *Bamboo* (Dendro-calamus strictus). The undergrowth in the *sāl* forests consists principally of Woodfordia floribunda, *Kurchi* (Holarrhena antidysenterica), Croton oblongi-folius and species of Gardenia and Randia. Mixed with the *sāl* are also a number of characteristically Central India trees, which do not cross the Gangetic plain, such as Cochlospermum, Soymida, Boswellia, Hardwickia and Bassia. In the villages there are groves of mangoes (Mangifera Indica), but few of the better fruit-bearing varieties are found. *Jāmun* (Eugenia Jambolona), *Karanj* (Ponamia Glabra), *Tetar* (Tamarindus indica), *Bael* (Aegle Marmegos), *Jack-fruit* (Autocarpus integrifolia), *Pipal* (Ficus religiosa) and *Bar* (Ficus Bengalensis) are common around village sites. The *Palās* (Butea frondosa and Butea Superba) is often gregarious in cultivated and waste lands, and its wealth of scarlet blossom in the hot season is a striking sight. The convolvulaceous creeper (Porana Paniculata), the well-known bridal creeper, displays a mass of white flowers along the *ghāts* in November, and a large variety of tree and ground-orchids are to be found in the jungle. Palms are seldom found but the dwarf palm (Phœnix Acaulis or *Khajūr* (is found on the upper edge of the *ghāts*.

Of the timber-yielding trees the most important are the *sāl*, *gambhar*, *tun*, *sisu*, *kend*, *asan* and *simal*. The principal fruit trees are the mango, *jāmun*, jack-fruit, and *mahuā*; but many other forest shrubs and trees yield fruit which affords a valuable food-supply to the aboriginal inhabitants in years of scarcity. Mr. Slacke, in his report on the Settlement operations of the Chotā Nāgpur estate, enumerates twenty-one species of seeds and the fruits of forty-five uncultivated trees which are used as food, in addition to thirty-four trees, the leaves of which are used as *sāg* (vegetables), and eighteen species of edible roots. Even this long list is probably not exhaustive. Mr. Slacke also gives the names of ninety-seven forest products used as medicines, twenty-eight used as oils and gums, seventeen used as dyes, and thirty-three creepers or bark of trees used as rope-fibres. The length of these lists shows the economic value of the jungles to the aboriginal inhabitants. Various trees, such as the *kusum* (Schleichera trijuga), *palās* (Butea frondosa), *dumar* (Ficus hispida), *bair* (Ziziphus jujuba) and *karam* (Adina Cordifolia) are used for the cultivation of lac, but the best lac is obtained from the *kusum* and *palās*. Economic uses.

In former times Rānchi was a happy hunting-ground for the sportsman, but this reputation is no longer deserved, and, though returns show that wild animals and game of all descriptions are to be found in the district, yet Rānchi now compares very unfavourably with the adjoining districts of Singhbhūm and Palāmau, and the enthusiastic sportsman or naturalist may spend many months scouring the jungle without finding anything worth preservation. Various causes have contributed FAUNA.

to this result. Cultivation, and the clearing of jungles for this purpose, has been widely extended during the last twenty years, and even from the few strongholds, such as Bāns Pahār in the extreme north-west corner of the district, or the jungles of Samsera and Malsarā on the border of Gāngpur in the south of the Simdegā subdivision, the game is rapidly being driven by the exploitations of timber-contractors and the unrestricted depredations of native *shikāris*. The aboriginal *shikāri* has no respect for age or sex, and with his bow and arrow or muzzle-loading gun will shoot any animal, large or small, that comes within range, and the wholesale destruction of smaller game which has gone on unchecked for years has driven the larger carnivorous animals to more favoured parts. For the preservation of the fauna of the district the establishment of sanctuaries for game is very necessary, or, failing this, the strict enforcement of the game laws, prohibiting the slaughter of females and immature males throughout the year, and of all game during the hot weather. A reduction in the number of gun licenses might assist game-preservation, but even if gun licenses were considerably reduced, the slaughter of deer and small game would go on unchecked, as the bow in the hand of the aboriginal is as useful a weapon as the gun. Gun licenses have been freely given in the past, to protect the inhabitants against the larger carnivora, and the total number of licenses at present in force is over 1,800. The destruction of wild animals has also been encouraged by the grant of rewards. The ordinary rewards are Rs. 25 for a tiger, Rs. 5 for a leopard or wolf, Rs. 2-8 for a bear or a hyæna.

Tigers.

Bordered as it is by Singhbhūm, Jashpur and Palāmau, all containing reserve forests and large uncultivated tracts, the district is naturally visited by tigers who are stragglers or excursionists from those more favoured parts. Owing to the dearth of deer and small game, tigers are ordinarily cattle-destroyers and frequently man-eaters. In the thanas in the south and west of the district hardly a month passes in which half a dozen to a score of cattle are not reported to have been killed by tigers and in the three years 1911, 1912 and 1913 the average number of cattle killed by tigers in the district was 1,122. In these three years also 177 persons were killed by tigers, and at the beginning of 1913 there were six known man-eaters at large. To rid the district of these pests, rewards of Rs. 500 were offered for every tiger killed in thanas Torpa, Bano, Kolebira, Kochedegā and Chainpur. The offer of these rewards had the desired effect, no less than five man-eaters being killed soon after they were proclaimed. In the year 1915 no less than four tigers were killed in Biru, and rewards of Rs. 500 were paid for each of them. During the three years 1911 to 1913 thirty-four tigers were said to have been killed in the district, but, though the majority of these were no doubt killed within its borders, there is good reason to believe that native *shikāris* are induced, even by the ordinary rewards of Rs. 25, to bring into the subdivisional headquarters at Gumlā the skins of tigers killed in the adjacent native States. Though the aboriginal is fearless in attacking even a tiger, the most common way of destroying a man-eater or cattle-destroyer is by means of a trap set with a poisoned arrow. A six-foot bamboo bow is fixed flat on, or a foot above, the ground, with a poisoned arrow on the bow string, aimed so as to command the path by which the tiger is expected to approach. Across the path, about eighteen inches above the ground, a string is drawn and is attached to the stick which keeps the bow taut, in such a way that the least touch will release the arrow. To protect men and cattle from walking into the trap, two strings are fastened breast high across the path but, in spite of this device, cases occur in which men are fatally injured by the poisoned arrow.

Leopards.

Leopards or panthers (Felis Pardus) are very common and show the same phenomenon as the woodcock. Certain places always hold leopards and no sooner is one killed than another takes his beat. Biru Pahār and Pālkot are typical rocky hills where leopards are to be found, and from the former no less than eight leopards have been killed in one year. The distinction between the rock and the wood panther, though admitted by few naturalists, is very clear in this district. The former is smaller, the spots closer and without any resemblance to a finger print; the head bullet-shaped and the ears small and pricked. This animal is rarely dangerous and confines its depredations to goats, pigs, and even fowls. The larger species is frequently a cattle-destroyer, and in the years 1911 to 1913 leopards were reported to have killed 1,720 head of cattle. During this period also 207 leopards were killed for rewards.

Bears.

Bears are also common. The rocky bolder-strewn hills which are a distinctive feature of the district provide luxurious covert for the Ursus Melursus, and in April the falling *mahuā* flowers and other fruit attract him to the neighbourhood of the villages. The bear is held in greater dread by the Kol than the tiger himself, and especially in November and December shows a savage and vindictive temper. Cases of mauling and scalping are common, and the wounds, though not very dangerous, are liable to set up blood-poisoning or tetanus, if not properly cleansed.

Wolves.

Wolves are occasionally found, but are not nearly as common as in the neighbouring district of Hazāribāgh, where a pack proved so destructive of children and cattle that a special reward of Rs. 50 a head had to be offered for their extermination. Only ten wolves have been produced for rewards in the last three years.

Hyænas, etc.

Hyænas and jackals are common, and the killing of the former, for which a small reward is paid, forms a regular source of income to some raiyats. The Bengal fox is found throughout the district. Wild cats are fairly common, but the tiger and leopard cats, if they exist, have not been brought to notice. Wild dogs, the worst destroyer of game in any jungle, are not common. The lynx, if it ever is found, is a wandering specimen from the south. Wild pig are plentiful throughout the forest tracts of the district, especially in Biru and Bāns Pahār. Badgers and porcupines are also found.

Ungulata.

The district formerly held a fair number of bison (Bos gaurus), but they are now very rare and only visitors from the reserve forests of Palāmau or Surgujā are to be found in the jungle in the north-west of the district. One old bull was shot in March 1913, so exhausted that its last charge left it unable to rise. Its condition and the fact that it was accompanied by three calves clearly showed that it was a fugitive from some distant jungle. Were the jungles of Bāns Pahār and the neighbourhood to be preserved for a few years, there is no doubt that bison would soon fill the coverts, for the bison multiplies freely when undisturbed. The bison is considerably smaller than the Assam variety (Bos frontalis), being little over fourteen hands in height. *Sāmbar* (Cervus unicolor) are also rapidly diminishing in number, and their extinction is due to the shooting of hinds by aboriginal *shikāris*, whether raiyats or zamindars. They are still fairly common in some parts, such as Konpāla, Udni, Onigara and Samsera. The Chital or spotted deer (Cervus axis) is found in small bands or pairs in most of the lighter jungles. Its scarcity is probably due to tigers who have a special liking for this species. The Chinkara or ravine deer, common in Hazāribāgh, does not appear to be found at all in Rānchi. His fatal curiosity has no doubt made him an easy prey to the hunter. The little four-horned antelope, or *kotra* (Tetracerus quadricornis) and the barking deer (Cervulus muntjac) occur in all jungles. Hog deer are not found, but the smallest of the deer tribe, the mouse deer (Tragulus Meminua) has been found in jungles inhabited by *sāmbar*. The *nilgai* or blue bull (Boselaphus tragocamelus) was formerly very common, and is still found in a good many jungles, such as those of Onigara in the north-west of Lohardagā thana. The blue bull is very destructive to crops and his extermination is hardly a matter of surprise or regret. Hares are common, and in every beat two or three fall victims to the axes or arrows of the beaters.

The most noticeable game bird in the district is the pea fowl which is found everywhere, especially on the sides of the rocky hills on the outskirts of villages. Jungle fowl and the painted spur fowl are less frequent but cling to certain jungles, such as those of Jamgāin on the borders of Ghaghrā and Lohardagā thanas. The grey partridge is to be found in the *patras* and small *nullahs*, and quail are found occasionally. The lower *don* lands usually contain a good number of snipe, and, though the lands are not large enough to give big bags, there are few places in which three or four couple cannot be got in a good year. Snipe are popularly supposed not to breed in this part of India, but an egg of an ordinary snipe has been found in Biru at the end of February. Ducks are not as plentiful as in districts where tanks and jhils abound, but the larger tanks and *bāndhs*, such as those at Rātu in Rānchi thana or at Toto in Gumlā thana usually hold some birds. The most common varieties are the gadwall, widgeon, white-eyed pochard, and cotton teal. The brahminy duck is found on some of the larger rivers, and on the Sankh wild geese are occasionally seen. Pigeon, both rock and green, are abundant and two species of sand grouse occur, though not in large numbers. Game birds.

Reptiles.

Snakes are not very common in the district, but are most numerous in the lower plateau. The statistics show that 76 persons and 9 cattle died of snake-bite in 1913, but such statistics are of little value. The cobra and the *karait* are the most common species; *dhamans* of considerable size are occasionally found and python are sometimes seen in the hilly tracts. Various species of harmless grass-snakes occur.

Fish.

There are no fisheries in the district and it is only in the tanks and *bāndhs* in and near the town of Rānchi, where there is a large demand for fish both for the European and the Bengali community, that species such as the *rohu, katla* and *mirgel* are reared. The larger rivers of the district are said to contain mahseer, while the *bachuā* is found in the deep pools of the River Sānkh. The aboriginal inhabitants of the district amuse themselves at some seasons of the year by catching fish in the water-logged *don* fields and streams with a bamboo trap known as a *kum* or *jhimri*, and on the occasion of the Sarhul festival the youth of an Orāon village make a fishing expedition to a tank or stream.

CLIMATE.

The climate of the Rānchi plateau is unsurpassed in the Province. The elevation of over 2,000 feet above sea-level gives it a uniformly lower range of temperature than the districts of Bihar. It is only during the months of April or May that the temperature rises to any great height, and for a few weeks a day temperature of more than 100°, which occasionally rises to 104° or 107°, makes one sceptical of Rānchi's claim to be considered a hill station. But in spite of the high day temperature, the nights are cool and the atmosphere is so dry that the heat is by no means so oppressive as that of Bihar or Bengal, even though the thermometer stands many degrees higher. During this period of the year occasional thunderstorms and nor' westers cause a refreshing fall in the temperature. The rains break usually before the end of June and the climate during this period of the year compares very favourably with that of many hill stations. Thanks to the excellent natural drainage, the rain flows away quickly and, unlike the Himalayan slopes, the plateau does not remain for days or weeks enveloped in fog and mist. Occasional breaks in the rains make life unpleasant, but they do not usually last for many days, and even during a long break the air is neither so saturated with moisture nor so enervating as in the plains of Bihar or Orissa. The end of the rains is irregular; they sometimes end in the last week of September, but there is often a heavy fall of rain during the first fortnight of October. The cold weather may be said to begin with the first week of November. In December and January the temperature on the grass sometimes falls to freezing point, and in the early morning hoar-frost covers the grass in the higher and more exposed parts of the district and does damage to the upland crops and young trees. A strong cold wind blows throughout January and the climate during this period of the year is extremely bracing and is not inferior to that of many health resorts in European countries. At the end of February the day-temperature rises considerably and continues to rise till it reaches its maximum in April or May. In the lower plateau the temperature is considerably higher than in the rest of the district and the moist enervating climate is the same as that of Mānbhūm.

Temperature and Humidity.

The mean maximum temperature falls as low as 73° in December and January and rises to 96° in April and 99° in May. During the four months of the rainy season the mean maximum is 83° or 84°. The mean minimum temperature never rises higher than 75·5° in May and June. In July, August and September it falls to 73° and 72° and during the next six months it averages about 57·5°, falling to 51° in December and January. The mean daily range of temperature varies from 24° in April to 10° or 11° in July and August. The humidity is at the lowest point in April when it is 42. It rises to 51 in May, 72 in June, and reaches its maximum of 89 in August. During the cold-weather months it averages about 63.

Rainfall.

The following table, which is based on statistics since 1878, shows the average rainfall recorded in the town of Rānchi, month by month :—

Month.	Rainfall.	
——	Inches.	Days on which rain falls.
January	0·78	1·5
February	1·55	2·9
March	1·30	2·7

Month.	Rainfall.	
—	Inches.	Days on which rain falls.
April	1·09	2·8
May	2·29	4·6
June	9·13	11·6
July	15·23	18·1
August	12·83	18·9
September	9·52	12·2
October	2·46	3·9
November	0·22	0·6
December	0·22	0·6

Though the rainfall varies from year to year at the different recording stations, these figures may be taken as typical of the district. During the four cold-weather months the rainfall is very slight, and frequently one or two rainless months are experienced, though it is said that formerly the district never enjoyed a rainless month. Rain during November and December causes considerable damage to the harvested crops, but a fall of rain in January or February soften the fields for ploughing. In March thunderstorms and showers give a normal rainfall of over an inch, but April is comparatively dry. During May the cyclonic storms, which come up from the Bay of Bengal in advance of the monsoon, give nearly 2½ inches, and in June when the monsoon breaks, there are, on the average, eleven rainy days. During July and August the rainfall is heaviest and there are, on the average, eighteen wet days in each of these two months. The rainfall in September averages over nine inches and is the most important of the year, as, if the monsoon fails early in the month, the rice crops on the higher lands wither and there is scarcity or famine.

The following table shows the average annual rainfall at ten recording stations in the district. It will be seen that the rainfall is heaviest in Kurdeg, in the south-west, and in Chainpur, in the west, and lowest at Tamār, Bano and Lohardagā :—

Average Annual Rainfall.

Stations.	Average.
Lohardaga	47·15
Ranchi	58·39
Silli	51·55
Pālkot	56·17
Bano	45·07
Tamār	40·26
Kurdeg	66·30
Gumlā	52·51
Chainpur	60·60
Khunti	50·32

CHAPTER II.

HISTORY.

EARLY HISTORY.

EXCEPT for the hazy legends of the aboriginal races, there is little material even for conjecture as to the early history of Chotā Nāgpur, previous to the settlement of the Mundās and Orāons. The Mundā legend of Sing Bōngā refers to the race of the Asurs, and perhaps celebrates the triumph of that race over the original inhabitants of the country, possibly the ancestors of the small iron-smelting tribe of that name, which still speaks a language akin to Mundāri. In various parts of the district there are tumuli which are known by the Mundās as "the burial-grounds of the Asurs". Some of them have been found to contain relics of an earlier civilisation. Traces of the Stone Age have been found in the modern districts of Mānbhūm and Singhbhūm and in parts of Rānchi district, quartzite axes and spear-heads have been discovered in the Jheria coal-fields, and a number of chert flakes and knives at Chaibassa and Chakradharpur; in this district a beautifully made celt was discovered in 1867 at Buradih in Tamār and in recent years many stone celts, including some very fine specimens, have been found in various parts. Copper celts have also been found, but in many instances their archæological value was not appreciated and they have not been preserved. Recently, however, twenty-one celts were found in a village in Basiā thana. They are the common, Indian, flat, battle-axe type and in fashion and design appear to be of a primitive type. There are also other traces of the copper age, and cinerary urns are occasionally found, in the shape of large earthenware *gharas*, containing pieces of brass and bits of copper, the remains apparently of ornaments. The pottery is of an entirely different type from that now made among the Mundās, being stronger and more ornate. All these remains go to corroborate the Mundā legend of an earlier race and to prove that a civilised race dwelt in the country long before the immigration of Kolarian tribes.

References to the country, now called Chotā Nāgpur, are to be found in the earliest historians. Thus Pliny mentions that in the interior, south of Palibothra (Patna), dwelt the Monedes and the Sauri. These tribes have been identified, solely on the ground of similarity of name, with the Mundās and the Savaras, who, though they no longer speak a dialect of Mundāri, are probably Mundāri by race. Ptolemy also refers to these two tribes, under the names of the Mandalai and the Sutrarai, Cunningham's interpretation of Hwen Thsang, the Chinese pilgrim of the 7th century A. D., places the district of Rānchi within the kingdom of Kie-lo-na Su-fa-Ia-na or Karna Suvarna, ordinarily identified with the Subarnarekhā river.

The origin of the Mundās and of the Dravidian Orāons is a problem that has often been discussed. Some ethnologists have evolved the theory that the Mundā speakers entered India from the north-east and the Dravidian speakers from the north-west. There is, however, little solid foundation for it, and further ethnological investigations go to show a connection between the so-called Dravidian races and the races to the south and east of the Indian Peninsula. At a later date these races appear in north-western India and the legends of the Mundās and the Hindus point to a struggle between these races and the Aryan invaders, in which the former were gradually driven eastward.

Settlement of the Mundās and the Orāons.

Though there is no evidence which enables us to fix the date at which the Mundās and Orāons settled in Chotā Nāgpur, there is little or no doubt that the Mundās were the first to come and, entering the district from the west and north-west, gradually passed into the country which they now occupy in the east and south-east of the district.

The ancestors of the Mundās and the Santāls crossed the Son and advanced along the borderland that separates the present district of Hazāribāgh from the districts of Rānchi and Palāmau. The Santāls crossed the Dāmodar, and first resided in the district of Hazāribāgh and then, following the course of the river, settled in Mānbhūm and the Santāl Parganas. The Mundās preferred to make their way into the higher forest plateau of Nāgpur and found their way to it, according to one tradition, through the pass of Omedanda in Burmu thana. The Orāons, according to their own tradition, came from the stronghold of Rohtās which had probably also at an earlier age been a resting-place of the Mundā race. Driven from this stronghold by some more powerful tribe, of which the identity is uncertain but which may have been the Cheros or Kharwārs, the Orāon race split into two parts. One branch, the ancestors of the present Māle tribe, proceeded down the Ganges and settled in the Rājmahāl hills. The second division, by far the larger of the two, proceeded up the North Koel river and, passing through Palāmau, emerged in the north-west of the Rānchi district. Here they found the forest country already opened up for them by their precursors, the Mundās, and, according to their own tradition, were received in friendly fashion by them. Traces of the Mundā occupation of the west and north-west of the district, now occupied almost solely by Orāons, may be found in the Mundāri *sasān diris*, or burial-grounds, which occur in many places, in the Mundāri names of the villages, and in the organization of the Orāon villages, which in many particulars resembles that of a Mundā village. In Orāon villages at the present day the priest, or *pāhān*, is occasionally a Mundā, and the reason given is that this descendant of the original settlers is better qualified to appease the local gods and spirits. The Mundās have the following tradition of their migration within the district. A compact body of twenty-one thousand under the leadership of Risa Mundā moved eastwards and settled in the village of Murima; a follower of Risa, Korumba by name, settled in the village, now known as Korāmbe after its founder, while another follower, Sutia, founded the village which came to be called Sutiāmbe. These two villages, Sutiāmbe and Korāmbe, are still mentioned by the Mundās of the central plateau as the cradle of the "Konkpāt" Mundas. This tradition clearly reflects the gradual eastward movement of the Mundās, who gave way before the more prolific Orāon race and sought refuge once more in distant jungles. A portion of the race probably also split off and, following the course of the South Koel, settled in Singhbhūm and became the ancestors of the Hos of the Kolhān.

Organization of the Mundās

The Mundās who first reclaimed the virgin jungle of Nāgpur had no idea of individual ownership of landed property. All land was in the joint ownership of a family, or a group of agnate families. Each family made its own clearances, which came to be called *hatu*, village, and later *khuntkātti-hatu*, or village of the family of the original settlers. The original village family gradually branched off into a number of separate families belonging to the same *kili*, or sept. Their organization was patriarchal, the founder of the village, or the oldest representative of the founder, being the chief both in secular and religious matters. As religious head of the village community, he was known as the *Pāhān* and was required to offer the public sacrifices in the *sarnā*, or sacred grove, to propitiate the gods and spirits of the village and so protect the community from the ravages of wild animals and secure for them satisfactory harvests. As the head in secular matters, he presided over *panchāyats* for the settlement of disputes, inflicted punishment for offences against established custom, and represented the community in its dealings with outsiders. Gradually the secular and religious functions became distinct, and the next most prominent and influential man in the village became responsible for secular affairs and was known as the *Mundā*, a term which eventually gave its name to the tribe. The two offices were hereditary and neither the *Mundā* nor the *Pāhān* had any rights superior to those of the other *bhūinhārs*, or descendants of the original founders of the village.

Over and above this village organization, the Mundās in course of time came to have a tribal organization. The descendants of the original settlers increased in number, the jungles and fields of the original settlement no longer afforded adequate subsistence for all, fresh hamlets were opened up and the inhabitants of the new villages, who had at the outset maintained their connection with the parent villages in respect of public worship in the *sarnā* and burial in the common *sasān*, eventually established their own burial-grounds and public sacrifices, and formed an independent village community. With the parent village, however, they continued to constitute, for social and political purposes, the group of allied villages, known as the *pārhā* or *patti*. The *pārhā* was in ancient times simply a wider brotherhood than the village, designed so as to afford greater protection to the communities against the aggression of other village units that surrounded them. A leader being required, the *Mundā* of the parent village, or the strongest and most influential of the headmen, became the *Mānki* of the *patti* and presided over the *panchāyat* composed of the *Mundās* and *Pāhāns* from the villages which formed the group. A similar organization was adopted by the Orāons, the head of the *parhā* being known as the Rājā, a title remembered by them from the days when they lived among the Hindus in Rohtās.

Election of a Feudal Chief.

According to the tradition of the two races, this organization was found to be defective and the Mānkis and Pārhā-Rājās about the 6th century A.D. selected one of their number to be the Chief Mānki or Rājā. The Mānki so selected was the Mānki of Sūtiāmbe, from whom is descended the present family of the Nāgbansi Rājās of Chotā Nāgpur. The family legend of the Mahārāja of Chotā Nāgpur, which is given in detail in the Gazetteer under the description of the village Sūtiāmbe, agrees in many respects with the Mundā and Orāon tradition. The first Rājā is said to have been the son of the great snake-god, Pundarīka Nāg, by Pārvati, the daughter of a Benares Brāhman, and to have been born at the village of Sūtiāmbe near Pithauriā, while his parents were on a pilgrimage to Puri. Pundarīka Nāg, being forced to reveal his identity to his wife, forthwith disappeared in his proper form in a pool of water, and Pārvati, in great agony of mind over the result of her womanly inquisitiveness, immolated herself on a funeral pyre. The child, whose name was announced to be Phani Mukut Rai, was brought up by Madra, the Mānki of Sūtiāmbe, with his own son. When both the boys were about twelve years of age, Madra found the adopted son to be so much cleverer than his own son that he named him as his successor, and the other Mānkis and Pārhā-Rājās unanimously elected Phani Mukut Rai to be their Chief. This event is said to have taken place in Sambat 121 or 64 A. D., but this date is undoubtedly too early, and it may safely be put some five centuries later. It was certainly subsequent to the migration of the Hos into Singhbhūm, as they have no such tradition among their legends.

The Chief Mānki, or Rājā, in whatever manner he may have been appointed, had originally exactly the same position in the group of *pattis* that the Mānki had in the group of villages. By degrees he came to acquire the position of a feudal overlord. It is not difficult to picture the stages by which this position was reached. During the military expeditions, in which the Rājā was the national leader, services were rendered, and contributions paid, by the Mānkis; on ceremonial occasions and at festivals, presents, or *salāmi*, were given; gradually the contributions were increased and, instead of being given occasionally, came to be given regularly. The Rājās also became Hinduized, and formed marital alliances with families long recognized as Hindu; Rājputs and Brāhmans from Hindustan were invited to settle in the country and to assist the Rājā in his expeditions against neighbouring States or in controlling his own vassals. They were rewarded with grants of land or villages, and began to dispossess the village communities of their rights. Thus began the struggle between the aboriginal cultivators and the alien landlords which has continued unceasingly till the present day.

MUHAMMADAN RULE.

To the Aryans and to the Muhammadan historians the whole of Chotā Nāgpur and the adjoining hill States was known as Jhārkand, or the forest tract. It was an inaccessible frontier country and was probably one of the last conquests of the Mughals in Hindustan.

The first mention of the district is found in the Chronicles of Ahmad Yadgar* who relates that the Emperor Sher Shah sent an expedition against the Rājā of Jhārkand, in order to secure possession of a famous white elephant, named "Syām Chandra†", which had the peculiarity of never throwing dust upon its head. The expedition achieved its object and Sher Shah regarded his capture of the elephant as an omen that he would one day be Emperor at Delhi. It was not till three-quarters of a century later that an attempt was made to bring the country into subjection. In 1585, the 30th year of Akbar's reign, Shahbāz Khān sent a detachment to "Kokrah, the well-cultivated district between Orissa and the Dakhin ruled over by Madhu Singh". The result of the expedition is thus described in the Ain-i-Akbari: "As the country is inaccessible, the Rājā thought he was safe and assumed an independent attitude. Our men, however, entered the district and carried off much plunder. The Rājā became tributary (Mālguzār) and was thus fortunate to get under the shadow of the Imperial Government".

The Muhammadans were no doubt attracted to the country by its reputation for diamonds, and, in the early years after their conquest, the Governors of Bihar sent frequent detachments

---

* Mss. Pages 170—175.

† The Bengali name "Syām Chandra" goes to show that this expedition was only against that part of Jhārkand which now forms the district of Mānbhum and did not penetrate to Chotā Nāgpur proper.

into the country and were satisfied with a tribute of two or three diamonds. The Chiefs also rendered service to the Emperor, and in 1591 Madhu and Lakhmi Rai of Kokrah served in the detachment commanded by Yusuf Chak Kashmiri, which marched over Jhārkand to Midnapore and joined the imperial army under Man Singh in the conquest of Orissa.

The Emperor Jahāngīr sought to bring into more complete subjection this country in which diamonds were said to be found of the value of a lakh of rupees each, and he directed Ibrāhīm Khān, on his appointment as governor of Bihar, to "invade the district and drive away the unknown petty Rājā". Ibrahīm Khān invaded Chotā Nāgpur in 1616, refused to be satisfied with the few diamonds and elephants which the Rājā sent him, overran the country and took possession of its diamond washings. The Rājā was captured and sent to Delhi, with his diamonds and twenty-three elephants. According to the tradition of the Chotā Nāgpur Rāj, the defeated Rājā was the 45th Chief, Durjan Sāl. He was removed from Delhi to Gwalior, where he was kept in confinement for twelve years, but secured his release owing to his skill in testing diamonds. He is said to have pointed out the flaw in a diamond, over which the Court jewellers were at variance, and, to prove that he was right, to have tied it to the horns of a fighting ram and set it to fight with another ram on whose horns an unblemished diamond was fastened, with the result that the former split while the true diamond was uninjured. The Emperor was so pleased at this that he not only gave him his release but granted his prayer that the other Chiefs imprisoned with him might be set at liberty. Durjan Sāl was restored to his former rank and ordered to pay an annual tribute of Rs. 6,000. During the next century and a half, the Rājā's relations with the Muhammadans appear to have been peaceful, except for occasional expeditions to enforce payment of the tribute. Thus, in 1724 the Subadār of Patna marched to the foot of the hills, but stopped his advance on receiving from the Rājā's agent a *nazarana* of a lakh of rupees, of which Rs. 4,500 were in cash and the rest in diamonds. An expedition in 1731 was arrested in a similar way, the Subadār meeting with considerable resistance and being glad to compromise his claim by receiving Rs. 12,000 from the Ghātwāl of Rāmgarh on account of the Nāgpur Rājā. The Rājās of this time claimed to be the overlords of the Ghātwāls of Rāmgārh and Palāmau, but the overlordship was probably only nominal, as the Chiefs of Nāgpur were fully occupied in keeping in subjection their own immediate vassals.

Introduction of Hindu Settlers.

During this period there must have been a considerable immigration of Muhammadans into the country, as villages composed entirely of Muhammadans are found scattered over the district. The Rājās also succeeded in consolidating their power over the aboriginal inhabitants by the introduction of Hindu settlers, who were given grants of villages on easy conditions. Many of the settlers, either of this, or an earlier, period, were required to render military service and to keep a standing militia for the assistance of the Rājā in his expeditions against external enemies or against his own subjects. That the Rājās of this time did much to spread the Hindu religion is shown by the temples in various parts of the district. The palace and temples at Doisā were built between the years 1683 and 1711; the temple at Chutiā bears the date 1685 and that at Jagannāthpur 1691. At Borea there is an inscription on the temple to the effect that it was begun in 1665 and completed in 1682, at a cost of Rs. 14,001, and at Tilmi a well in the fortress of the Nāgbansi Thākurs of that village bears the date 1737. The Brāhmans who flocked to the Rājā's court had to be supported and received *brit* grants of lands or villages. These holders of service tenures were only entitled to the supplies and services formerly given to the Rājā, but they did not rest content with this small share of the produce. They enhanced their demands for supplies and services, they collected a certain portion of the rent payable by the raiyats, or *parjas*, to the members of the *khuntkātti* family, and gradually acquired a proprietary right to the lands which they called by name of *rajhas* or "the Rājā's share". A more detailed account of the manner in which the village communities were gradually spoiled of their rights will be found in another chapter, but it is necessary to mention it in this place, as the gradual growth of the power of the Rājā and his jāgīrdārs accounts for many of the agrarian troubles of the 19th century.

British Rule.

In 1765 on the grant of the Dīwāni of Bengal, Bihar, and Orissa to the East India Company, Chotā Nāgpur, as part of the

Subah of Bihar, passed to the British, but it was not till some years later that they made any effort to occupy the country. In 1769 Captain Camac entered Palāmau, in order to reinstate the local Rājā and bring that part of the country under British subjection. The Rājā of Nāgpur at this time was in difficulties, not only from the petty Rājās who had made themselves independent of his authority but also from the Hos or Larkā Kols of Singhbhūm who were ravaging the southern parganas, in revenge for the attempts which he had made to subjugate them. He also had a long-standing feud with the Rājā of Rāmgarh, Māchchān Singh, who, he asserted, had acquired power by being employed for the Nizamat and had usurped authority over him. Rājā Dripnāth Sahi, accordingly, went to Captain Camac in 1772 and, after exchange of turbans with the Company's representative, duly acknowledged himself a vassal of that power, gave a *nazarāna* of Rs. 3,000 and agreed to do service against the Marāthās. In return for this Captain Camac recommended that he should be allowed to pay his revenue direct to Government instead of through the Rājā of Rāmgarh, and represented to the Council at Patna the importance of securing in their interests the Rājā of Chotā Nāgpur " whose country would form an effective barrier to the incursions of the Marāthās, thus covering Bihar and Birbhum and at the same time giving them the command of the passes into the Deccan ". The Rājā also offered to pay Rs. 12,000 in lieu of Rs. 6,000 which had been previously extracted. The Council at Patna accepted the offer and made a settlement for three years (1772-1775). The Rājā assisted the British troops in subduing Rāmgarh, but subsequently fell into arrears over the payment of his revenue owing to the incursions of the Marāthās and the refusal of the petty Rājās of Silli, Tamār, Bundu, and Barwe to pay their tribute, and in 1773 Captain Camac was forced to send troops into the country to make him fulfil his obligations. In 1774 the settlement was renewed for a further period of three years, but the Rājā stipulated to pay an enhanced amount, *viz.*, Rs. 15,001.

The Rājā was, however, a constant defaulter in the payment of revenue and refused to meet the officers of Government who were sent to induce him to pay his dues.* Mr. Ramus, who succeeded Captain Camac in charge of the military collectorship of Rāmgarh, reported to the Board of Revenue, in 1778, that "many of the zamindars have paid no attention when summoned to attend. The Rājā never hears. Whenever any force is sent into his country, he immediately flies into the Marāthā country. He is very capable of paying his revenue but always evades and can never be compelled to obedience, save by force". To assist the Rāmgarh Collector in his dealings with these recalcitrant zamindars, a force of five companies of sepoys had been established at Chatrā in 1778, and it was only the presence of these troops who were operating in Barwe under Captain Camac that induced the Rājā in that year to execute his agreements.

Military Collectorship, Rāmgarh.

The Rājā was allowed a free hand in the internal administration of the country, though it was nominally included in the military collectorship of the district of Rāmgarh, which was formed in 1780, with headquarters at Shergati, in the Gaya district, and at Chatrā, in the Hazāribāgh district. The district embraced the whole of the present districts of Hazāribāgh and Palāmau and parts of the districts of Gaya, Mānbhūm and Monghyr, as well as Chotā Nāgpur proper. The district officer combined the functions of Judge, Magistrate and Collector, but paid little attention to matters other than the collection of revenue.

Administration of the Rājā.

Under the terms of his *kabuliyat*, the Rājā agreed to be responsible for the safety of travellers and to arrest thieves and dakaits and bring them to justice. There were no police thanas and matters were left pretty much to his discretion. "He administered," says Colonel Dalton, "justice and the police under the feudal system that had previously prevailed, working through his vassals, some of whom were Rājās like himself of the old race, holding extensive estates, some of whom were brethren of his own in possession of maintenance grants and some persons on whom he had conferred *jāgīrs* on condition of their supporting him". His administration was hardly successful. In 1793 the Collector invited him to Chatrā with the object of making some arrangements for the punctual payment

* The traditional reason for this conduct is as follows :—On the occasion of the meeting of Captain Camac and the Rājā, the latter was wearing a jewelled turban of great value. Captain Camac persuaded him to exchange head-dresses and the Rājā was so wrath at being deprived of his jewels in this way that he vowed not to meet the British Representative again.

of his revenue and also of persuading him "to adopt some scheme for checking the excesses which had been and are practised in his zamindari, which has been for a long time past the receptacle for murderers, thieves, vagabonds and all disturbers of the public peace". Signs of unrest among the aboriginal population of the country were also in evidence and occasionally attracted the notice of the authorities. In 1789, there was an insurrection in Tamār, which was only put down by an expedition, and disturbances in this part continued till 1795. A lurid picture is painted of the disorders prevailing in the district by Captain Roughsedge, Commandant of the Rāmgarh Battalion, in a letter dated 27th October 1806, and his description of the murder of the Rājā of Barwe by the agents of the Rājā of Nāgpur throws a flood of light on the state of the country. "I cannot avoid mentioning, however, the treacherous and cruel murder of Harirām Singh, the Rājā of Barwe, in the year 1801. This person's pargana was overrun and conquered by the neighbouring Rājā of Sirguja, and being unsupported by his immediate superior, the Rājā of Chotā Nāgpur, he was obliged to submit to the invader, whose troops kept possession for some years but retreated on the intelligence of Colonel Jones' approach. The Rājā of Chotā Nāgpur availed himself of these circumstances to attempt the recapture of Barwe; but his troops would have had no chance of success, had not Captain Jones and Mr. Smith (at that time Magistrate of Rāmgarh) addressed letters to the Rājā of Barwe, inviting him to submit on an assurance of personal safety. On the faith of these letters and the solemn promises of his captors, he was induced to place himself in the hands of the Rājā of Chotā Nāgpur, whose officer sent him two days afterwards under an escort to Pālkot. Within one mile of this place, he was taken out of his palanquin and put to death in cold blood by the party who attended him and who had been sent by the Rājā for this particular purpose. I do not believe that any judicial enquiry was ever made or complaint instituted on account of this atrocious act, and, as the present Rājā of Chotā Nāgpur is not concerned, I should not have thought it applicable to my subject, did it not seem to prove that the want of proper authority in the district is of no recent date, and that the protection accorded to this person by the chief local officers of Government was thus contemptuously rendered ineffectual by an individual calling himself a British subject and in a district declared to be amenable to British laws".

The Rājā was in fact thoroughly disloyal, and Captain Roughsedge in another letter wrote of him as follows:—" I hope I have not unsuccessfully shown the necessity for reforms, and to these facts and arguments brought forward I will only add that the slightest mark of attachment or loyalty to the Government shown by any individual in Chotā Nāgpur at the present day is sufficient to bring down upon him the undisguised and serious displeasure of the Rājā and his officers". An attempt was made to remedy this state of affairs and in 1806 Mr. Blunt, the Magistrate of Rāmgarh, obtained the sanction of Government to the introduction of a system of police under Regulation XVIII of 1805, but the measure was never carried into effect, the Rājā being evidently opposed to the proposal.

Disturbances of 1807 and 1808.

Further disturbances occurred in 1807 and 1808. Owing to the disputes of the Rājā with his brothers, Captain Roughsedge again marched into the country. The Rājā's Diwān, Din Dyal Nāth, who had established a complete ascendancy over him and was primarily responsible for the disputes, fled the country with his followers and was arrested in Calcutta and brought to Chatrā. The Rājā met the British officer, paid up his arrears of revenue and settled his quarrels with his brothers. To secure better administration in future, he was ordered to keep up police thanas, six of which were established in 1809. The year 1809 is thus a noteworthy one in the history of the district, for it marks the beginning of the disappearance of the feudal authority of the Rājā.

Introduction of Police.

The police system then originated was, however, at first no more successful than the feudal system which it had superseded. The Rājā was not unnaturally opposed to a measure which diminished his authority and increased his expenditure and did all he could to nullify its effects. In 1819 he was deprived of his control over the police, in consequence of his failure to render any assistance to the Magistrate in the detection of a case in which a woman was murdered for having practised magical arts against the Rājā's son and daughter. Another cause of the failure of this system of government was that the new police officers were foreigners from Bihar or the North-West, who joined with the alien *jāgirdārs* in oppressing the people. The aboriginals had no hope of obtaining justice. "The Rājā by no means satisfied at his own loss of dignity and authority gave but surly answers to complainants who came before him. The darogas, or native police officers, the highest resident officials under the British Government, declared that it was not competent for them to decide on the grievances which most harassed the Kols, who complained that they had been dispossessed by foreigners, Muhammadans, Sikhs and others. It often happened that the unfortunate Kol who with difficulty made his way to the far off station of Chatrā or Shergāti found the tables turned on him when he got there. A host of witnesses in the pay of the opposite party were already on the spot, prepared to prove that he had not only no rights in the land but was a turbulent rebel besides". Typical of the state of country were the disturbances which broke out in Tamār in 1820. Major Roughsedge, who had been appointed in 1819 to be the first "Political Agent to Government in South Bihar and the recently ceded districts adjacent to that Province" and was responsible for the tranquillity of the country, reported that the disturbance was due to the oppression practised by the Rājā of Tamār upon one of his vassals, Raghunāth Singh. Raghunāth Singh in the hope of redress went to the court at Chatrā, but the evidence kept in readiness for him by the Tamār zamindar caused his committal to the Court of Circuit and his condemnation to transportation or imprisonment for life. Tamār had been in a disturbed state for some years and in 1820 two Mundās, Rudu and Kantu, at the head of three hundred followers, attacked a Mānjhi whom they regarded as responsible for a drought in the previous year, murdered his son, burnt his village, and then proceeded to vent their wrath upon other landlords. For a long time they defied the authorities and were not reduced till military operations on a large scale had been taken against them.

The Insurrection of the Kols, 1831-32.

After the suppression of this disturbance, the country was temporarily tranquil, but the smouldering discontent of the aboriginals at last broke out in the great Kol Insurrection of 1831-32. The immediate occasion of the rising was an incident which occurred in pargana Sonpur. The Mahārājā's brother, Kuar Harnāth Sāhi, had received the pargana as a maintenance grant and gave out the villages in farm to Sikhs, Muhammadans and others, over the heads of the Mānkis and Mundās. Twelve villages belonging to Singhrai Mānki were leased to a Sikh who, not content with taking away his lands, carried off his sisters as concubines. A graphic description of their grievances is given in the statement of Bindra Mānki, Singhrai's brother, taken at the time by the Magistrate of Chatrā. He narrates that a *bania* of Sonpur carried off all their cattle in return for two old buffaloes which they had borrowed from him; that they took the law into their own hands and recovered two bullocks with the aid of some men lent by the Rājā of Bandgāon, that a complaint was lodged against them at Shergāti and that they were seized by the Munshi and Jamadār of Chakradharpur, but after being kept in the stocks for fifteen days they effected their escape; that in revenge for their escape, the Munshi and Jamadār carried off and ravished their wives; that they told their grievances to the Rājā of Porāhāt who merely told them to do as they pleased, but to be careful not to get him into trouble. The end of the statement is pathetic: "We returned home, invited all the Kols, our brethren and caste, to assemble at the village Lankha in Tamār, where we had a consultation. The Pathāns had taken our honour and the Sikhs our sisters and the Kuar had forcibly deprived us of our estate of twelve villages. Our lives we considered of no value and being of one caste and brethren, it was agreed upon that we should commence to cut, plunder, murder, and eat. We said if any were hanged, it would be we four; if any put in irons, we should be the four. It is with this resolution that we have been murdering and plundering those who have deprived us of both honour and homes, conceiving that committing such outrages our grievances would come to light and if we had any master, notice would be taken of them and justice rendered".

The principal leaders of the revolt came from Porāhāt in the district of Singhbhūm, and these joined with the Sonpur Mundās to carry into effect the resolution made at Lankha. On December 20th a number of villages, held in farm by the Sikhs, Hari Singh and Diyal Singh, were plundered and burned by a body of seven hundred Kols under Surga, the aggrieved Mundā of Singhbhūm and Singhrai. A few days later the villages of two Muhammadan *thikādārs* were also burnt, the servant of one of them being thrown into the fire. Jafār Ali Khān, the farmer of village Gingria, had incurred the special hostility of the Mundās by refusing to pay fair prices to the Mundā women who came to sell iron; his village was destroyed and ten inmates of his house, including some Mundā women whom he had seduced, were burnt alive. It was probably the intention of the insurgents to confine the plundering and looting to Sonpur and its immediate neighbourhood. In January 1832 the number of insurgents was estimated to be 1,000 or 1,200, but the arrows of war were circulated through the whole country and by the middle of January the Orāons had joined the Hos and Mundās. The Nazir of the Shergāti court, who was sent to tranquillize the country, only succeeded in aggravating the situation by arresting one of the leaders; to his proclamation that they would recover their lands if they desisted from their campaign of rapine and bloodshed, the Kols indignantly replied that they would obey none but the Mahārājā and leave not a foreigner alive in Nāgpur. In every village the *Sads*, or Hindus, and the *Dikus*, or foreign landlords, were murdered or, receiving warning in time, fled the country. Even the petty Rājās of Rahe, Bundu, Tamār, and Barwe, though neither *Sads* nor *Dikus*, narrowly escaped with their lives, when those places were sacked and destroyed. The British authorities were entirely unprepared for an outbreak of such magnitude. Captain Wilkinson, with a few troops, reached the outskirts of the plateau in the middle of January and compelled Pithauriā and the neighbouring villages to submit and had some hard fighting round Nagri. By the middle of February sufficient troops were collected to form three flying columns which swept the country in parallel lines, as they advanced from south to north. The columns met with little resistance, save in Sonpur where the insurgents had abandoned their villages and taken to the hills. All the columns concentrated in this country and secured the surrender of the leaders on March 19th, 1832. To Captain Wilkinson belongs the credit for bringing the operations to such a successful issue. He cultivated the acquaintance and the friendship of the Mundās of Tamār, persuaded them and their Mānkis to dissociate themselves from the Larka Kols and to keep them out of the dominions of the Rājā, and also made friends with the *Sardārs* of the Larkas in Porāhāt. Many are the stories which the Mundās relate about "Alkinsun Sahib", the name by which they remember Captain Wilkinson, the first Agent to the Governor General in the South-West Frontier Agency.

Causes of the Insurrection.

Though the occasion of the insurrection was the treatment of the Sonpur and Porāhāt Mundās by the Sikh and Muhammadan *thīkādārs,* the causes were more deep-seated, as the following extracts from the report of the Joint Commissioners, Mr. Dent and Captain Wilkinson, will show :—

"The Kols throughout Nāgpur had within the last few years had their rents increased by their *ilākādārs,* zamindars and *thīkādars* by 35 per cent. They had made roads through the pargana without payment, as *begarries* (forced labour). The Mahājans, who advanced money and grain, managed within a twelve month to get from them 70 per cent., and sometimes more. They disliked the tax upon liquor, which was fixed at four annas a house, but more than that amount was levied very generally, besides a rupee *salāmi* on almost every village and a *khasi* or goat. The thana establishments were also complained of, and a *dāk* establishment was kept up, the expense of which fell upon the Kols of those villages which were situated on the lines of road traversed by the *dāk.* The raiyats of the Rāj's *bhandar* (*khās*) villages complain that the present Diwān had within the last five years taken from them double the quantity of *saika* grain (produce-rent) which he did formerly. The peons collecting rents in the *bhandar* villages formerly received one *paila* of rice or one anna per diem. They now take four since the present Diwān came into power. The *dhāngārs,* who go as labourers into Bengal and other parts of India, are on their return forced to pay one rupee to the owner or farmer of the village. Many people from below the ghāt have settled in Nāgpur and it was one of the subjects of complaint among the Kols that within the last five years several of these settlers, to whom they had become deeply indebted, had pressed so hard for payment that many of the Kols had executed *sewak pattas,* that is, had sold their services till the debt was discharged, which was in fact binding themselves to give their whole earnings to their creditor, receiving from him food and clothing, or to work for him exclusively, thus becoming his bondsman for life. The complaints against the thana *amlā* were loud in our progress through the country, but the number of instances of exaction are by no means as numerous as we anticipated". The Commissioners did not consider that there was any truth in the allegation that the Rāja had stirred up insurrection, though there were many reasons why he should wish to be rid of British interference. He had been deprived of his influence and authority over the *jāgīrdārs*, who now merely paid him rent, but formerly, before the country became subject to the Regulations, had been liable to forfeit their estates if they failed in rendering him services. He had also been a pecuniary loser, as he had been prohibited, in 1783, from collecting *madad* in addition to the rent, and also the *panchpownea*, or tax on certain castes and trades, and contributions on occasions of mourning and rejoicing in the royal family.

Administrative reforms.

The suppression of the revolt was followed by a number of administrative reforms. In Sonpur, the Mānkis and Mundās were all reinstated in their villages on reduced rentals, and the *thīkādārs* were referred to the Kuar for the adjustment of their claims. The proposal to introduce opium cultivation was dropped, and collections on account of excise and the *dāk* cess were temporarily suspended. But the chief lesson learnt by the insurrection was the necessity for a closer administration and more effective control by British officers on the spot. Accordingly, the whole system was changed, and the South-West Frontier Agency was established in 1834, with headquarters at Kishanpur (Rānchi). The Agency included all Chotā Nāgpur proper as well as Palāmau, Kharakdiha, Rāmgarh, Kundu, the Jungle mahals (except Bishenpur, Sainpahari, and Sherghar), pargana Dhālbhūm and the dependent Tributary Mahals. Within the territory so constituted, the operation of the Regulations and of the rules for the administration of civil and criminal justice and the collection of revenue was suspended. By the rules framed under the Regulation, the Agent was given very wide powers. He was vested with the same powers as were exercised by Commissioners of Revenue and by Civil and Sessions Judges, but was enjoined to conform to all orders from the Sadar Dewani and Nizamat Adalat, the Sadar Board of Revenue, and the Board of Customs, Salt and Opium. Subordinate to the Agent were the officers styled "Principal Assistants to the Agent to the Governor General", who were in charge of the divisions known as the Mānbhūm, Lohardagā, and Hazāribāgh Divisions. Captain Thomas Wilkinson was appointed the first Agent, and one of his Principal Assistants, Lieutenant Ouseley, was placed in charge of the Lohardagā Division, which corresponded roughly to the present districts of Palāmau and Rānchi, with headquarters at Lohardagā.

Civil and Criminal Courts.

The most important result of the establishment of the Agency was that, for the first time since the cession of the Dīwānī, a regular system of Police and Courts for the administration of justice by British officers was instituted. For the administration of Criminal Justice, the Assistants had powers similar to those exercised at the present time by the Deputy Commissioners. In addition to ordinary magisterial powers, they were able to pass sentence of imprisonment for a period of seven years. Their proceedings were subject to revision by the Agent, who had power to confirm, annul, or modify them at his discretion. For the administration of Civil Justice, there were two Munsifs, one at Lohardagā, and one at Rānchi, while the Principal Sadar Amin at Gola also appears to have exercised jurisdiction. The Principal Assistants tried some original civil suits and heard appeals from the decisions of the Munsifs. For the guidance of the Courts, a simple Code of rules was drawn up by Captain Wilkinson, which, though not sanctioned by Government, appears to have been followed till the introduction of the Code of Civil Procedure (Act VIII of 1859). Two salutary rules, drafted by Captain Wilkinson, may be mentioned. One, with the object of discouraging vexatious litigation, prohibited vakils from practising in any courts and allowed suits to be conducted only through the agency of Mukteārs, or authorized agents; the other, declaring that no sale, mortgage or transfer of landed property was valid without the consent of the Agent was intended to prevent disputes over transferred property and to discourage the old landlords from running into debt. An interesting side light is thrown on the distrust with which the Courts were regarded by the aborigines by the existence of a rule which prohibited the Munsifs from granting *ex-parte* decrees against Mundās, Mānkis, Kols, and "other such ignorant people". The Principal Assistant, Dr. Davidson, first issued and enforced this rule in 1838, and its wisdom is shown by the fact that when this rule was superseded by the Code of Civil Procedure, numerous fraudulent *ex-parte* decrees were passed against the Mundās and were one of the causes of the subsequent agrarian discontent.

Improvement in the Police administration

The system of zamindāri Police was introduced. A thana was maintained at Government expense at Lohardagā, and zamindāri thanas were set up at Pālkot, where the Rājā resided, and on the estates of the zamindārs of Barwe, Bundu, Tamār, Silli, and Bantahajām. The cost of the latter was at first defrayed by the Rājā, but in 1838 the zamindārs agreed to pay an additional four per cent. to meet this charge, and by a subsequent arrangement the Rājā and his subordinate zamindārs were authorized to collect a police cess of Rs. 2 or 3 from each village from their under-tenure holders and raiyats. The Rājā exercised the powers of a *darogā* within the jurisdiction of Pālkot thana, and the zamindārs similar powers within their own estates.

Though this system was intended to vest an authority in the Chiefs to whom the people had been accustomed to look for its exercise, it did not prove a success. Mr. Ricketts, Member of the Board of Revenue, reporting in 1855, wrote as follows :—

Failure of the system of zamindari Police.

" The Principal Assistant represents that the zamindāri police is inefficient, that the zamindārs are generally ignorant and either unwilling or unable to perform their duties, and that the establishments employed under them are so underpaid that it is impossible to expect any good service from them. The Muharrirs receive Rs. 6 a month and many of the barkandazes Re. 1-8, which is a quarter less than is paid to a coolie for the commonest manual labour. No information is procurable as to the terms on which the police were originally left in the hands of the zamindārs. Whether they are bound to keep them in a state of efficiency, whether the expenses were limited cannot be ascertained. The Principal Assistant is of opinion that for the sum paid by the zamindārs a more efficient establishment could be kept up, were the police directly under the Assistant. There is no doubt that an honest, able and active zamindār with the power of a *darogā*, might afford most efficient assistance to good government, while the powers of a zamindār of opposite character to do mischief is measureably increased by leaving the police in his hands ".

The system continued till the introduction of the new constabulary in 1863 when, according to the terms of Act V of 1861, the police powers of the zamindārs were abolished.

Defects of the administration.

Nor did the new system of government succeed in improving the condition of the aboriginals in other ways. The *jāgīrdārs* still continued to oppress the cultivators and extort from them illegal contributions and *abwābs*. Dr. Davidson, writing in 1839, says :—

"In point of fact there was no regular Police or Administration of Justice till the present Agency was established in 1834. That the Kols are frequently imposed on by their landlords is not for want of comprehension, but that they have been so long completely left to their mercies, and so entirely deprived of any protection from them, that it is difficult for them to make up their minds to resist". Mr. Ricketts, in the report already quoted, refers to this opinion and adds: —"Though there was no complaint preferred to me, there seems reason to apprehend that the people of the district suffer much from the foreign middlemen introduced by the Rājā. Major Hannyngton tells me that, 'In Chotā Nāgpur the *bhuinhāri* lands which exist in every village have been exposed to the rapacity of the middlemen, aliens who are hated by the people, and who, to obtain these lands, spare no species of force or fraud. Against these our Courts do not afford any facile remedy and the day may be not far distant when the people goaded beyond endurance may take the law into their own hands".

Further reforms.

To improve the administration of justice, the Agent was relieved of his duties as Civil and Sessions Judge, and in 1843 an officer was appointed, under the title of Deputy Commissioner, to carry out these functions. The Deputy Commissioner corresponded to the present Judicial Commissioner and received that title in 1861. In 1854 a further change in the administration was made. By Act XX of that year the Agency was abolished, and the duties and powers conferred by Regulation XX of 1833 were vested in an officer appointed by the Local Government, and Chotā Nāgpur was administered as a non-regulation Province under a Commissioner. The officer in charge of the Lohardagā district was first styled Deputy Commissioner in 1861. The headquarters of the Principal Assistant to the Agent had previously, in 1842, been transferred from Lohardagā to Rānchi.

Arrival of Christian Missionaries.

The year 1845 is a memorable one in the history of the district, for it witnessed the arrival of the first Christian Missionaries. In November 1845 four German pastors, sent out by Pastor John Gossner of Berlin, pitched their tents in Rānchi. For a few years their work met with little success, and it was not till 1850 that any converts were obtained. After that year the number of converts rose rapidly, and by 1857 there were 900 baptised members of the Lutheran Church and 2,000 enquirers. The education and teaching given by the missionaries had a great effect on the oppressed aborigines. Captain Davies, the Senior Assistant Commissioner, writing in 1859, says :—" With Christianity has naturally come an appreciation of their rights as original clearers of the soil, which rights in many instances they have asserted and established ; this, independent of other causes which induce the higher castes of natives to view with displeasure the spread of Christianity, caused great alarm among the landholders".

The Mutiny of 1857 caused a temporary set-back to the spread of Christianity and the departure of the British authorities gave the landlords an opportunity of oppressing their Christian raiyats.

THE MUTINY.

At the time of the Mutiny, Rānchi was the headquarters of the Rāmgarh battalion, which consisted of a full infantry battalion, with cavalry and artillery attached. About one-third of the battalion were men of Chotā Nāgpur but of the higher castes, and the remainder were recruited from Bihar and other parts of India. A number of aboriginal Kols had at one time been recruited, but, though good and courageous soldiers in some respects, were found to be led by their intemperate habits into many derelictions of duty, and the commandant of the battalion anxious to have it as much like a line regiment as possible had discontinued recruiting them. At Hazāribāgh there were companies of the 7th and 8th Native infantry, which had been possessed with a spirit of unrest ever since the first news of the revolt had reached them from the North. News of their disloyalty reached Rānchi, and it was decided to send two companies of the Rāmgarh infantry, thirty horsemen and two guns, under Lieutenant Graham, to disarm them. The force left Rānchi on August 1st but had not proceeded far on its march, when news was received that the Hazāribāgh troops had actually mutinied and were marching towards Rānchi. On receipt of this news, the Rāmgarh infantry, who were with Lieutenant Graham, mutinied, seized the guns, ammunition and four elephants, belonging to Colonel Dalton, the Commissioner, and made preparations to march back to Rānchi. The cavalry alone remained loyal and went on with Lieutenant Graham to Hazāribāgh. News of the mutiny of this detachment reached Rānchi early on August 2nd. At first Colonel Dalton and the military officers continued their preparations for meeting the men of the 8th Native Infantry, who were said to be at Burmu, 20 miles north of Rānchi, in spite of the fact that the loyalty of the troops at Dorānda was by no means certain. On the afternoon of the 2nd, some of the mutinous sepoys of Lieutenant Graham's detachment arrived at Dorānda, and the Commissioner and the Commandant of the Corps, seeing that it was now hopeless to rely on the loyalty of the troops, decided to vacate Rānchi and march to Hazāribāgh by the direct route *viâ* Pithauriā. The decision was not made a moment too soon; about an hour after departure, the mutineers of the Rāmgarh infantry arrived, burnt the court of the Deputy Commissioner and some of the officers' bungalows, released the prisoners from the jail, fired their guns at the German Mission Church, and looted the treasury. Colonel Dalton, with the troops who still remained loyal, arrived at Hazāribāgh without meeting any opposition; for this they were indebted to the Parganāit, Jaggat Pāl Singh, of Pithauriā, who had set up earthworks across the road by which the Hazāribāgh troops were marching on Rānchi. The troops, thinking the entrenchments were held by men of the Rāmgarh battalion and that Rānchi would be found to be well-defended, turned off in the direction of Lohardagā, and ultimately joined the rebels in the Tributary Mahals, taking no further part in the mutiny in Chotā Nāgpur.

Colonel Dalton, with the few troops under his command and with the men supplied by the Rājā of Rāmgarh, succeeded in restoring order in Hazāribāgh, recovered a large quantity of plundered property and a number of prisoners, re-opened the courts and caused business to be resumed in the bazar. Reinforcements, however, did not arrive and, thinking that the small force, even if it remained loyal, was insufficient to withstand an attack, Colonel Dalton reluctantly decided to fall back on the Grand Trunk Road at Barhi and Bagodar, though well aware that the abandonment of Hazāribāgh would encourage the mutineers. Barhi was reached on August 13th, and here the Commissioner was forced to remain inactive till reinforcements were available. At last, on September 1st, 150 men of Rattray's Sikhs arrived, and with their help he again occupied Hazāribāgh.

During this time the mutinous troops had remained at Dorānda, uncertain what movement to make. Disappointed at the failure of the Hazāribāgh troops to cross the Pithauriā Ghāt and join them, they set about trying to win the zamindārs on to their side; but in this they met with little success. The Mahārājā and most of the leading zamindārs remained loyal. Thākur Bisnāth Sāhi, of Barkagarh, who had long been regarded as disaffected, openly joined the mutineers and was reported to sit daily in one of the Cantonment bungalows administering justice. He also assisted the mutineers by cutting several breaches in the road over Rāmgarh Ghāt, with the obvious intention of making it difficult for troops advancing against Dorānda. Another disloyal zamindār was Ganpat Rai, of Bhaunro, an ex-Diwān of the Mahārājā, who, it is said, was formally installed by the mutineers as their Commander in-Chief. The prime mover of the Rānchi mutiny was, however, Jamadār Madho Singh, of the Rāmgarh battalion. It was not till the first week of September that the mutineers decided to leave Dorandā, taking with them four six-pounder guns, a large quantity of ammunition, the treasure and heaps of plunder, and to proceed, if possible, *viā* the Tika Ghāt, through Palāmau so as to effect a junction at Rohtāogarh with Kunwar Singh, to whom the guns and treasure would have proved acceptable. Before leaving Rānchi, they plundered the townspeople, attempted to burn the jail and the kachahri, and flung the records into a well; they also beheaded an old native doctor, named Budu, who was attached to the jail. The progress of the mutineers was slow, as the transport of the guns, treasure, and plunder was no easy matter at that season of the year. The zamindārs did much to hinder their march, and, in particular, Hari Singh, Barāik of Charya, entrenched the ghāts against them and only abandoned his position when the guns were brought against it.

A few days after the departure of the mutineers, on September 22nd, Colonel Dalton, with 150 Sikhs and 150 men of the 53rd Regiment under Major English, reached Rānchi. He was anxious to start off in pursuit of the mutineers, who had by this time reached Balumath (in Palāmau district) and were reported to be uncertain whether to advance through Palāmau or towards Chatrā, but was unable to carry this plan into effect, as the 53rd Regiment were ordered to go back to the Grand Trunk Road. When Major English with the troops under his command reached Hazāribāgh, he received orders to march against the rebels at Chatrā. On the 2nd of October he came up with the rebels, who now numbered over 3,000, and completely defeated them, capturing the guns and ammunition and recovering a large amount of the treasure and plunder. Colonel Dalton thus describes the effects of this victory :—

"Nothing could have been more favourable to the thorough re-establishment of the authority of Government and the speedy restoration of order than the circumstance under which the mutineers were signally defeated. Chatrā is one of the largest and wealthiest towns in the division, where there is always a collection of people from all parts of the country. Moreover, the mutineers had pressed into their service hundreds of the working classes of Chotā Nāgpur. All these were present during the engagement and many witnessed the complete extinction of the force, that had for a month occupied the headquarters of the Province in a manner that will be long recollected as a reign of terror, and whose progress through the villages had been marked by devastation and ruin. They then hastened back to their homes, and long before I received even the first brief news by express from Major Simpson, the news had spread and was known to every one in the neighbourhood".

Although the courts had been re-opened after Colonel Dalton's return to Rānchi on the 23rd of September, desultory warfare continued for some time, as the local rebels were still at large. Thākur Bisnāth Sāhi and Pānde Ganpat Rai had been taken with the mutineers on their march from Dorandā to Chatrā, in order to ensure the safe passage of the ghāts, but both they and Jamadār Madho Singh, the insurgent leader, escaped after the battle. Madho Singh was not heard of again, but in December the Thākur and Pānde were reported to be on the border of Pālāmau, intriguing with the Bhogtā insurgents, who had been giving considerable trouble in that part of the country. In March 1858 depredations were committed by local insurgents on some villages in pargana Nawāgarh, and the Barwe police-station was looted. To operate against these local insurgents, Colonel Dalton assembled an escor of the Rāmgarh Irregular Cavalry and 200 men of the new Kol Levy, which was raised and trained soon after the return to Rānchi. Thākur Bisnāth Sāhi and Ganpat Rai were captured and hanged, in April 1858, their estates being confiscated to Government.

Spread of Christianity and conflicts between raiyats and landlords.

During the fifty years which have elapsed since the Mutiny, the history of the Rānchi district is one of agrarian discontent, culminating in the *Sardāri Larāi* and the Birsā rising. It is also the history of the spread of Christianity. During the Mutiny the Christian community was broken up but their dispersion over the district seems to have given a considerable impulse to Christianity, as the number of converts largely increased after the restoration of order. An impression rapidly gained ground that to become Christian was the best way of shaking off the oppression of the landlord. "The result of this", says Colonel Dalton, "has been a great accession of strength to the ranks of nominal Christians. A reasonable desire to be reinstated in *bhūinhāri* lands actuated some, a dishonest idea to become one of this favoured family of *bhūinhārs* seized others. The next step was to profess Christianity, and coming to the Mission at Rānchi they returned with their hair, puritanically, cropped and ready to assert their rights and defy their landlords. Conflicts between the Christian aboriginals and their landlords were of frequent occurrence; the Christians sought to take forcible possession of the lands, of which they considered themselves to have been dispossessed by the landlords, while the latter retaliated by bringing false charges of dakāiti and robbery against the tenants and subjecting them to illegal confinement and duress. Towards the end of 1858 the conflict assumed a serious aspect, and troops had to be sent from Rānchi to Gobindpur to preserve order in Basia and Sonpur. The authorities, however, realized that the only effectual method of preventing a repetition of such outbreaks was to remove the grievances that had caused them. Accordingly, in 1858, Lāla Lokhnāth Sāhi, a Nāgbansi zamindār, was deputed to prepare a register of all *bhūinhāri* lands. He continued to work till his death in 1862, and made enquiries in 572, and completed the register of *bhūinhāri* lands in 429, villages. The knowledge that an attempt was being made to restore them to their lands temporarily pacified the Mundās, and parganas Lodhma and Sonpur, where the greater part of the work was carried out, and which had previously been the most troubled, were reported to have become, since the completion of the register, the least disturbed of all the parganas in which such tenures existed. The decisions of the Lāla were on the whole more favourable to the landlords than to the *bhūinhārs*,

Register of bhūinhāri lands.

but were to some extent a settlement of the question and placed a limit on further encroachments. When the survey was discontinued, disputes again broke out, and in 1867 a petition was presented to the Local Government, purporting to be signed by 14,000 Christians. Though this petition was grossly exaggerated and contained many unfounded complaints against the Mahārājā and even against the Commissioner, Colonel Dalton, it served the purpose of impressing Government with the necessity of completing the survey begun by Lāla Lokhnāth Sāhi. Accordingly, the Chotā Nāgpur Tenures Act (Act II B. C. of 1869) was passed. Under this Act, special Commissioners were appointed who had power to survey and demarcate the privileged lands of the tenants (*bhūinhāri*) and of the landlords (*mānjhihas*). The operations, which were begun on April 1st, 1869, and were not completed till 31st March 1880, extended to 2,482 villages.

Result of the Bhuinhāri Survey.

The operations undertaken under the Act, though successful to some extent in the areas in which they were carried out, were a mere palliation of the grievances which prevailed throughout the country. Government in their Resolution on the final report of the Commissioners admitted that " the success of the Act has fallen short of the expectations generally entertained on its introduction. The operations have not removed every cause of disagreement, and disputes are still of frequent occurrence. This partial failure appears to be due to two causes ; first, to the fact that *rājhas* tenures were not included in the scope of the Act, and, secondly, to the extravagant claims and expectations of a section of the *bhūinhārs*, which rendered it impossible to satisfy them by any settlement which aimed at preserving the just rights of both parties". A third cause was that some landlords persuaded the *bhūinhārs* to conceal their status by representing that Government intended to impose a special tax upon them. The Special Commissioner, Babu Rākhāl Dās Hāldār, had shown in his final report how the exclusion of *rājhas* had opened a door for further disputes involving expensive litigation both in the criminal, revenue, and civil courts. The landlords, seeing that the exorbitant claims of *bhūinhārs* had been disallowed, sought either to dispossess them of all lands other than the demarcated *bhūinhāri* land, or to increase the rent payable for such lands. Further, small advantage was taken of the provisions of the Act permitting the commutation of prædial conditions and services for cash payment. Only 1,161 applications were received. "The Mundās and headmen showed great indifference on the subject and the landlords resorted to all means in their power to render this portion of the Act nugatory; while the landlords, however, valued the services more highly than money payments, the raiyats also seemed to prefer giving the accustomary amount of labour to paying additional rent, especially when no remunerative employment was available". The Government of Bengal, however, did not consider it necessary to undertake a thorough survey and settlement of the whole district, though this was recommended by the Commissioner. They considered that the settlement of the Chotā Nāgpur estate which was being undertaken would be a further step in the solution of the disputes over a large portion of the district, and that in the remaining villages, which were held by *jāgīrdārs*, maintenance-holders, and farmers, the provisions of the Chotā Nāgpur Landlord and Tenants Procedure Act of 1879, which had recently been passed, were sufficient for the protection of the raiyats against illegal enhancement, while securing to the zamindārs their fair rental. The new Act provided that the rent of *bhūinhāri*, *khuntkātti* or *korkar* lands was not liable to enhancement, except under certain conditions and circumstances, and that the rent of other occupancy raiyats should not be enhanced, except on application to the Deputy Commissioner. The Act also repeated the provisions of the previous Act for the voluntary commutation of services. Like the Act of 1869, it disappointed the hopes of its framers. The landlords contrived to evade its provisions; rents were enhanced, and prædial services increased, frequently by the device of bringing a suit for arrears of rent at rates greatly in excess of what was actually paid, often by forcing or cheating the raiyats into agreeing to higher rates. The landlords, however, were not invariably successful; in many cases the raiyats succeeded in improving their position at the expense of the less wealthy and less powerful landlords. In villages where the majority of the inhabitants were Christians, *begāri* (or prædial service) was not rendered, and in some cases the landlords were forcibly deprived of their *khās* lands.

Agitation of the Sardārs.

The main grievances underlying the Sārdāri agitation and the agrarian discontent during the last fifteen years of the 19th century were the system of *beth begāri*, or compulsory labour, the exaction of prædial conditions (*rākumāts*), the illegal enhancement of rents of *rājhas* lands, and the question of the status of the Mundā proprietors of *khuntkātti* villages, which had not been included in the *bhūinhāri* survey. With these very real grievances in the minds of the aboriginals, the Sardārs, who have been rightly described as an unscrupulous and dishonest band of cheats, found little difficulty in stirring up an agitation, and collecting money, ostensibly for the purpose of bringing their complaints to the notice of the authorities. They began to bombard Government with petitions in which the most extravagant claims were put forward. Their principal prayer, that of being allowed to form themselves into village communities directly under Government, was found to be unreasonable and extravagant, and the petitions were all necessarily rejected, "as their entertainment would subvert the progress which has been made during a lengthened period in the Chotā Nāgpur division". The missionaries sought in vain to convince the Sardārs of the futility of these petitions, with the result that they left the Church and set up a violent opposition to the mission work. During all the time that the earlier memorials were under discussion, the aboriginals did not do anything that was punishable under the law. In 1881 an incident occurred, which foreshadowed the Birsā rising fifteen years later. A party calling themselves the children of "Mæl" and headed by "John the Baptist" set up a "Rāj" at Doisā, a former seat of the Rājās of Chotā Nāgpur. The ringleaders, who were promptly punished, were not proved to have any connection with the Sardārs. By the beginning of 1887 the movement had assumed considerable dimensions. Many of the Mundās and Orāons refused to pay rent to their landlords, on the ground that they had got a decree declaring them to be the owners of the soil and only bound to pay rent direct to the "Sarkār". Meetings were held in various places with the object of collecting subscriptions and inciting the people to take possession of the *mānjhihas* lands and to dispute the authority of the local officers, but the actual outbreaks were few in number and were easily suppressed by the civil authorities. At Tilma the Christians opposed the cultivation of the *mānjhihas* lands, and in Tamār they seized and cultivated the *mānjhihas* land of the Rāni, but the prompt arrest and imprisonment of the principals had the effect of stopping further trouble, and when the harvest of 1887 was reaped, no breaches of the peace occurred.

Disturbances of 1889 over beth begāri.

The Sardāri agitation of 1887 was followed by disturbances in the west of the district in 1889. These were due to the spread of Christianity among the Orāons of these parts, who had hitherto been beyond the field of the work of the Lutheran and Anglican Missions. The Roman Catholic Mission had established stations at Burudi in the Khunti thana in 1874 and at Dorandā in 1883, but no great progress was made till the Rev. Father Lievens began to preach among the Mundās, Orāons, and Khariās in the south-western and western parts of the district. Within three or four years over forty thousand nominally joined the Church and the movement was, as before, viewed with fear and suspicion by the landlords. In the year 1889 a number of landlords sent up a petition to the Commissioner, alleging that the Roman Catholic Missionaries were unsettling the minds of their raiyats and converting them by thousands to Christianity. They complained that the Jesuits held out hopes to the aboriginals which were incapable of fulfilment and thereby induced them to join the Church; though this complaint was exaggerated, there is no doubt that the sympathy with which the missionaries listened to the complaints of the aboriginals about the burden of their prædial services, encouraged them to believe that the only way of escaping from oppression was to become a convert. The claim of the landlords to exact unlimited services from the raiyats was preposterous, and the missionaries very properly advised the raiyats only to render those services which had received the sanction of custom. The immediate result of such advice was that a spirit of resistance filled both Christians and non-Christians. The landlords refused to abate their demands, and the raiyats refused to pay their ordinary rent or render their customary services. The disturbances were not very serious; and the officials, though apprehensive of disturbances on a large scale, had little difficulty in maintaining the peace of the district as a whole. The Christians in some villages tried to coerce their unconverted brethren into accepting the new religion, and forcibly cut off their top knots; in other villages they forcibly cut and carried off the crops from the *mānjhihas* lands. In 1890 the Lieutenant-Governor, Sir Stewart Bayley, visited Rānchi and held a Conference, at which several missionaries, representative landlords, and officials were present and it was generally agreed that a wholesale commutation of services and prædial dues was the only true solution of the problem of agrarian discontent, but this measure was not undertaken. A proclamation issued by Mr. Grimley, the Commissioner, with the authority of Government, prescribed a scale of service renderable for each holding, according to the custom of the district. The total amount of labour amounted to fourteen days in the year. These orders were in no way binding on the landlords or the tenants, and, though partially successful, their effect was transient as a solution of the problem. During the next four or five years, while Government was engaged in considering the question of the amendment of the Tenancy Act, the country was comparatively free from disturbances, but the Sardārs still continued to collect subscriptions, in some cases extorting them by threats or violence, and between the years 1893 and 1895 several Sardārs were prosecuted on charges of extortion and assault. Their operations extended throughout the whole of the Mundā country and the northern portion of the Porāhāt estate of Singhbhūm. The total collections are estimated to have amounted to over a lakh of rupees, the greater portion of which was paid over to certain lawyers of Calcutta for drafting a memorial to Parliament, and the rest was misappropriated by the Sardārs themselves.

The Birsā rising of 1895.

In 1895 the ferment in the Mundā country again broke out, when a leader was found in the person of Birsā, a Mundā of the village Chalkad in Tamār thana. Birsā was a convert of the German Mission and had received a little education and a smattering of English at the Mission School at Chaibāsa. His influence over the Mundās and Orāons was extraordinary. He quickly won for himself the reputation of a worker of miracles, and both Mundās and Orāons flocked to the village of Chalkad to see the new prophet and to be cured of their ills by his miraculous powers. Birsā soon gave himself out to be the prophet of a new religion, which, he said, he had received from Sing Bongā himself. The new religion was a mixture of Hinduism and Christianity. The Mundās were to give up worshipping, and sacrificing to a number of *bongās* or subordinate deities and to worship only one God, Sing Bongā; they were to lead good lives, abstain from eating animal food, and wear the sacred thread of the twice-born Hindu castes. Later, Birsā began to regard himself, and to be regarded by his followers, as the incarnation of the deity, and announced that on a given day fire and brimstone would descend from heaven and destroy all men on earth except those who had the good sense to repair to his village of Chalkad and stay near him on that occasion. Chalkad and the neighbouring hills and villages became a large camp; stores of rice were collected and temporary huts erected, and crowds of armed Mundās, especially from the Sardāri villages, assembled there. Birsā's teaching now began to assume a political aspect; he advised his followers to defy the authorities, informing them that the *rāj* of the Mahārāni (Queen-Empress) was over and that the Mundā *rāj* had commenced. He prophesied that if Government opposed him, the rifles of its soldiers would be turned to wood and their bullets to water, and he issued an injunction to the raiyats that they were to pay no rents in future but hold their lands rent-free. These proceedings naturally alarmed the authorities, and the Superintendent of Police was sent out to arrest him. Mr. Meares, the Superintendent, reached Chalkad on the night of August 24th and succeeded in penetrating to the place where Birsā was sleeping without the knowledge of the multitudes who surrounded him. The police overpowered the guard, and Birsā was well on the way to Rānchi under arrest before the crowds of his followers even knew that he had been arrested. He and fifteen of his followers were tried and convicted under section 505 of the Indian Penal Code and sentenced to two years' imprisonment. Illustrative of the faith which the Mundās had in Birsā was the rumour which went round the country that the jail walls fell down when he entered the jail gates. The only foundation for the rumour was that the mud-wall of a small grain-store collapsed.

Release of Birsā and second rising.

During Birsā's confinement the excitement in the Mundā country subsided. He was released before the expiry of his sentence, on the occasion of the Diamond Jubilee of Queen Victoria, and soon gathered a band of his followers round him. His first move was to visit and desecrate the old Hindu Temple at Chutiā, probably with the object of asserting his claim to the Chotā Nāgpur Rāj, of which Chutiā was an ancient seat. Some of his followers were arrested on the spot, but Birsā himself escaped and vanished for a period of two years. Towards the end of 1899 he reappeared, and he and his chief followers began to tour round the country and stir up the people to attack the landlords and the authorities. The day fixed for the outbreak was Christmas Day, 1899. A large number of preconcerted murderous attacks and acts of incendiarism occurred in various places in thanas Khunti, Tāmar, Basiā, and Rānchi. A German merchant, Mr. Caesar, was shot dead in a village in the depth of the jungles of pargana Sonpur, and attacks were made on the Anglican Missionary at Murhu and the Roman Catholic Missionaries at Sarwadā. At Burju a police constable and four chaukidars were put to death, and at Khunti the police-station was attacked, one of the constables killed, and some of the houses burnt down. The Commissioner, Mr. Forbes, and the Deputy Commissioner, Mr. Streatfeild, hastened to Khunti with 150 men of the Native infantry stationed at Dorandā, and on the 9th of January came upon the main body of the Mundās at Dumari Hill. The insurgents refused to surrender, and the troops were compelled to use their rifles and storm the hill. A number of the insurgents were killed or wounded, and the rest dispersed. Birsā himself was arrested in Singhbhūm on the 3rd February, and he and his chief followers were placed on their trial. Birsā died of cholera in Rānchi Jail during the course of the trial in June 1900; of his followers two were hanged for murders committed during the rising, while others were sentenced to various terms of transportation or imprisonment.

Lessons of the Birsā rising.

The Birsā insurrection, following the Sardāri agitation which has lasted for so many years, impressed upon Government the necessity for removing once and for all the grievances which had been the cause of all the agrarian discontent in the district. Before the Birsā outbreak, a fresh attempt had been made to remove the grievances about *rakumāts* and *begāri* by passing the Commutation Act of 1897. The Act reproduced the provisions of Act I of 1879, under which the Courts had power to commute prædial conditions and services into cash payments, on the application of one of the parties, and power was also taken in it by the Local Government to order a compulsory commutation when it was considered expedient to do so. But this Act, like its predecessors, disappointed the expectations of its framers. No commutation was ever ordered by Government, and, though a number of applications for commutation were received from both landlords and raiyats, they amounted to a very small percentage of the whole. The raiyats, especially those who became nominal

Christians, preferred to cease to render services rather than enter upon expensive litigation, which usually resulted in a substantial increase of their rent, while the landlords were unable to prove to the satisfaction of the Courts that their demands were authorized by custom and hence were reluctant to apply.

Settlement operations, 1902-1910.

It was at last recognized that the preparation of a complete record-of-rights for the whole district, and particularly for the Mundā country, was absolutely necessary, and also that the compulsory abolition of the *beth begāri* system must be taken in hand. Accordingly, it was decided, in 1901, to effect a survey and settlement of the Mundā country. The work was taken up in 1902, and, after the Mundā country had been dealt with, the operations were extended to the rest of the district. All prædial services were commuted throughout the district, and with them the præd ial conditions (*abwābs* and *rukāmuts*) which were a secondary cause of dispute; and thus both questions were finally set at rest. The law relating to landlords and tenants was amended and improved in the light of the experience gained in the course of the Settlement operations by Act V of 1903, which dealt principally with the *Mundāri khuntkātti* tenancies and, finally by the present Chotā Nāgpur Tenancy Act (Act VI of 1908) which re-arranged and consolidated the enactments previously in force and embodied certain provisions of the Bengal Tenancy Act and some additional provisions which confirm local customary rights and usages. Of the immense benefit conferred on the district by the Settlement operations there can be no doubt. Apart from the advantages resulting from the abolition of *beth begāri* and *rukumāts*, the raiyats have now a final and conclusive record of their lands, their rent, and their miscellaneous rights in jungle and waste lands, and there is a general consensus of opinion that the settlement records have definitely put a stop to the harassing litigation which has ruined so many landlords and tenants. Criminal cases have decreased in number, for many of the criminal cases of the district were paddy-theft cases and cases of trespass on land in assertion of a supposed or real right. Civil suits, which were usually filed by parties who had failed in the criminal courts, show a similar decrease. In the Munsif's courts at Gumlā and Khunti the number of title suits fell from 137 and 244 in 1907 to 62 and 70 in 1910, respectively, and the average number of suits filed annually during the last four years is only 72 at Gumlā and 74 at Khunti. Suits for arrears of rent, which formerly involved protracted disputes as to the amount of rent and *rukumāts*, are now easily disposed of at a single hearing, the only question to be decided being whether the rent has been actually paid or not, and, as most of the landlords are now in the habit of granting receipts, this question is easily settled. Litigation is in fact no longer the gamble which it formerly was. Both landlords and tenants are, on the whole, satisfied with the result of the operations, though some landlords no doubt consider that they have been deprived of their prescriptive rights while some missionaries and other friends of the raiyats consider that more might have been done to restore the ancient status of the cultivators. The raiyats, appreciating the security of their tenure, are taking steps to improve their lands, and there is reason to hope that the next half century will see a great improvement in the methods of agriculture.

Apart from the Settlement operations, other important steps were taken to improve the administration of the district. It was realized that the outlying parts of the district were so far distant from the headquarters at Rānchi that the people preferred to submit to any compromise rather than undertake the trouble and expense of making a long journey to the courts. The result was that the zamindārs and police were omnipotent in such out-of-the-way tracts as Barwe and Biru, and deeds of lawlessness were committed which were a disgrace to the administration. Murder cases and other very serious offences were usually brought before the courts, but offences of lesser magnitude went unpunished. Even murders were frequently concealed. The control over the police was so ineffective that they were the real rulers of the country. The Chaukidāri force was equally corrupt and was responsible for many of the cases of *dakaiti*, theft, or burglary. In order to bring the administration of justice nearer to the homes of the people, the Gumlā subdivision was opened in November 1902, and the Khunti subdivision three years later, in December 1905. The areas included in these subdivisions which were formerly hotbeds of lawlessness may now be said to be among the most peaceable and law-abiding parts of the Province.

Recently a further step has been taken to improve the administration of the district. The Gumlā subdivision proved too large for efficient administration and the southern portion of the district has been formed into a subdivision with head-quarters at Simdega, a few miles south of Biru.

Removal of German Missionaries.

The outbreak of war between England and Germany in 1914 rendered it necessary to take precautionary measures against the missionaries of the Lutheran Mission who were resident of the district. Soon after the outbreak of war, those missionaries who were of military age were recalled to the head quarters of the Mission at Rānchi and not permitted to take any part in the missionary work. The older missionaries, many of whom had spent the greater part of their lives in Chotā Nāgpur, were allowed to remain in their mission stations and were placed on parole. In 1915, in accordance with the decision of the Government of India to intern or repatriate all German subjects, the missionaries were removed from the district, those of military age were sent to the concentration camp at Ahmadnagar, with the older missionaries with the women and children were detained for a few months at Dinapore, and later repatriated to Germany. Though the missionaries have been removed the work of the Mission still continues; the educational side of the work being supervised by the Bishop of Chotā Nāgpur and by members of the S. P. G. Mission, while the parochial work is carried on by the Indian pastors and catechists.

CHAPTER.

THE PEOPLE.

Census.

THE first attempt at an enumeration of the people was made by Captain Depree at the time of the Topographical Survey of Chotā Nāgpur in 1868. The population of 128 houses, selected at random, was found to be 811, yielding an average of 6·34 persons a house. The number of houses, ascertained by the survey to be 139,116, was multiplied by this factor, and the total population of Chotā Nāgpur, with an area of 7,120 square miles, was estimated to be 881,995 persons. In 1872 a careful census was made by a special salaried agency under the supervision of the regular police. Owing to the sparseness of the population no attempt was made to effect a simultaneous census but a gradual enumeration was carried out. The total population of that part of the Lohardagā district which now forms the district of Rānchi was found to be 813,328, or 115 persons to the square mile. The average number of persons per house was found to be 5·1, a fact which accounts for the higher figure obtained at the rough census of 1868. In 1881 the first regular simultaneous census was carried out and the total population was found to be 1,058,169. At the subsequent censuses of 1891, 1901 and 1911 the population was 1,128,885, 1,187,925 and 1,387,516.

Density and growth of population.

The density of the population at the census of 1911 was 195 to the square mile, as against 166 in 1901, 158 in 1891, and 148 in 1881. It diminishes from the north-east to the south, south-west and west, the Rānchi subdivision having 256, the Khunti subdivision 226, and the Gumlā subdivision only 146 persons to the square mile. The population is most dense in thanas Rānchi (367), Silli (324), and Bundu (321), and least dense in thanas Bishunpur (77), Kolebirā (115) and Kurdeg (116). In spite of the drain caused by increasing emigration, the population of

Rānchi grew steadily between 1881 and 1901, the increase being 6·7 per cent. during the first decade and 5·2 per cent. during the second. The growth during the ten years ending in 1901 was retarded by several years of bad harvests and general depression, actual famine prevailing in some parts in 1897 and 1900, when the flood of emigration was greatly increased. After allowing for the effects of emigration, it was estimated that the true increase of population was about 13 per cent. The decade ending in 1910 was a period of agricultural prosperity broken only by one bad year. In the first five years good crops enabled the people to recover from the effects of the famine of 1900. A bumper harvest followed 1906 in leading to heavy exports, but the people, with the improvidence characteristic of aboriginals, squandered their gains and were left with little to tide over the scarcity of 1907-08. Famine was declared in the west of the district, but elsewhere the people managed to hold out with the assistance of loans. In 1908 the crop was fair, but the mortality was very heavy, for distress lowered the general vitality of the people and diminished their power of resistance to disease. Cholera and small-pox broke out in epidemic form and caused nearly 10,000 deaths between them, and the death-roll from fever was also heavy. The birth-rate was high throughout the period and was in excess of the death-rate in every year except 1908 and the net result was an excess of births over deaths amounting to 196,000. The total addition to the population was 190,591 or 16·8 per cent., a large increase which must be attributed to the increased prosperity of the people, the high birth-rate natural to prolific aboriginal races, and improved enumeration in tracts previously difficult of access.

Emigration. The opening of the Purulia-Rānchi Railway has greatly facilitated emigration, and emigrants at the census of 1911 outnumbered immigrants by 271,666, while the number of persons born in the district but resident elsewhere was in 1911 30,058 more than in 1901. No less than 99,000 persons born in the district were engaged in clearing land and cultivating tea in Jalpaiguri, while there were 92,000 emigrants from Rānchi to Assam. The readiness of the people of the district to emigrate is explained by three factors, *viz.*, that the aboriginal inhabitants are multiplying rapidly, they pursue an uneconomic system of cultivation, and they have thriftless habits. The Mundā or the Orāon is not industrious and takes little thought for the morrow ; what savings he makes in a good year are spent at the local liquor shop, and when a period of stress occurs he has little to fall back upon and is forced to seek for remunerative employment outside the district. The soil of the district is generally poor and unfertile and, though new areas are being constantly opened up, the increase in cultivation does not keep pace with the increase in population. Often too the aboriginal who has been deprived of his ancestral land by a rapacious landlord wishes to earn money to enable him to bring a law suit, to repurchase his farm, or to acquire new land in the vicinity. Formerly, too, there was considerable migration across the border into the adjacent Feudatory States, the aboriginals being anxious to take up new land in these undeveloped parts and escape from the oppression of their landlords. The Settlement operations, however, have given the raiyats greater security of tenure and stopped this cause of migration.

Towns and villages.

The only three towns in the district are Rānchi, Lohardagā, and Bundu. The population of Lohardagā is practically stationary, though the opening of the railway may lead to an increase in the next decade. The population of Rānchi has risen from 18,443 in 1881 to 32,994 in 1911 and has increased still further since it became the temporary headquarters of the Government of Bihar and Orissa. The population is almost entirely immigrant, and consists for the most part of the persons who have been attracted by the work of the courts and Government offices or by trade. Bundu, which is a large market and the centre of the lac industry, has a growing population which has risen from 5,469 in 1901 to 6,950 in 1911. The remainder of the population lives in 3,925 villages, of which 3,152 have a population of less than 500, but even this figure does not give a correct idea of the nature of the village. For census purposes the *mauza*, or settlement village, was taken as the unit, and the *mauza* often comprises a very large area and consists of numerous scattered *tolas* which contain only two or three houses apiece. The villages are generally built on a ridge or near the crest of a slope. They consist of a cluster of mud-huts huddled together in the most perfect disorder. Winding alleys and pathways, often leading to an infinite series of *cul-de-sacs*, form the only thoroughfares. In the rains they become extraordinarily filthy, manure pits surround the houses, and every pit and ditch, filled with stagnant water, forms a fine wallowing ground for the pigs which abound in every aboriginal village. In the centre of the village there is usually a large tree and near it the *akhrā* or dancing ground. Immediately outside the village is the *sarnā,* or grove sacred to the village deity. In many villages the *sarnā* consists of only one or two large *sāl* trees, the sole survivors of the primeval forest. Ancient custom forbids anyone, even the Bhuinhārs of the village, to cut the wood, and even if a branch falls, it can only be taken on payment of the price to the Pāhān or Māhto of the village. In Mundā villages a conspicuous object on the outskirts of the village is the group of monoliths, which form the *sasān* or burial-ground of the Bhuinhārs.

The houses are built of mud with a roof of tiles or thatch. In the central plateau, where the people are more prosperous and jungle products less easily obtainable, tiles have displaced thatch, but in the more jungly parts of the district thatched houses are common, and often a wall of saplings plastered over with mud or cowdung replaces the mud-wall. The average house consists of three buildings, one of which is the sleeping apartment, one a kitchen and the third a cattle shed. In the houses of the Mundās, the *māndi ōra,* or eating-room, includes also the *ading* or shrine where the spirits of deceased ancestors are worshipped. The rooms are arranged on three sides of a quadrangle, and on the fourth side there is the *bāri* or garden, used for the cultivation of vegetables and spices. Before building a house, the site has to be carefully selected, and it is the custom of the Orāons and of some other tribes to put a few grains of rice on the intended site ; next morning the householder returns, and if he finds that the rice has disappeared, having been eaten by white-ants or birds, he abandons the site as ill-omened ; if it is untouched, he begins to build. In the villages inhabited by Hindus, more elaborate houses are found, built of sun-dried bricks and decorated with crude drawings of animals or gods.

The furniture of a cultivator's house is scanty. A few mats woven from palm leaves by the women form the only beds ; in the houses of well-to-do raiyats a *khātiā,* or string bedstead, and a *mānchi,* or string stool may be found. Brass utensils, such as *tharis* and *chipnis* (plates), *dubhās* (cups) and *lōtās* (jugs) are purchased by those who can afford to do so. The poorer classes have to be content with the earthen pots made by the local Kūmhār, such as the *gharā,* a large vessel used for drawing and storing water and the *chūkā*, used for the same purposes as the *lotā*. Bamboo baskets of various sizes and shapes are used for storing grain, and *pitis*, or boxes of split bamboo, for storing the precious records of law suits and other cherished possessions.*

Over nearly the whole of the Rānchi district the language of the settled Aryans is a corrupt form of the Bhojpurī dialect of Biharī, which has undergone modifications partly by the influence of the Magahi dialect, which surrounds it on three sides, and of the Chhattīsgarhi spoken to its west, and partly owing to the influx of words into its vocabulary which belong to the languages of the non-Aryan population. The dialect is generally known as Nāgpuriā, or the language of Chotā Nāgpur proper.† It is locally known as Sadān or Sadri and is called by the non-Aryan Mundās "Dikkū Kāji," or the language of the Dikkū or Aryans. On the east of the district, in the sub-plateau area of the Five Parganas, the language is not Nāgpuriā but is a form of Magahī, known as Pānch Parganiā. In the south-east corner of the district a colony of Jains speak the variety of western Bengali known as Sarāki. Finally in the north of the district a colony of 20,000 immigrants from Hazāribāgh still speak Magahī, the language of their mother-country. The following table taken from the Linguistic Survey of India shows the languages of the Rānchi district and the number of persons speaking them at the time that the Survey was made :— Languages. Nāgpuriā.

Name of language.	Spoken by
Bengali—	
Sarākī	48,127
Bihārī—	
Standard Magahī	20,141
Pānch Parganiā Magahī	8,000
Nāgpuriā Bhojpurī	297,585
Mundā Languages	406,086
Dravidian Languages	325,860
Other Languages	23,086

* A detailed account of the houses of the Mundās and of the household utensils and agricultural instruments used by them will be found in "The Mundās and their Country" by Mr. Sarat Chandra Roy. Mr. Roy has also published a similar book about the Orāons. A collection of articles in common use among the Mundās and Orāons has been made by Mr. Roy for Government and will be placed in the Patna Museum.

† Nagpuriā has the advantage of being well illustrated by the Rev. E. H. Whitley whose "Notes on Nāgpuriā Hindu" has recently been republished. The gospels have been translated into Nāgpuriā by the Rev. P. Eidnæs.

The languages of the aboriginal tribes of the district may be divided into two classes, those which belong to the Mundā family of language and those which belong to the Dravidian family. The late Professor Max Muller was the first to distinguish between these two families and to designate the languages spoken by the Mundās, Santāls, Hos, Bhumij, etc., as the Mundā family. Various other suggestions have been made for the designation of these languages and they have been called by other authorities Kolarian or Kharwarian. Sir George Grierson in the Linguistic Survey of India has adopted the denomination introduced by Max Muller and places in the Kharwāri group of the Mundā family the following languages spoken in the Rānchi district:— Mundārī, Birhōr, Tūrī, and Asurī.

Mundāri. Mundārī is spoken by rather more than half a million people, of whom 350,000 are in the Rānchi district. It is spoken by 94 per cent. of the Mundā race and also by the inferior artisan castes living in the Mundā villages, such as the Pāns and Lohrās. The most idiomatic Mundāri is spoken in the Mānkipatti, south-east of the town of Rānchi. The Orāons in the neighbourhood of Rānchi town also speak a form of Mundārī which is known as the *Horo-liā-jhagar.**

Tūri. The Tūrī language agrees with Mundāri in most essential points, though in a few characteristics it follows Santāli. At the census of 1911 it was spoken by 2,300 persons.

Asuri. Asurī, the dialect of the Asurs, according to information collected for the Linguistic Survey, was spoken by 8,000 persons, but according to the figures of the recent census only by 3,100. This language, with the kindred dialect of Agāriā which was spoken only by 40 persons in 1911, appears to be rapidly dying out. Closely akin to Asurī is Korwā, the language of the Korwās, who are found principally in the west of the district and in the bordering district of Palāmau and the states of Jashpur and Surguja. According to the census of 1891 it was spoken by 5,000 persons in Rānchi district alone, but by 1911 the number had fallen to 1,200. In all the Kharwāri group of the Mundā

* The most important grammar of the Mundāri language is by the Rev. J. Hoffman, S.J., who has also published a Mundāri First Reader. The Bible has been translated into Mundāri by the Rev. Dr. Nottrott, formerly Head of the G. E. L. Mission.

family, the whole character of the language has been preserved with great fidelity, though Aryan principles have of late begun to influence the grammar.

Khariā. Included also in the Mundā family is the Khariā language, which has been largely influenced by Aryan languages and has been described as like a palimpsest, the original writing on which can only be recognized with difficulty. At the time of the Linguistic Survey, Khariā was spoken by about 80,000 persons, of whom 68,000 were inhabitants of this district. At the census of 1911 it was returned as the language of 57,000 persons in the district.

Kūrūkh. Kūrūkh, the language of the Orāons, belongs to the Dravidian family which includes all the languages of Southern India. At the census of 1901 the language was found to be spoken by 585,000 persons in the districts now included in Bengal, Bihar and Orissa and Assam, of whom 315,000 were inhabitants of the Rānchi district. At the census of 1911 the numbers had risen to 677,000 and 358,000, respectively, the increase being probably due to the greater accuracy of the returns and not to any actual increase in the number of speakers. The Orāons, especially the men, usually know Nāgpuriā though they speak Kūrūkh in their own homes.*

Tribes and Castes. The population of the district may be subdivided into pure Hindus and Muhammadans, semi-aboriginal castes claiming to be Hindus, and aboriginal tribes. The Hindus, who number 550,715, represent the settlers from Northern India, Bihar, and Bengal, who were introduced by the early Rājās of Chotā Nāgpur, or who migrated in large numbers to the country during the early years of the last century. The principal Hindu castes are Brāhman (10,146), Rājputs (23,318), Kāyasth (3,569), Teli (28,662), Kurmi (56,335), Koiri (8,101), Goālā (Ahir) (41,617), Sunri (6,431), Baniya (2,387), Chamār (4,256), Dhobi (5,536), Dosādh (4,269), Hajjām (9,038), Rauniār (Noniār) (9,095). The Brāhmans include a large number of Brāhmans from Orissa. The Kurmis include not only the Hindu cultivating caste but also the aboriginal tribe of Kurmi Mahtos, whose residence is chiefly in the Mānbhūm district, and also in Silli thana on the eastern border of the Rānchi district. Of the Muhammadans 22,882

* Rev. Ferd Hahn has published the following books on the Kūrūkh language; Kūrūkh Grammar, Calcutta, 1900; Kūrūkh-English Dictionary, Part I, Calcutta, 1903; Kūrūkh Folk-lore, collected and transliterated, Calcutta, 1905.

are Jolāhās, many of whom are no doubt descendants of persons who settled in the country at the time of the Mughal conquest; 5,111 are Pathāns, mostly itinerant traders and money-lenders, and 15,069 are Sheikhs. Of the semi-aboriginal tribes the most important are the Chik Barāiks, of whom 25,509 were classified as Hindus and 3,428 as Animists ; the Ghāsis (14,523 Hindus and 6,185 Animists); Gonds (8,258 Hindus and 259 Animists); Mahlis (16,897 Hindus and 5,114 Animists); Pāns (14,051 Hindus and 649 Animists); and the Lohārs (30,317 Hindus and 16,055 Animists). Separate figures have not been given in the census statistics of 1911 for the Bhogtās, Jhorās, Rautiās and Gorāits who, though probably non-Aryan, claim to be, and are recognized as, Hindus. At the census of 1901, there were 17,294 Bhogtās, of whom only 12 were classified as Animists, 2,208 Jhorās, 20,301 Rautiās, and 6,277 Gorāits, all of whom were classified as Hindus. The principal aboriginal tribes are the Mundās, Orāons, Khariās, Tūris, Asūrs, Korwās, Birhors and Nāgesias ; the three first mentioned tribes alone numbering over 800,000.

ABORIGINAL TRIBES.
The Mundās.

The Mundās are the most numerous of the Kolarian tribes inhabiting the Chotā Nāgpur Division. In the census of 1911 the total number of Mundās in the Rānchi district was 343,721, of whom 66,992 were returned as Christians, 56,720 as Hindus and 220,009 as Animists. Although less numerous than the Dravidian Orāons, the Mundās have a universally admitted precedence over the other aboriginals in virtue of their older occupation of the country, their traditions of rule in it, and their establishment of the Nāgbansi Mahārājās. The great bulk of the Mundās occupy the southern, south-western, and eastern parts of the district. They are most numerous in Khunti and Tamār thanas, where they form nearly 75 per cent. of the total population.

Name.

The Mundās call themselves *Horo-ko* (men) and their race the *Horo* (man), and the word Mundā is the title of the temporal headman of the village or, if used as an adjective, means rich or influential. As the Mundā was the official who represented the tribe in their dealings with their Hindu neighbours, the title came to be used by them to designate the tribe. The name Kol was, and is, often used to designate the Mundās and other allied tribes but, whatever the origin of the word may be, it has acquired an opprobrious suggestion and is strongly resented by the Mundās themselves.

Appearance, Dress and Character.

The Mundās are one of the darkest races in India, the colour of the skin being a black-brown, often of a shade approaching black. The head is long, the nose is thick and broad and sometimes depressed at the root, the lips thick and the cheek bones prominent. In build they are stout and muscular and in stature somewhat below medium height.* Both men and women when young may be described as comely, and their cheerful laughing countenances are far from displeasing. The dress of the Mundās is very simple and scanty ; the men ordinarily wear a loin-cloth, with a coloured border at the two ends, called *botoi,* and use a piece of cloth as a wrapper for the upper portion of the body, known as *barkhi* or *pichowri.* The women wear a long piece of cloth, called *pāriā,* round the waist allowing a portion of it to pass diagonally over the upper part of the body. Shoes are seldom worn, and the head is usually uncovered, though well-to-do Mundās wear *pāgris.* In the rains they often carry bamboo-umbrellas (*chātōm*) or wear circular rain-hats, called *chūkūri* and made of leaves of a creeper found in the jungles. Both the young men and young women are very fond of personal decoration. A young man wears round the waist a sort of belt made of cocoon-silk or plaited thread (*kārdhāni*) and his long hair, well-oiled and combed, is tied up at the side in a knot, with a wooden hair-comb (*nāki*) stuck into it. Strings of coral or china beads or of silver four-anna pieces adorn his neck, and in times of festival flowers are used to decorate the hair or as garlands. The Mundā girls greatly appreciate jewellery and deck themselves out with ear-rings, necklets, bracelets and anklets of brass, or of some more precious metal, or of lac and coloured glass. The poorer Mundā women wear a peculiar ornament in the ear, called *tār-sākōm,* which consists of a roll of palm-leaf, dyed red and set off with tinsel and lac. The Mundās tattoo their girls by way of ornamentation; three parallel lines are pricked on the forehead and two lines on each of the temples; a few marks are made on the chin; the back, arms and hands are also tattooed. In former times Mundā boys were subjected

* Of the one hundred Mundā specimens measured by Sir Herbert Risley, the average head measurements are as follows :—Length, 185·9. Breadth, 138·6 and cephalic index, 74·5. The average dimensions of the nose were, height, 44·7; breadth, 40·2 ; nasal index, 89·9. The average stature was 158·9 centimetres.

to the Spartan treatment of having their arms burnt with a red-hot iron rod, the circular marks being regarded as a decoration, but this custom is now falling into disuse. The chief characteristics of the Mundā race may be said to be their conservatism and their instinctive antipathy to aliens. The best qualities of a Mundā are his keen sense of self-respect, his love of truth and honesty, and his courage; his worst qualities are his inordinate love of drink and his improvidence. Intercourse with foreigners, and in particular the evil surroundings of the law courts, have done much to contaminate him, and the Mundā has often been driven by injustice and oppression to use the methods of his adversaries against them. He is impetuous and sensitive, but repents a rash action committed on the spur of a moment. A Mundā who has killed a man in sudden anger often voluntarily gives himself up to justice and appears before the Magistrate with his blood-stained weapon still in his hand.

Tribal organization.

The Mundā tribe is divided into a number of exogamous clans, or septs, known as *kilis*. Though exogamous as regards the *kilis*, the Mundās are endogamous as regards other tribes, and marriage with members of other Kolarian tribes, such as the Santāls, Khariās, Asūrs, etc., is not permitted. The only exception to this rule is that the Mundās of Tamār still intermarry with the Bhumijs of Mānbhūm, who are in origin probably of the same race. The *kilis* are totemistic and derive their names from some natural object, such as an animal, bird, fish, reptile, or plant, and the members of the *kili* are forbidden to eat the totem after which it is named. When the Mundās first migrated into Chotā Nāgpur, the number of *kilis* was no doubt comparatively small, but as they multiplied, the existence of a small number of large *kilis* became inconvenient, and new septs were formed. A few *kili* names are shared by the Mundās and Santāls and may be held to date back to the days when the two races were united, but the majority of the names are peculiar to the Mundās. Various legends are given by the Mundās themselves as to the origin of the totems of the different clans, thus the *Horo* or *Kachuā kili* owes its origin to the fact that the ancestor of the clan was assisted to cross a swollen stream by a giant *kachua* or tortoise; the ancestor of the *Nāg Kili* was a snake-charmer and, when he died while returning from a distant village, the snake coiled itself round his body and carried it back to his family, who out of gratitude kept the snake in their house and gave it plenty to eat and drink.

According to Mundā tradition, all the members of a *kili* are descended from a common ancestor; descent is counted through the father, and the children belong to the paternal *kili*. The possession of the same *kili* name is, therefore, the first proof of membership in a given clan or family. There is also a religious bond between members of a *kili*, consisting of a communion in the same sacrificial offerings. Members of one *kili* may on no account partake of the offerings made by members of a different *kili*. As during life members of a *kili* are united by a common name and by common sacrifices, so after death they are united in a common burial ground. Every *kili* has its own burial ground, or *sasān*, and the bones of every member of the family, even if he may happen to die away from the village, are, on the occasion of the annual festival, called the *jāng-tōpā*, placed beneath the stone slab, or *sāsāndiri*, of his clan. The well-known saying "*Sasāndiriko-Hoɩ onkoāpatā*" (their burial stones are the title-deeds of the Mundās) owes its origin to this custom, and a Mundā can only prove that he is a member of a particular clan or of a particular village community by proving that the bones of his ancestors were buried under the *sāsāndiri* of the clan.

The social system of the Mundās being of the patriarchal type, the head of the family is at the same time the priest of the family, who, in case of illness or distress, has to offer sacrifices to propitiate the domestic and other *bōngās* (spirits). But the village community being composed of families descended from common ancestors looks on it itself as a family, and hence requires a special representative to exercise over the whole village functions similar to those exercised by the head of the family in the household. This representative is called the ***Pāhān***, and his functions were originally both religious and civil. His religious functions, which were the more important, consisted in offering the public sacrifices to propitiate the local spirits, and so to preserve the village from the ravages of wild animals, to obtain good harvests and to ensure successful hunts. As the civil head of the village, he had to preside over the *panchāyats* for the settlement of disputes, inflict punishment for breaches of tribal custom and collect and transmit the quit-rent due to the proper authorities. In these civil functions he was assisted by the next most prominent member of the community, the Mundā. The functions of the Mundā and Pāhān gradually became distinct, the Pāhān devoted himself to the religious duties, while the Mundā undertook the more distasteful civil duties which involved intercourse with aliens and foreign landlords.

In course of time, as the number of members of each *kili* increased and one village proved insufficient for the residence and cultivation of all, some members were forced to move away and form new villages in the neighbourhood of the parent village. At first they shared the *sasān* of the parent village and joined in the public sacrifices at the *sarnā*, or sacred grove, but later instituted their own sacrifices and made their own *sasān*. Though separate in these respects, the daughter and parent villages still continued to act together in social and administrative matters and the group of allied and associated villages was constituted into a *parhā* or *patti*, the latter being the name given to the organization by the Nāgbansi Rājās. The head of the *parhā* was the *Mānki*, whose functions in respect of the group were similar to those of the Mundā in respect of the village. This organization exists to the present day, but in two different forms, according to the area in which it is found. East of thana Khuntī is the Khuntkātti area and west the Bhūinhāri area. The Bhūinhāri area may be said to show the social organization of the *pārhā* in its purest form, while the Khuntkātti area shows the clearest examples of the political organization of the *patti*. In the former each *parhā* consists of eight to twelve villages; all the *bhūinhārs*, or descendants of the original settlers, in these villages being members of the same *kili*. All trace of the Mānki has disappeared, doubtless owing to the length of time since the Hindu landlords destroyed their independence, arrogated to themselves the functions of the Mānki, and discontinued the use of the title. In each *parhā* there is a standing committee, or *panchāyat*, with permanent officers, whose titles, such as Rājā, Dīwān, Thākūr, Lāl Pānde, and Kartā, have been borrowed from their Hindu neighbours. Complaints are lodged to the Rājā or Dīwān by the Mundā or Pāhān of the village in which the offence has been committed, and orders are given to the Pānde to convoke the assembly. All members of the *kili* are entitled to attend. The proceedings are opened with a feast and there are certain officers to whom special duties are assigned, thus the "*Sākām-hcānī*" gathers the sāl leaves which serve as plates, the *Chārichātāni* makes the leaf-cups for drinking, the *pān khāwās* distributes the lime and tobacco and *pān*. The Rājā, as president, explains the complaint or cause of dispute to the assembly and, after evidence and statements have been taken, pronounces their decision. The most common causes of complaint are offences against the marriage laws; if the offender is repentant and promises to leave the woman, he is let off after having drunk the blood of a white he-goat or a white cock. Otherwise, he is fined, the fine being realised by the Diwān and his *sipāhis*; if he refuses to pay, he is beaten and out-casted. Apart from complaints of this kind, the *panchāyat* is often convened to discuss questions of social custom, such as the abolition of *jatrās* and dances, in view of the immorality to which they lead, or matters of political importance, such as the *Sārdari Lārai*, a movement which aimed at the expulsion of all Hindu zamindārs.

In the Khuntkātti area the title of Mānki still survives and the *pattis* of which the area was composed consist of ten to twelve villages. The *pattis* are for the most part broken up, except in the locality known as the *Mānkipatti*. Unlike the Bhūinhāri area, the *patti* is not composed exclusively of members of the same *kili*. There is no standing committee and there are no permanent officials, and the *panchāyat* is composed, when occasion requires, of the two headmen of the villages included in the *patti*, under the presidency of the Pat Mundā, or occasionally of the Mānki. The proceedings differ little from those of the *parhā panchāyat* in the Bhūinhāri area which have been already described.

In the case of minor disputes, a private *panchāyat*, consisting generally of members of the same *kili*, is convened by the aggrieved persons. A president, or *sir panch*, is elected, and he, with the aid of two assessors selected by each party, decides the question at issue. In former times the decision of a *panchāyat* was regarded by the Mundās as inspired and not to be disregarded, but now a party dissatisfied with the decision seeks his remedy in the courts. As at the *parhā panchāyat* a feast is a necessary preliminary and is provided by the parties. Oaths and ordeals are sometimes used to detect guilty persons. In the *lolo-dā*, or hot-water ordeal, the suspected persons are required to pick a coin out of a vessel of boiling water, the Mundā believing that the hand of the innocent man will be unscathed, while that of the guilty will be scalded. In boundary disputes a curious ordeal is sometimes practised; a hole is dug on each of the boundary lines claimed by the two parties and is filled with powdered rice; a representative of each party then has one leg buried in the hole, and the false claimant is the one who is first compelled by exhaustion or the biting of ants and other insects to cry out to be released.

Marriage Customs.

In the old days a Mundā youth was not considered old enough to marry till he could fashion a plough with his own hands, and a Mundā maiden till she could weave a palm-leaf mat and spin cotton, and in those days the young men were left free to select their brides. In modern days the marriage is generally arranged by the parents or guardians, though the consent of the boy is frequently sought for and obtained. A go-between (*dūtām*) is sent to the guardians of the girl, and if the answer is favourable, the *dūtām* and the boy's guardian and friends, and sometimes the boy himself, start for the girl's village, and on their way keep a sharp look-out for good or bad omens. This observation of omens is known as *chenre-uri*, which etymologically has the same meaning as "augury". If they meet unfavourable omens, such as a person carrying an axe, spade, or shovel; a cow lowing, but not in response to her calf; sweepings being thrown away from a house; rice being carried; clothes being washed with ashes, etc., the whole matter is at an end; but if the omens are good and they hear a cow and calf lowing in response to each other, or see a person carrying paddy, clean clothes, or a pitcher of water, or making a plough or yokes, or meet a tiger, they proceed to their destination, where they are hospitably entertained, and in return invite the girl's guardians to their village. During the journey of the girl's relatives, a similar observation of omens is made, and if all is favourable, the *joārni*, or spokesman for the bride's party, makes a set speech beginning: "Now for this boy and this girl, in the presence of Sing Bōngā in heaven and the Panch on earth, the omens have been all right", and ending: "To-day the boy's father and the girl's father will thatch two roofs with one bundle of straw (*i.e.*, become members of one family). May the roofs ever remain thatched like this". The next ceremony is the *bālā* or betrothal, at which after the usua feast the bride-price is settled, not by naming the demand, but by symbols. Thus the number of clay marbles and *sāl* leaves given to the bridegroom's father represent the number of rupees and *sāris* which the bride's father requires, and the number sent back represent the amount which the former is willing to give. The terms being agreed upon, the ceremony is completed by the Mundā or Pāhān of the bride's village clasping the hand of the Mundā or Pāhān of the bridegroom's village and both agreeing to pay a fine if the betrothal is broken. The bridegroom now sits on the knees of the bride's maternal uncle or of the Mundā or Pāhān of her village and receives a new piece of cloth and a necklace from the bride's father. The ceremony of presenting the bride-price (*Gōnongtākā Iditūkā*) and of selecting the day (*lōgōntōl*) usually take place at the same time. The betrothed girl sits on the knee of the boy's maternal uncle, while a girl friend sits on the knee of the Mundā or Pāhān of the boy's village, and "gives *lōgōn*" by handing some rice, turmeric, and betel-nut spread on a new cloth to him. Last comes the *ārāndi* or marriage ceremony proper. For three days before the marriage, the bride and bridegroom sit for a short time on the *māndōā*, a rectangular mud platform, with *sāl* saplings at the four corners and saplings of *sāl*, bheloā and bamboo in the centre, erected in their respective homes, and are anointed with mustard-oil mixed with turmeric juice by a female relative. On the evening before the wedding comes the *chūmān* ceremony, at which the bridegroom clad in a cloth dyed with turmeric juice, is touched on the feet, thighs, shoulder-joints, and cheeks by his female relatives who hold some rice in their folded hands. A similar benediction ceremony takes place at the bride's house. The marriage procession next starts from the bridegroom's house and the bridegroom, if he can afford it, is carried in a *pālki* or, failing that, on the arms of his relatives till the limits of the village are reached. At the first mango tree the procession halts for the *ūli-sākhi* ceremony, at which the bridegroom receives the blessing of his mother. At the confines of the bride's village, her relatives meet the procession with music and dancing, and the parties join, walk round the boundary of the village, and proceed to the bride's house. In the courtyard the bride's mother and her female relatives sprinkle the boy with water and again perform the *chūmān* ceremony. The bride is brought out in a bamboo basket and carried three times round the bridegroom's *pālki*. Bride and bridegroom then throw three handfuls of rice at each other's foreheads and are conducted into the house. Next the bride has an *ūli-sākhi*, in which she makes the mango tree a witness to the marriage by marking it with flour and tying a thread round it. In the morning the preliminary ceremony of *sasāng-goso*, or anointing with oil and turmeric, is performed, both bride and bridegroom being anointed by the female relatives of the other, and each in turn having a little blood drawn from the finger. The blood is put on a rag, called *sinūi*. In the forenoon, having been carried by their relatives three times round the *māndoā*, they are made to stand upon a large plate of *sāl* leaves, the bridegroom facing west and the bride facing east. He presses the toes of her left foot with the toes of his right foot, and three times touches his neck and that of the bride with the blood-stained rag. They change positions, and the bride does the same with her rag. Reverting to their positions, they exchange garlands of flowers, and each places three vermilion marks first on his, or her own forehead, and then on the forehead of the other. This is the binding part of the ceremony. Their garments are then knotted together and they are conducted into the house, the bride walking behind her lord, who has to pay toll to the bride's elder sister before he obtains entry. Four maidens, two from each party accompanied by Ghāsi musicians, now proceed to the nearest spring followed by the other women. The maidens fill their *gharās* with water, and place them on their heads. Two elderly women, one carrying a sword, and the other a bow and arrow, stand with their backs to the water-carriers, and pass the sword and arrow back over the neck so as to touch the jars of water. The procession then returns to the house, the woman with the sword brandishing and whirling her weapon, and the other women imitating her. The maidens next pour the water over the bride and bridegroom, who in fresh array are seated on a straw-covered plough-yoke in the courtyard. Having again assumed their yellow garments and daubed one another's forehead with *sindūr*, the young couple sit down upon a mat in the courtyard. Ceremonial water is given to the bridegroom and a sword is put into his hand, with which he kills a goat. Amidst much ceremony and consumption of rice-beer, the fathers of the bridegroom and bride drink from the same cup **and** embrace one another; the mothers do likewise, and there is mutual felicitation. Bride and bridegroom then wash the feet of the guests who place on a brass plate their wedding gifts, usually in cash, each paying from two pice to a rupee. At the bridal feast, the bridegroom places a *sāl* leaf beside each guest, and the bride puts a pinch of salt on it. Both sit beside the Mānki, or senior village official wash his hands and serve salt to him. The men having dined, the women sit down to their meal. Before the departure of the bridegroom, the bride performs a curious ceremony. Seated with her back to her mother, who is seated on the threshold of her house, she throws three double handfuls of paddy over her shoulder to her mother, who catches it in her cloth. She is then made over to the bridegroom by the Mundā or Pāhān of the village in presence of the Panch or assembled elders. The bridegroom is next compelled to pay toll to the bride's girl friends, and after a demonstrative leave-taking, he carries away his bride by the mode of conveyance in which he arrived. At his house the *chūmān* ceremony is again performed, and a dinner follows at which the bridal pair distribute salt to the guests. Next day a party of the bride's relatives come to be entertained, and a week or two later, when the bride's parents come to take the married couple to their village, their son-in-law uproots the saplings from the middle of the *māndōā*, and a sumptuous feast again takes place.

Family life is happy in the aboriginal tribes, the wife usually making herself a comrade to her husband. But divorce is not attended with many difficulties. If the husband will not maintain his wife, or if she refuses to live with him, a *panchāyat* of the relatives is held, and the person desiring the divorce, who selects three out of the five members, snaps a *sāl* leaf in token of the dissolution of the marriage. If the wife is the unwilling party, the bride-price is returned. Divorced persons and widows marry in the *sagāi* form which simply consists of a feast at the bride's house; and the issue of such marriage is legitimate. The same applies to most of the lower Hindu castes. The funeral ceremonies of the Mundās are described in the subsequent paragraph on their religion.

THE ORAONS.

The Orāons are the most numerous tribe in the district, and at the census of 1911 numbered 388,768, of whom 7,343 were classified as Hindus, 88,647 as Christians and 302,778 as Animists. They dwell principally in the west, north-west, and centre of the district, and also in Palāmau and the Feudatory States of Jashpur and Surguja, the total Orāon population of the province being over 640,000. Large numbers have migrated to the tea gardens of Assam and the Duars, and 90,000 were enumerated at the last census in Jalpaiguri district. Small colonies of the race are also found all over Bengal, and in parts of Tirhut where they work as labourers, and are known by the name of *dhāngars*, a Kūrūkh word signifying a "youth" and then "a youth who labours for another". *

Name.

Extremely little is known of the early history of this Dravidian tribe. They call themselves Kūrūkh, a name which is sometimes traced to one of their mythical kings called Karakh. It is more probable that it is derived from some obsolete Dravidian root, meaning "man," or it may possibly be connected with the Dravidian word *Karugu*, an eagle, and be totemistic in origin. Colonel Dalton was inclined to think that the name is derived from Konkan, which is supposed to have been the cradle of the race, Konkan having been converted into Kūrūkh owing to the Orāon partiality for gutturals. Another interpretation given by some literate Orāons themselves is that Kūrūkh is a variant of Coorg, where they formerly lived. The name "Orāon" is said by Colonel Dalton to have been given them as a nickname, perhaps because of their many migrations and partiality to roam, and, according to Sir George Grierson, the Hindus say that the word "Orāon" is simply the Indo-Aryan "Uran," a spendthrift, the name being an allusion to the alleged thriftless character of the people. Dr. Hahn agrees that the name was coined by the Hindus, but considers that it is based on *orgora*, a Kūrūkh word for "hawk," the totem of one of the septs.

Early History.

It is probable that the Orāons originally came from Southern India, as philologists have traced in the language of the Kanarese and other Tamulian languages a close resemblance to the Kūrūkh tongue. Another theory that has been put forward is that the Orāons accompanied the Mundās in their migrations from the

* Colonel Dalton interpreted the name as "hillman" and derived it from "Dang" or "Dhang," a hill.

north-west of India before the Aryan invaders; but this does not appear to be supported by either Mundā or Orāon tradition. Though the Orāon tradition agrees with the Mundā tradition in naming Azimgarh, Hardinagar, Pipragarh and finally Rohtāsgarh as homes of their race, it is possible that the tradition was merely borrowed from their neighbours. The most certain legend of the Orāons is that they dwelt in Rohtās, but were driven from the stronghold by a treacherous attack of their enemies, who took advantage of the drunken revelry in which they were engaged at the Sarhul festival. Who the enemy were is uncertain. According to an explanation of some Orāons themselves, it was the Muhammadans, but as the Muhammadans did not conquer Bihar before 1193 A. D. and Rohtās before 1539 A. D., this is inconsistent with their own tradition that they were settled in Chotā Nāgpur long before the days of Phani Mukut Rai, the first Rājā. In other accounts they refer to the enemy as Mlechchhas, an appellation given by the Hindus to all impure tribes; and, according to one theory, Mlechchhas were the Kharwārs or Cheros who at one time occupied the Rohtās plateau. There is, however, no doubt that Rohtās was once their home, as Orāons are still found in these hills. Dislodged from Rohtās, the tribe split up into two branches, one branch proceeded down the Ganges, settled in the Rājmahāl hills, and became the ancestors of the present Mālē tribe; another, and larger section, proceeded up the Son and then along the valley of the North Koel into Palāmau till they reached the highlands of Chotā Nāgpur, which they found already sparsely populated by Mundās. There is no tradition of war between the two tribes and, according to Mundā tradition, they allowed the Orāons to settle, on condition that they ate meat and discarded the sacred thread which they wore. According to Orāon tradition, they were the more civilized race and introduced the use of the plough and the construction of the terraced *don* lands. The Mundās gradually retreated before the more prolific and numerous Orāons and left them in undisputed possession of the north-west of the district. Like the Mundās, the Orāons formed their village communities into groups, known as *pārhās*, under the presidency of the headman of one of the villages, who was known as the *pārhā Rājā*, and the Orāon and Mundā *pārhās*, when the tribes were living together in the central plateau, elected one of their chiefs to be the Rājā of the country.

Appearance and characteristics.

The colour of most Orāons is the darkest brown, approaching to black; the hair is jet black, coarse, and rather inclined to be frizzy. Projecting jaws and teeth, thick lips, low narrow foreheads, broad flat noses, are features which strike a careful observer as characteristic of the tribe.* The eyes are often bright and full, and no obliquity is traceable in the opening of the eyelids. The Orāons are of good physique, capable of carrying heavy burdens and travelling long distances. An Orāon can carry a load of two maunds thirty to thirty-five miles in a day and continue to do so for several days in succession. In character, the Orāons are cheerful and light-hearted; when young, they delight in physical exercise, especially dancing. On the occasion of their festivals the young men and maidens of an Orāon village spend two, three or more nights in dancing, with but short intervals for sleep. The worst vice of the Orāons is their improvidence and inordinate love of drink. They are not so conservative as the Mundās, and Colonel Dalton remarks on their adaptability to the ways and customs of the persons among whom they live. This adaptability is said even to change their outward appearance. Orāons who have lived long in the Duārs become tawny in complexion, while the Orāons themselves say that those who have lived long among Muhammadans grow beards and whiskers.

Dress.

The clothing of the Orāons is similar to that of the Mundās. Both sexes are extremely fond of ornaments. The young men adorn themselves with a girdle (*kārdhāni*) of twisted black cotton-thread, or silk, which also serves the useful purpose of carrying his keys, purse, lime box, and small iron pincers, or *chimta*, which are used for extracting thorns from the feet. Necklaces of coloured beads are often worn. The most noticeable ornaments of the women are the heavy brass bracelets on the arms, and the ornaments of various kinds which are thrust through the lobe of the ear. At their dances their head-dresses are often adorned with plumes of heron feathers.

* Of the one hundred Orāon specimens measured by Sir Herbert Risley the average head measurements are as follows:—Length, 184·6; breadth, 139·3; cephalic index, 75·4. The average dimensions of the nose, height, 46·2; breadth, 39·8; nasal index, 86·1. The average stature is 162·1 centimetres.

A peculiar feature of Orāon villages is the *dhūmkūriā* (*jōnkh-erpā* in Kūrūkh) or bachelors' hall, an interesting survival which is still found in the older villages. The Orāons are very reticent about this institution, but Mr. S. C. Roy of Rānchi has recently collected much information about this institution and its counterpart, the *pel-erpā* or maiden's dormitory. These institutions cannot be said to conduce to the morality of an Orāon village; they are gradually falling into disuse and are not countenanced in villages of which the inhabitants have become Christians. The inmates of the *dhūmkūriā* form a fraternity into which boys are admitted after curious ceremonies, and take a prominent part in many of the religious and social customs of the tribe. Its object appears to be to "make men" of the boys, to make them successful hunters and to train them in their social and other duties. It is undoubtedly a survival from the primitive days, when the tribe was dependent on hunting. Dhūmkūria.

Like the Mundās, the Orāons are divided into numerous exogamous septs, known as *gotras*, which take their names from some bird, fish, animal, plant or mineral. These totems are regarded as sacred by the sept named after them and are respected by them as ancestors: thus a *Panna* will not touch iron with his tongue or lip; a *Kujur* will not use oil made from the creepers of that name, a *Kispota* will not eat pigs' entrails; septs whose totem is an animal will not eat flesh of that animal, *e.g.*, *larka* (tiger), *kaya* (wild dog), *tiga* (field-mouse), *tirki* (young mouse), *orgora* (hawk), *toppo* (woodpecker), *minj* (eel). The sept name descends in the male line. There is no objection to a man marrying a woman belonging to the same sept as his mother, but generally marriage with a maternal aunt or first cousin on the mother's side is disallowed. Marriage with members of other tribes is entirely prohibited. At the head of the village community is the Pāhān or Baigā and the Māhto. The difference in the functions of these two officials is expressed by the Orāons in their saying *Pāhān gāon banāta hai, Māhto gāon chalāta hai, i.e.*, the Pāhān appeases the deities and demons of the village while the Mahto looks after its secular affairs. In some villages the Pāhān is a Mundā by caste and occasionally a member of some other aboriginal tribe, it being held by the Orāons that the descendant of the first settlers in a village is Organization.

better qualified to deal with the village gods. The duties of the Pāhān are the same as those of the Pāhān in a Mundā village, but whereas among the Mundās the office is hereditary and is held for life, among the Orāons the Pāhān is selected triennially from among the members of the Pāhān family or by means of the magic *sūp* or winnowing basket. The selection of the religious head of the village rests on the knees of the gods, and the *sūp* is used as a divining-rod to conduct the person holding it to the house of the man most fitted for the office. In some cases, after the proper ceremonies, a stone is rolled through the village, and he at whose door it stops is the fit person. The Pāhān has special lands assigned to him and is assisted in his religious functions by the *Pujār* or *Pānbhara,* whose duties are to carry water and cook on the occasion of village sacrifices.

The Māhto is also elected, usually triennially, from among the members of the Māhto khunt. In some villages where the Orāons have been driven by their zamindārs to abandon their customs, his election has to be approved by the zāmindar and in new villages he is almost a servant of the zāmindar.

As with the Mundās, groups of villages are united into *pārhās,* which must have been of considerable political and social importance in old days.

Panchāyats.

The *Parhā panchāyat* still survives ; it consists of the leading men from a group of villages, *e.g.*, the Pāhān, Māhto, and the leading *bhūinhārs* and *jeth* raiyats. It meets only once a year and deals with matters affecting whole villages and not merely individuals, such as matters of religion, dates of festivals, and also with disputes about the flags which each village has as its distinctive emblem. It also punishes villages which take an unfair advantage over their neighbours and do not observe the customary rules of sport on the occasion of the annual hunt. The *Panchora panchāyat* resembles more closely the *Pārhā panchāyat* of the Mundas : it is presided over either by a *Kartaḥā* or a *Mukhiā*. The office of the former is hereditary, that of the latter is only held as long as the holder is considered fit to perform the duties. It deals with grave offences against caste rules and tribal custom and also is a sort of court of appeal against the decisions of village *panchāyats.* An important function of the *panchora panchāyat* is to re-admit an out-caste into caste. After it has been decided to re-admit the out-caste and the fine which he is to pay has been fixed, the actual ceremony of re-admission takes place. The out-caste goes round and tells the members of the date of the assembly. He then fasts for a certain period, during which he is guarded by two *sipāhis*, who are specially deputed to see that he takes no food or drink except turmeric water. When the assembly meets, the *Kartahā* sacrifices a white cock or white goat, and the out-caste has to drink the blood. He then serves the *Kartahā* and each member of the assembly with food and pays the former his fee (*patri tāri*), which varies from Rs. 5 to Rs. 15. The *Kartahā* is the first to touch the food prepared by the out-caste, and the moment he raises it to his lips is the signal for all present to hurl their rice at his head. The *Kartahā* is thus a scape-goat who, on his return home, atones for having eaten the food of an out-caste by a feast to his caste men, paid for out of the fee which he has received.

The marriage ceremonies of the Orāons are generally similar to those of the Mundās which have already been described in detail. During the preliminary negotiations there is the same observation of omens, and, if the omens are inauspicious, the proposal is dropped. If all goes well, there comes the settling of the price or *pānbandhi*. At the actual marriage ceremony, the bride and bridegroom stand on a curry-stone under a bower, the boy touching the heels of the girl with his toes. A long piece of cloth is put round them to shield them from the public gaze, and the boy dips his finger into a cup of *sindūr* and makes three lines on the bride's forehead and the bride does, or attempts to do, the same to the bridegroom. Water is thrown over the couple, who retire into the house. A little later a special ceremony takes place to invoke the protection of the ancestors. The final ceremony is the *khiritengua handia*, at which the oldest member of the assembly as representing the *panchāyat*, solemnly addresses both bride and bridegroom and exhorts them to remain true to each other in sickness and in health. Marriage Ceremonies.

The Khariās are a Dravidian tribe, classed on linguistic grounds as Mundā. They are found scattered over a wide tract of country from the district of Bankura to the Chhattisgarh States, but their chief stronghold is in the south-western parganas of Rānchi district. The total Khariā population of the district KHARIAS.

is 50,710, of whom 19,273 are Christians; about 1,000 returned themselves as Hindus at the recent census.

Appearance and character.

In appearance the Khariās resemble the Mundās, but have rather coarser features and are not so well proportioned. In Singhbhūm and other districts, they are found in a very wild state, dwelling on the hills and in the jungles, but in Rānchi they have settled down to become cultivators. Though the settled Khariās of Rānchi are considerably in advance of the wild Khariās of the hills of Mānbhūm and Singhbhūm and are, on the whole, industrious cultivators, yet they have a bad reputation for intemperance and immorality, their dances on the occasions of their marriage ceremonies and festivals frequently degenerating into vicious orgies. Though not over-fastidious feeders, they are said to profess to be very exclusive in regard to cooking and eating, and Colonel Dalton writes of them as follows:—"This characteristic, I found, most developed in villages of Chotā Nāgpur, where Khariās are associated with Orāons under Brāhman proprietors. It is a common saying that every Khariā must have his own *hānria* or cooking pot. He may not even allow his own wife to cook for him, and, if a stranger enters a house in which he keeps his cooking pots, every vessel is polluted and the whole are destroyed or thrown away. This class of Khariās are specially filthy in their habits, and it is not improbable that Hindus may have been more than ordinarily harsh in excluding them from their kitchens and inner apartments and that the Khariās retaliated by out-casting everybody".

Origin.

According to one tradition, their ancestors were originally settled between Rohtās and Patna, but they quarrelled with their relations and fled into the jungles and wandered till they came to the Koel River, where, finding unoccupied lands to suit them, they settled first at a place called Pora on the river, whence they were driven into Biru and Kesalpur by the aliens who were granted farms of their villages. Another tradition is that they came from Mayurbhanj in the south and ascended the valley of the South Koel till they came to their present location. Colonel Dalton endeavoured to reconcile these traditions by the theory that they may have fallen back from the Gangetic province, passed through the Vindhya range and come gradually round to the south-east water-shed of Chotā Nāgpur, but legends of this kind, which often refer to comparatively recent migrations of a small portion of the race, are of doubtful value in giving any clue to their ancient history.

Organization.

The Khariās are divided into four sub-tribes, Dhilki-Khariā, Dudh-Khariā, Erengā Khariā and Mundā Khariā. The Dudh Khariās affect a leaning towards Hinduism and will not touch beef but will eat the flesh of the buffalo. They are also subdivided into numerous exogamous septs, all of which are totemistic, but the rule making the totem taboo is not universally observed. The Khariās have a *panchāyat* system similar to that of the Orāons. The chief functions of the *panchāyat*, which is not a permanent body, are to decide questions of caste custom, to re-admit persons who have been outcasted for a breach of caste custom, such as killing a cow or bullock among the Dudh-Khariā class, and to settle questions of inheritance.

Marriage customs.

Girls are usually married after the age of puberty, but infant marriage has been adopted by a few of the richer members of the tribes in imitation of the Hindu custom. The chief characteristic of the marriage ceremony is the revelry and dancing which takes place and which bears "more directly than delicately on what is evidently considered the main object of the festivities, the public recognition of the consummation of the marriage". After the preliminary negotiations by the parents, the bride is escorted to the bridegroom's house and is met by the bridegroom's party on the outskirts of the village. A revel takes place, and large quantities of *hānria* are drunk. Early next morning the bride and bridegroom are anointed with oil and taken to bathe. Five bundles of straw are placed on the ground, and the yoke of a plough is placed upon them. The bride and bridegroom stand facing each other on the yoke, and the bridegroom smears vermilion on the bride's forehead and the parting of her hair, while she makes a small round spot of the same colour on his forehead. This completes the marriage ceremony, and the parties sit down to feast at the bridegroom's expense. While the feast is going on, the bride is brought before the company and washes a cloth in hot water, in token, apparently, of her willingness to do any form of household work.

Religion.

The religion of the Khariās may be defined as a mixture of animism and nature worship. In many respects they have borrowed from the Orāons or Mundās and it is difficult to say what was the original belief of the tribe. The head of the religious system is Bar Pahāri, who appears to correspond to the Mundā Sing Bōngā or the Orāon Dharmes. Colonel Dalton also mentions the sun-god, under the name of Bero, to whom every head of a family must offer five sacrifices in his lifetime, the sacrifices being always made in front of an ant-hill as an altar. Other gods are those attached to certain places, such as Dorho Dubo, the god of the springs, Pat Dubo, the god who resides in rocky hills, Gumi, the god of the *sarnā* or sacred grove; while others have power to spread disease among persons or cattle, or to give good crops, and have to be appeased with sacrifices. For such sacrifices the Khariās employ the service of the Pāhān of the village, of whatever caste he may be. Like other tribes, they believe in the power of the spirits of deceased persons, especially those who have died a violent or unnatural death, to do harm and have recourse to the *sokha* or exorcist in the case of illness or trouble. Like other animistic tribes, the Khariās delight in dancing, and their festivals, like their marriage ceremonies, often degenerate into orgies.

Funerals. The Khariās observe a curious distinction in their funeral rites; the bodies of married people are burned while persons who die unmarried are buried. The ashes of the dead are put into an earthen vessel with some parched rice and thrown into a pool or tank, if possible, in the *bhuinhāri* village of the deceased.

Asurs. The Asurs, a small non-Aryan tribe, are found in the north-west of the district and live almost entirely by iron-smelting. They also practise a form of cultivation akin to *jhuming* on the *pāts*, or level hill-tops. Extremely little is known about the origin of this tribe. Colonel Dalton was inclined to connect these with the Asurs who, according to Mundā tradition, were destroyed by Sing Bōngā, and it has been conjectured that they are the descendants of the original inhabitants of the plateau, who were driven out by the Mundās and of whom the only traces now to be found are a few scattered *tumuli* and occasional stone or copper celts. Another conjecture is that they are a branch of the Mundās, who, like the Turis, split off from the rest of the tribe on account of their profession. Whichever theory is correct, it is certain that the Asurs resemble the Mundās both in appearance and language, and, like them, are divided into exogamous totemistic septs. Of their religion little is known; according to Colonel Dalton, they worship Sing Bōngā, and also the great hills, in which they dwell, under various names. At the census of 1911 there were 3,383 Asurs in the district, of whom 284 were classified as Hindus. The Agarias, who number only 250 persons, are probably akin to, and perhaps a sub-caste of, the Asurs.

The Turis are a non-Aryan caste of cultivators and bamboo-workers who, from their physical type, language and religion, appear to be an offshoot of the Mundās, and like the Mahlis and Lohrās, may have separated from the parent tribe owing to the profession which they follow. Sir Herbert Risley in the "Tribes and Castes of Bengal" says there are four sub-castes of Turis, *viz.*, Turis or Kisān Turi, Or, Dom, and Domrā, distinguished by the particular modes of basket and bamboo-work which they practise, but the two latter classes usually speak Hindi, are socially inferior to the Turis and Ors, have little resemblance, either in appearance or customs, to the Mundās and appear to be more akin to the Doms of Bihar. The Turis are divided into exogamous septs, which are for the most part totemistic and correspond closely with those in force among the Mundās. In religion they are becoming Hinduized, and at the census of 1911, 3,937 were classified as Hindus and 2,592 as Animists. The veneer of Hinduism, however, is slight and in many villages Turis are found holding the office of Pāhān, a fact which goes to show that they entered the district along with the Mundās. Large numbers of Turis have embraced the tenets of the deistic sect known as Sri-Nārāyani, but, though professing this religion, have not broken with their old belief and in cases of illness have recourse to the regular aboriginal methods of propitiating the spirit who is believed to be afflicting them. Turis will eat cooked food with Mundās and Orāons and are as lax as these tribes in the matter of diet. TURIS.

The Birhors are a jungly tribe with no fixed habitation, who roam from forest to forest, living on game and monkeys and by the manufacture of drums and the sale of jungle products. They speak almost pure Mundāri, and the fact that their name Birhor =jungle-men in Mundāri) includes the word *horo,* which the Mundās apply exclusively to themselves, points to their being an offshoot of that tribe that has preferred a wandering life in the jungles to the settled life of a cultivator. At the census of 1911, BIRHORS.

927 members of the tribe were found in the district, of whom 500 were classified as Animists and the rest as Hindus. In Risley's "Tribes and Castes of Bengal", their religion is said to be a mixture of Animism and Hinduism, and they are said to seek to harmonize the two systems by assigning to Devi the chief place in their Pantheon, and making out the animistic godlings to be her daughters and grand-daughters.

NAGESIAS. The Nāgesiās are a small tribe consisting of some 4,700 members, all of whom were classified as Hindus in the census of 1911. They are described by Colonel Dalton as of dark complexion, short stature and very ugly features, and are probably Dravidian in origin. They are found in remote jungly villages, and their sections bear totemistic names, such as are found among the Mundās and among many other Dravidian tribes. There are two subtribes, one of which uses vermilion in its marriage ceremonies and is known as Sindarā, while the other uses oil and is known as Teliā.

KORWAS. The Korwās in Rānchi district number less than 2,000, their principal habitat being Palāmau and the Feudatory States of Jashpur and Surguja. They are less wandering than the Birhors and do a certain amount of cultivation in a spasmodic way, but their occasional lapses into predatory savagery mark them out as one of the lowest of the aboriginal tribes.

Of the castes which are probably non-Aryan in origin but which have become recognized as Hindus, the most important are the Rautiās, Bhogtās, Binjhiās, Bhuiyās, Jhorās and Gonds.

RAUTIAS. The Rautiās are a well-to-do land-owning and cultivating caste, probably Dravidian in its original affinities but since refined in features and complexion by a large infusion of Aryan blood. The name Rautiā suggests some connexion with Rajpūts, and the cognate term Raut is used in some districts to denote an inferior Rajpūt. Their traditions say that they formerly dwelt in Sinhaldwip (Ceylon) whence they migrated to Barhan in Mirzapur. Some Rautiās were serving as sentinels in Gwalior, when Rājā Durjan Sal was imprisoned there, and, in return for their good offices, the Rājā on his release rewarded them by grants of lands and villages. The tradition appears to contain a substratum of truth, and there is no doubt that the Rautiās were the feudal militia introduced by the Chiefs. The leaders of the caste were granted *jāgīrs* and given the titles of Barāik, Gonjhu and Kotwār, and, in return, kept up a standing militia for the assistance of the Rājā against his external and internal enemies, and their descendants now hold tenures for which a quit-rent is payable to the Mahārājā. The rank and file of the caste became raiyats, paying light rents and possessing occupancy rights.

The Rautiās are divided into two endogamous sub-castes, Bargohri and Chhot-gohri. The origin of the two sub-castes is obscure, but it may be that the Chhot-gohri were the first settlers who were out-casted for some breach of tribal custom, or that they are the offspring of alliances between the Bargorhi and women of inferior caste. The Chhot-gohri at the present day eat fowls and wild pig and drink spirits, all of which things are forbidden to the Bargorhi. Each sub-caste is divided into sections (*paris* or *got*) with totemistic, territorial, and eponymous names, a fact which goes to prove their mixed descent. The Chhot-gohri Rautiās have a representative assembly for groups of from five to fifteen villages, called *mandli*, which decides caste questions. It is presided over by a hereditary official known as the *mahant*. The Bargohri have no standing assembly but summon a *panchāyat* as occasion requires. Organization.

Their marriage customs contain several features of a primitive and non-Aryan character. In the first instance both parties go through the form of marriage to a mango tree. The essential and binding portions of the ritual are the knotting together of the clothes of the bride and the bridegroom and *sindūrdān*, which is effected by smearing on the bride's forehead a drop of blood drawn from the little finger of the bridegoom, and *vice versâ*. Sākadwipi Brāhmans officiate at the ceremony. As with other similar castes in Chotā Nāgpur, the custom of succession among the Rautiās is that the whole property goes to the eldest son, subject to the condition that he creates maintenance grants in favour of his younger brothers, each younger brother gets a smaller share than his immediate elders, and sons by a *sagai*, or second, wife less than sons by a *bihāi*, or first, wife. Marriage customs.

The dead are usually disposed of by burning, and a regular *sraddh* ceremony is performed with the assistance of a Kanaujiā, or, failing him, of a Sākadwipi Brāhman.

The religion of the Rautiās is a mixture of the animism prevalent among the aboriginal tribes and the debased form of Religion.

Hinduism disseminated by the Brāhmans of Chotā Nāgpur, who are markedly inferior in point of learning and ceremonial purity to the Brāhmans of the great centres of Hinduism. Rama, Ganesa, Mahadeva and Gauri are the favourite deities whose worship is conducted by Brāhmans, in more or less orthodox fashion, but besides these there are spirits which, in the imagination of the aboriginals, inhabit the hills, rivers, rocks, and trees, and cause disease and distress to man and beast, such as Bar-pahār (the Marang Buru or mountain of the Mundās), Burhā-Burhī, the ancestors of mankind; the seven sisters who scatter cholera, small-pox and cattle-plague abroad, and Goraiā, the village god. Like the aboriginals, the Rautiās believe that the ghosts of women who die in child-birth, of persons killed by a tiger, and of all *ojhas*, or exorcists, are liable to re-appear and trouble the living, and they employ the exorcist (*ojha* or *mati*) to identify the spirit at work and appease it with gifts of money, goats, fowls, or pigs. They also believe in witchcraft and employ the services of the *ojha* to detect the witch or wizard who has caused a particular illness.

Socially the caste ranks fairly high, and Brāhmans will take water and sweetmeats from their hands. The Bargohri are more particular in matters of food than the Chhot-gohri, and will not eat cooked food, smoke, or drink, except with members of their own sub-caste. The Chhot-gohris are equally particular about cooked food, but will smoke with, and take water from Bhogtās, Ahirs and Jhorās. They also drink spirits and fermented liquors, and eat wild pigs and fowls.

BHOGTAS. The Bhogtās of the Rānchi district claim to be entirely distinct from the Kharwār Bhogtās of Palāmau. In appearance and customs they closely resemble the Rautiās; they claim to be, and are recognized as, Hindus and frequently call themselves Singh. According to their own tradition, they were introduced into Rānchi from Brindaban by one of the Mahārājās, and it is probable that, like the Rautiās, they were a feudal militia.

BINJHIAS. The Binjhiās are an agricultural and landholding tribe found in the south of the district. At the census of 1911, 3,785 were recorded as Hindus and 40 as Animists. They are divided into two sub-tribes, the Pahāriya Binjhiās and Dānd Binjhiās, so called from living, respectively, in the hills and the plains. The latter are divided into four exogamous septs, They claim to have come from the Vindhya Hills from which they derive their name, and the fact that they often talk Oriya points to their having come from the district of Sambalpur and the Feudatory States of Gāngpur and Patna. Though they eat fowls and wild pig, the Binjhiās, especially the Dānd Binjhiās of the south, are recognized as Hindus and enjoy much the same social rank as Rautiās. Brāhmans are employed in the worship of the greater gods, including Devi, who under the name of Vindhu-basini is regarded as the patron goddess of the caste, and Jagannath. Their minor deities are Chadri Devi and Giansri, the goddesses who preside over the village. The gods of the Pahāriya Binjhiās are Debi, Sing Bōngā, Nind Bōngā, or the moon, and Mahadeo, who are worshipped by a Binjhiā priest, called the Baigā Pāhān, and his assistant, the Dīwān, who offers the sacrifices, while the Pujāri, or consulting priest, determines what the sacrifice should be. For the decision of questions of caste usage, the Binjhiās, like other tribes, have a representative assembly consisting of delegates from every household, presided over by the Kartahā, whose office is hereditary. As with similar tribes the more wealthy members have become Hinduized.

The Bhuiyās who are found in the south of the district call themselves Khandāit Pāiks and claim that they and the members of their caste in Gāngpur, Bonai, and Orissa, are entirely distinct from the degraded Bhuiyās of Gaya, Hazāribāgh, and Palāmau. Sir Herbert Risley, in "The Tribes and Castes of Bengal," puts forward the plausible theory that the Bhuiyās had their original settlements in the Feudatory States to the south of the Chotā Nāgpur plateau. Radiating out from there, their social fortunes were determined by the character of the people with whom they came in contact. The stronger non-Aryan tribes, the Mundās, Hos, and Santāls, cut like a wedge through the line of the Bhuiyā advance to the north; a few successfully established themselves in Hazāribāgh and Gaya, while those who travelled furthest north fell under the domination of the Hindus and were reduced to the servile position which they now occupy. Those who went southward to Orissa rose rather than declined in the social scale, and some of the leading families have come to be chiefs of the petty Orissa States, and have established their claim to be Rājputs. The Bhuiyās of Rānchi district stand half-way BHUIYAS.

between these two groups, they have not degenerated to the position of serfs, like the Musahar Bhuiyās of Bihar, nor have they risen to the status of landlords. They are a respectable class of cultivators, who, as the name Khandāit or swordsman suggests, may have been employed as a militia to guard the southern frontier of the Rājā's country.

The Bhuiyās of Rānchi have advanced somewhat on the path of orthodox Hinduism. They do not regularly employ Brāhmans, except for their marriage ceremonies, but sometimes call them in to recite *mantras*. They believe in a host of communal ghosts and spirits, who have ill-defined functions and a capacity for mischief and malevolence and must be appeased by offerings of goats and fowls, and practise exorcism. At the census of 1911, 16,700 were returned as Hindus and rather more than 300 as Animists.

JHORAS. The Jhorās are a small caste, found principally in Biru pargana, who were believed by Colonel Dalton to be a sub-tribe of Gonds. The zamīndār of Biru, who is a Jhorā, claims to be a Gangabansi Rājput and is generally acknowledged as such, and other members of the tribe, both landholders and cultivators, claim similar rank. The caste profession of the Jhorās was originally gold-washing in the auriferous sands of the Sānkh River. Colonel Haughton was told in 1854 that a man could earn as much as ten to twelve annas a day, a sum greatly in excess of the wages of an ordinary labourer, which at that time could not have been more than one anna. A recent experiment showed that only two or three annas worth of gold could be extracted in a day. As gold washing with their primitive appliances is a very poor business, the majority of the members of the tribe have become ordinary cultivators. The Jhorās employ Brāhmans as their priests and burn their dead in the usual way by the side of a river, but they contribute also to the sacrifices of the village *pāhān*, of whatever caste he may be, and also follow the custom of the Mundās and Orāons in bringing the spirit of a deceased person back to his home.

GONDS. The Gonds number over 8,000, of whom all but 250 were classified as Hindus. Those who belong to the sub-caste of Rāj Gonds claim precedence over other members of the tribe and have undoubtedly become more Hinduized.

Certain other castes are probably non-Aryan in origin, but have remained low in the social scale and have not become Hinduized to the same extent as the Rautiās and other castes described above.

The Ghāsis are a Dravidian fishing and cultivating caste found in the Chotā Nāgpur Division, the district of Sambalpur and the Feudatory states. Of the total number of 70,000 nearly 21,000 are inhabitants of the Rānchi district, of whom 14,500 were returned as Hindus and 6,200 as Animists. The caste profession is to act as musicians at weddings and festivals and to perform menial offices of all kinds. Ghāsi women act as midwives and nurses. Their marriage ceremony is a debased form of that in ordinary use among orthodox Hindus. Widow marriage and divorce are freely practised and polygamy is permitted. The Ghāsis eat beef and pork and are greatly addicted to drink. Colonel Dalton regarded them as Aryan helots and says :— GHASIS.

"Far viler than the weavers are the extraordinary tribe called Ghāsis, foul parasities of the Central Indian Hill tribes and submitting to be degraded even by them. If, as I surmise, they were Aryan helots, their offices in the household or communities must have been of the lowest and most degrading kinds. It is to be observed that the institution of caste necessitated the organization of a class to whom such offices could be assigned and when formed, stringent measure would be requisite to keep the servitors in position. We might thence expect that they would avail themselves of every opportunity to escape and no safer asylums could be found than the retreats of the forest tribes. Wherever there are Kols, there are Ghāsis, and though evidently of entirely different origin, they have been so long associated that they are a recognised class in the Kol tradition of Creation which appropriately assigns to them a thriftless career and describes them as living on the leavings or charity of the more industrious members of society".

The Gōrāits are a non-Aryan caste of musicians, comb-makers and cotton-carders. They are also village watchmen and messengers, and in fact their functions may be aptly described as these of the village drudge. One family of Gōrāits is usually found in every village. They profess to be Hindus, but have not yet attained to the dignity of GORAITS.

employing Brāhmans. They worship Devi Mai and a tribal spirit called Purubia, to whom a goat is sacrificed once a year. On occasions of illness an exorcist is called in to detect the spirit or witch who is giving trouble. If the exorcist attributes the visitation to the wrath of the tribal god, the Pāhān is called upon to offer a sacrifice. The Gōrāits observe few restrictions in the matter of food or drink and in social status rank with Lohrās and Ghāsis.

LOHARS. According to the Census figures for 1911 the total number of Lohārs in the district was 46,946, of whom 30,317 were Hindus, 16,055 Animists and 574 Christians. The Lohārs consist partly of immigrants from Bihar who are known as Kanaujiā Lohārs and partly of indigenous blacksmiths who are known as Nāgpuriā Lohārs or Lohrās. The latter are a recent accretion from the ranks of the aboriginals and are often called Kol Lohārs. They are divided into two sub-castes, *viz.*, Sad Kamār and Lohrā proper. The former have abandoned their caste occupation and are engaged in agriculture. They still speak Mundāri and in some villages follow the Mundā custom of burial in a *sasāndiri*. They do not take meat other than of fowls or goats, do not drink *pachwai*, do not take cooked food from Mundās and will take water only from those who observe the same distinctions in the matter of food as themselves. On the other hand, they admit into caste the children of Mundā women though the woman herself is regarded as a concubine. The Lohrās are much lower in the social scale than the Sad Kamārs; they observe very few restrictions about food and drink, for they take cooked food from both Mundās and Orāons, and even eat the carcases of dead animals. Inter-marriage between Sad Kamārs and Lohrās is unknown. The religion of the Lohrās is mainly animistic; they worship their gods without the intervention of any priest, and resort to exorcism in case of illness or trouble.

MAHLIS. The Māhlis are a Dravidian caste of labourers, palanquin-bearers, and workers in bamboo. Sir Herbert Risley conjectures that the group comprising the Bānsphor, the Sulānkhi, and the Tānti Māhlis, is a branch of the Santāls, separated at a comparatively recent date from the parent caste, and bases his conjecture on the ground that the totemistic sections of the Māhlis correspond with those of the Santāls. It is equally probable that the outlying sub-caste of Māhli Mundās, found in the Rānchi district, parted from the Mundās because they followed a profession held to be degrading by the tribe. The Māhlis occur in very old Mundā traditions, and even in their mythology, and are said to have been out-casted for unclean eating. They eat beef, fowls, and pork, and, though the latter is the totem of the race, they avert the consequences of breaking of the taboo by throwing away the head. They are also much addicted to spirituous liquor. The religion is a mixture of half-forgotten Animism and Hinduism imperfectly understood. They worship Bar Pahāri (the mountain god of the Mundās), Manasa, the snake goddess and other godlings of the animistic tribes. They have not yet risen to the dignity of employing Brāhmans. The Māhlis have a bad reputation as thieves, and have a sort of thieves' jargon of their own.

PANS AND CHIK BARAIKS.

In Risley's "Tribes and Castes of Bengal" the Chik Barāiks are said to be a sub-caste of Pāns, but, apart from the fact that the profession of each caste is weaving, their connection with the degraded tribe of Pāns found in Orissa is doubtful. The Chik Barāiks claim to be Aryans and Hindus, and are certainly fairer and more Aryan in appearance than the Pāns or Pānrs who are found in Mundā villages, often speaking Mundāri and following many of the Mundā customs. The latter are most probably Dravidian, though Colonel Dalton suggests that they are "in all probability the remnants of the Aryan colonies which the Hos subjugated". This theory is doubtful, for there is little evidence to prove that there was an Aryan civilization in Chotā Nāgpur before the incursion of the Dravidian races, but it may be that the Chik Barāiks, who are considered locally to be the social superiors of the Pāns, are the descendants of some Aryan weaving caste which settled in Chotā Nāgpur at an early date. Both castes now claim to be Hindus, and at the census of 1911 out of 29,000 Chik Barāiks and 14,600 Pāns, only 3,400 and 600, respectively, were classified as Animists.

RELIGIONS

According to the census statistics of 1911, of the total population of 1,387,516, 550,715 were Hindus, 51,158 Musalmans, 177,473 Christians and 607,820 Animists. "Animism is the term used to cover the miscellany of superstitions which prevail among primitive tribes in all parts of the world. These tribes are very vague in their religious conceptions, but they all agree in the presence on earth of a shadowy crowd of powerful and malevolent beings who usually have a local habitation in a hill, stream or patch of primeval forest, and who interest themselves in the affairs of men. There is also a general belief in magic and witchcraft. From the point of view of the Census Animism is used as the name of the category to which are relegated all the pre-Hindu religions of India."* The practical difficulty is to draw the dividing line between Hinduism and Animism. Many semi-aboriginals lay claim to be Hindus, though Hindus scorn their pretentions, and in the Rānchi district the entries in the Census schedules depended largely on the caste of the enumerator. In the case of the purely aboriginal tribes, such as Mundās, Orāons, Khariās, Asurs, nearly all who were not converts to Christianity were recorded as Animists, but members of the semi-aboriginal tribes, such as Ghāsi, Turi, Lohār, Dom, Gond, who worship some Hindu gods and have adopted some Hindu customs, were entered as Animists if the enumerator was a Hindu, but as Hindus if the enumerator was a Christian or an educated aboriginal. The description of the various castes and tribes given above shows the extent to which Hindu customs have been adopted. The number of Christians has increased largely in the district during the last forty years and has risen from 343 per 10,000 of the population in 1881 to 1,283 in 1911. The conversions have been wholly from the aboriginal races, and the number of Animists has fallen from 5,471 per 10,000 in 1881 to 4,381 in 1911. This remarkable spread of Christianity has had a great effect on the district and the story of Missionary work in Chotā Nāgpur has been described at length in another chapter.

Birsaites. A small number of persons in the district were enumerated in the recent census as Birsaites, or followers of Birsā Mundā. Birsā's religion was a mixture of Hinduism and Christianity. The central doctrines are that there is one God, that Birsā is his incarnation on earth, and that

* Census of India, 1911, Volume I, Part 1, by Sir E. A. Gait, K.C.S.I., C.I.E., I.C.S.

purity of character and habits are the essential things demanded of man by God. A Birsaite must wear the sacred thread, must abstain from animal food, must not work on Thursdays (the day of Birsā's birth) and must not cut down *sāl* trees on Tuesdays. Many Mundās had, and still have, a belief in his supernatural powers. When he was in jail, no Mundās believed that he was really confined. They alleged that he had gone up to heaven and that the authorities had only a clay figure in jail which they pretended was Birsā. After his death from cholera during his trial, his body was shown to certain Mundās but they refused to be convinced that it was his corpse, and some Mundās even now believe that he will come again. There is said to be a movement to induce his younger brother to revive the cult, but the latter has not the enterprise or enthusiasm of Birsā and the religion seems doomed to die of inanition. Only fifteen persons were classified as Birsaites in the recent census.

In the account given above of many of the smaller tribes, their religious beliefs have been briefly described. The beliefs and superstitions of the Orāons and Mundās are not only better known, but also may be regarded as typical of the animistic religion of the aboriginal races and thus merit a more detailed account.

Religion of the Mundās.

The cult of Sing Bōngā and ancestor worship are characteristic features of the Mundā religion. Subordinate deities and spirits have also to be worshipped, or rather propitiated, and the word *Bōngā* now is used to denote all spirits which exert an influence for good or evil, and, when used alone, those spirits or subordinate deities who cause sickness and other evils, if not appeased with sacrifices. Sing Bōngā is the sun-spirit or god of light, he is the invisible supreme being who created all the other *bōngās* and is essentially and wholly good. All men's lives are in his hands, though power to do mischief is given to the inferior deities. There is no specific worship of Sing Bōngā, but he has to be saluted every morning and in times of special calamity receives a sacrifice of a white goat or white fowl. The sacrifices are not offered either to Sing Bōngā or to any of the inferior spirits because they stand in need of food or drink, and the Mundās explicitly maintain that they take only the honour of the sacrifice.

Ancestor Worship.

The spirits of the ancestors are known as *Ora-bōngāko*, or gods of the household. Some two or three days after the death of any person, except infants or women dying in child-birth, the ceremony known as *Umbu'-adar*, or bringing in of the shade, is performed. The procedure is as follows:— In the evening two persons enter the deceased's house, bolt the doors, place some food in a cup and sprinkle ashes over the whole floor. Meanwhile the villagers or relatives of the deceased go to the place where his body lies buried or was burnt, and one man addresses the deceased as follows:—" Here now we have come to recall thee home. Thou hast been long enough out in the field in the chill and cold". A procession is formed to the house of the deceased and, arriving at the door, the speaker asks in the name of the shade that the door may be opened. A short dialogue ensues, and the persons inside the house express misgivings as to the intentions of him who seeks admission. When the replies of the shade have satisfied them, the door is opened, and the floor and leaf-cups are examined. If there is any real or apparent foot-print in the ashes and any real or apparent disturbance of the food, all are satisfied that the spirit has taken up its abode in the *ading*, a side room used for the storing of rice. If no traces are found, the ceremony is repeated. After three unsuccessful attempts, the spirit is held to have taken up his abode in some tree or rock. The bones of the deceased or a portion of them are buried under the common tombstone of the *kili* on the occasion of the *jāng-tōpā* and the tomb is anointed in honour of the dead with any oil that the members of the family have with them.

The *Ora-bōngāko* receive daily worship, and before every meal a Mundā drops a few grains of rice on the floor as an offering to them; similarly a few drops of rice-beer are given to them before drinking. There is also a special feast every year in their honour, which is known as the *Sarhul* or *Bā-Parob* (flower feast), and they are also worshipped along with other deities on other occasions. An *Ora-bōngā* is regarded as having power to afflict the living with the disease of which he died, and hence sacrifices have to be offered to them; as a preventive of evil the shade is propitiated by a gift of some stimulant, such as rice-beer or tobacco, of which the deceased was in his lifetime particularly fond; and in time of illness a sacrifice, either of urid, cooked rice, cooked fish, a black fowl, red goat, or sometimes a bullock, is offered. If a newly-married woman gets frequently ill, her illness is held to be caused by one of the *Ora-bōngās* of her father's house who has followed her to her new home. Such spirits are known as *Horatenkoa bōngā* or traveller's *bōngā,* and must be appeased by a sacrifice offered by the woman and her husband on the road leading to her home.

Other deities. The other deities of the Mundās are those which are associated with certain natural features of the country, such as hills, rivers, pools, woods, trees, etc. Thus *Buru Bōngā* is the god who resides in the hills and is associated with any high or conspicuous hill, especially the remarkable hill Marang Buru near the village of Lodhmā, to which not only Mundās and other aboriginals but also Hindus and Muhammadans resort to offer sacrifice. The *Pangrua bōngā* is associated with a waterfall near the village of that name in Khunti thana. The *Ikir Bonga* rule over, and have their abode in, tanks and lakes while the *Nage Era* haunt low swampy places. The *Deswali Bōngā* with his wife, *Jaher Burhia,* is found in every village and has his abode in a particular *sāl* tree in the *sarnā,* or sacred grove, a patch of the forest primeval left intact to afford a refuge for the forest gods. Each god has his peculiar powers of doing evil and has to be propitiated with appropriate sacrifices. To account for the origin of these gods the Mundās tell the Asur legend, which is recited yearly at some festivals.

Asur legend. The Asurs, says the legend, were famous iron-smelters who prided themselves on their strength and numbers and defied even Sing Bōngā. Sing Bōngā became angry at the smoke of their furnaces which ascended up to his seat in heaven and sent various birds as messengers to tell the Asurs to stop their work. But the messengers were treated with contumely ; the king-crow, which was formerly white, was covered with coal dust, the tail of another bird was pulled out to an abnormal length, the king-vulture was hit on the head with a hammer, and the treatment given to the bird-messengers permanently changed their appearance. At last Sing Bōngā determined to visit earth himself and stop the practices of the Asurs. He adopted the disguise of a leprous boy, and being rejected with horror by the Asurs, was taken in by a childless old couple of Mundās named *Lutkum Haram* and *Lutkum Burhia.* By some miraculous deeds, such as smashing balls of iron with eggs and causing the paddy of the old couple to multiply, he won the respect of the Asurs. He also caused their iron-ore to fail and their furnaces to fall in. In distress they came to him for help, and he advised a human sacrifice. As they were unable to obtain a victim, he agreed to be sacrificed by being burnt alive in one of their furnaces. The Asurs accordingly shut him up in a furnace, but when the furnace was opened, Sing Bōngā appeared, bright as the sun and laden with gold, silver, and precious stones, and persuaded the greedy Asurs that, if they too entered the furnace, they would find a large store of the precious metals. The men believed him and entered the furnace, while their wives blew the bellows. Thus all the male members of the tribe were destroyed. The Asur women, in distress at the loss of their husbands, entreated Sing Bōngā to give them sustenance. He agreed to do so if they promised obedience and respect. On their making the promise, Sing Bōngā rose to heaven with the Asur women holding on to his garments. When they had risen to a certain height, he threw them over the country and they became the *bōngās* of the spots on which they fell. Sing Bōngā promised that henceforth the Pāhān would sacrifice to them, and thus they would get sustenance.

These deities are not generally malevolent, but must be appeased occasionally with sacrifices. A more malevolent class of spirit are the sprits of persons who have died unnatural or violent deaths, such as *Churins, Muās, Apsans,* etc. These evil spirits are distinguished from the spirits of the ancestors and the gods of the village, and are termed *banita bōngās* or spirits which have to be propitiated in contradistinction to the *manita bōngās* who have to be adored. The detection and propitiation of these spirits as well as the detection of the witches or wizards who have the power to stir them up to do evil is the special function of the ghost-finders, the *Najos, Matis, Deonras* and *Sokhas,* whose methods are described in a subsequent paragraph.

Hinduism among Mundās.

A large number of Hinduized Mundās are to be found, especially in the Five Parganas, who no longer join in the old national worship. In most cases, however, they still make use of the services of the Pāhān to offer sacrifice to the village gods whose influence over the affairs of the village is never questioned.

Mahādeo is a favourite god with these Mundās, and Devi-Mai (Sakti) also receives homage and worship.

Religion of the Orāons.

The Orāon religion resembles that of the Mundās in many respects, especially in its recognition of an omnipotent benevolent deity and in the worship of ancestors.

The supreme Being is called Dharmes, whose abode is in the Sun, but who is not identified with the sun and is regarded as almost immaterial. Dharmes is not malevolent but has given the management of the affairs of the world into the hands of spirits who have to be appeased. It is only as a last resource that an Orāon who has failed to get rid of disease by propitiation of the evil spirits will turn to Dharmes with the words "*Akkum ninim ra-adai*". "Now art even thou," meaning "now the case rests with thee". Vows are made to Dharmes and sacrifices are promised if a recovery is obtained. The sacrifice to Dharmes, as to Sing Bōngā, consists only of a cock or a goat which must be white in colour. Dharmes is also called by the Hindu name of Bhagwān.

Ancestor Worship.

According to the belief of the Orāons every man has two shades ; the heavier goes to *markha,* the heaven of the Orāons ; the lighter remains on earth. On the day of the burial of a corpse, the ceremony known as *Chhain Bhitrāna* takes place. A miniature hut of straw is built near the home of the deceased, and one of the men of the village sets fire to it and, striking together a plough-share and sickle, calls the name of the deceased and summons him to come back, as his house is on fire. The shade promptly returns and on his return his nearest relative sacrifices a cock and pours the blood into a corner of the house, to induce him to remain there. A later ceremony is the *Koha Benja,* or great marriage, when the ashes of the corpse are deposited in the ancient burial place or *kundi.* This may be either in a field, covered with a huge stone, or in the bed of a river. The relics of the deceased are carried round the village and the ceremony is believed to cause his spirit to be admitted to the circle of the departed spirits in the other world. Sacrifices are offered to the spirits of departed ancestors, partly to ensure their repose and partly to obtain help from them. At the festivals, and in particular at the *Naya Khani* or eating of new rice, some morsels of food and drops of liquor are thrown on the ground for the benefit of the ancestors. In times of great distress, the spirits of the ancestors are invoked and they are also asked to protect a new-born child or newly-married couple. It has been suggested by Father Dehon that this was the original form of worship of the Orāon tribe and that the worship of other deities through the agency of the Pāhān or Ojha was borrowed from the Kolarian tribes among whom they dwelt. He considers this to be proved by three facts, first that members of the tribe themselves believe it, secondly, that in these ceremonies a pure form of the language unmixed with Hindi is used, and thirdly, that Orāons prefer, if possible, to have as their Pāhān a member of a Kolarian tribe.

To explain the origin of the minor deities and spirits, most of whom are malevolent and have frequently to be propitiated, the Orāons tell the legend of the destruction of the Asurs which differs only in details from the Mundā legend already given. Thus, one of the minor deities, *Baranda,* is said to be the son of an Asur woman who was pregnant at the time of the destruction of the Asur men. He was kept by Dharmes and given his post to reward the labour of his mother. He is regarded as the cause of misfortune and poverty, if he takes up his abode in a house. As Father Dehon puts it, the Orāons look upon God as a big zamindār who does nothing by himself but keeps a *chaprassi* or *tahsildār*. *Baranda* is the *chaprāssi* who has all the defects common to the profession, and complicated ceremonies have to be performed, which probably represent the payment to Baranda of his *dasturi,* without which he cannot be induced to leave the house.

The minor gods and spirits may be divided into those of the household and those of the village. *Baranda* belongs to the former class. The *Erpa-nad* or house demon is represented in the house by a wooden peg, and sacrifices of fowls and goats have to made to her in cases of illness. The village spirits are *Khunt, Bhula* and *Churil,* which are really generic names. Thus *Khunt* is the generic name for all the *bhūts* who have taken up their abode in the village, of whom the fiercest are *Darha* and *Dakhin* his wife. To *Darha* only must human sacrifices be paid at least once in each generation, the victim, usually a boy or girl, being known as *Olonga*. Such sacrifices may perhaps still be made, as it is easy for a village to unite in a conspiracy of silence. *Churil* is the generic name for the spirits of women who have died in pregnancy. They appear in the form of women, but with their feet turned backwards, and are especially dangerous to new-born children and women who are confined. Various means are taken to prevent such spirits haunting a village, and, if a woman dies in childbirth, her ankles are broken and stakes driven through her feet before she is buried in a lonely place far away from the village. *Bhula* are the spirits of all persons who have died violent deaths; the word literally means "wanderers" and the spirits are supposed to wander about, still bearing the scars of the wounds from which they died. The chief of the village deities are *Pat* with his chaprassi *Duharia* and *Chola Pacho* or *Sarnā Burhi*. The former dwells in a hill near the village and the latter in the sacred *sāl* grove, while her sisters dwell in other trees. She is credited with giving good crops. *Deswali*, her servant, is said to cause mortal disease among men and cattle. *Chandi* is the goddess of hunting to whom sacrifices must be made to ensure a plentiful supply of game. All the village *devtas* and *bhūts* must be appeased by the sacrifices of the Pāhāns.

The above account is based chiefly on the interesting account of the "Religion and Customs of the Orāons" contributed by the late Father P. Dehon, S.J., to the Asiatic Society of Bengal,* which refers principally to the Orāons of Barwe and Chhechhari among whom he worked. The religious beliefs of the Orāons, as of other Animists, are very amorphous and vague; new gods are invented, new customs are adopted, new festivals are introduced, and in other parts of the district no doubt many variations in detail would be found. But the account applies equally to all Orāons in that it shows how they believe themselves to be surrounded by a crowd of deities and spirits most of whom are malevolent and who are on the look-out for any opportunity to do them harm.

The belief in malevolent spirits is the origin of the belief in witchcraft. To detect the malevolent *bhūt* or the witch or wizard who is stirring him up to do mischief is the function of the witch-doctor or augur. The witch or *dain bisāhi* is usually an ugly old woman who is supposed to have acquired the power of commanding the *bhūts*. The *bhūts* sometimes of their own accord attack people but are often stirred up to do so by the

Exorcism and witchcraft.

* Published in the Memoirs of the Asiatic Society of Bengal, Volume I, No. 9, pages 121—181, 1906.

witch. When sickness attacks a villager, the first thing to be done is to find out who is the malevolent spirit or the witch, and the only person competent to do this is the *ojha*, *deonra*, *sokha*, or *mati*. The person who believes himself to be the victim of the wrath of the *bhūt* goes to the ghost-finder. The latter takes some rice and oil, lights a small earthen lamp, and places the rice on a *sūp* (winnowing fan). He then concentrates his gaze on the lamp, chants numerous *mantras* or incantations, in which the names of all the spirits are mentioned. As each name is mentioned some rice is thrown into the flame, and the presence of the guilty *bhūt* is revealed either by the flame flaring up when his name is mentioned or by the winnowing fan moving in a mysterious manner. The next step is to propitiate the *bhūt* by sacrifices and the *ojha* tells the victim what sacrifices are appropriate. Father Dehon gives an interesting account of the ceremony whereby the *ojha* among the Orāons imprisons the *bhūt* and thereby prevents him causing further trouble. The *bhūt* is present in the lamp, for the *ojha* has seen him. To make him captive, he places a cone of *sāl* leaves over the lamp-wick, buries the cone in an ant-hill, and offers sacrifices to his patron *deota* to persuade him to guard the *bhūt* carefully in his feeble prison. Next comes the *niksāri* ceremony whereby the *bhūt* is confined in a stronger prison. When the man has collected the victim for sacrifices, the *ojha* gets an iron cone prepared by the village blacksmith and after the usual incantations places the lamp-wick in the iron cone (or *singhi*), closes it securely and buries it in the ant-hill. Sacrifices are then offered to Dharmes and other gods, and the *bhūt* is thus effectually prevented from doing further mischief. The method of detecting a witch is similar to that of detecting a *bhūt*. A visit is paid to the *ojha* or *sokha*, the latter being generally a Hindu or low caste Muhammadan or even an Orāon Bhagat. The *sokha* selected is usually one living 15 or 20 miles from the village, so that the people may be sure that there is no imposture. The witch doctor lights his lamp and falling into a sort of trance begins to describe the appearance of the witch. The people soon fix his description on to some unfortunate old woman of the village and returning home proceed to vent their wrath on the witch, calling on her to produce the sacrifices with which to appease the *bhūts*, and, if she fails to do so, beating her and driving her from the village and in many cases putting her to death. Cases of the murder of witches even now occasionally come before the courts, and there is little doubt that cases also occur which are never reported and that the *sokhas* are dangerous members of the community.

Another curious custom whereby Orāons seek to protect their village from the attacks of disease is the *Rog Khedna*. In one form of this ceremony all the inhabitants of the village carry out old earthen cooking-pots, pieces of mat, etc., and place them outside the boundary of the village, to show the evil spirit who caused the mischief the way out of the village. Another form is to take the herdsman of the village, tie a cow-bell round his neck and drive him beyond the boundaries. A fowl is then sacrificed and the head buried. A string is then fastened to the head and drawn across the road, and any person who passes by and touches the string with his right foot will get the disease and free the patient from it. According to Father Dehon, the sacrifice is to *Duharia* who is regarded as the Chaukidar *deota*, whose special function is to keep the *Bhulas* in order, the string being set so that, if the *Bhulas* try to re-enter the village he will be awakened.

Festivals of the Orāons and Mundās.

The festival of the Orāons and Mundās differ only in detail and may conveniently be described together.

The Māgē festival takes place in the month of *Pous* (January) after the crops have been harvested. The spirits of the deceased ancestors and other minor deities are worshipped, in order that good crops may be obtained in the coming year and that the village may not be visited by any calamity or disease. The festival is a great occasion of rejoicing and often degenerates into an orgy; *Māgē Kaji* or words used at the festival being a synonym for obscene language. At this time labourers are released from their contracts and engaged for the new year.

The Phaguā festival corresponds to the Holi of the Hindus and is observed in order to ensure a successful hunt. Sacrifices are offered by the Pāhān to the deities of the hills and forests.

The Sarhūl festival, known by the Orāons as *Khaddi*, takes place in May when the *sāl* trees are in bloom. *Sāl* flowers are gathered and taken to the *sarnā* and sacrifices offered to various gods. During this festival no Mundā or Orāon will touch his plough. According to Father Dehon the festival celebrates the marriage of the Sun-god (Bhagwan) with the earth goddess (Dharti Mai).

The Batauli festival, called by the Orāons *Kedletta,* is celebrated in June before the reploughing of the low-lying rice fields and the transplantation of paddy. Sacrifices are made by the Pāhān to various deities to ensure a good crop.

The Kolom Sing festival, also known as the *Khalihān puja,* takes place in Agahan (November), before the harvest is threshed. No villager may thresh his corn before the Pāhān has prepared his threshing-floor (*Kolom*) and offered sacrifices of fowls.

The Jom Nawa or Naya Khāni is celebrated when the *gora* paddy is harvested before the new rice is eaten. When the *gora* paddy is ripe, the Pāhān sticks an arrow in a field and proclaims that harvesting may begin. As each household begins to reap, they make a private feast of the occasion, and the Pāhān and other villagers offer sacrifices of fowls. The festival is not universal among the Mundās, and in the localities where it is practised it is probably borrowed from the Hindus.

The *Karam* festival is also probably borrowed from the Hindus by the Mundās and Orāons. On the eve of the day fixed the boys and girls fast and go together to the nearest jungle and bring back a branch of the *Karam* tree, dancing and singing in triumph. The branch is planted in the middle of the *akhrā* and the whole night is spent in dancing and singing round it. Next morning the branch is thrown into the river.

The Sohrai festival takes place in Kartik (October-November) and is properly the feast of the cattle to whom the people wish to show their gratitude. A lamp is hung in the cowshed and kept burning all night and sacrifices are offered to Goreā, the deity presiding over cattle. The cattle are anointed with oil, garlanded with flowers, given a good feed of corn and turned out to pasture.

The Ind Parab is celebrated by the Mundās in a few villages only, generally in those of which the landlord is a Nāgbansi. Two large umbrellas are raised in honour of the first Nāgbansi chief, and, at the village of Sutiambe, in honour of Madra Mundā, the foster-father of the first Chief.

The aboriginal tribes have borrowed other festivals from

the Hindus, such as the Dasahara, and in fact miss no opportunity for feasting, dancing and merriment. At all these festivals large quantities of rice-beer are drunk, and the young men and maidens spend the nights in dancing. An excellent account of the dances and songs will be found in Mr. S. C. Roy's books on the Mundās and Orāons. The *Jātras* of old were, as Mr. Roy points out, the great social congress of the Orāons; here the young men of one clan selected brides from the maidens of a clan other than their own; while the tribal dances were supposed to ensure success in hunting and good crops. At the present time the *Jātras* have not the same importance; they undoubtedly conduce to intemperance and immorality, and the Missions have sternly set their face against them. Immorality is to be deplored, but it would be a great matter for regret if these festivals, survivals from a primitive age, were entirely abandoned.

CHAPTER IV.

PUBLIC HEALTH.

Vital statistics.

A COMPARISON of vital statistics before 1892 is of little value. The registration of deaths was introduced in 1869, the duty of reporting them being imposed on the village chaukidar, and, though it has been continuously carried on, there have been many changes of system and in the area of the district since that date. In the Rānchi Municipality births were first registered in October 1873 and Act IV (B. C.) of 1873, which makes compulsory the registration of births and deaths, was extended to that area in 1887, and to the Lohardagā Municipality in 1890. Registration of births was begun in rural areas in 1877, and the system now in vogue, whereby the chaukidars report deaths and births at the weekly parade at the thāna, was introduced in 1892.

The agency for reporting births and deaths is not more reliable than in other districts, while the size of the areas within the jurisdiction of each police station and the long distances from headquarters render it more difficult for police and medical officers to check the chaukidars' reports. The statistics of births and deaths, however, are probably more accurate than in the plains, as the aboriginal population have no prejudice against reporting the deaths and births of females, but the causes of death are hopelessly confused. Cholera and small-pox may be diagnosed, but all other diseases are classified by the chaukidar under the general head of "fever."

The decade ending in 1902 was generally considered an unhealthy one, probably because of the mortality in the famine year of 1897, but the average birth-rate was 37·14 per thousand, and the death-rate only 25·56. In the famine year of 1897, the death-rate rose to 46·48, but in the following year it dropped to 18·51, the lowest rate found in any district of the province. In the ten years 1901-10, the birth-rate averaged 44·54, but the death-rate (28) was slightly higher than in the preceding period. In 1908, a famine year, the death-rate rose to 46·05, but in the two years of good harvest which succeeded the famine the birth-rate rose to 44 and 52, while the death-rate fell to 26 and 29. The average birth-rate during the five years ending 1915 was 41·14 while the death-rate for this period was 21·93.

The birth-rate is, as might be expected, highest among the aboriginal population in the less developed parts of the district, especially in Chainpur, Lohardagā and Gumlā thānas. Even allowing for the inaccuracy of the statistics, it is not surprising to find that with this high birth-rate the population of the district rose by over half a million between the years 1872 and 1911 and that between the two last censuses of 1901 and 1911, in which great accuracy was obtained, the population increased from 1,137,000 to 1,387,000.

Principal diseases, Fever.

The term "fever" used in the published statistics must be held not merely to mean malaria, but to include all kinds of febrile complaints, such as respiratory diseases and measles, as the reporting chaukidar classifies all such diseases indiscriminately under the one name.

There is no doubt, however, that the inhabitants of, and immigrants to, the district do suffer severely from malaria, and it is probable that many of the true fevers are malarial in origin. Malaria is not an uncommon cause of attendance at the dispensaries at all times of year, but particularly during August and September and at the end of the rains. Major Fry, I.M.S., who has made a special study of the subject, states that all three varieties are met with : Malignant tertian, benign tertian and quartant, the latter being particularly common in the sub-plateau areas which are associated with high spleen rates. Major Fry's observations show that the Rānchi plateau is not an endemic area, though the edges of it are hyperendemic, perhaps because the residents descend frequently to the lower plateau. The largest number of cases and the worst type of fever occur in the lower plateau, in Tamār and the south-west of the district, and though slight enlargement of the spleen is not uncommon throughout the district, the splenic index is only high in those areas. The resident population of the district have established relative immunity from the disease, but new settlers or casual visitors are very susceptible. A notable fact is that the police stations are usually highly malarious, apparently because of the aggregation of visitors from infected areas. The villages compare unfavourably as regards sanitation with Bengal, every hollow near the houses is used as a receptacle for manure, with the result that the water-supply is polluted, and the pools round the villages form most favourable breeding grounds for anopheline mosquitoes. The mosquitoes most numerous are Myzomyia Rossi, Myzomyia Culcifacies, Nyssorhynchus Fuliginosus and Pyretophorus Jeyporensis. Of these, the second and fourth are common in the hyperendemic regions, and as they are well known to be the most prominent carriers in India, are most probably the cause of the distribution of the disease.

For the ten years ending 1902 the death-rate from fever was reported to be 14·13 per mille and for the ten years ending 1910, 17·83, the total mortality during these periods being 25·56 and 28·006, respectively. In 1908, a famine year, there was abnormally high mortality, the death-rate for fever alone being as high as 25·06 per mille. In the year 1915, when the total mortality was 26·53, the mortality from fever was reported to be 18·93 per mille.

Cholera. In normal years the number of deaths from cholera is small. The natural drainage of the district is excellent and it is only after a very defective monsoon that the well and the *dāris*, or springs in the terraced rice-lands, fail to give a supply of water, which with care is potable. The conditions favouring a spread of the disease are present only in abnormal years when the failure or early cessation of the monsoon causes a shortage of good drinking water, and the epidemics which have occurred in famine years have been severe. During the years 1893 to 1902, the average mortality from cholera was only ·80 per mille, while in the following period, 1901-10, it was slightly lower. In 1908 the disease broke out in epidemic form, both in the famine area to the west of the district and in the town of Rānchi, and the death-rate in this area rose to 7·01 per mille. In 1911 only 17 deaths from cholera were reported in the whole district, but in 1912 there were 347 deaths in all or 25 per mille. There was a virulent outbreak in the village of Hatmā Karamtoli, near Rānchi, which caused 27 deaths out of 40 cases in a period of three weeks. The infection was also conveyed through milk to Rānchi Bazar, where several deaths occurred. In the Khunti thana there was also a severe outbreak and, in spite of the devoted efforts of the English Mission doctors at Murhu, the mortality was above 60 per cent. A similar outbreak occurred in 1915, when the death-rate rose to ·56. These epidemics occurred at the close of the hot weather, and a copious rainfall in July and August stopped the further spread of the disease, by replenishing the water-supply and destroying flies and other germ-carriers. Outbreaks such as these may be said to be typical of the disease in normal years.

Small-pox.

Serious epidemics of small-pox are not common, and as a rule the death-rate is low, the average mortality for 20 years being only ·20 per mille. In the epidemics of 1892, 1908 and 1909, the mortality was 1·97, 1·28 and 1·14, respectively, but in no other year did the death-rate exceed ·50.

Plague.

Plague is practically unknown at present in the district; only four or five deaths have occurred in the last ten years, and these were of persons who were already infected with the disease, before they entered the district.

Bowel complaints.

Dysentery and diarrhœa are more common than in the neighbouring districts and cause considerable mortality during the hot and rainy seasons. Bad drinking water is a principal cause of these diseases and little care is taken to keep the tanks and *dāris*, which form the water-supply of a village, free from pollution. A contributory cause is the large extent to which the aboriginal population feed on jungle fruits and roots, and coarse grain, such as *gondli*, and it is for this reason that the mortality from bowel diseases is highest in, and after, years of scarcity. In such years the *gondli*, which ripens in August and is eaten unmixed with rice, creates the disease in constitutions already enfeebled by a sparse diet of jungle fruits and roots. In 1897 the mortality was exceptionally high (4·97), and in 1907 and 1908 it was over 3 per mille, but these figures are certainly considerably underestimated. It is difficult to believe that in a normal year, such as 1912, there would be only 1,650 deaths from this cause.

Tuberculous diseases.

Tubercle of the lungs, joints and abdominal viscera is becoming more common in the town of Rānchi. The over-crowding of buildings and the multiplication of schools and boarding-houses must be held responsible for this unfortunate development. Healthy boys from country villages are brought into close contact with phthisical town-children, and in many cases either become victims of the disease themselves or, on settling permanently in the town, raise up families, whose powers of resistance to the disease appear to be very feeble.

Rabies.

As in other parts of India, rabid jackals and dogs are frequently found in the towns and bazars, and, though accurate returns of the deaths they cause are not procurable, there is no doubt that a considerable mortality must occur in the remote parts of the district, where there is no possibility of sending the patient to Kasauli. In the town of Rānchi alone, in 1912, five patients went to Kasauli, while two persons who were bitten by a mad jackal refused to undergo the treatment and died in a few weeks.

Other diseases.

Throat affections, such as quinsy, are common, especially towards the end of the rains. Pneumonia is prevalent in the cold weather and rains. The aboriginals are generally supposed to be racially immune from goitre but several cases have been known. The glare of the laterite soil and the dust of the uplands are contributory causes of diseases of the eye, especially conjunctivitis, but cataract is rare as compared with other parts of India. Rheumatic affections often cripple permanently the persons whom they attack, and skin-diseases and several species of intestinal worms are common. Cancer of the lips occurs among elderly males and is attributed to the habit of chewing tobacco mixed with lime. Venereal diseases are very rare in the district and are practically confined to the non-aboriginals of the towns.

Infirmities.

In the census of 1911 the record which was made of infirmities included insanity, deaf mutism, blindness and leprosy. The total number of persons afflicted in Rānchi district was 2,541 or ·18 per cent. of the total population. Leprosy is uncommon as compared with the neighbouring district of Mānbhūm, and only 160 cases were recorded. There is an Asylum for Lepers at Lohardagā, which is maintained by the Mission to Lepers in India and the East, and was started in 1884 at the instance of the Rev. F. Hahn of the Lutheran Mission; it contains accommodation for twenty-seven patients. Total blindness is also not very common, and only 1,454 persons were returned as suffering from this affliction. In 1895 a Blind School was started at Rānchi, in connection with the English Mission, by Mrs. O'Connor. The male inmates of the school are taught to do cane and bamboo work, and the women are taught mat-making. Reading and writing are also taught on the Braille system.

Lunatic Asylums.

Rānchi has been selected by Government as the site of a large Central Lunatic Asylum for European lunatics from Northern India and of an Asylum for Indian lunatics from the provinces of Bengal and Bihar and Orissa. For these two large institutions land has been acquired in the village of Kānke, about five miles north of Rānchi : the construction of the European Asylum, at a cost of over thirteen lakhs, has been almost completed, while plans are being prepared for the Indian Asylum which will accommodate 1,500 patients.

Hospitals and dispensaries.

Till 1902, the only dispensaries in the district were those maintained by the municipalities of Rānchi and Lohardagā. The Rānchi dispensary was established in 1855, and was for a long time in charge of an Indian doctor, paid from local funds. A new building to accommodate eighteen in-patients was opened in 1872, and in that year the in-patients numbered 146 and the out-patients 1,789. During the last twelve years the hospital has been entirely rebuilt and considerably enlarged. In 1902 it consisted of one *kutcha* building, which contained both the in-patient and out-patient departments, and was stigmatised by the Commissioner as the dirtiest and most dilapidated dispensary he had ever seen. In 1902, from subscriptions raised for the Queen Victoria Memorial Fund, a new operation room and male surgical ward were erected, and in the following year the hospital was enlarged by the erection of a male medical ward and a new female ward. In 1916 four cottage wards were opened for patients willing to pay a small sum for their occupation ; in 1913 two wards for infectious diseases were constructed, and, finally in 1914, a new out-patient building was completed at a cost of Rs. 20,000, as a memorial to King Edward VII. The hospital now contains sixty beds and is well equipped. It will not be out of place to mention that the hospital owes much to the liberality of Rai Sahib Thakur Das of Rānchi, who bore the whole of the erection of the female ward, was a liberal subscriber to the King Edward Memorial Ward, and has recently met a considerable portion of the cost of an X-Ray installation to complete the equipment of the hospital. The hospital is under the Civil Surgeon, and in the year 1915, 17,466 patients were treated.

The Lohardagā dispensary was opened in 1881 and has recently been rebuilt and enlarged at a cost of Rs. 15,000. In 1915 the total number of patients was 6,751. Since 1902, the District Board has done much to bring medical relief within reach of the inhabitants; dispensaries were opened at Bundu and Chainpur in 1902, at Gumlā in 1903, Silli in 1906 and Khunti in 1907. The dispensary at Gumlā has accommodation for twelve in-patients and is in charge of an Assistant Surgeon. The remainder are in charge of Sub-Assistant Surgeons or local Indian doctors. At the outlying dispensaries the bulk of the work is the treatment of out-patients, either at the hospitals, or at the bazars which are visited by the medical officers, and in 1915, 22,231 patients received treatment. The aboriginal is still somewhat shy of the dispensary, and prefers to trust to his own jungle drugs or to apply to his missionary for assistance. He is impatient of slow medical treatment, but will readily submit to a surgical operation or come to the local hospital for the treatment of wounds, received either from his own kinsmen or from wild animals.

Aided and private institutions.

The most sucessful private dispensary is that at Murhu, in the Khunti subdivision, maintained by the S. P. G. Mission and aided by the District Board. The dispensary was opened by the Rev. Dr. Kennedy in 1905, with accommodation for 16 in-patients and in the first nine months nearly 3,000 cases were treated and 50 major operations performed. The hospital was enlarged in 1911 and the staff now includes an Indian doctor and a trained European nurse, in addition to the Missionary in charge. In 1910 a dispensary was started by this Mission at Itki in Bero thāna, to carry on medical work among the Orāons. Buildings were erected in 1912, and consist of a dispensary, four small wards and an operating theatre, and the staff consists of a European Lady doctor and a compounder. The hospital at the headquarters of the S. P. G. Mission in Rānchi is in charge of a Sub-Assistant Surgeon and a European nurse.

The Lutheran Mission maintain the Elizabeth Dispensary at Rānchi, and at Lohardagā, in addition to the dispensary, there is a home for incurables and the small leper asylum, which has been mentioned above.

Vaccination.

Vaccination was introduced into the district in 1867, and Act IV (B. C.) of 1865, prohibiting the practise of inoculation by itinerant *tikaits,* was extended to the Division in 1869. The compulsory Vaccination Act, Act V (B. C.) of 1880, is in force only in the Municipal areas, where the cost of the establishment is met from Municipal funds, and in the Civil station of Dorandā. In rural areas vaccination is performed by licensed vaccinators, numbering about forty-five, who receive two annas for each successful operation. There are also four inspecting officers whose pay is met from provincial funds. The average number of successful vaccinations performed annually during the five years ending 1914-15 was 50,958. The value of the protection is keenly appreciated, and in 1914-15 out of 51,818 persons vaccinated 38,189 were infants, or about 79 per cent. of the surviving infant population. Revaccination is not so popular, and the people who have been accustomed to inoculation do not realise that vaccination is only a temporary preventive, and it is only in times of an outbreak of small-pox that they will go to the trouble and expense of the operation. In addition to the prescribed fee, the vaccinators are usually required to do *pujà* for the speedy recovery of the patients and receive a few annas remuneration for this essential service.

A vaccine depôt has recently been opened at Nāmkum, a few miles from Rānchi on the Purulia road, from which the supply of lymph required for the province is drawn.

Sanitation.

Two factors combine to render the problem of sanitation less acute in Rānchi than in other districts. In the first place the natural drainage, owing to the configuration of the ground, is excellent, and in the second place, there are no very large villages and bazars. The main problem is the supply of good drinking water. The town of Rānchi has plenty of good wells, and the water-supply was sufficient for the population before the town became the temporary headquarters of the Local Government. The increase in the population has made it necessary to consider the possibility of a water-supply scheme, but the schemes which have been prepared are too costly to be undertaken for some years to come. Two small pumping stations have been erected, one at Rānchi to supply water to Government House and the quarters occupied by officers, and one at Hinu to supply water to the quarters occupied by clerks. The villages rely for their water-supply on rivers, tanks, and *dāris*, or springs which are found in the low-lying paddy-fields, while at the more important bazars and villages the District Board have constructed masonry wells. Many more such wells are needed, and an increase in their number will improve greatly the health of the district, by removing one of the chief causes of dysentery and other bowel complaints. In the town of Rānchi considerable improvements have been made of recent years in the scavenging and conservancy arrangements, but the arrangements are still far from satisfactory and a proper drainage system is urgently needed in the more congested parts. At Bundu and Gumlā Union Committees, financed by the District Board, have recently been instituted to look after the sanitation of these large bazars.

CHAPTER V.

AGRICULTURE.

THE cultivable land of the district is divided into two classes, *viz.*, *don* and *tānr*. The *don* lands are the terraced low lands on which rice only is grown, and the *tānr* are the uplands which produce a coarse form of rice, known as *gora*, millets, pulses and oil-seeds. In the Khunti subdivision these lands are known as *loyong* and *piri*, respectively. Classes of land.

The *don* lands are prepared by levelling and embanking the slopes, so that they may retain the water. They are classified according to the amount of moisture they naturally retain. Fields lying at the bottom of the depressions between the ridges are known as *garhā don*, and, as they retain the moisture well, produce excellent crops in normal years and good crops even in years of drought. The most valuable *garhā don* is *kudar*, that is, land kept permanently moist by a rivulet or spring flowing through it. *Garhā don* in the Bengali-speaking portion of the Five Parganas is called *bahal* or *dabar*. Lands lying next above the *garhā don* are known as *sokrā*, while those at the top of the slopes and immediately below the *tānr* lands are known as *chaurā* or *bade*. Such lands are extremely liable to drought, and those parts of the district which have the highest proportion of *chaurā* lands are most liable to famine. In the Settlement record *don* lands have been divided into four classes, *viz.* :—

Don I.—Land which is continually wet and grows both the ordinary winter rice crop and a summer rice crop known as *tewa*.

Don II.—Lands which produce the winter rice crop, which is cut in the month of Agahan (December).

Don III.—Lands which produce the winter rice crop which is usually cut in Kartik (November).

Don IV.—Lands which produce the autumn rice crop which ripens in Bhado and Aswin (October).

These four classes correspond to the *kudar*, *garhā*, *sokrā* and *chaurā don*, respectively.

The area which produces two crops in the year is very small and only amounts to 760 acres, of which nearly half is in Khunti thāna. For all practical purposes the land which is classified as *Don* II may be regarded as the best rice-producing land in the district, and of the total cultivated area of the district 12 per cent. has been included in this class, the percentage being slightly higher in the Khunti and Sadar subdivisions than in the Gumlā subdivision. Twenty-one per cent. of the total cultivated area is included in the two lowest classes; in the Sadar subdivision, where the population is more dense and the rice cultivation consequently more extended, the percentage is 28 while in the Gumlā subdivision it is only 16. From crop-cutting experiments made by officers of the Settlement Department, the produce of an acre of the two first classes of land has been ascertained to be about 19 maunds of paddy while that of the two lowest classes is about 12 maunds.

The uplands are also subdivided by the inhabitants according to their productiveness. The land nearest the village site which profits most by the manure and drainage of the houses is known as *dihāri dānr*. This includes the *bāri* or small garden which is immediately adjacent to the house and is used for growing maize, vegetables and spices, and the *bira-bāri*, in which paddy seedlings are grown for transplantation. Further away from the village site come the ordinary *tānr* lands which are divided according to the fertility of the soil, the worst being that which is very stony, with little depth of soil (*rugri tanr*). The Settlement Department have also divided *tānr* into classes. *Tānr* I corresponds to the *bāris* round the houses. *Tānr* II is level land more remote from the village, but with good depth of soil. *Tānr* III is the stony or sloping land usually furthest away from the village site, with little depth of soil and little or no capacity to retain moisture. Lands of the two latter classes usually lie fallow once in two or three years, and, taking this fact into account, the produce of the three classes in terms of paddy may be said to be, *Tānr* I eight maunds per acre, *Tānrs* II and III three maunds per acre.

The soil is generally very poor in quality. From the earliest days of the British administration, the district was regarded as infertile and therefore of very inconsiderable value. Mr. Grant, in his "Historical and Comparative Analysis of the Finances of Bengal," written in 1787, refers to "the area commonly called Nāgpur, from the diamond mines of that place" as "barren in almost everything except the most precious jewels in the world". The soil is an infertile laterite. In the lowlands there is a large admixture of clay, but the soil of the uplands consists mainly of sand and gravel and only thinly covers the rocks beneath. As is to be expected from its gneissic origin, the soil is rich in potash but very deficient in lime and phosphates. The chief vernacular names for the different varieties of soil are (1) *pankua*, or alluvial soil, found chiefly in the Five Parganas; (2) *nagra*, called *chite* in the Five Parganas, a black sticky clay soil; (3) *khirsi*, a loam consisting of equal proportions of clay and sand; (4) *rugri*, or gravelly soil; (5) *bala*, or sandy loam; (6) *lāl matia*, the red ferruginous sandy loam, found in the *tānr* lands. Soil.

The cultivator of the Rānchi district is practically entirely dependent on a good rainfall for his crop of rice. There is very little artificial irrigation in the district. Some of the zamindārs have constructed tanks or *bāndhs* for the irrigation of their lands, and the raiyats in some few cases derive benefit from these. But many of the zamindārs are in too bankrupt a condition to undertake any works of improvement, and are, or have been, on such bad terms with their raiyats that they are reluctant to combine with them in carrying out any large works. The raiyats also are notoriously improvident, and though they have shown themselves capable of united action in the struggle against landlords, they have not yet shown themselves capable of joining together to carry out any large irrigation schemes, such as utilizing for their crops the water of the numerous rivers and streams which intersect the district. In the less developed parts of the district they are still able to reclaim lands from the jungle or to make new fields by embanking and terracing the lands in the bed of a stream, and they rest content with extending their cultivation in the manner which has been followed for centuries. In the more populous parts of the central plateau, the limit of extensive cultivation Rainfall.

appears to have been reached, and if the population increases rapidly the raiyats will be compelled to learn what are to them new methods of cultivation, to improve their uplands by the use of manure, and to make good crops a certainty in their lowlands by means of irrigation. Under present conditions the rice crops are dependent on a good rainfall, or rather on a well distributed rainfall. If the monsoon ceases in the latter half of August or early in September, the rice crop on the *chaurā* lands perishes and the raiyats are unable to get a good crop of *gorā* rice, pulse, or oil-seeds from their *tānr* lands. The dependence of the crops upon a well-distributed rainfall is illustrated by the facts of recent years of scarcity and famine. In 1899 the prospects were favourable till the end of July; in the next three months the rainfall was 15 inches below the normal. Again in 1904 the total rainfall of the year was above normal, but the early cessation of the rains caused the crops to be very poor. In 1907 the rain was normal, or above normal, during August, but no rain fell after the 9th of September.

Cultivation of Rice.

Rice is the staple food-crop of the district. The rice grown on the uplands is known as *gorā* and includes many varieties of coarse rice, such as *alsanga* and *karanga*. It is sown broadcast as soon as the first rains break, and is reaped in September. The total area under *gorā* paddy was ascertained in the Settlement operations to be 317 square miles, or 13·17 per cent. of the net cropped area of 2,483 square miles, and the produce of this area in a normal year may be taken to be 1,464,960 maunds of paddy or 732,480 maunds of rice.

The lowland paddy may be divided into two classes, the bhadoi and the aghani. The bhadoi crop corresponds to the *lauhan*, or light rice, crop grown on the *chaurā don* and includes many varieties of coarse rice, such as *jhalar-genda* and *mughdi*. The aghani crop, which is reaped in November, corresponds to the *garuhan* or *barka* rice, grown on the lowest and best lands, and includes the finer varieties of rice, such as *kalamdani*, *tilasar* and *rai-muri*. The total area under bhadoi and aghani rice is 756 and 447 square miles, respectively, and the total produce about 10,778,880 maunds of paddy or 5,383,440 maunds of rice.

There are three processes for the cultivation of lowland paddy, viz., *bunā*, *lewā* and *ropā*. *Bunā* is sowing the rice on dry fields shortly after the first rain of May or June, *lewā* is sowing in mud, at the end of June, seed which has been brought to the point of germination by being soaked in water for twenty-four hours, and *ropā* is the transplantation of seedlings which have been reared in a nursery. Before sowing or transplantation the fields are generally ploughed three or four times; the first ploughing (*chirna*) is done as soon as possible after the winter rice is harvested, or after the winter rains; if the *bunā* process is to be carried out, the fields are ploughed again in February or March, the clods broken up and the field harrowed and levelled; the second and third ploughing being known as *dobarna* and *uthaona*. The fields are manured sometimes in the month of Chait by spreading cowdung over them. The final ploughing just before the seed is sown on the pulverised soil is known as *puraona*. For the *lewā* process the field is thoroughly ploughed again after the first heavy rainfall of June or July and brought into a state of liquid mud. For transplantation, the seedlings are reared in the *bira-bāri* near the homestead and, after the wet field has been ploughed, are planted out by the women of the household. The fields are weeded three times, first before the seed is sown, secondly, in July or August, with the help of the plough and harrow, and, lastly, by hand in August or September. When the crop is ripe, it is harvested by both men and women, and carried off to the *khalihān*, or threshing-floor, which is preferably a flat piece of bare rock (*chatān*), or failing that, a plot of waste land in a *bāri* or mango-grove, which has been carefully levelled and smoothed. The threshing is done by men and bullocks, and the grain is stored in large bundles made of twisted straw rope known as *morās*, or in large cylindrical baskets made of split bamboo and plastered inside with mud and cowdung, called *chatkās*.

Other crops.

The principal bhadoi crops grown on the uplands, apart from the *gorā* rice, are cereals, such as *gondli*, or small millet (Panicum miliare) and *marua* (Eleusine coracana), pulses, such as *urid* (Phaseolus Roxburghii), and oil-seeds, such as *surguja* (Guiyotia Oleifera). The upland crops are usually sown in rotation. In the first year the ground is manured and a crop of *marua* sown; this is followed by a crop of *gorā* paddy, which profits by the manure given in the previous year. In the next year *urid* is sown and in the last year *gondli*, which thrives even in a poor soil and which, being reaped early in the summer, can be followed in the same year by a crop of *surguja* or *kurthi*. Frequently *rahar* (Cajanus Indicus) is sown with the *gorā* or *gondli* and reaped in the *rabi* harvest, while *bodi* is sown along with *marua*. In most villages, as the soil of the uplands is extremely poor, they are left fallow by turns for one, two, or three years at a time. The net area under the principal crops other than rice was found in the Settlement operations to be:—*Urid*, 127 square miles; *gondli*, 300 square miles; *marua*, 110 square miles; *surguja*, 157 square miles. Maize, spices, and vegetables are grown in the enclosed *bāris* near the houses. The *rabi* crops are not important. Wheat and barley are not grown in large quantities, the uplands being too dry during the cold-weather months and irrigation from wells being an expensive labour which the aboriginal cultivator will not undertake. *Rahar* (Cajanus Indicus) and *sarson* or mustard (Sinapis dichotoma) are the principal *rabi* crops.

Tobacco.

Tobacco is grown only in the alluvial soil of the Five Parganas; about 230 acres were found to be cultivated with tobacco in Tamār thana at the time of the recent Settlement operations. A detailed account of the cultivation of tobacco is given in Hunter's Statistical Account of Lohardaga district, but the crop is not sufficiently important to call for a repetition of that account. The tobacco consumed in the district is imported from Bihar and that produced locally is smoked in the form of small cheroots by the inhabitants of the Five Parganas.

Sugarcane is also grown in a few villages of the Khunti subdivision, chiefly in thānas Sonahatu and Tamār.

Cotton or *kapās* (Gassypium Herbaceum) occupies about 11,000 acres in the Gumlā subdivision and is grown by aboriginals, semi-aboriginals, and Kurmis, who appreciate the stout homespun cloth that can be manufactured from it.

Market gardening.

Market gardening is almost exclusively practised by Koiris and is confined to the town of Rānchi and the surrounding villages, and to the neighbourhood of Lohardagā. Chutiā in particular has a large colony of Koiris, originally immigrants from Bihar, and the aboriginal inhabitants of that village have also devoted themselves to the cultivation of vegetables. English vegetables do well in gardens during the cold weather, and some of them, such as tomatoes, may be found growing in the *bāris* of Christian aborigines, who have been induced to grow them by the European missionaries. The well-to-do aboriginals sometimes grow

Indian vegetables, such as brinjals, onions, pumpkins, gourds and sweet potatoes, and spices, such as turmeric (*haldi*) and chilli.

Fruit trees.

In nearly every village there is a grove of mango trees, planted by the Hindu landlord, the fruit of which is the common property of the village ; the trees are frequently barren and the better varieties of mangoes are not obtainable. Jack trees are also common and, according to the custom of the country, both the tree and the fruit are the property of the man who planted it. Theft of jack-fruit is a frequent subject of complaint in the courts. The fruit of the tamarind and the *karanj* (Pongamia glabra) is also the exclusive property of the owner of the tree. The fruit of the *karanj* is not eaten but is made into oil and used for various purposes. It is used to kill the insects which infest the hair of the people, and it is also said that wood coated with the oil resists the attacks of white-ants. Its principal use is, or rather was before the days of Kerosine oil and Dietz lanterns, as a lamp oil. The fruit of other trees, such as *mahua*, *jāmun*, *kusam*, etc., which are found round the village, are, like mangoes, the common property of the villagers. Plantains, guavas and limes of various kinds are grown principally by the Hindu inhabitants, and a Hindu village can often be distinguished from an aboriginal village by the plantains or papeyas growing round the houses.

Tea.

The cultivation of tea in the district of Rānchi dates back to 1862 and owes its origin to Mr. Stainforth, a retired civilian who settled at Rānchi. He started two gardens, one at Hotwar, about three miles north of Rānchi, and the other at Palāndu, about 12 miles east, on lands leased from the Barkagarh Estate which had been confiscated by Government after the Mutiny. In 1872 the whole area of the Palāndu garden (184 acres) was under mature plants and yielded 20,500 lbs. of leaf, all of which was manufactured into black tea. Of the Hotwar Estate only 35 acres were under mature plant and the yield was 3,200 lbs. Since that date a number of new gardens have been opened, all under European management, and there are now 21 gardens with an area of 2,070 acres, while the produce is over 300,000 lbs. The leaf is now practically all manufactured into green tea. Coffee also does well in Chotā Nāgpur, but the cultivation is not carried out on any extensive scale.

Silk.

The rearing of tasar cocoons is carried out in portions of thanas Tamār and Khunti, bordering on Singhbhūm, but nowhere on a very large scale. Wild cocoons are very rare and tasar is usually obtained from cocoons reared on the *asan* tree (Terminalia tomentosa). By custom no payment is made for trees used for the cultivation of cocoons, whether on cultivated land or waste lands and jungle. The Roman Catholic Mission at Khunti are endeavouring to encourage the industry among their converts.

Lac.

The cultivation of lac is sporadic throughout the district. It is most common in the Khunti subdivision and in a portion of the Sadar subdivision, but in some parts, though the conditions appear equally favourable, little lac is produced. Lac is the resinous incrustation which is produced on the twigs of several varieties of tree round the bodies of colonies of the lac insect (coccus lacca). Originally lac was merely collected from trees on which it was found, but with the development of the trade, cultivation has become widespread. The method of propagation is simple; twigs of a tree utilized in the previous year and crowded with larvæ are bound to the twigs of a tree to be brought under cultivation. The insects are gradually hatched out from the larvæ and proceed to feed on the resinous sap of the tree which exudes from their bodies and forms a hard crust of lac over the whole twig. The trees most suitable for lac are *palās* (Butea frondosa) and *kusum*, (Schleichera trijuga), but it is also grown on the *bair* (Zizaphus jujuba) and other trees. The lac of a *kusum* tree commands the best price, and a fair-sized tree produces two crops in a year, in the hot weather and again in the beginning of the cold weather, and the annual value of the lac is not less than Rs. 10.

Cattle.

The cattle of the Rānchi district are very small and undersized, and this is largely due to the lack of good pasturage and of good fodder. In the remote parts there is still ample pasturage in the jungles, but owing to the extension of cultivation the area is rapidly decreasing. In the more extensively cultivated parts, the cattle are grazed on the waste lands of the village, or on the fields after the harvest has been cut, and in the hot weather are in a wretchedly poor condition. In the rains grass grows rapidly, and they pick up and become some what fat. The aboriginals seldom feed their cattle in stalls, and only paddy straw is stored for use as fodder. Cows are not kept for milk. The Mundās in fact think it almost a crime to drink the milk of a cow which they consider should be left entirely to the calf. Cows are habitually yoked to the plough and are known as *gundri* or plough cows. Buffaloes are not bred in the district, but are imported from North and South Bihar and from Palāmau. They are used for ploughing the heavier *don* lands.

The agricultural stock list compiled during the Settlement operations shows a total number of 540,000 bulls, bullocks and cows, 137,000 buffaloes and 201,000 calves, or between three and four head of cattle to each cultivating family. Though the inhabitants of the district have no objection to eating beef, they cannot afford to kill their cattle for this purpose. The hides of cattle are usually the perquisite of the Lohār or Ahir of the village and cases are not uncommon in which they resort to poisoning cattle for the sake of the hides. There is a considerable export of hides and skins from Rānchi.

Cattle disease is extremely prevalent in the district. Epidemics of rinderpest and hæmorrhagic septicæmia are common, and cause great mortality, while foot-and-mouth disease causes the plough cattle to deteriorate. The official statistics for the year 1914-15 show nearly a thousand deaths from rinderpest and over two hundred and fifty from hæmorrahagic septicæmia, but these figures are of little value as the majority of the deaths are not reported. The aboriginal is extremely apathetic in taking any preventive measures against the disease; he regards such calamities, which he cannot account for, as due to the malignant spite of one of the village *bhūts* and beyond trying to appease the spirit by sacrifices takes no steps to prevent the spreading of the infection. The Christian population are beginning to appreciate the benefits of inoculation as a prophylactic against these diseases. An interesting and promising experiment has recently been made. Twenty boys nominated by the Heads of the three Missions were trained in Rānchi in the work of inoculation and then sent out to the various Mission stations to tour and inoculate cattle in the surrounding villages, under the supervision of the Missionary in charge. During the year 1913-14 no fewer than 67,900 cattle were inoculated. Members of the Roman Catholic Co-operative Society are encouraged to get their cattle inoculated by being unable to obtain loans for their purchase, if the cattle of their village have not been inoculated in spite of the opportunity being given. It is too early to say whether this experiment has resulted in decreasing the mortality, but the measure gives great promise of success.

Besides cattle the cultivators keep large numbers of sheep and goats, mainly for food purposes. In an aboriginal village there are pigs innumerable, as the sacrifice of a pig, and the subsequent feast on its flesh, forms an important part of their religion. Horses and ponies are not numerous, and the possession of a pony is regarded as a sign of wealth.

Veterinary dispensary.

The District Board has a well-provided Veterinary dispensary at Rānchi under the charge of a Veterinary Assistant, and employs two itinerant Veterinary Assistants, one of whom has his headquarters at Gumlā.

District Agricultural Association.

The District Agricultural Association, which was formed in 1905, has devoted its attention to the improvement of methods of agriculture but, like similar associations in other districts, has not met with any great success in overcoming the conservatism of the agriculturist. The need for irrigation has already been mentioned. Improvement in the breed of cattle and in the fodder supply is also much needed. With the gradual deforestation of the district the problem of pasturage becomes more acute and unless the breed of cattle is improved, such improved methods of agriculture as deep ploughing cannot be adopted. Attempts to induce the cultivator to use an improved form of plough are always met with the reply that their cattle are not sufficiently strong. In many villages the limit of extensive cultivation has already been reached, and with the increase of population a more intensive cultivation will have to be carried on. In the past there was plenty of waste land waiting to be cultivated, and the need for improved methods of cultivation was not apparent, but the problem of the next century in the district of Rānchi will be how to improve the soil so as to produce sufficient grain for the increasing population.

The Association holds an Annual Agricultural Show on the site of the old *mela* at Chutiā. The exhibits are fairly numerous but come for the most part from Rānchi itself, the most conspicuous exhibits being usually the collections of English vegetables produced by the Missions or by the Jail.

CHAPTER VI.

FORESTS.

Extent of Forests.

The name Jhārkand, or the "forest tract," shows that the whole of Chotā Nāgpur was at one time a huge forest, consisting no doubt mainly of *sāl* trees, from which stood out isolated hills covered with "upper mixed" forest. The forest has gradually been destroyed by the axes of the cultivators, and at the present time the whole of the central plateau has been almost completely cleared and there remain only the jungle-clad hills on the outskirts of the district. In the early days of British administration the destruction of the forests went on unchecked. Their value was not appreciated; the economic effects of denudation were not recognized, and it was generally accepted that nothing should be done to prevent the extension of cultivation. In 1883 Mr. Hewitt, the Commissioner, called attention to the rapid destruction of private forests in the Division and to the "incalculable misfortune resulting from their wholesale destruction not only to the Chotā Nāgpur country but to the Bengal districts lying below the plateau". In 1885 Dr. Schlick reported that "in a general way it may be said that the Hazāribāgh and Rānchi plateau contains now comparatively little forest". Dr. Schlick probably referred only to valuable forests, though the correctness of his opinion is open to doubt.

Statistics compiled during the recent settlement operations shows that there are still 2,281 square miles of jungle in the district, or 32 per cent. of its total area. Of this area 889 square miles have been classified as culturable jungle, and 1,392 square miles as unculturable jungle. In the Sadar subdivision, with an area over 2,002 square miles, there are only 600 square miles of jungle, both culturable and unculturable, principally in thānas Burmu, Angara, and Lohardagā, which comprise the hills fringing the north and north-west of the central plateau. In these thanas jungles still cover more than 45 per cent. of the total area, but in the remaining seven thanas less than 23 per cent. of the area is jungle, the greater part of which is growing on land which can never be brought under cultivation. In the northern and western half of the Khunti subdivision and in the eastern part of the Gumlā subdivision the country is similar to that in the Sadar subdivision and thānas Karra, Khunti, Torpa, Sisai, Ghaghrā and Gumlā only contain 281 square miles of jungle, or 15 per cent. of the total area. In the whole of this central plateau the country is dotted at intervals with sharp rocky peaks practically devoid of vegetation. Low rocky ridges also occur, covered sometimes with a meagre growth of scrub but more frequently without any forest growth whatever. In a few places patches of stunted *sāl* are seen and at rare intervals isolated trees of fair size appear, growing on the most precipitous slopes, apparently devoid of all soil. In some villages the *sārnās*, or sacred groves, are still of considerable size, but in most villages only small clusters of trees remain, the only proofs that these tracts were ever under forest. Indeed, if they did not exist, it would be difficult to believe that a forest had ever grown on them. In the sub-plateau tract, consisting of thānas Silli, Sonahatu and Bundu, similar conditions prevail, 22 per cent. of the total area being jungle-covered, and that principally on the *ghāts* which cut off the lower from the higher plateau. In thāna Tamār, which forms the southern border of the lower plateau, there is still a large tract of jungle, extending over 140 square miles. But it is in the south and west of the Gumlā and Simdegā subdivisions that the largest and most important forest areas are found and it is only in this part of the district, where the population is still comparatively sparse, that there is any hope of taking effective steps to prevent further denudation. In thāna Bishunpur 64 per cent. of the total area is jungle. The long range of hills, which runs north from Pālkot to the borders of Palāmau and forms the watershed between the north and south Koel, is generally covered with forest containing only *sāl* of very poor growth, and scrub, consisting of such shrubs as Woodfordia and Cleistanthus. The steepness of the slopes and the poverty of the soil render the production of any forest of value an impossibility, while in the small areas of level ground the forest has been cut down and burnt by the cultivators so that a crop may be raised from the soil rendered temporarily fertile in this way. The slopes of the Rājāderā plateau, to the west of Tendār and Bishunpur, are covered with a poor type of forest sufficient for the needs of the inhabitants but containing few large trees. The Rājāderā plateau itself, at an elevation of 3,500 feet, is now mainly denuded, but must have been covered with jungle at a comparatively recent date. Round the village of Rājāderā some of the original forest still remains, but it contains few large trees, as, owing to its elevation, the maximum girth which *sāl* will attain probably does not exceed 4½ feet. The Sankh river rises in these forests and leaves the plateau through a narrow gorge containing virgin forest of fair hill type, with *sāl* trees up to five feet in girth, but the forest is gradually being destroyed by the inhabitants of a village situated in the gorge, who are rapidly extending their cultivation and by contractors. In the undulating plateau of Barwe, through which the Sankh flows, the country is almost devoid of jungle, even the steepest slopes being flecked with cultivation. The destruction of the forest in this tract is of comparatively recent date and missionaries who have resided here for the last twenty years state that on their first arrival dense forests surrounded their stations. In the valley of the Sankh, south of Rāidih, patches of better forest are found. Between Kondrā and Kulukerā on the western border of the district there is a large tract of forest, but as it has been worked for some time past by contractors for sleepers, it contains few large trees. The flat country south of Kulukerā is practically denuded of jungle, but the rocky ridge in Kurdeg thāna, near the southern border of the district, is well covered with second class forest, free from cultivation. Further east, in thānas Kochedegā, Kolebirā and Bano, the country appears at first sight to be covered with thick jungle but on a closer examination the forests of Biru, Bhaunrpahār and Pālkot are found to contain few large trees and to have suffered from reckless cutting by timber contractors. The following table shows the area under jungle in the western and southern thanas of the Gumlā and Simdegā subdivisions :—

Thana.	Area in square miles.	Area of culturable jungle.	Area of non-culturable jungle.	Total jungle area.	Percentage of jungle to area of thana.
Bishunpur	237	42	111	153	34
Chainpur	407	19	131	150	37
Rāidih	198	38	42	80	40
Kurdeg	309	55	114	169	54
Kochedegā	530	92	153	245	46
Kolebirā	396	111	100	211	53
Bano	212	41	49	90	42
Pālkot	223	30	64	94	42

Causes of deforestation.

Of the causes which have led to deforestation the most important is the extension of cultivation, for, while other causes, such as the exploitation of forests by contractors, or reckless cutting for timber and fuel by the cultivators, tend to lessen the density of the jungle and to prevent the growth of large trees, reclamation of jungle areas for purposes of cultivation causes its total destruction. It is difficult to estimate the extent to which cultivation has been extended at the expense of the forests during the last quarter of a century, as no detailed survey of the district was made till the recent settlement operations. A comparison, however, has been made between figures obtained during the recent survey and those obtained during the survey of the Chotā Nāgpur estate in 1882—84, and it has been found that in fourteen villages the average net decrease in the area under jungle was 11 per cent. These villages were in the central plateau, and it is probable that in outlying tracts, in which the population has increased very rapidly during the last 25 years, the area brought under cultivation, either temporary or permanent, is considerably larger. Though the reclamation might have been better regulated, extension of the cultivated area was necessary in the interests of the growing population, as a very high percentage of the waste land, not under forests, is unfit for cultivation. The landlords have in most cases consented to the reclamation, in return for a *salāmi* or increased rent; and it is only in the case of absentee landlords that the reclamation has been carried out without their consent, and sometimes without their knowledge. "Jhuming", or a form of cultivation akin to "jhuming", obtains in the remote parts of the district. Under this system, the trees are felled from patches in the jungle, and burnt on the ground with the undergrowth, and the land thus cleared yields poor crops for a few years and then is abandoned. The practice is undoubtedly very destructive of forests, and the value of the forest destroyed is entirely disproportionate to the value of the crops raised, but the practice can hardly be said to be very prevalent in the district.

The second main cause is the sale or lease of forests to contractors and others. The felling of large trees is open to no objection, but, even if the contractor is given a carefully worded lease, the owner of the forest is not able to supervise his work, or that of his agents, or to prevent them recklessly thinning out the forest. Over-exploitation by contractors is very obvious in the jungles of Biru, Tamār, Basia and Bhaunrpahār, which were mentioned by Dr. Schlick, in 1888, as important *sāl* forests, but now hardly contain a tree from which a sleeper can be made. This cause has always been in operation but has been more marked of recent years. The opening of the railway to Rānchi and Lohardagā and the improvement of communications by road has made timber more marketable and has led to the sale of jungles previously untouched. Moreover, since the settlement operations commenced, the abuse by the tenants of their customary right has given an impetus to sales, as the landlords naturally try to obtain as much profit as possible from the jungle, before all the valuable timber is felled.

Apart from the sale of jungle to contractors and timber companies, much damage has been done to the jungle by the raiyats themselves. The decrease in the area of the jungles and the increase in population has greatly enhanced the demand for timber both for building purposes and for fuel, especially in the neighbourhood of Rānchi and the railway. By the custom of the district, a raiyat has no right to sell wood cut from the village jungle but in some villages, where the relations between landlord and tenants are strained, the raiyats have exceeded their right and cut the jungle wholesale for purpose of sale, without the consent of the landlords. The practise is difficult to stop; if the raiyat is found cutting wood in the jungle, he asserts that it is for his own use; if he is found selling it in the bazar, he denies that it came from the zamindār's jungle. In some villages the landlords exact a payment of so many rupees or annas from each family for the exercise of the right to cut wood and sell it at the weekly bazar. This system is known as *bankatti* and, though it has the advantage of securing some profit to the landlord, yet, as no restrictions are placed on the amount cut, it has as much effect in lessening the density of the forest as the abuse by the raiyats of their customary rights. Apart from cutting timber for sale, the raiyats are also most wasteful in cutting wood for agricultural purposes. A large tree will be felled to make a plough or a door-post, or even to secure the honey secreted in its top. One of the worst forms of waste is the indiscriminate cutting of *sāl* saplings to make a fence round a house, or even to make a temporary enclosure for a wedding, when other less valuable wood would serve the same purpose.

Other minor causes, which, if not active causes of deforestation, prevent the progress of natural reafforestation, are indiscriminate grazing, and the practise of firing the jungle. Grazing, especially of browsers, destroys the young trees. Firing, if carefully regulated, does not cause any very serious damage. The destruction of the undergrowth helps the growth of the larger trees, and it is only the firing of young plantations which would cause any very marked denudation of the forest area. The total damage caused by firing in the district is probably not very great as the zamindārs usually take steps to prevent the firing of young jungles.

Effects of deforestation.

The indirect effects of the destruction of forests are difficult to estimate. Scientific investigations go to show that forests under some conditions increase the rainfall, by lowering the temperature of the surrounding air and thereby provoking the precipitation of rain. In Rānchi district the masses of barren rock, from which all soil has been washed and on which all vegetation have been killed, were undoubtedly formerly covered with trees, and it is possible that this change in the physical aspect of the country has had its effect on the climate, but there are no statistics to show that the rainfall has decreased, or even that there has been any marked variation in the distribution. There is also no evidence to prove that the level of the sub-soil water has become lower. Considering the large areas still under jungle, and the fact that the country, as a whole, is well wooded, it is safe to conclude that deforestation in Rānchi has not yet reached the stage at which these serious effects are noticed.

The direct effect of the loss of the forests are more obvious but are apt to be exaggerated. Many of them are purely local, and it is incorrect to draw any wide generalizations and to assert that the district as a whole has become less fertile or is more liable to famine and scarcity than it was in the days when the forests were more extensive. A few fields may have become unfit for cultivation owing to the loss of moisture caused by the radiation of heat from the barren rocky hills; in a few villages the inhabitants may be forced to use cowdung for fuel and thus to rob the fields of the only manure they ever get; in some areas the population may be unable to obtain jungle produce in such quantities as formerly and are thus deprived of one of their chief sources of food in years of bad harvests; but it is fallacious to say that, because no famines are known to have occurred before 1897, the three famines since that date were due to, or were intensified by, the diminution in the jungle area. Though generalizations, such as these, are exaggerated, there is no doubt that the deforestation of the district is rapidly reaching a stage at which these effects will make themselves felt. Formerly the raiyats obtained without difficulty all the wood needed for fuel or for the construction of their houses or agricultural instruments, and there was ample grazing-ground for ther cattle within a short distance of their villages. Already in the more cultivated tracts the raiyats are put to trouble or expense in getting timber. The diminution of the areas from which timber can be obtained leads to excessive cutting in the remaining jungles, while the decrease in the grazing area similarly tends to over-grazing of existing areas and thus prevent the natural regeneration of the forest. The effects of deforestation, in fact, become in time the causes of further deforestation, and when, in addition to this, it is remembered that the cultivators are accustomed to cutting timber in the most wasteful and extravagant manner, and that the landlords on their part are endeavouring to make as much immediate profit as possible by the sale of their property to contractors, it will be recognized that measures are urgently required for the preservation of the existing forests.

Various suggestions have been made as to the protective measures to be adopted, but before describing these, it is necessary to give an account of the rights of the landlord and tenants in the jungle.

Right of landlords and tenants.

Generally speaking, it may be said that the proprietary right in the jungles of the Rānchi district rests with the landlords, while the raiyats, who represent the ancient village communities, retain a right of user for certain purposes. This condition has arisen gradually. The aboriginal tribes, who first entered the district, found it covered with virgin jungle and reclaimed land for cultivation. Jungle lands were abundant, and each village community extended the limits of cultivation and cut timber for domestic and agricultural purposes, as it thought fit. Later, feudal chiefs imposed their authority, and received a small tribute and exacted certain services, but in no way dispossessed the descendants of the original settlers of their proprietary rights either in the cultivated or uncultivated land. The chiefs, however, gradually became Hinduized and both the chiefs themselves and the Hindu settlers introduced by them came to acquire the position of landlords and were recognized by the Courts as the owners of the soil. In early days, as the jungle land was still abundant, the landlords did not prevent the raiyats cutting all the timber they required for their own use, and neither raiyats nor landlords realized that timber had any commercial value. It is only within comparatively recent years that the jungle question has arisen. With the increase of population, the decrease in the area of jungle, and the improvement of communications, both by road and rail, timber came to be a marketable commodity. Landlords began to assert their proprietary right, and met with no opposition from the raiyats, provided they were still permitted to cut for their own requirements. By degrees the landlords imposed restrictions, in some cases reasonable, and designed merely to prevent waste, in other cases unreasonable and designed to reserve the exclsuive proprietary right to themselves. The villages of the Rānchi district now present the jungle rights in three different stages of development. In the intact *khuntkātti* villages of the Mundā country the proprietary right in the jungles still rests with the *khuntkattidars*, who have jealously and successfully opposed any interference with that right by the superior landlords. In the majority of villages the proprietary rights of the descendants of the original clearers of the soil have passed to the landlord and the raiyats merely retain the right to cut timber for fuel and domestic purposes. In a few villages the landlord has succeeded in establishing his sole proprietary right and some jungles are found, especially in the Sadr sub-division, which are designated *rākhāwat*, or reserved jungle of the landlord, in contradistinction to *katāwat*, or jungle in which the raiyat still has the right to fell trees.

Settlement record of jungle rights.

In the record-of-rights prepared by the Settlement Department the customary rights of the raiyats have been carefully recorded. The tenants of village have —

(1) the right to cut trees for the purpose of building and repairing their houses, for agricultural purposes, such as making ploughs, and for fuel;

(2) the right to graze their cattle in the jungle;

(3) the right to collect the fruit of the *mahuā* and other forest trees, and to gather other kinds of forest produce for *boná fide* domestic purposes. They have no right to fell timber or gather forest produce for sale.

These rights are subject to a quantitative limitation. Thus the raiyats have no right to cut certain valuable trees, such as *jāmun, mahuā, āsan, haria, kusum, palās* and *ām*; nor can they cut *sāl* trees beyond a certain girth, about 27 inches in circumference at a height of three feet from the ground, or, if they are needed for the *boná fide* purpose of making ploughs or carts, of a girth not exceeding three feet. Tenants of villages, in which there is no jungle remaining, usually have the right to cut wood from the jungles of an adjacent village. This right is really a survival from the days when all jungles were open to all inhabitants of the district. The raiyats are not allowed to reclaim waste or jungle land without the permission of the landlord.

The landlords have a full right to sell the timber of the jungles but, though the question has never been raised in the Courts, this right must be considered as subject to the restriction that, in so doing, they must not deprive the tenants of their right of user. In other words, the landlords can only sell surplus trees, that is, trees which the raiyats have not the right to fell, and such trees as are not reasonably required for the satisfaction of the present or future *boná fide* reasonable requirements of the tenants.

Proposal for the protection of forests.

The difficulty of the problem of forest preservation in Chotā Nāgpur lies in reconciling these conflicting interests. In 1909 the Government of Bengal appointed a Committee to make local enquiries as to the extent of deforestation in Chotā Nāgpur and Orissa, and, on the report of the Committee, decided that the preservation of large tracts of jungle in these areas was an administrative necessity, and that, as there was no hope that the progress of denudation would slacken, since the natural causes all tended to its increase, it was the duty of Government to take action in the interest of the people. The provisions of the Bengal Forest Act VII of 1878 were not considered suitable. Under this Act a landlord may apply to have his forest managed by Government as reserved or protected forest, but experience had shown that landlords had not taken advantage of this provision in the past and there was no reason to anticipate that the landlords of Chotā Nāgpur would make use of it in the future, as they do not yet appreciate the benefits of scientific management, which may secure for them large future profits but deprive them of all present profits. Nor was it considered desirable to apply to Chotā Nāgpur those sections of the Act which give Government the power to take over certain tracts and enforce certain prohibitions, subject to the condition that the owner may claim to have the forest acquired. It was thought that the cost of acquisition was a bar to any action on these lines and that, apart from this, such action would not be acceptable either to landlords or tenants and would cause considerable friction between them, as they would have to adjust their joint claims to new conditions. It was therefore proposed to introduce a private Forests Bill, the objects of which were—

(1) to empower the Government to intervene, in the public interest, to preserve private forests from destruction; and

(2) to facilitate, or in some cases direct, the afforestation of private waste lands.

The Bill gave power to the Forest officer in charge of any forest of which Government had assumed control, to scrutinize leases, to supervise cutting and growing, and to prevent fires. Both landlords and tenants were to be left as free as possible to exercise their customary rights, but in extreme cases the Forest officer would have power to close entirely blocks of forest and fines could be inflicted on the village communities or on the proprietors if damage was done to such closed blocks, either by felling timber, by cultivation, or by grazing of cattle. The Bill was submitted to public criticism and the criticisms received, both from the landlords and the missionaries who voiced the opinion of the aborigines, showed the great difficulty of reconciling their conflicting interests. Both parties admitted the necessity, but the landlords viewed with disapproval a measure which would result in expropriating them from their forests, for a term so extended that it would in practise amount to permanence, without giving them any adequate compensation, and the raiyats feared that the powers given to the Forest officers to enforce prohibition would result in depriving them of their customary rights, in particular of their right to take jungle produce and to graze their cattle in the jungle, and that the management of the forests would let loose a number of forest subordinates who would practise extortion in various ways. In view of the opposition which the introduction of the Bill would inevitably stir up, the Government of Bihar and Orissa decided not to proceed with it.

The system of State management which the Bill contemplated, bristles with difficulties, and an alternative suggestion that certain blocks of forest lands should be acquired by Government appears likely to meet with greater success. In such acquired blocks all rights both of landlords and tenants would be extinguished, and the blocks would be so selected as to leave in each village sufficient jungle to provide fuel and timber for the inhabitants and grazing for their cattle. The objection to such a measure is of course the expense involved, for, even though the forests reserved in this way would become of considerable commercial value, the initial expenditure would be probably very high, while it would also be a task of some difficulty to calculate the present value of the jungle. Complete reservation, however, in this way would have the advantage that certain areas would become covered with dense jungle, and, if it be a fact that forests do affect rainfall, such jungles would have considerable effect on the amount and distribution. As an alternative to acquisition, it has been suggested that as a large number of estates in the district are under the management of Government under the Encumbered Estates Act, Government in its position as landlord of these estates should apply for the reservation and protection of certain areas under the Bengal Forest Act, thus setting a good example to other landlords in the district. There is no doubt that much good could be done in this way; and during the long period that heavily encumbered estates are under the management of Government there would be ample time for the recuperation of the forests. It is true that on the release of the estates the zamindār would have full power over the forest and might again dispose of it to contractors with a view to getting a large immediate profit, but the principal objections to the proposal are that in many cases the estates are so insolvent that they could with difficulty bear the cost of an effective system of management by the Forest Department, and that this procedure could only be followed in a very limited area and would involve the imposition of restrictions and prohibitions by the Forest officer which would be regarded by the tenants as infringements of their customary rights. A further solution that has been proposed aims at doing away with the antagonistic rights of landlords and tenants by partitioning the jungles. Each party would have full proprietary rights in its share, and there are reasons to anticipate that both raiyats and landlords, if they were in sole possession, would come to realize the value of their property and take steps to prevent its wholesale destruction. Though the aboriginal takes little thought for the morrow, and still less for future generations, even the aboriginals, and especially the Christian aboriginals, might easily be persuaded through the influence of the Missionaries to take the necessary steps for the preservation of their own property. In the course of the Settlement operations some examples were found of efforts on the part of the villagers themselves to preserve their forests. In some villages of Bero thana in which the jungle area was small, the raiyats and their landlords had adopted a regular system of cutting blocks of the jungle in rotation for purposes of fuel, each block being left uncut for four or five years. The objection that is usually raised to this proposal is that the partition could not be settled without friction between the parties. It is doubtful whether this objection is valid, as the antagonism which was formerly rife between landlord and tenants has died down as a result of the recent settlement operations and, though there is a remembrance of the agrarian disputes of the last half century, the main causes of dispute have been removed and both parties might be willing to accept a compromise of this nature.

Reafforestation.

Apart from the problem of the protection of existing forests there is the problem of reafforestation. At Tendār an interesting experiment was conducted by the people themselves ; *sāl* seed was sown some twenty years ago with satisfactory results and there is now strong *sāl* copse covering several acres, but this experiment is the only instance of reafforestation by the raiyats themselves. The raiyats are reluctant to plant trees because there is no specific provision of the law that the man who plants and rears the tree should become its owner. If the law was altered there is some hope that the raiyats and landlords might be encouraged to carry out such work themselves. Though in many places the soil has been washed away and re-afforestation thus rendered impossible, there are undoubtedly still large tracts in which forests might be raised, of greater value than the meagre crops at present cultivated.

CHAPTER VII.

NATURAL CALAMITIES.

FAMINE, Causes of famine.

FAMINE due to deficiency of rainfall may be said to be the only natural calamity from which the inhabitants of Rānchi can suffer. Floods are rendered almost impossible, except for a very short period and within the narrowest limits, by the physical conformation of the country and the rapid discharge of the surface drainage. The crops in the lowest fields are sometimes injured to a small extent by very heavy falls of rain. When famine or scarcity has occurred, it has been due almost invariably to the failure of the rains in the latter part of August and in September and October. The crops are in fact entirely dependent on the rainfall, as there is very little artificial irrigation in the district. Zamindārs occasionally construct tanks and *bāndhs* for the benefit of their *khās* lands and the raiyats sometimes derive benefit from these reservoirs, but of the total cropped area of the district (2,483 square miles), the irrigated area only amounts to 3,058 acres. Though the country is intersected by numerous streams and rivers, practically no attempt is made either by landlords or tenants to utilize the water for irrigating the crops. Under present conditions a serious failure of the rain means famine through a large part of the district, while a partial failure causes scarcity and distress. The water drains away from the uplands and even the higher lowlands with great rapidity, and unless the crops on those lands receive a plentiful and continuous supply of water, they wither and die very quickly.

Two instances may be given of the benefits of irrigation. In 1908, when famine conditions prevailed over a considerable part of Rānchi district, there was no scarcity in the Dhalbhūm pargana of Singhbhūm. The conditions were exactly similar; but in Dhalbhūm the aboriginal villagers, in concert with the headmen, have constructed tanks and *bāndhs* for irrigation, and by damming the streams and small rivers make use of the water for the fields of the villages on their banks. The inhabitants of the tract are thus not dependent entirely on the rainfall and can resist periods of scarcity which play havoc with the people of Rānchi. In this same year, Ghāghrā thana was part of the area in which distress prevailed and famine was declared, but in three villages, in which irrigation *bāndhs* had been constructed, little distress was experienced and good *rabi* crops were obtained.

The most important crop is the autumn and winter rice. The total area under rice amounts to 1,530 square miles, or 61·61 per cent. of the total cropped area, and of this the area under *bhadoi*, *aghani* and *gorā* rice is 756, 447 and 327 square miles, respectively. The *gorā* rice which is grown on the better class of uplands (*tānr*) is the first to suffer from an early cessation of the rains, and, next, the rice grown on the *chaurā*, or higher lowlands, and in years of scarcity famine areas will generally be found to correspond with the areas in which there is the greatest proportion of the classes of land entered in the settlement record as Don III and Don IV, with a high proportion of uplands. Such areas are found in villages in the more backward tracts, where the land has been cleared at comparatively recent dates. In villages in the more intensely cultivated areas there are large stretches of low-lying rice lands, classified in the settlement as Don I or Don II, which remain moist for the greater part of the year, and such villages are little liable to scarcity. The areas most liable to famine are, thus, thānas Bishunpur, Chainpur, Rāidih, Kurdeg, Kcchedegā, and part of Ghāghrā adjacent to Bishunpur. Bishunpur is probably the area which is least able to resist conditions of scarcity.

Though the importance of the rice crop cannot be overestimated, there are other factors to be taken into consideration. In the Khunti subdivision, the lac crop has an important bearing on the prosperity of the people. If lac is abundant and good prices are obtainable, the people can resist famine, and their power to resist has been greatly increased by improved communications. Before the opening of the railway, importation by road was slow and difficult, but supplies from other districts can now be easily obtained, and there is little doubt that in 1908 the distress, at any rate in the parts round Rānchi, was alleviated by the importation by rail of over 6,000 tons of rice. Jungle produce, in particular the *mahuā* crop, also plays an important part in the economy of the district, and has been estimated to be equivalent to a two months' supply of food. Both in 1897 and in 1900, the partial failure of the *mahuā* crop greatly aggravated the distress.

Early famines. There is no record of famine in early times. There was severe drought in 1820, 1823, 1827, and 1837, but in none of these years was the distress sufficient to cause famine. Even the great famine of 1866 did not seriously affect the district. On the plateau coarse rice rose to the unprecedented price of 11½ seers to the rupee, but though the people felt the pressure of scarcity to some extent, there was no approach to actual scarcity, except in one or two places on the border of Mānbhūm where the price of rice rose as high as eight seers to the rupee, probably owing to heavy exports.

In 1873 the rains began so late that only a portion of the *bhadoi* crop could be sown. Later in the year, they fell in such torrents as to beat down the young crops, while from the 13th September till the following January there was an unbroken stretch of dry, hot weather. Distress was confined to the Five Parganas, and even in this tract the construction of a few roads and the issue of land improvement loans amounting to Rs. 2,360 were the only relief operations required. A bumper crop of *mahuā* and of jungle fruits in 1874 served to dispell any apprehension of serious distress. The experience of those years led to the conclusion that famine need not be anticipated in the district, and that even scarcity would be confined to the Five Parganas, where the proportion of *chaurā* to *garhā don* is high. Subsequent experience has shown this conclusion to be false. Since 1888 there have been three famines, in 1896-97, in 1899-1900, and in 1907-08. Whether the distress was really greater in these than in previous years, is uncertain. Greater knowledge of the district, owing to improved communications, may have resulted in relief measures being taken to meet distress, which in former times would have passed unnoticed. But it is probable also that the destruction of the forests has led to a decrease of jungle products, and thus deprived the people of one of their chief means of resistance to famine. In each of the recent famines the distress was greatly aggravated on the outbreak of the rains, when the collection of jungle produce was no longer possible, and on the first two occasions, there were a partial failure of the *mahuā* crop.

Famine of 1897.

In 1897, though famine was never actually declared in the district and relief operations were only carried on for a few months on a small scale, there is reason to belief that the sufferings of the people were great. The harvest of 1895 had been deficient, and in 1896 the monsoon was very weak in August and September, the rainfall being only 8·08 and 3·08 inches, respectively, in those months against a normal fall of 13·67 and 8·76 inches. In October no rain fell. The rainfall was also badly distributed, and in some places excessive rain did damage to the *bhadoi* crops. The whole district was affected, and the outturn of the rice crop was estimated at only eight annas. As the crop of the previous year had only been ten annas, the stock of food-grains was very low, while the high prices obtainable in other districts tempted the people to a reckless export of their stocks and drained the district of what little grain it contained. At first no apprehension of serious distress was entertained, and the only relief measures undertaken in April, May and June were the opening of a few kitchens at Rānchi and Lohardagā and work on the Bundu-Silli road. The price of rice had, however, been steadily rising. In the second half of October 1896, it had risen from 11 to $9\frac{1}{2}$ seers, and, though the price fell slightly during the next two months, it rose steadily from February 1897 till it reached $6\frac{5}{16}$ seers in June and $5\frac{6}{16}$ seers at the end of July; in many markets only four seers could be obtained for the rupee. Contributary causes to the distress were the partial failure of the *mahuā* crop and the total failure of the mango crop, while the break of the monsoon stopped the collection of jungle produce. The isolated position of the district and the deficiency of carts precluded the importation of grain during the rains, and it became clear that the people would not be able to surmount the calamity without assistance from public funds. The outbreak was sudden, sharp, and short-lived; and immediate relief operations had to be undertaken in an area of 700 square miles, south-west of Rānchi, the worst tract being one of 100 square miles, west of the unfordable Kāro river, in Lāpung, Basia and Sisai. Test works were opened, but failed to attract labour, as the people preferred to support life on a meagre diet of jungle products, without working, to obtaining a ration insufficient to compensate them for the expenditure of physical energy. In all, 52,710 persons in terms of one day received relief in return for work; the average daily number being 675, and the cost per unit per day being 9 pies. Gratuitous relief was the chief means of meeting the distress, 153,200 units in all being relieved in this way, the average daily number being 2,042. The acute stage was of short duration and scarcely last two months. A bumper crop of *gondli*, seasonable weather and an increase in the importation of rice, owing to a bounty of one rupee per maund being given, had the effect of lowering prices, and the relief works were closed at the end of August, and the kitchens in the following month. The total expenditure from public funds was Rs. 1,80,000. Only three deaths from actual starvation were reported, but cholera broke out in epidemic form, and there was an exceptionally high mortality from bowel complaints, probably the result of an unwholesome diet of *gondli*, unmixed with rice, upon constitutions already enfeebled by a low diet of jungle fruits and roots. In August and September alone the mortality was 21·18 per mile.

Famine of 1900.

The famine of 1900 was entirely due to the early cessation of the rains in 1899. The monsoon was normal in June and July, but in the next three months the average rainfall (except in thanas Silli and Tamār) was 9·08 against a normal district average of 24·85, and in thanas Lohardagā and Chainpur only 6·60 and 7·76, respectively. As a result, the winter rice crop was a failure; the outturn for the whole district was only six annas, while in thanas Toto, Sisai, Lohardagā and Bishunpur, it was only three annas. The *bhadoi* crops were fair, but the *rabi*, which is of little importance, failed absolutely. The mango and *mahuā* trees, which might have yielded a three-months' food-supply at a time when it was specially needed, produced, in March 1900, the worst crop known for years. In spite of these unfavourable circumstances, the people showed great powers of endurance, and until April distress was nowhere so severe as to amount to famine. Test works were opened during March, April and May in various parts of the district, but it was not till June, that famine was declared in thanas Chainpur, Khunti, Sisai, Karrā, Toto, Bishunpur, Lohardagā, Basiā and Pālkot.

The total area affected was about 2,180 square miles, with a population of 320,251, and comprised roughly a tract, about 70 miles long and 30 miles wide, running from the centre of the district to its extreme north-west corner. The areas, in which the distress was most severe, were thana Karrā and the adjacent parts of Sisai, and thanas Chainpur and Bishunpur. Test works were also opened in thanas Rānchi, Māndar, and Kochedegā, but the distress in these parts was neither very general nor very acute.

By the end of July 60 relief works and 14 test works had been opened, on which 10,271 persons were employed; the number gradually increased, till, in the first week of September, over 14,000 men, women and children were at work. Gratuitous relief was first given in July and was confined as far as possible to relief in kitchens, only those for whom such relief was unsuitable being given dry doles. The attendance reached its maximum of 8,561, in the week ending the 18th of August. Both relief works and kitchens were closed in the middle of September, when a good *bhadoi* crop had been harvested and there was a promise of a good crop of winter rice. The cost of the relief operations was Rs. 2,02,936; of which Rs. 1,11,636 were expended on wages, Rs. 20,190 on doles and rations, and Rs. 54,472 on establishment. The relief works undertaken were the construction of tanks and reservoirs, or of roads. The former are far the more useful, but the people preferred work on the latter.

The famine of 1908 ought to have found the people in a position to surmount it. Normal harvests from 1900 onwards had been succeeded by bumper crops in 1905-07, but the bulk of the grain was exported owing to the impetus given to trade by the failure of crops elsewhere. The lac crop was also on the whole good during these years, though the price of lac had fallen by more than 50 per cent. owing to depression of trade in America. These favourable circumstances, combined with the fact that, during the pendency of the settlement operations, many raiyats withheld their rent, should have caused more cash than usual to remain in the district. Unfortunately the aboriginal cultivator never looks ahead, and recklessly spends his ready money on clothes, amusements or drink; and he was in no better position to tide over the bad harvest of 1907 than in previous years. Famine of 1908.

The famine was again due to the early cessation of the rains of 1907 and was intensified by the large export during that year. The total rainfall, though in excess of the normal, was very badly distributed; August, with 25·61 inches of rain and the first week of September were abnormally wet, but, except for one or two local showers, there was no rain after the 9th of September. The result was that the *gorā*, or early paddy, suffered from the absence of sun in August, and gave an average outturn of only eight to twelve annas, while the winter rice, especially on the higher, or *chaura*, lands dried up owing to insufficient moisture, and though the outturn varied throughout the district, it did not average more than eight annas, and in Chainpur and Tamār thanas did not exceed three annas. The oil-seed crops completely withered and the *rabi* was a total failure. Distress was general throughout the district, but the distribution of nearly three and a half lakhs of rupees in seed loans assisted two-thirds of the district to tide over the crisis. Famine was declared only in the Gumlā subdivision, in thanas Kurdeg, Kochedegā, Chainpur, Bishunpur, and Ghaghrā, an area of 2,261 square miles with a population of 237,238. Relief works were also necessary in Sisai thana and in part of Sonahatu, and test works were opened in Burmū and part of Tamār. The distinguishing mark of the famine was the unprecedentedly high price of rice throughout the district. By December 1907 it was higher than in the famine of 1900 and nearly as high as in 1897, and it rose gradually from eight seers to the rupee to five and, in some places, four seers. The classes chiefly affected were the poorer cultivators, whose holdings contained a large proportion of *chaurā* lands, and the land-less classes. The first test work was opened in Bishunpur in February, but the people held aloof as long as they could obtain a subsistence from jungle produce. Even when they came and prospected the work, they remained only a few days at a time, were very suspicious, refused to come far from their homes and loathed a set task to be done in a set time. The distribution of seed loans in April alleviated, and in some places entirely staved off, distress, and by the end of May only twelve relief works had been opened, the majority in Bishunpur and Chainpur thanas. The break of the rains, contrary to experience in other districts, intensified the distress and by the end of June twenty-three relief works had been opened. Famine was declared in the six thanas in the beginning of July and the number on relief works rose rapidly. Gratuitous relief, which began with the rains, developed very rapidly. The distress was at its height in July and August. The largest number of workers in one day was 12,221; in the middle of August 3·47 per cent. of the population of the declared area were employed on the works, which by that time numbered 35, while 2·47 per cent. were receiving gratuitous relief. Towards the end of August a good crop of *gondli* was harvested but afforded little relief, the price being 12 seers to the rupee as compared with 64 seers to the rupee in 1900. As soon, however, as the *gorā* crop began to come on the market, steps were taken to close the operations, gratuitous relief was terminated on 15th September, and all works were shut down by the 24th. During the hot weather all the relief works undertaken were the construction and repair of tanks and *bāndhs* for the storage of water; the rains made this work impossible and the construction of roads was taken up. Gratuitous relief was given in the form of money doles, distributed fortnightly at suitable village centres. The number of persons relieved, reckoned in terms of one day, was 1,273,799. The total expenditure, excluding seed loans, was Rs. 2,11,763, wages accounting for Rs. 1,12,958, gratuitous relief for Rs. 51,963 and establishment for Rs. 25,094, and the cost per unit was 31 pies. The railway which had recently been opened greatly facilitated the import of rice to Rānchi and the adjacent parts, and the large import had a great effect in steadying prices throughout the district, even though the rice imported did not reach the outlying tracts. The number of emigrants, especially to the tea gardens, was unusually high, and this too may be partly attributed to the increased facilities offered by the railway. The year was unhealthy, small-pox, fever and cholera succeeding one another, and the death-rate was 46·4 against an average of 23·4 per mille for the preceding five years.

CHAPTER VIII.

RENTS, WAGES AND PRICES. MATERIAL CONDITION OF THE PEOPLE.

ORIGIN OF RENTS.

IT has been shown in the Chapter on the history of the district that the aboriginal tribes who cleared the lands several centuries ago were the original proprietors of the soil and paid no rent to anybody. As time went on, chiefs arose who exercised an overlordship over the village communities and received some tribute and personal services from them. The chiefs by degrees became Hinduized and, to establish their supremacy on a firmer basis, encouraged Hindu immigrants to settle in the country and gave them grants of land and villages. The Hindu settlers were not owners of the soil and were entitled only to the tribute and petty services formerly rendered to the chiefs. With this they did not rest content; gradually they reduced the aboriginal proprietors of the soil to the position of ordinary tenants and succeeded in exacting more and more from the cultivators in the form of rent, prædial dues and personal services; they also deprived them of their cultivated lands or, taking possession of the jungles and waste lands, brought them under cultivation and settled them on rent with other tenants. At the beginning of the 19th century the agrarian struggle first took definite shape. The chiefs, or their grantees, sought to increase the charges on the land while the aborigines refused to comply with their demands, and the Kol insurrection of 1832 was the attempt on the part of the latter to get rid of the alien landlords and recover their ancient lands and rights. The suppression of the rebellion strengthened the hands of the landlords and the establishment of courts tended still further to improve their position. The officers who administered the law were often ignorant of local customs and failed to recognize the proprietary right of the Mundā or the Orāon who was in no way fit to compete on anything like even terms with his Hindu antagonists. Many of the disputes, however, were never brought to the Courts but decided in the villages themselves, success remaining with the stronger party, and this fact accounts for the wide divergence between the incidents of tenancies in different parts of the district. In a few villages, known as Mundāri *khuntkātti* villages, the ancient system of land-tenure still survives and the descendants of the original settlers are still the co-proprietors of the land included in the boundaries of the village, paying only a quit-rent to the superior landlord ; in others the ancient system is found in various stages of decay, the head of the village community, or his successor in interest, has acquired the position of a landlord, while the other members have been reduced to the position of ordinary raiyats but hold their lands on privileged terms ; and finally there are the purely zamindāri villages in which no trace of the ancient village community can be found, save perhaps in the existence of a few monolithic burial stones.

Mundāri Khuntkātti tenancies.

The Mundāri *khuntkātti* village usually contains three elements, namely—(*a*) the *khuntkāttidārs ;* (*b*) the *parjas* or raiyats, and (*c*) the subsidiary artisan classes. The *khuntkattidārs* are the descendants in the male line of the original founders of the village. They are the owners of the whole of the area included in the village boundaries and are responsible for the payment to the superior landlord of a fixed annual rent, which represents the tribute which the founders, or their descendants, agreed to pay for the support of their feudal chief. The rent is made up out of the *chāndās*, or subscriptions, of the various *khuntkāttidārs*, but the subscriptions of most of them have been reduced and the deficit is made up by the rents paid by the *parjas*, or raiyats, who hold land under the joint brotherhood. The duty of collecting the subscriptions and paying the quit-rent to the superior landlord rests with the Mundā, or civil held of the village community. Originally the Pāhān was the head of the village both in civil and religious matters, but he gradually left to the Mundā this distasteful task which involved intercourse with alien landlords and alien officials. The villages were also united into groups of ten or twelve known as *pattis*, and at the head of each *patti* was the Mānki, whose duty, like that of the Mundā, was to collect the *chāndās* of the villages and pay them to the landlord. *Pattis* are now found as a working unit only in the east of Khunti thana, which is known as the *Mānki patti*. The Mundā was not the landlord or owner of the village, nor was the Mānki the owner of the group of villages, but he was allowed to retain half the quit-rents collected by him as his share. The villages of a *patti* are thus divided into two categories, *thākur* villages, or those which pay contributions for the landlord's share of the rent, and *chaputa* villages, or those which contribute the Mānki's share. The *chāndās* payable by the members of the village community and by the various villages composing a *patti* appear to have been fixed in an arbitrary manner and vary enormously. The amount of the subscription of each *khuntkāttidār* no doubt corresponded originally with his share of the cultivated lands which he inherited, but as the individual *khuntkāttidār* had the right of reclaiming uncultivated lands, no such correspondence is now found to exist. The Mundā and Pāhān frequently pay nothing. After the rebellion of 1832 *pattas* were granted to the Mānkis fixing the rent payable by the *patti*.

In the recent Settlement operations 156 intact Mundāri *khuntkātti* villages were found, with an area of 144 square miles. The total rent payable by these villages to the superior landlords is Rs. 3,013, of which Rs. 1,735 are paid by the *parjas* holding land under the *khuntkāttidārs*. The average total rent of a village, including the commuted value of prædial conditions, is thus only Rs. 19-4-0, while in Khunti thana the average contribution paid by each of the *khuntkāttidārs* is only 14 annas. The excess amount collected by the Mundās from the *khuntkāttidārs* and *parjas* over the actual rent payable to the superior landlords is only Rs. 463 or less than Rs. 5 per village. This small amount is usually spent on entertaining the "Rājā's" peons and tahsildārs when they visit the village. The extent to which the Mānkis have been deprived of their position as heads of the *pattis* is shown by the fact that of the 156 Mundāri *khuntkātti* villages there are only 59, of which the rents are still payable to them. In the remaining villages the rights of the Mānkis have been permanently alienated to *khorposhdārs, jāgīrdārs* and others. The villages in which the old system still survives are with three exceptions in Khunti thana.

Special provisions for the protection of Mundāri *khuntkātti* tenancies were laid down in the Chotā Nāgpur Tenancy (Amendment) Act, 1903, and have been reproduced in the Act at present in force. The chief provisions are that such tenancies are not transferable by sale, whether in execution of a decree or otherwise; that mortgages or leases can only be given subject to certain restrictions and that no suits can be brought for arrears of rent, which are only recoverable by Certificate procedure.

Breakdown of the Khuntkātti System.

The Mundāri *khuntkātti* system no doubt at one time obtained over the greater part of the district. Various causes contributed to its breakdown. The Mundās themselves were ignorant, shy, and uncivilized, and were no match for the more advanced races with which they were brought into contact. The zamindārs and money-lenders were eager to obtain possession of the villages and reduce the *khuntkāttidārs* to the position of ordinary raiyats and were assisted in their attempts by the courts who were ignorant of the customs of the country and unable to appreciate the position of the cultivators. In many cases the process by which the communal system was broken down was somewhat as follows:— The headman of the village endeavoured to secure for himself a superior position. He did so in various ways; he appropriated to himself the rents paid by the *parjas* for additional lands which they were allowed to cultivate, though any such payments should have been used to reduce the contributions payable by each of the members of the community; he assumed control over the jungles and waste lands and disposed of them without reference to the co-proprietors. He ran into debt, borrowed money from the local money-lender, and executed a document in his favour, in which he pledged the whole village as his security. He failed to pay the quit-rent to the superior landlord, often because the other *khuntkāttidārs* became jealous of him and refused to pay their contributions. He was sued in the courts, either for his debts or for the arrears of rent, and the courts, finding him to be the rent-receiver, not unnaturally regarded him as the sole proprietor and sold the village in execution of the decree to the money-lender or superior landlord. The intruder, who thus succeeded to the interest of the Mundā, carried on the process. He sued the *khuntkāttidārs* for their arrear contributions as if they were ordinary raiyats, dispossessed them of their holdings, and either cultivated them himself or settled them with other, preferably Hindu, cultivators. Thus in many cases the breakdown of the system was due to the greed of the Mundā ; in a few cases it was due to political agitation. The Sardārs, especially during the years 1888-92, refused to acknowledge obligations to any landlord below the State and induced the *khuntkāttidārs* to withhold their rents from the Mānki. The Mundās were sued, and being wrongly regarded by the courts as proprietors, the whole village was sold. Both Revenue and Civil courts showed themselves equally ignorant of local customs, and even Government officials have been responsible for the destruction of the system. An example is to be found in pargana Siri which at the time of the Mutiny was found to be an intact *khuntkātti* area. The *jāgīrdārs* of a portion of this area endeavoured to get some of their lands recorded as *mānjhihās* in the Bhuinhari Survey, but the Special Commissioner found that the area was *khuntkātti* and that no *mānjhihās* land could exist in it. The estate soon after came under the management of Government under the Encumbered Estates Act, and the Manager, whether through ignorance or through a mistaken zeal for the estates under management, accepted an *ex-parte* statement of the proprietor that there was *mānjhihās* land in the village for which the headmen paid rent, brought a suit for a declaration to this effect and obtained a decree. The tahsildārs made further encroachments and at the time of the recent Settlement operations the original status of the village had been so far destroyed that the *khuntkāttidārs* paid rent individually and had lost their proprietary rights in the village jungle and waste. In the neighbourhood of Tamār the system was destroyed by the constant aggression of the " Rājās " of Tamār who, for three generations, have taken advantage of accidents, such as the minority of a Mānki or a Mundā, or even employed downright force in breaking down the rights of the Mundās.

At the recent settlement 130 square miles were found to be in possession of Mundāri *khuntkāttidārs,* apart from the intact Mundāri *khuntkātti* villages which have been described above.

Bhūinhāri tenancies.

From the Mundāri *khuntkātti* tenancies we may pass on to describe the *bhūinhāri* tenancies. *Bhūinhāri* is a local variant for the word *khuntkātti,* and many of the *bhūinhāri* villages are villages in the same stage of decay as the broken Mundāri *khuntkātti* villages. The term, however, has a somewhat wider significance than the term *khuntkātti* and includes not only lands held by the descendants of those persons who settled in the district long before the landlords established themselves, but also lands reclaimed by more recent settlers, who cannot, therefore, claim the same proprietary right as the *khuntkāttidārs.* It was to protect these tenures and to put a stop to the numerous disputes between the aboriginals and the landlords over them that Act II (B. C.) of 1869 was passed. Under that Act special Commissioners were appointed who had power to survey and demarcate the privileged lands of the tenants (*bhūinhāri*) and the privileged lands of the landlords (*mānjhihās*). They also had power to restore to possession persons who had been dispossessed of lands of *bhūinhāri* or *mānjhihās* tenure at any period within twenty years before the passing of the Act. The record was declared to be final and conclusive of the incidents of the tenures recorded, and it was further provided that after the publication of the records no lands not mentioned in the register should be held to be of *bhūinhāri* or *mānjhihās* tenure. The *bhūinhāri* tenancies are thus all the lands recorded in the register which was prepared between the years 1869 and 1880 under this Act. The record was in many ways defective ; no definition of "*bhūinhāri*" was given, and the decisions of the Commissioners must have been to some extent arbitrarily made, while many cultivators, either from ignorance or owing to the persuasions of their landlords, failed to claim their lands. In spite of these defects, the record had the great advantage of finality, and in the recent Settlement operations the Settlement officers had no difficulty in identifying these privileged lands. Included in the term *bhūinhāri* are certain cognate tenures :—

(*i*) *Bhūtkhetā,* or devil's acre ; this term is applied to lands which are dedicated to the worship of the village spirits (*bhūt*). The lands are either the property of a particular *khūnt*, or class, and are cultivated by a member of the *khūnt*, who devotes the proceeds to propitiating the family ghost, or they are the property of the village community and are made over to the Pāhān, whose special duty is to sacrifice to the village *bhūts*. In the Mundā country, the office of Pāhān is hereditary, but in the Orāon country a new Pāhān is usually selected with the aid of the magic *sūp* or winnowing basket from the *Pāhān Khūnt* every three years. In both areas the land is seldom actually cultivated by the Pāhān, but is settled by him with an under-raiyat for a period of three years.

(*ii*) *Pāhāni* and *dalikatāri*.—These lands are also held by the village priest for the performance of certain sacrifices.

(*iii*) *Pānbharā*.—These lands are held by the Pāhān's assistant in return for carrying water and cooking during the sacrificial rites.

(*iv*) *Māhātoi Mundāi*.—These are service tenures held by the village headman, who is known as the Mundā in the Mundā country and the Māhto in Orāon villages. The Māhto is usually elected from the *Māhto Khūnt* and in some villages the election has to be approved by the zamindār. In new zamindāri villages the Māhto is practically the agent of the landlord.

Bhūinhāri tenancies are usually held rent-free or on payment of a small quit-rent. The holders also had to pay certain prædial dues and render certain services, which have now been commuted into a cash rent. A *bhūinhāri* tenancy is not liable to any enhancement of rent; it is a tenure under the law but for all practical purposes may be regarded as a raiyati tenancy, held under certain favourable conditions.

The total area of *bhūinhāri* lands found in the recent settlement operations was 215 square miles; at the time of the *Bhūinhāri* Survey the area was larger, but since that date a considerable proportion has passed to the possession of the landlords by sale, dispossession and abandonment.

Cultivating tenancies.

The land in possession of cultivating raiyats is known as *rājhās*, in contradistinction to the *mānjhihās* land which includes all land cultivated by the landlords or their servants. The *rājhās* land includes *chattisa*, *uttakar* and *korkar*. *Chattisa* is a tenancy consisting of lowlands (*don*) with a quantity of uplands (*tānr*) thrown in. For such lands a higher rent is usually paid than for other classes of lands, no doubt because they are of superior quality. In addition to the cash rent, prædial dues (*rakūmāts*) were ordinarily leviable and prædial services (*begāri*) were rendered, but all such conditions have been commuted into cash rent in the Settlement operations. If there is no complementary upland, or *lagān tānr*, the tenancy is known as *murli chattisa*.

Uttakar, or *balkat*, is also a tenancy of *don* only, usually of inferior quality to that contained in a *chattisa* holding. Such lands are assessed to rent generally at half the rates of *chattisa* lands and sometimes at an even lower rate. No *rakūmāts* are payable. The name *uttakar* is said to be derived from the fact the raiyat only paid rent (*kar*) in the years in which he raised (*uthao*) and cut a crop (*bal*), and it is stated by Mr. Webster in his report on the tenures of Chotā Nāgpur, written in 1875, that by the custom of the country no length of possession gave the holders any rights of occupancy, and that it was only in one or two villages that any such claim was put forward and then only by alien tenants who wished to introduce the Bihar custom. This distinction, however, appears to have lapsed and tenants of *uttakar* lands now have the same rights as the tenants of *chattisa* lands. *Korkar* is the general term applied to a tenancy consisting of rice lands which have been made by the raiyat himself by the conversion of uplands, jungle, or waste lands. Dr. Davidson reported, in 1839, that no rents were payable for these holdings, the tenants only being liable for about 15 days' service, apparently irrespective of the area of the holding. This custom no longer prevails, though in a few villages, in thanas Māndar and Kuru, *korkar* lands have been found to have been held rent-free since before the *bhūinhāri* Survey. The general custom of the district is that during the preparation of the lands, *i.e.*, for the first three or four years, no rent is payable; after that lands are assessed at half the rate payable for *chattisa* holdings. The custom, however, i not uniform. In Biru, where the area of such lands is large and where the preparation of new *korkar* lands is going on apace, the same rates are levied as for *chattisa* holdings; in Silli ten-sixteenths of the ordinary rate is charged; in some areas half the rate for *uttakar* holdings is levied. The custom of half-rates is recognized to be equitable by both landlords and tenants, but some powerful landlords have succeeded in overriding the custom. By a well-established custom which has been recognized in the present Tenancy Act, a raiyat who prepares *korkar* acquires a right of occupancy in it at once, and it is also a general custom that the raiyat shall obtain the consent of the landlord before preparing such lands. It was, however, formerly a common practice for landlords to allow a raiyat to prepare *korkar* for three or four years and then, when the land had become valuable, sue him for ejectment as a trespasser. This practice has now been prevented by the Tenancy Act which requires the landlord to bring the suit within two years from the date on which the cultivation of the lands was begun.

According to the custom of the country, uplands (*tānr*) are complementary to the holding of lowlands (*don*), and hence no cash rent is payable for them. It is only in the more intensely cultivated portion of the district that *tānr* lands are found in addition to those which are included in the *chattisa* holding. When a cash rent is assessed on such lands they are known as *damgat tānr*; when a rent-in-kind is paid, of the quantity of seed required for the fields, they are known as *maswār tānr*.

Prædial conditions.

Prædial conditions are defined in the Tenancy Act as "conditions or services appurtenant to the occupation of land, other than the rent, and include *rakūmāts* payable by tenants to the landlords, and every *mahtut*, *mangan* and *madad*, and every other similar demand, howsoever denominated, and whether regularly recurrent or intermittent". These conditions are locally known as *rakūmāts* and *begāri*. In the recent Settlement operations all prædial conditions have been commuted into a cash rent, and the record and commutation are final and conclusive. Under the present Tenancy Act no tenancy can be created with prædial conditions attached nor can new prædial conditions be imposed on any existing tenancy. Thus both *rakūmats* and *begāri* have been finally abolished and may be said to be now only of historical interest.

Rakūmāts.

It has sometimes been contended that both *rakūmāts*, which are a species of *abwāb* and *begāri* are not leviable in Chotā Nāgpur, inasmuch as zamindārs were enjoined by section 54 of Regulation VIII of 1793 to consolidate all such charges and were prohibited by section 55 from imposing any new *abwābs* or *mahtuts*. Regulation IV of 1794, however, specially exempted the zamindārs of "that part of Zila Rāmgarh which is included in the Soubah of Bihar" from the operation of the rules contained in section 54 of Regulation VIII. The landlords were thus not forced to consolidate existing charges but were forbidden to impose new ones after that date. But the law was not known to, or was not observed by, the landlords of Chotā Nāgpur, and the claims of the landlords to levy additional *rakūmāts* were upheld by the civil and revenue courts. In 1793, the *rakūmāts* and *begāri* leviable were no doubt insignificant, but the Hindu *jāgīrdārs*, anxious to get as much profit as possible from the land, gradually increased them, and during the whole of the 19th century there was a long-continued struggle over their imposition. Attempts were made to put a stop to them by executive order. In 1827, the Magistrate of Rāmgarh issued a proclamation enjoining their total abolition, which apparently met with some success, as Dr. Davidson, Principal Assistant to the Agent, wrote in 1839 as follows :—" These *abwābs* were a fruitful source of oppression to the Kols, but fortunately they have been abolished for the last ten or twelve years by an order of the Magistrate of Rāmgarh. The Rājā complains greatly of the hardship of this order and at my first coming here I made some enquiry into the subject, but found the demands so enormous that to enforce them would ruin the whole country. They are well got rid of and ought never to be revived in any shape". The landlords, however, continued to levy these duties and to add to their number, in spite of these orders and in spite of a decision of the High Court, in the case of Urjan Sahi *versus* Anand Singh, that no cesses could be legally levied in Chotā Nāgpur in which Act X of 1859 was in force. It is doubtful whether this decision was correct, but whether correct or not, it certainly did not stop the levy. The landlords also had some claim for consideration for, as Mr. Oliphant, the Deputy Commissioner, pointed out in 1875, " it was obviously improper to prohibit the levy of all cesses without affording the zamindārs an opportunity in the first instance of commuting these dues to rent''. *Rakūmāts*, too, or some of them, may be regarded as a species of produce rent for the *tānr* lands and, as such, were not prohibited by any of the Acts or Regulations. The legality of their imposition was at length recognized by Act I of 1879, which provided for their commutation. Little use was made of these provisions, and during the last twenty years of the 19th century the landlords became more exacting in their demands, especially of compulsory labour (*begāri*), while the tenants, aided by the Christian missionaries, became more strenuous and successful in their refusal. The Commutation Act of 1897 permitted either party to apply for commutation and, though many applications were made, nothing like a general commutation of prædial conditions took place. It was not till the Settlement operations of 1902—1910 that the problem was finally solved, and a stop put to these exactions which had been the most fruitful source of agrarian discontent. The commutation then carried out was fair as far as possible to both parties. The criterion of liability was local custom or usage, or contract, and, though in some cases the landlords have suffered a diminution of income owing to the fact that illegal and unauthorised dues, not sanctioned by custom, were disallowed, yet it may be said that on the whole they have been liberally treated. The levy of any new cesses had been forbidden in 1793 and though this levy had been at first tacitly and afterwards openly recognized, yet there is no doubt that the landlords had in many cases carried these exactions to excess, and by so doing had hindered the development of the country.

The most common kind of *rakūmāts* were payments of *urid, sarguja, gondli*, cotton, paddy, straw, and *kher*, and were in reality a produce-rent consisting of a fixed quota of the produce of the uplands included in a *chattisa* tenancy. The other class of *rakūmāts* were miscellaneous, and sometimes irregular, dues, payable on certain specific occasions or for certain specific purposes. The following examples will suffice to show their nature : *Dasai*, a payment made to the landlords on the occasion of the *Dasāhara* festival, sometimes in the form of goats or buffaloes for sacrifices, sometimes in cash (*dasāin salāmi*). *Laurdan ghi* was a small quantity of *ghi* given at the same festival.

Bhatta was a payment, usually in kind, to meet the expenses of the landlord and his servants when they visited the village. *Nawakhāni* was a contribution of rice made at the winter harvest. *Nimako Dhān* was paddy taken by the landlord in lieu of salt. The landlords used to import salt and exchange it at the rate of one seer of salt for a *kāt* of paddy. The payment was still made, even after the import of salt was discontinued. *Dāk mashāra* or dâk cess was a cess originally levied by landlords to meet the expenses of the Government cess. The dâk cess was abolished in 1907, and though some landlords continued to levy it, it was not commuted in the Settlement operations, as it was not paid for the use or occupation of land. *Rasid Likhāi* was the charge made for writing rent receipts. As landlords are now required by law to give rent receipts, free of cost, its value was not allowed in the commutation proceedings. *Mahuā* oil and *mahuā baheri* were taxes paid for the right to take *mahuā* flowers and fruit. *Panriai* and *Diwāni* were contributions paid by the *jāgīrdārs* to the Mahārājā's record-keeper (*pānre*) and *diwān*. Formerly the landlord used to exact from the villagers the best bullock of the herds but, after the custom was discontinued, a cash payment known as *bardoch* was made. *Thāna Kharcha* was a cess levied for the upkeep of the police, for which the Mahārājā and the *jāgīrdārs* were responsible, and continued even after the police were taken over by Government.

At the time of the settlement it was found in most villages that the payment of *rakūmats* in kind had ceased and that their money values were collected instead, and in some cases they had been commuted to Re. 1 or Re. 1-8 per unit of land. Some of the miscellaneous charges such as *dasai* were levied on *korkar* and *uttakar* as well as *chattisa* tenancies. The incidence of *rakūmāts* varied considerably from village to village.

Begāri consists of a number of days' labour given by the raiyats free of charge to the landlord for the cultivation of his *khās* lands, or as personal service. There is no doubt that from the earliest times the landlords exacted a considerable amount of service from their aboriginal raiyats. What was the ground for this is uncertain; Dr. Davidson in his report of 1839 advances the theory that the labour was given for their *bethbegāri*, or service holdings and for their *bhūinhāri* and *korkar* lands which they held rent-free or at a quit-rent. The special commissioners of Begāri.

the *Bhūinhari* Survey also found that *bhūinhāri* land was held rent-free, but that the holders had to render, sometimes, as much as 30 days' service. The enquiries of the Settlement officers go to show that it was a recognized incident of every holding for nearly a century. Even in the earliest times the system was much abused; Dr. Davidson in 1839 issued a proclamation that under no circumstances should landlords levy more than a fair amount of *begāri*, which was reckoned to be about 15 days. Similar proclamations were issued at other times, and in 1890 when the disputes over *begāri* had become very acute, owing to the spread of Christianity, Mr. Grimley, the Commissioner, with the authority of Government, issued a proclamation limiting it to 14 days. The incidence of *begāri* varied from thana to thana and village to village in the same way as the incidence of *rakūmats*, and the amount of service rendered depended on the relative strength of landlords and tenants. In villages such as those in Chainpur, Kochedega and Kurdeg thanas, in which the aboriginal inhabitants had become Christians *en masse*, it was found by the Settlement Department that no *begāri* had been levied for periods varying from seven to twenty years. The landlords had been forced to give way to the united opposition of their tenants and either lease out, or cultivate by hired labour, their *khās* lands. On the other hand, several zamindārs claimed that their right to *begāri* was only limited by their requirements, and in Bishunpur thana one landlord was found to have actually succeeded in levying 50 to 60 days' labour annually from each of his raiyats. The *begāri* rendered in a typical village was found to be about 10 to 15 days, made up as follows :—

- 3 days' ploughing (*har*),
- 3 days' digging (*kori*),
- 3 days' planting or sowing (*ropni*),
- 3 days' cutting (*kātni*),
- 1 day's thrashing (*misni*),
- 1 day's storing the grain (*mōrābāndhi*),
- 1 or 2 days' carrying the landlord's burden on his journeys (*des bides*).

In each case the period of labour was generally limited to about half a day, and, as the raiyat received food and drink from the landlord, the cash value of a day's service rarely exceeded one anna, and was therefore commuted at this rate by the Settlement officers.

Cash rents. System of Land Measurement.

Land measures in the ordinary sense of the term do not exist in Rānchi district. The local term for the area for which rent is payable does not represent any uniform superficial area but the amount of land for which a certain quantity of seed is required. Thus a *kāt* of land represents the area for which a *kāt* of paddy seed is required. A *kāt*, however, as a measure of quantity, is itself indeterminate and varies in different parts of the district from twenty seers to one maund, according to the size of the *pailā* or measure used. Further, the amount of seed depends upon the fertility of the soil, and it is thus impossible to express these units in the terms of any standard measure, such as acres or *bighas*. The area of a tenancy is usually described with reference to the unit in vogue for the lowlands (*don*) and these units are known as *pawās*, *annās* and *kāts*. The *pawā* and the *annā* are the units most generally used but they are even more indeterminate than the *kāt*, which is used for both lowlands and uplands in the Mundā country; thus in Ghāghrā thana a *pawā* corresponds to the area which can be sown with two to ten *kāts* of seeds according to the locality. The subdivisions of the *annā* and *pawā* differ in various parts of the district. Thus in parganas Khukrā, Korambe, Kuru, Lodhma, Jaspur and Omedanda, 2 *kānis* make 1 *kanwā*, 2 *kanwās* make one *pawā* and 4 *pawās* make one *khari*; in pargana Belkaddi, 2 *kānis* make one *kanwā*, 4 *kanwās* make one *pawā* and 4 *pawās* make one *khari*; in parganas Biru, Basiā, Doisa and Pālkot, 2 *kānis* make one *kanāsi*, 2 *kanāsis* make one *kanwā* and 4 *kanwās* make one *annā*. In some villages the *kanwā* denotes the same area as an *annā*. In some parts of the district the rupee is used and in this measure four annas equal one *pawā* and four *pawās* equal one rupee, and it is probable that this measure denoted originally the area for which one rupee of rent was paid. The *kāt* is subdivided into two *khandis* and forty *pailās*. In Tori pargana *don* land is measured by *pattis*; 20 *dhurs* equal one *katha*, 20 *kathas* equal one *kara* and 3 *karas* equal one *patti*; the area of a *patti* varies from two to four *bighas*. In parts of Chainpur and Bishunpur thanas, on the level hill-tops, known as the *pāts*, land is measured in *hāls* or ploughs, and the rent is assessed on the number of ploughs which the raiyats possess.

Another reason for the difference in the size of the unit, even in the same village, is that *pawās* or *annās* which abut on uplands have been increased in size by the cultivator who has enlarged his rice-land by terracing and taking in portions of the upland while other cultivators having land in less favourable surroundings have to be content with their original *pawā*. Further, when new cultivators settle in a village, they are usually required to pay a higher rent, and a simple way of doing this was to give them a smaller *pawā* but make them pay the customary rate. By this system rents were often illegally enhanced. In the settlement record the area of all tenancies has been recorded in acres and decimals and the people are gradually becoming acquainted with this standard and are realizing the advantage of a determinate measure over the indeterminate measure previously in force.

Enhancements of rents.

During the agrarian struggles of the 19th century the landlords not only increased the prædial conditions but also largely enhanced the cash rents. The enhancement of the rents of holdings other than *korkar* by private contract was prohibited by the Chotā Nāgpur Tenancy Act of 1879, but the decisions of the courts rendered this wise provision of the law futile. The landlords frequently persuaded or forced the raiyats into agreeing to an enhancement of rent. They paid for a time, but when they fell into arrears and were sued, the courts decreed the amount which they had actually paid, even though it was admitted to have been enhanced quite recently. Another favourite device of the landlords for obtaining the sanction of the courts to enhanced rates of rent was to sue the raiyats for a sum in excess of what they had actually paid. False account books and *jamābandis* were prepared for the benefit of the court, receipts for the enhanced rates, and not for the sums actually paid, were given to the raiyats, who, owing to their illiteracy, were unable to detect the fraud; a certain number of raiyats who were friendly to the lāndlords were produced as witnesses, or even made defendants, and admitted the higher rates, and the court not unnaturally misled by this volume of evidence decreed the suit in favour of the landlord. Another method of enhancing rent was to sublet a village on a temporary lease to a *thikādār* at a very high rate with the deliberate object of making him extract, by fair means or foul, higher rents from the raiyats. In many cases the arbitrary and exorbitant demands of the landlords defeated their own objects. They became involved in harassing and expensive litigation and the raiyats driven to desperation either attacked the landlord and his servants or abandoned the village. The victory too was not always with the landlords. Christian aboriginals have exhibited remarkable powers of combination and have often defeated the landlord with his own weapons. Just as the landlords brought suits for enhanced rates, so the tenants deposited their rents in the treasury at reduced rates. Wealthy and influential zamindārs who kept proper books of accounts were easily able to disprove the correctness of such deposits, but the poor and illiterate zamindārs were reluctant to embark on expensive litigation and after accepting the amounts deposited were unable to obtain subsequent decrees for enhanced amounts. It must be remembered too that enhancement of rates is not necessarily synonymous with an increase of rent. Raiyats frequently included new lands in their old tenancies without paying additional rent, and in the absence of any definite system of land measurement, it was easier for the landlords to enhance the rate, the normal area remaining the same.

Incidence of rent.

In the record-of-rights all holdings have been entered in acres and decimals and as all prædial conditions have been commuted to rent, it is possible to give statistics showing the incidence of rent per acre. Statistics giving the average rate per acre over the whole district or over a large tract are of little value, as the rates vary considerably from village to village. It has been calculated by Mr. Reid in his Settlement Report that the incidence of rent per cultivated acre is ten annas in the Sadr subdivision and five annas in the Gumlā and Khunti subdivisions. The gross rental of the lands occupied by all classes of raiyats has also been calculated to be only one-eighteenth of the volume of the produce in a normal year. Mr. Reid remarks: "The incidence of rent throughout the district is not heavy. The disputes about rents are due rather to the arbitrary and illegal manner in which the charges have been increased and to their unequal distribution than to the heaviness of the burden".

Produce rents.

The amount of land held on produce rent in the district is comparatively small. Three systems are in vogue, *viz.*, *ādh batāi* or *sājhā*, *saikā*, and *maswār* or *kar*. Under the *sājhā* system half the produce is payable, under the *saikā* system a fixed amount, and under the *maswār* system an amount of the produce equivalent to the seed sown. Under the *saikā* system the contributions are generally heavy, as the lands held are often part of the landlord's privileged lands. Many applications for commutation of these produce rents were received by the Settlement officers.

Rent of trees.

In many parts of the district the raiyats make considerable profit by the cultivation of lac. By the custom of the district the owner of a tree is the person who planted it, or his successor in interest, and he has a full right to grow lac on his tree. Landlords, however, have, in some cases, ignored this custom of ownership and enforced the payment of rent for privately-owned trees. On trees growing in the jungle the raiyats have not the same customary right to grow lac free of rent. But the rates payable are by no means uniform and vary with the market price of lac. In Kochedegā and Rāidih thanas no payments are made. In Rānchi thana the landlord charges from 8 annas to Rs. 3 per tree. In Gumlā and Ghaghrā thanas the raiyats pay sometimes half the value of the produce.

Wages.

From circumstances not peculiar to the Rānchi district wages have steadily risen during the last sixty years. In 1856 day labourers received four to five or six pice, and in 1886 six or eight pice. Two annas was the standard wage for a long period, but the general rise in the price of food-grains, the increased demand for labour, especially in Rānchi town, and also the greater facilities for emigration to Bengal and the tea districts have all contributed to raise wages, and at the present time an unskilled labourer can obtain a daily wage of two or three annas in any part of the district, while in the town of Rānchi he can obtain four or even five annas. The wages of women and boy labourers also show a corresponding increase. Women who, in the eighties, received three to four pice a day and, till recently, five to six pice, can now obtain two annas, while boys can get five to six pice. Cash wages, however, are still the exception rather than the rule in the district, and it is only labourers in and near Rānchi or those employed on Government work who receive payment in cash. Grain payments vary in amount from $2\frac{1}{4}$ to $4\frac{1}{2}$ seers and in value are approximately equivalent to the cash payments.

Wages of skilled labour.

Masons and carpenters who, in 1856, received two or three annas a day and for a long period continued to receive a standard wage of six annas can now obtain eight annas or more. Skilled blacksmiths obtain equally high wages, but the village blacksmith, like other village artisans, still receives annual payments in kind. The *lorhā* receives a certain measure of paddy, usually a maund, annually for every plough owned by each cultivator who requires his services. He is paid separately for his services in making or mending other tools and implements. Ahirs receive a similar remuneration for each pair of cattle which they graze, and also a certain proportion of the milk. Basket-makers, such as Turis, Ors, Mahlis, are paid for each article, and potters also receive a fixed sum for their work.

Monthly wages. Monthly wages have also risen, and an unskilled labourer now commands five to seven rupees a month while women can obtain four rupees or even more. Since the railway was opened, and especially since Rānchi became the headquarters of the Local Government, wages have risen to an abnormal degree, and a servant if provided with food and clothing receives four rupees or double that amount if food and clothing are not given.

Dhāngrai. Daily or monthly wages, whether in cash or kind, cannot be said to be typical of the district. Before the commutation of *begāri* the raiyats of a village ploughed, sowed, and harvested the landlord's fields, while permanent field servants, or *dhāngars*, were also employed. A *dhāngar* is often a younger member of a respectable raiyat's family who takes service under the zamindār for a year in order to earn a lump sum for his family. He is hired usually in the month of *Māgh* (January) and receives wages in kind varying from six to twelve or even to eighteen *kāts* of paddy and a cash wage which has risen from Rs. 4 a year to Rs. 12, or even to Rs. 18 in some localities where the labour, such as that involved in irrigation, is heavy. He also receives a ration of food at midday. In some parts of the district, in lieu of receiving paddy, the *dhāngar* is fed and clothed by his master and lives as a member of the family, while in other parts he is given a parcel of land, or receives a portion of the land which he has helped to cultivate.

Pasri. Another form of hired labour is known as *pasri*. A *pasridār* is a man who has no ploughs or plough-cattle of his own and enters into an agreement with some wealthier cultivator, by which the latter agrees to lend his plough in return for manual labour during the cultivating season.

Prices.

In Rānchi, as elsewhere, the prices of grain have risen largely during recent years, and the rise is apparently permanent. An old proverb "*sab dhān bais paseri*" refers to the days when one rupee purchased from 110 to 154 seers of paddy, and persons still living can remember when paddy was sold at three maunds to the rupee, but in those early days money was not in large circulation and transactions were all by exchange, and hence these figures hardly represent the true value of the commodities. Even in 1859 common paddy was sold at two maunds to the rupee and rice at one maund; by 1870 the price had only increased by 35 per cent. In 1888 rice sold at two rupees a maund, and from that date prices, though varying with the season, have steadily risen; in 1902 fifteen seers of rice could be obtained for a rupee in Rānchi and sixteen at Lohardagā and Pālkot, and in 1914, after a moderately good harvest, rice was selling in Rānchi at eight or nine seers while in the outlying parts one or two seers more were obtainable. The large rise in prices in the Rānchi market during the last two years is due partly to the large increase in the population of the town since it became the headquarters of Government. There are still great variations between the price of grain in Rānchi and in markets accessible to the Railway and that in the inaccessible parts of the district. This variation is most marked just after the harvest is reaped, the improvident aboriginal being anxious to sell his crop and pay his rent and the dealer being anxious to buy in the cheapest market. As the year proceeds, prices tend to become more level throughout the district and when the *gora* crop is reaped in August, rice is in defect owing to export and consumption, and prices rule nearly as high in the south and west as in the east of the district.

Material condition of the people.

From the fact that the incidence of rent is not heavy, that wages have risen during the last quarter of a century and that the inhabitants of the district readily emigrate to the tea gardens of Assam and the Duars where remunerative employment can always be found, it might be inferred that the material condition of the people is good. A further argument in support of this inference which is sometimes put forward, is the fact that the excise revenue is increasing yearly and that the inhabitants of the district spend more than 15 lakhs a year on liquor. Yet the inference is not wholly true ; and, though the material condition of the people has no doubt improved considerably in recent years and there are hopeful signs of a more marked improvement in the future, yet the cultivator under present conditions cannot tide over years of scarcity and is forced to borrow at heavy rates of interest from the money-lender and to become heavily involved in debt.

From data collected during the Settlement operations it has been calculated that the average holding of a cultivator is 12 acres, of which 4 acres is *don*, or lowland, and 8 acres *tānr*, or upland. On the basis of crop-cutting experiments, the average annual produce has been ascertained to be about 80 maunds of paddy and, assuming that the cultivator's family consists of 5·3 persons and that each member requires half a seer of rice a day for his sustenance, 24 maunds of rice, or 48 maunds of paddy, are required for home consumption. Out of the remaining 32 maunds, 6 maunds must be set aside for seed and there are thus only 26 maunds, the market value of which is about Rs. 32-8, out of which the cultivator has to pay his rent and purchase necessaries, including clothes, salt and tobacco. The rent charges of an ordinary raiyat's holding are equivalent to about one-eighteenth of the gross value of the produce, but after the necessaries of life have been purchased, the balance out of which the rent charges have to be paid is extremely small and in bad years it vanishes altogether. It is true that most cultivators have a supplementary source of income. Each raiyat keeps some poultry, goats, sheep, cattle or pigs. One or two members of the family work as labourers or emigrate to Assam and the Duars and their earnings help to increase the family income. Many raiyats also make a considerable income by the cultivation and sale of lac, and it is from these additional sources of income and not from the produce of the cultivated land that the rent is paid. The average raiyat has thus in a good year a bare margin for the purchase of luxuries, or for any expenditure on the improvement of his holding. Many holdings, however, are below the average and their produce affords a bare minimum of subsistence for the cultivator and his family.

In these circumstances it is not surprising that the capacity of the cultivator to tide over periods of stress, engendered by a Indebtedness.

partial failure of the crops, is small. The aboriginals and semi-aboriginals can, it is true, subsist in conditions which would play havoc with more civilized races and can maintain life, even when their crops fail, on jungle fruits and vegetables, but even in good years they frequently have recourse to loans to meet some extra expenditure, such as on a marriage, or borrow the seed for their holding at exorbitant rates of interest from the *baniā* who is to be found in nearly every aboriginal village. Interest at seventy-five per cent. per annum is the normal, but not the maximum, rate of interest charged to the cultivator, and once he gets into the clutches of the money-lender, it is no easy matter for him to extricate himself. The oppression of the money-lender in former days reduced some of the cultivators and labourers almost to the position of serfs and frequently drove whole families to migrate to the labouring districts. Attempts have been made at various times to protect the raiyat from the results of his improvidence. Restriction on the transfer of holdings were introduced in the Tenancy Act of 1903, the object being to stop the sale of raiyati holdings by improvident raiyats and to restrict all forms of mortgage and thereby save the aboriginal population from becoming the serfs of the money-lenders. These restrictions were reproduced in section 46 of the present Tenancy Act. Transfer by raiyats of their rights in their holdings for any period exceeding five years are prohibited ; but a raiyat may enter into a *bhugut bandha* mortgage for any period not exceeding seven years. A *bhugut bandha* mortgage is one in which the loan is repaid by the profits arising from the tenancy during the period of the mortgage. The restrictions of the transfer of Mundāri *khuntkātti* tenancies are similar and the provisions of section 46 were made applicable to *bhūinhāri* tenancies in 1908. During the Settlement operations, statistics were collected showing the extent to which all cultivated lands, whether held by tenure-holders, tenants or raiyats, are sublet under mortgage leases, mortgages and *bhugut bandhas* entered into after the passing of the Act being shown separately. In the whole district 9,725 acres of *don* and 4,932 acres of *tānr* were mortgaged before the passing of the Act. After the passing of the Act, the amount of *don* mortgaged was 5,111 acres, and the amount of *tānr* 2,285 acres. The amount of land sublet in *bhugut*, both before and after the passing of the Act, was comparatively

Restrictions on the transfer of lands.

small and amounted only to 340 acres of *don* and 133 acres of *tānr*. The total area of cultivated lands affected by mortgages of both kinds was 35 square miles or 8·2 per cent. of the land cultivated by raiyats, while the total recorded indebtedness amounted to Rs. 7,83,141. The average amount advanced per acre of *don* and *tānr* was, before the passing of the Act of 1903, Rs. 39-4-0 and Rs. 10, respectively. The Act of 1903, while not diminishing the number of transfers, had the unexpected effect of increasing the security value of both classes of land: that of *don* lands increasing to Rs. 61-4-0 per acre. This increase, though partly due to the large increase in the value of lands during the last seven or eight years in the Sadr subdivision, is mainly due to the fact that the security afforded by the mortgage of a raiyati holding for a period of five years is considered by the money-lenders not to be less than the value of a mortgage on the same holding for an indefinite period. Even if the mortgagor demands to be put in possession of the land at the end of the period, the money-lender can still attach and sell his movable property, including his crops. As a matter of fact, experience has shown that the raiyat seldom demands to be put in possession and often agrees with the money-lender to execute a second mortgage for a period of five years. Another method by which the intention of the law is defeated and the sale or permanent transfer of raiyati holdings effected is for the raiyat to make a collusive surrender of the holding to his landlord, who then resettles the land with the money-lender. Thus the restrictions on the transfer of land have not proved a success, and it appears desirable to amend the law and to permit the transfer of holdings, provided the transfer is approved by the Deputy Commissioner. This would prevent raiyats selling or leasing their lands at unfair rates.

At the time of the settlement it was found that *bhūinhāri* and *khuntkātti* holdings had also been largely mortgaged and that in all 43 square miles had been mortgaged by tenure-holders, *bhūinhārs*, and *khuntkāttidārs*, of which probably more than half was mortgaged by the two latter classes. It was accordingly decided to grant loans under the Agriculturists' Loans Act to Mundāri tenants in all cases in which the value of the land exceeded the amount of the debt, to pay off the mortgagee and restore possession of the land to the mortgagor. In all a sum of Rs. 1,48,600 was given out in loans under this scheme, but the scheme did not meet with the success that was anticipated, and there is little doubt that in many cases the lands were remortgaged shortly after the original mortgage had been redeemed. It will be seen from this that the attempts to improve the economic condition of the people by legislation or Government action have been partial failures. There are, however, signs that the people themselves are beginning to take steps to improve their own condition. Government and the Christian Missions are doing much to spread education among the aboriginals and thus to improve their moral and material condition, for education not only opens the door to employment of various kinds but also makes the people realize the folly of improvidence. The non-Christian Orāons and Mundās are following the example of their Christian brothers and are making efforts to qualify their children for some additional employment besides their hereditary occupation of agriculture. Recently an Association called the "Orāon-Mundā Sikhsa Sabha" has been started to raise funds to assist boys in prosecuting their studies at schools and colleges. With the spread of education it may be hoped that the Orāon or Mundā will conquer his improvident habits, will give up the vice of intemperance, and will devote the profits of his land to improved methods of agriculture, and especially to the development of irrigation. The Settlement operations have given to the raiyat security of tenure, and he now appreciates the fact that any improvement of his holding will result in profit to himself and is well aware that he is not liable to be deprived of his land through the rapacity and oppression of his landlord. The most remarkable feature of the history of the last four or five years has been the spread of the Co-operative movement, which is due partly to the efforts of missionaries and other persons interested in the welfare of the aboriginals, and partly to the growing desire of the people for an improvement of their material condition.

Co-operative Societies.

The movement has now taken firm root among the Christians of Chotā Nāgpur and societies under the supervision of missionaries are in a very flourishing condition. Without close supervision the societies languish and fail, and there is little prospect of the non-Christian aboriginals forming societies of their own accord. The benefit derived from co-operation is great, and, as the history of the last half century shows the successful struggle of the Mundās and Orāons against the serfdom which the landlords endeavoured to impose, the coming half century will witness the struggle between the cultivator and the *mahājan*, and it may be confidently anticipated that the development of the co-operative movement will end in setting free the cultivator from the toils of the money-lender, as effectually as the publication of the record-of-rights has set him free from the oppression of the landlord.

The first societies in the district were established by the late Mr. Lonsdale in the Anglican Mission Stations of Kachabāri and Bargari, and these and eight other societies in the parish of Itki flourished under his supervision. Since his death they have received little attention and a recent report shows them to be nearly all in a stagnant condition. The Bishop of Chotā Nāgpur has now taken up the matter, the existing societies are to be reorganized on denominational lines, new societies are to be started in mission centres, and ultimately there will be a central society at Rānchi. The ten existing societies have a membership of 365 and a working capital of Rs. 3,849.

The Lutheran Mission was also not slow to appreciate the benefits of co-operation, and the societies instituted and supervised by the Rev. Paul Wagner of Purūlia have achieved good results. There are in all ten societies attached to the Mission, eight of which are in this district, with 1,635 members and a working capital of Rs. 28,854. The societies originally started with a loan from Government, but this has been repaid, and they rely now almost entirely on the deposits, partly compulsory and partly voluntary, made by the members. The deposits amount to nearly 85 per cent. of the working capital. The societies are thus independent of outside aid and the system has the advantage not only of giving the cultivator loans at an easy rate of interest, when he needs them, but also of teaching him the lesson of thrift.

The societies of the Society for the Propagation of the Gospel and the Lutheran Mission are eclipsed by the giant society of the Roman Catholic Mission, started some five or six years ago by the Rev. Father Hoffman, which has now the distinction of being the largest society of the kind in India and practically in the world. The success of the movement among the Roman

Catholic converts is entirely due to the energy and enthusiasm of Father Hoffman. The society in 1915 had over 10,000 members and a working capital of over Rs. 1,00,000, and the rapidity with which the movement is spreading may be judged by the fact that the working capital has increased by over Rs. 60,000 in the last two years. The society is confined entirely to members of the Mission and though criticisms are sometimes levelled against it on this score, it is clear that were this not the case it could not possibly cope with the work thrust upon it.

The purposes for which loans are given show the needs of the aboriginal. Cattle-disease is always more or less prevalent in Chotā Nāgpur, and heavy mortality of cattle is one of the chief causes which tend to impoverish the raiyat. In 1912 more than one-third, and in 1913 nearly one-quarter, of the money given out in loans was for the purchase of cattle. Father Hoffman, however, did not rest content with assisting the members to replace their losses; he endeavoured with some measure of success to induce them to take prophylactic measures and so reduce cattle mortality. The training of aboriginal Christians in methods of inoculation and the attempts to make inoculation popular have been described in Chapter V.

Loans for the repayment of debts form a large item in the amount given out, but, though the urgent need of setting the cultivator free from the burden of his old debts is fully recognized. Father Hoffman has adopted the sound principle of placing thrift before credit and encourages the members of his society to work out by thrift their own salvation. The society also has its indirect effect in improving the condition of its members. Resolutions and rules demanding self-sacrifice are voluntarily accepted by the members. Two typical rules may be quoted:—Any member who gets drunk has to pay a fine to the society; any member who resides within five miles of a school and does not send his children to be educated, may be called upon to resign his membership.

Side by side with the Chotā Nāgpur Co-operative Society is the Chotā Nāgpur Catholic Co-operative Store which also owes its origin and success to Father Hoffman. The objects of the society are defined in its bye-laws :—

"The primary and immediate object of the society is to train the aborigines of Chotā Nāgpur to trade, and thus gradually render them fit to secure for themselves that share in their own country's trade to which they have the first right. The ultimate object is to secure for the members, whether cultivators, traders, or artisans, all that co-operative buying of raw materials and co-operative sale of produce and manufactured articles can procure. With these objects in view the store is open to all members and non-members alike for the sale of produce and the purchase of the necessaries and luxuries of life".

The store, or "*Gola*" as it is known in Rānchi, stocks most things—cloth, salt, oil, yarn are in great demand, but the main business is in rice. Rice is bought and sold at the market rate, and both sellers and purchasers enjoy the great advantage of fair measurement. Eventually rice will be purchased only from members, and this will secure that the profit of the land goes into the hands of the cultivator who is now compelled to sell his produce soon after the harvest in order to pay his rent and purchase the necessaries of life and who is liable to be cheated in both transactions by the *bania* whose success both as buyer and seller is reputed to depend largely on his sleight-of-hand. The members are at present somewhat suspicious of the system of commission sale and prefer hard cash for their goods, but eventually no doubt they will see the advantage of receiving a small percentage of the price at first and later on sharing in the profits made by waiting for the market. The business is rapidly increasing; in 1912 the turnover was Rs. 60,000; in 1913 it rose to Rs. 1,11,000. Branches have been opened at eight different centres throughout the district. Father Hoffman had many difficulties to contend with: but with the aid of a lay brother who had experience of a commercial firm in Calcutta, he built up the business upon sure foundations. Apprentices are now trained to manage the central store and to take charge of its branches, and the staff are learning by experience to avoid the pitfalls which beset amateur dealers.

In addition to the Co-operative Societies working under the control of the missionaries, there is a Central Bank at Rānchi, to which are attached 85 small societies, composed of Chamārs, Mehtars and other depressed classes, mostly in or near Rānchi town, or of weavers and aboriginal cultivators in the interior. The societies are not in a flourishing condition, in spite of the enthusiasm and energy of Rai Bahadur Radha Gobind Chaudhuri, their founder, of Babu Amarendra Nath Banarji, and of Babu Sarat Chandra Roy. The lack of success of these societies illustrates the difficulty of spreading the movement in villages, the inhabitants of which are of different races, different religions and different languages.

CHAPTER IX.

OCCUPATIONS, MANUFACTURES AND TRADE.

ACCORDING to the census of 1901, pasture and agriculture were the occupation or means of livelihood of 951,257 persons in the Rānchi district, or over 80 per cent. of the population. Of these 16,494 were engaged in stock-breeding and dealing, 13,530 were rent-receivers, 877,452 rent-payers (*i.e.*, ordinary cultivators) and 35,005 agricultural labourers. At the census of 1911 pasture and agriculture were the occupation or means of livelihood of 929,495 persons, or nearly 67 per cent. of the population. Of these 44,314 were rent-receivers, 723,683 rent-payers, 94,316 farm labourers, and 53,750 herdsmen, graziers, etc. These figures include both actual workers and dependants, the latter amounting to 375,315, or 40 per cent. of the total. The marked variation between the totals of all these classes is not due to any real decrease in the number of persons engaged in agriculture, but to the fact that in 1911 a different system of classification was adopted and greater accuracy was obtained. The classification, however, is still somewhat elaborate for a district such as Rānchi in which the enumerators, who are unskilled and often barely literate, find it no easy task to distinguish between a worker's primary and subsidiary occupation or to classify workers under their proper heads. The figures obtained require careful examination. For instance, the total number of persons engaged on agriculture, excluding those engaged on forestry and the raising of farm stocks amounts only to 868,340, or 62·6 per cent. of the total population, a smaller percentage than in any other district of the province, except Mānbhūm, but it must not be inferred

CENSUS STATISTICS.

from this that commerce and industry form the sole occupation of a large proportion of the inhabitants of the district. Nearly all the artisans of the district, the weavers, blacksmiths, potters, etc., have small holdings, while the money-lenders and traders also derive part of their income from agriculture.

The industrial population accounts for 8·2 per cent. of the total, and of these about 53 per cent. are actual workers and include 9,200 cotton-weavers, 6,300 workers in wood (carpenters, sawyers, basket-makers), 6,600 workers in metal, (principally blacksmiths), 8,200 potters, brick-makers, etc., 8,100 manufacturers of articles of food (grain-parchers, sweetmeat-makers, butchers, distillers), 9,200 tailors, barbers and shoe-makers. Trade and commerce support 113,752 persons, or 6·7 per cent. of the population, of whom 53 per cent. are dependants. Included under this head are 3,800 drivers and cart-owners, 5,600 brokers and bankers, *i.e.*, *mahājans*, 6,500 dealers in chemical products (drugs, dyes, petroleum, etc.), 16,800 dealers in food-stuffs, 6,300 dealers in fuel, charcoal, cowdung, etc., and 3,100 general dealers. The professional classes number only 11,379, or ·8 of the population, of whom 1,800 are priests and ministers of religion, 378 lawyers, muktars, etc., and 530 teachers. This class also includes nearly 1,000 musicians, *i.e.*, the Ghāsis, who perform at weddings and festivals. Apart from these four major classes, 71,218 persons were supported by domestic service, of whom 45,768 were actual workers; 2,400 were employed in the police or as village chaukidars; 1,764 were in the service of the State; 146,318 persons, of whom only 45,906 were dependants, were described vaguely as labourers, without any definite occupation being given; and finally 7,739 persons were included in the class of beggars, vagrants and prostitutes.

INDUSTRIES. Apart from the industries of the village artisans, the only industries of any importance in the district are the collection and manufacture of lac which is carried on principally at Bundu in the Khunti subdivision, and the manufacture of tea. A description of the methods employed in the manufacture of lac will be found in the Gazetteer of Mānbhūm and, as the methods employed in this district are similar, need not be repeated. According to the figures obtained at the industrial census of 1911 there were eight lac factories in the district, giving employment to 415 male workers and 222 female workers. The figures somewhat under-estimate the extent of the industry as at the time of the census several factories were not working. The war in Europe has again caused the trade to decline, and several factories have been closed. The lac industry owes its development to Mr. Stainforth who established a factory at Dorandā forty years ago. A description of the tea industry has been given in the chapter on Agriculture. At six gardens the manufacture of tea, principally green tea, is carried on and gives employment to 330 male workers and 205 female workers.

Cotton Weaving.

There are no large weaving centres in the district and cotton weaving is carried on only as a home industry, *i.e.*, production on a small scale for merely local consumption, by the weaving castes, such as the Chik Barāiks, Pāns and Muhammadan Jolāhās. The cotton used in weaving is often locally grown and spun by the women of a cultivator's family. The Mundās have a strong prejudice against taking up the industry of weaving, which they consider to be a degrading occupation, only fit for the Pāns of the village. The Roman Catholic Mission recently attempted to induce Mundā boys to take to weaving and thereby supplement their incomes derived from agriculture, and sought to overcome their prejudice by the use of the Japanese loom which was worked with the feet, but the attempt was unsuccessful and had to be abandoned.

Ironware and Cutlery.

The ordinary iron utensils required for domestic use are made locally throughout the district by the village Lohrās and Lohārs. Iron is extracted from iron ore by the Asurs and Lohrās, and sometimes by the Orāons and Mundās themselves. The appliances used by the blacksmith are primitive and the products of his hearth and anvil have no pretensions to fine work. The weapons used by the aboriginal tribes in hunting are sometimes good examples of rude work, especially the hunting axes, known as *balua* or *phalsa*, according to their shape. Heavy axes (*tāngi*) are also made for wood-cutting.

Gold-washing.

Attempts have been made at various times to develope the gold-washing industry in the Sonapet valley, but without success, and abandoned machines can still be seen there, to bear witness to the disastrous results of the Calcutta gold boom. The

Jhorās of Biru occasionally wash for gold in the auriferous sands of the Sankh and other rivers, but a hard day's work is well rewarded if the gold-dust obtained is worth three or four annas. Diamonds, for which the country was famous in historical times, are no longer found.

Other industries.

Other industries call for no special description; workers in brass and bell-metal, principally at Rānchi and Lohardagā, manufacture the ordinary vessels for household use; the village Kumhārs supply pottery of the most ordinary description; the carpenters turn out only rough work, but aboriginal boys, trained in the Industrial School at Rānchi, show some aptitude for wood-carving and wood-turning, and there are signs that this industry will develope. Basket-making is carried on by the Turis and Doms, who are scattered about the district. Rope is manufactured by Birhors and other the aboriginals from jungle grasses and fibres. Musical instruments, especially drums, so dear to the heart of the aboriginal, are also of local manufacture.

TRADE.

The chief centres of trade in the district are Rānchi, Lohardagā, Gumlā, Pālkot, Gobindpur and Bundu, and the importance of the two former markets has increased since the opening of the extension of the Bengal-Nagpur Railway. Trade from the southern portion of the district goes to the main line of the Bengal-Nagpur Railway at Chakardharpur, Rājgāngpur, and other stations. Apart from the railways, a considerable amount of trade still goes by road *viâ* Hazāribāgh and Chattrā to Gaya. In the wilder parts of the district pack-bullocks are regularly used as the only means of conveyance, and long trains of them may be seen passing through Barwe bringing oil-seeds from the Feudatory States of Jashpur and Surguja. Except at Rānchi and Lohardagā, there are no permanent markets, and trade is carried on by means of the weekly *hāts* held at various centres, at which the merchants purchase food-grains, oil-seeds, lac, hides, etc., from the cultivators and sell in return salt, kerosine oil, and Manchester goods. The chief articles of export after a good harvest are oil-seeds and rice. Stick lac is also exported, chiefly to the manufacturing centres in Mirzapur and Mānbhūm. Other items of export are hides and skins, tea, timber and bones. Sugar, salt, kerosine oil, coal and manufactured articles are the principal articles of import. An interesting attempt to do away with the *bania* and secure for the aboriginals the profit of their cultivation has been made by the Roman Catholic Mission by the establishment of a large Co-operative Store, of which an account is given in Chapter VIII.

Weights and Measures.

The standard *ser* of 80 *tolas* is practically only known in the larger markets and trade centres. In the Five Parganas the *solāhi ser* is used, and is equal to one-third of the standard *ser*; it is so called because it is equal in weight to sixteen Gorakhpuri pice. In other parts of the district the weight in most common use is the *athāisi kachi ser* which is equal in weight to twenty-eight copper pice, or half a standard *ser*. Seven *sers* make a *paseri* and eight *paseris* one maund. The *kachcha ser*, which equals 9·6 standard chitaks, is also in common use; six *kachcha ser* go to one *paseri* and 48 to the maund, which is thus equal to 28 standard *sers*.

Grain, however, is seldom weighed, and all transactions in grain are carried out by means of the measure known as the *paila*. The size of the *paila* varies, and to ascertain which merchant will give him the best price for grain the customer has not to enquire what the rate is but to see whether a large or small *paila* is being used. The following *pailas* are in common use; the *chhapnāhi paila*, so called because a *paila* of cleaned rice is equal to 56 common pice or one standard *ser* of 80 *tolas*; the *baragandi paila* which equals twelve *gandas* (48) of common pice and the *sawāi paila* which derives its name from being the equivalent to one-and-a-quarter of the *chhapnāhi paila* and is equal to five-fourths of a standard *ser*. In measuring grain for family consumption or the distribution of grain-wages the *rozni paila* is used.

Divisions of time are but vaguely recognized by the rural population, the time of day being usually fixed with reference to the position of the sun or to a meal or some agricultural operation, *e.g.*, taking out or bringing home the cattle. The day and night are each divided into four *pahar*, each *pahar* into four *ghari* and each *ghari* into two *dand*. A *ghari* varies in length according to the duration of daylight and is longer by day in summer and by night in winter; it averages about three-quarters of an hour. The Hindi Sambat year is used throughout the district.

The local measure of distance is the *kos* or league; it consists of sixteen *goli*, or gunshot distances, which consist of 440 *deg* or paces. The *kos* is a somewhat indefinite measure and is said to be the distance which a man can walk carrying in his hand a green *sāl* twig before it becomes withered. The system of land measurement is described in Chapter VIII.

CHAPTER X.

MEANS OF COMMUNICATION.

A CENTURY ago the only means of communication in the district consisted of jungle paths over which no wheeled vehicle could pass. On the establishment of the Agency in 1834, roads were constructed from Rānchi to the headquarters of the surrounding districts, but even in 1870 only 175 miles were maintained, the most important being the roads from Rānchi to Silli, and from Rānchi to Barkheta on the northern boundary of the district. Under the Road Cess Committee many new roads were constructed, and existing roads were improved, and in the year 1888 there were 700 miles of road, many of which were only fair-weather tracks. The improvement of the communications has been carried on by the District Board and there are now over a thousand miles of road. So great is the area of the district, and so small the resources of the District Board, that the metalled roads connecting Rānchi with the neighbouring districts are maintained at the cost of Government. The Public Works Department maintains 129 miles of metalled road which open up the north-west, north-east, and south of the district. The District Board is responsible for the roads connecting Rānchi with the subdivisional headquarters at Gumlā and with the west and south-west of the district, and also for the feeder roads to the railway. In all 901 miles of roads, including from village roads, are maintained, all of which, except for a few miles near Rānchi, are unmetalled. The more important roads are surfaced with red gravel, or "murram", which is found in great quantities in the district, but the majority are merely tracks over the high lands with drains cut on either side and brick or wooden culverts for drainage purposes. The physical conformation of the country makes the construction of roads difficult. Even in the undulating central plateau, there are numerous streams and rivers which, though dry in the hot weather, are impassable after a storm in the rains, and the roads have to be embanked where they cross the low-lying valleys between the ridges. In the west and south-west where the country is hilly and more broken, the work is even more difficult. The streams are more numerous and the roads have to pass over steep *ghāts*, or passes in the hills. In spite of these difficulties great improvement has been made in the roads in the last few years, and it is now possible for a motorist during the dry season to reach even the most distant parts of the district without encountering any insuperable obstacles. The detailed account of the roads which is given below shows the progress which is being made. On the roads maintained by the Public Works Department there are inspection bungalows every ten or twelve miles, while there are bungalows at several thanas, constructed and maintained at the cost of the *ghātwāli* fund.

Vehicles. The bulk of the trade of the district, except on the metalled roads, is still carried on pack-bullocks, and long streams of pack-bullocks and pack-ponies are met crossing the hills in the west of the district and bringing to the railway at Lohardagā or Rānchi the produce of Barwe, Biru, and the Feudatory States. Bullock-carts are numerous on the metalled roads radiating from Rānchi, and much of the trade with the Gaya district and South Bihar is still carried in carts along the road to Hazāribāgh, instead of by the circuitous railway route *viâ* Purulia and Asansol. For these large carts bullocks are imported from Bihar, as the small and undersized bullocks of Chotā Nāgpur are unable to pull anything heavier than the *sagar*, the ordinary cart of the district. The *sagar* which is a low cart with two solid wheels, built up of three blocks of wood, can traverse the roughest country with a light load and is used for bringing timber from the jungles and rice to the markets. The aboriginals and low-caste Hindus carry their goods by means of the *banghi*, a flat elastic wooden or bamboo rod, about four feet long, which is carried on the shoulder, the articles being placed in two nets which are suspended from the ends. For the conveyance of passengers, the *pālki*, similar to that in use in other parts of India, is used by well-to-do Indians, but the most characteristic vehicle of Chotā Nāgpur is the "push-push". This has been aptly described as "a bathing machine on two wheels, only not half so high or roomy". It is about four feet high inside, and stretched over the top is a semi-circular roof of matting, beneath which are the traveller's servants and luggage. The vehicle is propelled by from four to eight coolies. Before the Rānchi-Purūlia railway was opened, a "push-push" was the only form of conveyance for the journey of 75 miles from Purūlia, and even with fresh relays of coolies every eighth mile, the journey under the most favourable circumstances used seldom to take less than twenty hours. In the eighties visitors to Rānchi had an even longer journey in this uncomfortable conveyance, as the route from Calcutta was by rail to Giridih, and thence by road through Dumri, Bagodār and Hazāribāgh. Since the opening of the railway to Rānchi, the "push-push" is rapidly becoming a relic of the past, but it may still be seen at Rānchi railway station waiting to carry the traveller's luggage and servants to his destination, or met in the bazar conveying a Secretariat Assistant to his office, or his children to the school. With the improvement that has been made in the roads in recent years, and with the increase in the official population of Rānchi, since it became the headquarters of Government, motor cars have become very numerous and form a striking contrast to the primitive *sagar* and the cumbersome "push-push".

The four first-class roads maintained by the Public Works Department connect Rānchi with the headquarters of the Mānbhūm, Hazāribāgh, Singhbhūm, and Palāmau districts The first three are metalled with quartz, and the last with good gravel. Main Roads.

The Rānchi-Purūlia Road (74½ miles, 38½ miles in the district) is metalled and bridged throughout. The two largest bridges are across the Subarnarekhā—one a girder bridge at the 36th mile, on the boundary of the district, and the other a stone bridge a few miles outside Rānchi. Until the opening of the Rānchi-Purūlia railway this was the most important of the roads from Rānchi and carried a great volume of traffic, both in passengers and goods. Even now the number of bullock-carts using the road is considerable, and there is much traffic in goods to the intermediate stations between Rānchi and Purūlia and to the large bazars of Silli, Jonha, and Jhalda. Motorists also make great use of the road.

The surface of the road is so good and the gradient of the *ghāt* so easy, that the journey to Purūlia can be performed as quickly in a car as in the train, and the pleasure of the motor drive through the beautiful scenery is highly preferable to the tedium of the journey by rail. There are good inspection bungalows at Tatisilwāi, Angara, Jonha, and Kita. The dâk bungalow at Thulin (40 miles), formerly much used as a half-way house in the days of the "push-push" journey, is just outside the district.

The road from Rānchi to Hazāribāgh (58 miles, 20 in the district) is also metalled and bridged throughout. It decreased in importance on the opening of the railway to Purūlia, but much of the goods traffic to Bihar still follows this route to avoid the necessity for transhipment at Purūlia, while most of the coal used in Rānchi is brought by this road from the Rāmgarh coalfield. The road has a great attraction for motorists, and now that the bridge over the Dāmodar river at Rāmgarh has been completed, the journey presents no difficulties. Before the bridge was opened, the motorist could cross the river in the dry season by a temporary wooden bridge, but, if the river rose at all, he had to entrust his car to the tender mercies of coolies who slung it on poles and carried it on their backs, or, if it rose still higher, to load it on to a clumsy ferry-boat, which was slowly pushed to the opposite bank. There are inspection bungalows at Ormānjhi and Chutupalu. At the 18th mile from Rānchi a road branches off to the foot of the Ichadāg hill, on the summit of which (3,500 feet above sea-level) the District Board has erected a bungalow, to serve as a sanatorium for the inhabitants of Rānchi who find the heat of April and May too oppressive.

The Rānchi-Chaibassa road (88 miles, 38 in the district) has increased considerably in importance since the establishment of a subdivision at Khunti. It is metalled and bridged throughout. The Subarnarekhā at the 7th mile is crossed by a causeway, and bridges have recently been erected over the Kānchi river at the 15th mile, and the Tajna at the 20th mile. There are inspection bungalows at Kalamati, Khunti, and Murhu. The Rānchi-Chaibassa and Rānchi-Hazāribāgh roads form an important part of the Trunk Road which will link up Bankipore and Bihar with Cuttack and Orissa.

The Public Works Department also have charge of the Rānchi-Daltonganj road, of which 36¾ miles are in the district, and a portion of the Rānchi-Pithauria road. The former with the District Board road from Kuru links up Rānchi with Lohardagā but its importance has been considerably reduced since the opening of the Rānchi-Lohardagā Railway; the latter forms the approach to the Lunatic Asylums which are in course of construction, some six miles out of Rānchi, and has been improved by the erection of a bridge over the Potpoto river at the fourth mile. The road via Pithauria used to connect Rānchi with Hazāribāgh before the present road via Rāmgarh and Ormānjhi was constructed.

District Board Roads.

Of the roads maintained by the District Board, the most important are those connecting Rānchi with Gumlā and Biru in the west, and with Bundu and Tamār in the south-east, Lohardagā with Gumlā, and Khunti with Torpa and Basia. The Rānchi-Gumlā road (56 miles) is gravelled throughout and has masonry bridges over all the rivers, except the South Koel. An attempt was made to provide a ferry for this river but did not prove a success. During the dry weather the river is easily fordable but during the rains it is often uncrossable for days together, even in the primitive *donga*. Two roads link up Rānchi with the south-west of the district; the main route is via Khunti and Torpā to Basia and thence to Kolebira, Simdegā and Kochedegā; while another road passes through Lodhmā, Karrā and Jariā to Basiā. From Basiā a road goes to Pālkot and Gumlā. These roads are at present unmetalled and not surfaced with gravel, but the main road via Torpā is being improved by the erection of bridges and culverts, while the improvement of the road between Kolebirā and Simdegā is under consideration. A road will also be constructed, linking Simdegā and Biru with the B.-N. Railway near Rājgāngpur. The road to Bundu is bridged throughout, and will soon be metalled. The Lohardagā-Gumlā road (32 miles) has become of great importance since the opening of the railway to the former town and with the assistance of grants from Government the District Board is constructing bridges over the rivers and metalling the greater portion of the road, as it has been found by experience that gravelled roads are little better than *kutchā* roads if the cart traffic is at all heavy. The timber traffic in this part of the district is very heavy, as many of the *sāl* jungles in the north-west of the district are being exploited by contractors, and a large number of carts pass along the Ghaghrā-Netarhāt road which leaves the Lohardagā-Gumlā road at the 16th mile. Bridges are being constructed on this road which, apart from the timber traffic, owes its importance to the fact that it unites the potential hill station of Netarhāt with the railway and with Rānchi. The roads in the outlying parts of the district and the village roads are little better than cleared tracks, with drains cut by the side. In the famine of 1908, the roads in the famine areas of Biru and Barwe were improved by the construction of embankments, but the improvement has not been permanent. The chief need on all the roads in the district is the construction of masonry bridges over the small rivers and of permanent culverts, to prevent the surface drainage breaching the embankments.

Arboriculture. The main roads from Rānchi are lined with avenues of shady trees. Trees are also being planted by the side of the District Board roads, especially quick-growing trees, such as *pipal*, *bar* and *tun*, and fruit trees, such as jack, mango, *jāmun*, and *karanj*, which afford both shade to the traveller and profit to the planter.

The District Board has constructed wells at the larger bazars and villages on the main roads.

Water communications. There are no canals or navigable rivers in the district. The larger rivers are crossed during the rains in a *donga*, a primitive boat constructed of the hollowed-out trunk of a tree and propelled with long bamboo poles.

Railway communications. The opening of the Purulia-Rānchi branch of the Bengal-Nagpur Railway has made Rānchi easily accessible from Calcutta and elsewhere. The line was begun in 1905 and was opened by Sir Andrew Fraser, Lieutenant-Governor of Bengal, on November 14th, 1907. It is built on the 2′ 6″ gauge and is 72·55 miles in length, 36·63 miles being in the Rānchi district. There are six intermediate stations between Rānchi and Purūliā, those at Tatisilwai, Gunga Ghāt, Jonha and Silli being within the district boundaries. The journey from Calcutta to Rānchi can now be accomplished in 14 hours, and that from Bankipore to Ranchi in the same time. The extension of the line to Lohardagā was begun in 1911, and was opened for traffic in October 1913. The line passes midway between the Rānchi-Gumlā and Rānchi-Lohardagā roads and is 42·8 miles in length ; there are intermediate stations at Argora, Pisga, Tangārbansli and Naggira.

The effect of the Railway on the district is shown by the increase in the amount of goods exported between the years 1908, 1912 and 1914-15. In 1908 exports amounted to 5,803 tons, in 1912, to 16,818 tons, and in 1914-15, after the opening of the Lohardagā extension to over 21,000 tons.

The following table shows the chief exports from Ranchi stations.

—	1908	1912	1914-15
	Tons.	Tons.	Tons.
Grain and Pulses ...	306	214	223
Rice	1,489	5,513	228
Hides and Skin ...	567	851	435
Lac stick	1,662	2,007	1,427
Oil-seeds	963	6,897	3,618
Tea	105	172	107
Timber	101	171	641
Bones	313	527	344

Imports amounted to 24,362 tons in 1908, to 27,735 in 1912, and to 45,386 in 1914-15. The principal imports are :—

—	1908	1912	1914-15
	Tons.	Tons.	Tons.
Coal	1,905	2,747	10,032
Cotton Twist ...	805	912	1,021
Rice	6,241	46	1,017
Wheat	402	290	253
Wheat flour ...	467	462	720
Lime	119	1,802	3,630
Kerosine oil ...	875	1,496	1,719
Salt	4,659	5,610	5,856
Sugar	1,728	1,319	711
Mahua flowers ...	1,052	39	340

The Lohardagā branch promises to have an equally heavy export traffic, the import traffic being naturally considerably less than to Rānchi. The export traffic on this line in 1914-15 amounted to 12,251 tons and the import traffic to 4507 tons.

The figures for passenger traffic to and from Rānchi are as follows :—

	Outward.	Inward.
1908 ...	... 781,134	67,555
1914-15	... 131,885	146,913

Here again the figures show the great benefit of the railway in a famine year, the large number of outward passengers in 1908 being due to the emigration of coolies to Bengal and the tea districts to obtain work. The total number of passengers carried on the Lohardagā line in 1914-15 was over 76,000.

Postal communications. There are altogether 35 post offices in the district, including one head office, 11 sub-offices and 23 branch offices, and 475 miles of postal communication. The number of postal articles delivered weekly averages over 38,000, while the value of money orders issued in 1914-15 was Rs. 17,33,315, and of money orders paid was Rs. 8,71,910.

Six hundred and ninety-four accounts have been opened in the Savings Banks, the deposits amounting to Rs. 1,65,834 in the year 1914-15.

There are six combined post-telegraph offices in the district. The number of messages despatched was 17,905 in 1911-12 before Rānchi became the headquarters of the Local Government, and 73,856 in 1914-15.

CHAPTER XI.

LAND REVENUE ADMINISTRATION.

THE CHOTA NAGPUR ESTATE.

For purposes of Land Revenue administration the district consists of only one permanently-settled estate, that of the Mahārāja of Chota Nāgpur. The estate embraces the whole of the district, with the exception of a few villages which belong to the Padma Rāj estate in the district of Hazāribāgh, and the Kashipur Rāj estate in the district of Mānbhum. The land revenue of these villages is paid in the districts in which the parent estate is situated. The land revenue payable by the Chota Nāgpur estate is Rs. 15,042. Of the total area of the estate, 724 square miles are in the *khās* possession of the Mahārāja, the remainder being held by subordinate tenure-holders. Three of these tenures are in the direct possession of Government, having been confiscated after the Mutiny, and for these estates a rent of Rs. 678 is payable to the Chota Nāgpur estate and is set-off against the total land revenue demand.

Origin of the Estate.

Though the early history of the district, as indeed of the whole of Chota Nāgpur, is involved in obscurity, it is certain that the Mundās and Orāons entered the country at an early date, which cannot now be fixed with any precision, or dispossessed the Asurs, of whom traces are still found and reclaimed it from virgin jungle. The primitive village communities of the Mundās were united into *pārhās*, or groups of villages, over each of which a Chief presided. At a very early period, possibly the tenth century of the Christian era, the Chief of Khukhrā became the feudal superior of the other Chiefs. Whether he was elected or whether he succeeded in imposing his authority is doubtful, but it is certain that the original Chief of Chotā Nāgpur was a Mundā and that his authority was recognized both by the Mundās and by the Orāons and other inhabitants of the district, who agreed to render him certain feudal services and to pay some small tribute. The Chief of Khukhrā was the ancestor of the present Mahārāja of Chota Nāgpur. As the family prospered, the Chiefs intermarried with Rājput families of Pachet and Singhbhūm and gradually came to be recognized as Rājputs. Having thus become a member of the Hindu community, the Rājā sought to induce other Hindus to come and settle in the country, in order that they might afford him assistance, not only in protecting himself against the invasion of neighbouring Chiefs, but also in controlling his own turbulent vassals. He achieved his object by making grants of villages on easy conditions; frequently the grantees were only required to render personal service and to keep up a standing force of militia, and, in return, were left free to make what they could out of their villages. They were naturally not content that the village communities should render them merely a few petty services and pay an insignificant tribute and, as they were more civilized and better organized than the aborigines, they succeeded in ousting them from their position of proprietors of the soil, reduced them to the position of mere cultivators or tenants, imposed payments of various kinds and exacted greatly increased services. Thus it came about that the Mahārājā established his position as the overlord of the whole of Chota Nāgpur, the Hindu settlers introduced by him, and the members of his family to whom maintenance grants were given, became his subordinate tenure-holders, while the aborigines sank to the position of rent-paying tenants.

Tribute payable to the Muhammadans.

This was the condition of affairs when in 1585 A. D. the Rāja of Khukhrā, as the Chota Nāgpur Rāja was then called, became a tributary of the Muhammadans. The subjection was at first purely nominal; the Mughals exacted no yearly tribute and were content with making occasional raids into the country and carrying off as tribute a few diamonds which were found at that time in the Sānkh river. In 1616 the Emperor Jahāngir sought to make the subjection more real, and his lieutenant, Ibrāhim Khān, the Governor of Bihar, defeated Rājā Durjan Sal and carried him off captive to Delhi. Twelve years later he secured his release, owing, it is said, to his skill in testing diamonds, and agreed to pay an annual tribute of Rs. 6,000. Ever after this the

Muhammadans exercised but little control over the internal affairs of the district and were content if they received a portion of the stipulated tribute.

Payment of revenue to the British administration.

The district together with the rest of Chota Nāgpur came under British subjection in 1765, when the *diwāni* of Bengal, Bihar and Orissa was ceded by the Nawab. At first the British made little attempt to bring the country under their administration and it was not till 1769 that Captain Camac penetrated into the country. The revenue of Nāgpur which amounted to only Rs. 4,000 was paid at this time through the Rājā of Rāmgarh, but in 1771 the Rāja of Nāgpur applied to Captain Camac for permission to pay his revenue direct to Government and also for the restoration of some disputed tracts of territory. The Council of Patna agreeing with Captain Camac as to the importance of securing the good will of this Rājā "whose country would form a barrier against the incursions of the Mahrattas", made a slight rectification of the boundaries in favour of Nāgpur and made a settlement with the Rājā Drip Nath Sahi, by which he stipulated to pay an annual revenue of Rs. 12,000 including customs and transit duties. The agreement was for a period of three years (1772-5). The Rājā however, was very remiss in making payments, and towards the end of 1773 Captain Camac had to send an expedition to the country to make him fulfil his obligations. In 1774 the settlement were renewed for a period of three years and according to the *patta* the revenue was fixed at Rs. 15,001, of which Rs. 12,001 were revenue and Rs. 3,000 *nazarāna*. The apparent increase may be due to the exclusion of pargana Tori from the earlier settlement. In the *kabuliyat* given to the Rājā in 1787 he agreed not to levy *sayer* and other prohibited cesses, for which he had received a deduction; to be responsible for the safety of travellers and to arrest thieves and dakaits and bring them to justice. In case he failed to pay the stipulated revenue, his estate or such portions thereof as might be necessary were declared to be saleable. The terms of the *patta* and *kabuliyat* given at the time of the decennial settlement on the 3rd May 1790 are exactly similar to those contained in the *kabuliyat* and *patta* of 1787. The revenue agreed upon was Rs. 14,100-15-3, the difference of Rs. 900 as compared with the *jama* fixed at previous settlements being due to the remission on account of exchange. The settlement with the Rājā does not appear to have been formally declared permanent, but when the point was raised in 1799, the Board of Revenue, in reply to a reference, held that the revenue was fixed for ever under Regulation I of 1793, and this decision was upheld when the point was again raised by Collector of Rāmgarh in 1823.

Mode of collecting the revenue.

Up to 1799 the revenue of the esate was paid t) the Collector at Chatrā. The mode of collection was peculiar. A *Suzāwal* (agent), appointed by the Collector but paid by the Rājā, was attached to the estate. The Rāja made over to him a certain proportion of the harvests under the appellation of *taidad*. From this the *Suzāwal* realised the Government revenue and his own allowances, returning the balance, if any, to the Rājā. In 1799-1800 when the Collectorship of Rāmgarh was temporarily abolished and the district was annexed to the revenue jurisdiction of Bihar, the system of collection in vogue was discontinued and balances began to accumulate. In 1808, at the Rājā's request, a *Suzāwul* was again appointed and soon after a Deputy Collector was appointed at Rāmgarh.

***Sayer* and excise duties.**

A frequent subject of dispute between the Rājā and the British authorities about the year 1820 concerned the *sayer* and excise duties. The general policy of Government at the time of the Decennial Settlement was to take into their own hands the collection of these duties and to compensate the zamindars for the consequent loss of income by a remission of revenue. The conditions of Chota Nāgpur differed greatly from those of Bihar, and Mr. Leslie, the Collector of Rāmgarh, in June 1789, represented that the collection of the *sayer* by Government officials would stir up the opposition of the "jealous and uncivilized" people of the district, and in a letter written a few months later reported that "the *sayer* collections consist only of three articles at present, viz., '*gungeat*, *gauthwari* and *haut* duties,' none of which can be in my opinion discontinued without a disadvantage to Government; but as the *gungedt* is composed of two articles, viz., a duty on the sale of goods and one on passing through, called *nikhusai*, I think the latter ought to be struck off as a hardship to traders."

Though it is not quite clear what policy Government followed in the matter, it is certain that the Rājā did not receive any remission of revenue but that a remission was granted to the Rājās of Rāmgarh and Palāmau and that the covenants executed by him in 1790 contained the same conditions as those granted to these and other zamindars, and stated that a deduction had been made for *sayer*. He did not however, raise the question of remission till much later and appears to have gone on collecting the duties, the British authorities having but a weak control over the country and being unable or reluctant to raise any objections. The question of transit duties appears to have been raised in 1823, and the Collector, holding their collection to be prohibited by the Rāja's covenant, advised the merchants not to pay and to resist *viz et armis* any attempt to realise them. The Board of Revenue called on the Rājā to state his claim for a remission on account of the abolition of *sayer*, and he bazed his claim chiefly on the ground that his estate had been expressly exempted from the scope of the Regulations and that the *sayer* and *abkāri* collected by him for the last 35 years had been used to defray the cost of the police thanas and preserve the peace of the district. The Collector, in forwarding his petition, disposed of the argument that he was not bound by the Regulations by referring to a *parwana* of 1780, which directed the Rājā to discontinue the collection of *sayer* and produce *sayer* accounts, on which the remissions were granted, and contended that the Rājā was bound by the terms of the covenant which he had accepted without objection for many years. He also pointed out that the Rājā could claim no consideration on the ground of the expenditure incurred in the upkeep of the police, as he kept them heavily in arrears and allowed them to pay themselves by extorting money from the inhabitants under warrants granted by himself. The final orders of the Board in this matter are not extant but it appears that no remission on account of *sayer* was granted. Mr. Webster, a former Manager of the Chotā Nāgpur Estate, considered that the Rājā was hardly treated in this matter. At this length of time and in the absence of complete papers it is difficult to form an opinion, but it may be held that the Rājā was himself responsible for the mistake, if mistake it was, as he allowed the inclusion of the condition in his covenant to pass without protest and continued to collect the duties, both those which were legal and those which had been abolished.

With regard to the excise duties, there is no doubt that the Rājā received no compensation, when this source of revenue was resumed by Government in 1823 and the collection farmed out for the whole pargana for Rs. 6,500. The Rājā had for many years steadfastly opposed any attempts on the part of the authorities to take over the excise; he represented that the result of such action would be to drive the Kols back to their old home of Rohtās and to endanger the public revenue; he also concealed the true facts and pretended that the collections were no source of profit to him or his *jagirdars*. Thus in the case of excise also the Rājā was largely responsible for the failure to obtain any remission of revenue.

Status of the Raja.

Another question of some historical interest is whether the Rājā had any claim to be regarded as a Feudatory Chief. This claim is based chiefly on a Resolution of 1789, which exempted the district from the Regulations, and also on the fact that, in the early days of British administration, the Rājā was given a very free hand in the internal affairs of the district, the only interference being by the despatch of small detachments to secure the arrest of a criminal, or to assist the Chief in realizing his dues from his subordinate tenure-holders. The question was finally disposed of by the orders of Government issued in 1824, in which it was held that the district had only been exempted from the Land Revenue regulations and that the general regulations applied to Chotā Nāgpur in the same way as to other parts of the province.

SUBORDINATE TENURES.

The tenures subordinate to the Rājā of Chotā Nāgpur may be divided into three classes—(1) those of the dependent Rājās; (2) service tenures and (3) maintenance tenures.

Tenures of dependent Rajas.

The Five Parganas, i.e., the low-lying plateau in the east and south-east of the district, were undoubtedly in early days in the possession of independent Rājās. The tenures of these Chiefs were not creations of the Rājā of Chotā Nāgpur but the Chiefs gradually came to recognize him as their feudal superior. In most cases this recognition was enforced, in the first instance, by conquest; in many cases the Chiefs regained temporarily their independence, and it was not till the end of the 18th Century that they were finally reduced. In the early days of their subjection they rendered feudal services to the Rājā but when the necessity for such service disappeared, they agreed, or were forced, to pay a fixed quota of the revenue into his hand as rent. Tamār was formerly subject to Orissa and was apparently brought into subjection when the Chotā Nāgpur Chief accompanied the Muhammadans in their invasion of Orissa. Bundu and Rahe were compelled by the British authorities in 1793 to enter into agreements to pay rents. Silli was probably subordinate to Chotā Nāgpur before the cession of the country to the British. Apart from the estates of the Five Parganas there are other estates which have a similar origin. The Barwe estate was originally subordinate to the Rājā of Surguja but was annexed by conquest. The Rājā of Surguja, however, re-established his authority and it was not till 1799, that the Rājā of Chotā Nāgpur was able, with the assistance of British troops, to bring back the Chief to his allegiance. These tenures, not being in origin creations of the Chotā Nāgpur Chief, differ from other tenures in the district, in that they are not resumable on the failure of male heirs. The Chotā Nāgpur Estate has, it is true, endeavoured to deprive them of this privilege by contending that the present proprietors are not the legitimate descendants of the original Chiefs and in some cases have got the proprietors to accept *pattas* in which this condition is specially mentioned. Mr. Webster, a Manager of the estate, writing of them in 1875, says:—"All these estates are held under what are called *bhandowa pattas* and on the failure of heirs male to the original holder they escheat to the Chotā Nāgpur Estate." Rahe has in fact been resumed but the grounds on which the resumption was granted in 1845 have been declared unsound by a subsequent judicial decision and Tamār has been judicially declared to be non-resumable. The question of the status of the proprietor of Barwe is at present the subject of civil suit.

Service *Jagirs.*

The origin of the service *jāgīr* is as follows:—Prior to the establishment of British dominion, the Chiefs of Chotā Nāgpur were constantly engaged in petty warfare, sometimes with their own vassals, sometimes with the Chiefs of neighbouring States. To protect their country from the ravages of their enemies as well as to enable them to make reprisals on their neighbours, a standing force or militia was required. The Rājā accordingly gave lands in *jāgīr* to foreigners from other parts of India on condition that they were at all times ready to assist him with a certain proportion of armed followers. The *jāgīrs* are thus feudal tenures, "the counterpart", as Mr. Walpole described them in 1809, "to those engagements which existed in the middle ages to so great an extent in many parts of Europe." When the country became vested in the British Government the necessity for military service ceased, and it was deemed equitable that they should pay a cash rent and some praedial dues (*rakūmāts*), in lieu of the services formerly rendered. The holders of these tenures are usually members of the fighting castes, either Rājputs, or Rāutiās and Bhogtās who claim to be Rājputs. The holders of the tenures are known as *barāik*, *ghātwāl*, etc. Besides these feudal *jāgīrs*, other *jāgīrs* were given to the numerous officers and servants with which the Rāja surrounded himself in imitation of the pomp and pageantry of Hindu or Mughal royalty. Thus we find a village granted to a composer of *extempore* poems with which the Mahārājā of the day was well pleased, to a noted wrestler for his feats of strength, to domestic servants such as a *diwān*, "sepoy", *kotwāl*, or *hukabardar* (preparer of the Mahārājā's *hukah*), while others were granted in return for special services, as, for instanee, to persons who killed enemies of the Mahārāja under his orders. There are also religious *brit* tenures. As the Rājās adopted the Hindu religion, they introduced a number of Brāhman priests, erected temples to the Hindu deities throughout the country, and made *bramhottar*, *debottar* and other *brit* grants of lands or villages to the priests for their maintenance and for the upkeep of the temples and the worship of the gods. Two curious forms of such tenures, mentioned by Mr. Webster in his account of the estate written in 1875, are *Tanga* villages and *Chiba brit*. "*Tanga* villages", he writes, "usually belong to Brāhmans and according to tradition were obtained in this way :—If a Brāhman failed to obtain a village from the Mahārājā by fair means and was willing to sacrifice himself for the benefit of his heirs, all he had to do was to betake himself to a village and, taking care to select a good one, deliberately hang himself therein. The only way of expiating the guilt of possessing a village in which a Brāhman had hanged himself was by getting rid of the accursed spot and by giving it away in *jāgīr* to the heirs of the deceased. The origin of *Chiba brit* was said to be :—The Mahārājā having finished chewing his *pan* or betel threw it away. Some great admirer picked up the choice morsel and put it in his mouth and was recompensed for his devotion to the Mahārājā by the grant of a village or two."

Maintenance Tenures.

The Rāj family has always followed the custom of primogeniture, and hence it became usual for the Rājās to allot maintenance holdings to their near relatives, the Thākurs and Lāls, as the younger brothers of the Mahārājā and their descendants are called. At first it would seem that these grants meant nothing more than the assignment of the tributes or supplies which the Rājā got from the village communities, but, like the service *jāgīrdārs* and the Rājā himself, the *khorposhdār* gradually reduced the cultivators to the position of rent-paying tenants.

Incidents of service and maintenance tenures.

The incidents of these tenures are too numerous and too varied to be enumerated in detail and it must suffice to mention only the most important which are found particularly in the feudal *jāgīr* and in the maintenance grants. The term *jāgīr* connotes resumability, that is, the tenure lapses to the parent estate on the failure of male heirs and all such tenures are locally known as *putra putrādhik*. The maintenance grants are also resumable, though the condition is not always stated in the deeds under which the original grant was made, yet if the tenure was originally a *jāgīr*, the custom is none the less certain. Even *brit* grants lapse to the parent estate on the failure of male heirs of the original grantee, though, according to Hindu usage, such grants are not resumable under any condition by the grantor. Previous to the Permanent Settlement, the Mahārāja did in some cases exercise the right to resume at will, but the power to resume such grants as existed at the time of the Permanent Settlement, without the consent of Government, was expressly taken away by the *patta* granted to the Rāja of that time. *Jāgīr* tenures are also impartible and inalienable. The *jāgīrdārs*, maintenance-holders, and even tenure-holders subordinate to them, have adopted the custom of primogeniture which prevails in the Chotā Nāgpur family. The usage was recognized as long ago as 1800, as by Regulation X of that year the provisions of

Regulation XI of 1793, under which the estates of persons dying intestate were declared to be liable to be divided among the heirs of the deceased according to Hindu or Muhammadan law, were declared to be inapplicable to the jungle *mahals* of Midnapur and other districts. Colonel. Dalton, the Commissioner of the Division, who was for 18 or 19 years in Chota Nāgpur and made a special study of local usages, wrote in 1875: "The ordinary Hindu law does not apply to the estates (*jāgīrs*), as by custom and under the provisions of a Regulation passed in 1800 primogeniture is admittedly the *lex loci*, but judicial decisions based on a mistaken analogy with similar tenures in Bihar and Bengal have held the *jāgīrs* to be partible as well as transferable. Should further judicial decisions succeed in introducing a system of succession which is entirely opposed to local usage, the ancient estates of the district will become subdivided and in the end transferred piecemeal to money-lenders and other proprietors."

Other Tenures.

Apart from the tenures described above, the Mahārājās have at various times given leases of portions of the estate to the money-lenders, traders and other adventurers, who first began to find their way to Chota Nāgpur at the beginning of the 19th century. Some of these leases are permanent, (*doami* or *bemiadi thika*), others are perpetual leases on fixed rentals (*mokarrari*), others usufructuary leases (*zarpeshgi* and *bhugat*).

Of the whole estate measuring 7,052 square miles, only 724 square miles are now in the *khās* possession of the Mahārājā; 1,050 square miles have been given out by him, or his predecessors, as *khorposh*, while 4,480 square miles are in the possession of the feudal, and other, *jāgīrdārs*. *Brit* grants absorb 134 square miles, and the remainder is held on leases, viz., *Mokarrari* 22·55 square miles; *thika* 126 square miles; *zarpeshgi* 3 square miles, *doami* (permanent absolute grants) 493 square miles.

The cultivating tenancies, some of which are technically tenures, are described in the chapter on Rent.

Landlord's privileged lands.

All lands which are in the *khās* cultivation of a landlord are locally known as *mānjhihās*, a word which literally means the headman's share and is an interesting survival of the time, when the villages were ruled by headmen and landlords had no jurisdiction in the village economy. The landlords have appropriated this heritage and demarcated *mānjhihās* land now means land in the possession of the landlord and at his absolute disposal. The Chotā Nāgpur Tenures Act of 1869 provided for the preparation of a record of all *mānjhihās* and *beth-kheta* lands, or privileged lands of the landlords, of which they could prove their possession for a period of twenty years before the passing of the Act. *Beth-kheta* lands are, as the name implies, lands set apart for service. The villagers, who cultivate them, render special services to the landlords; or they are cultivated by the whole body of the villagers, who share the produce and in return render a fixed number of days' service to the landlord. No occupancy rights can accrue in such lands, however long the possession of the raiyat. In the recent settlement a record was prepared not only of *mānjhihās* and *beth-kheta* lands, demarcated at the time of the *bhūinhāri* survey, but also of all landlords' privileged lands. The latter are defined by the present Tenancy Act as all lands which are cultivated by the landlord himself, or which are leased to tenants for a term of years or year by year, and in which by local custom occupancy rights do not accrue to the tenants. This definition operated somewhat harshly on landlords who had been in the habit of leasing their *khās* lands to *thikadārs*, who in turn sublet them to raiyats for indefinite periods. As the definition of "settled raiyat" was introduced into the Tenancy Act of 1908, many of the raiyats to whom such lands had been leased had acquired rights of occupancy, and lands which were undoubtedly the landlord's *khās* lands have thus been converted into ordinary raiyati holdings. The record prepared by the Settlement Department shows that the *mānjhihās* and *beth-kheta* lands demarcated under Act IX of 1869 occupy 89 square miles, other privileged lands of the landlords 65 square miles, while 251 square miles are in actual cultivating possession of the landlords. The landlords thus hold 11·2 per cent. of the total area at present under cultivation of 3,614 square miles.

Exemption of estates from sale for arrears of debt.

The tenure-holders of Chotā Nāgpur are notoriously improvident; their estates produce no very large income and the proprietors, even in the earliest times, incurred heavy debts to money-lenders and traders. If estates belonging to ancient families were sold up in execution of decrees of the courts, and possession passed to alien landlords, there was fear of disturbances and discontent among the tenants. In the year 1795 the sale of the great estate of Pachet in Mānbhum for arrears of revenue had caused a general rising of the tenants, which was only put down by the cancellation of the sale. The purchase of the Palāmau estate by Government at a sale for arrears of revenue, in 1820, had made the people sullen and discontented, and they readily joined the Kol insurrection of 1831 and again gave considerable trouble both before and during the Mutiny of 1857. Profiting by these examples Government adopted the policy of stopping as far as possible the sale of estates. Under rules drawn up by Captain Wilkinson, the first Agent, and sanctioned by Government, the sale or transfer of landed property without the Agent's consent, on any account whatsoever, was prohibited, and it became customary for the Agent and his Assistants to interfere in, and decide summarily, questions between debtors and creditors. The practice in fact was to attach, and take under direct management, such estates as were likely to default or be sold up in the Civil Courts in execution of decrees for debts. Such procedure was purely executive and when Act VIII of 1859 (the Civil Code of the day) was extended to Chota Nāgpur, it was held that the power could no longer be effectively exercised. When, however, application was made to the Commissioner for sanction to the sale of estates, according to the terms of the provision of the notification extending the terms of the Civil Procedure Code to Chota Nāgpur, he ordinarily refused to allow the sale, when it was found that the assets were sufficient to meet the liabilities within a reasonable time.

Encumbered Estates Act.

To legalize the procedure which had been followed since the earliest days of the British administration, the Chotā Nāgpur Encumbered Estates Act (Act VI of 1876) was passed. The objects and reasons were stated as follows: "The accumulation of debts and the sale of large ancestral estates in satisfaction thereof is a process calculated to cause trouble in most parts of India. This is notably the case in the districts of the western portion of Bengal, which are comprised in the Chota Nāgpur province. In these districts there are many landed proprietors who are very improvident and apt to run into debt to an extent which exposes their estates to the danger of being brought to sale. If such sale takes place, trouble arises between the purchaser then villagers and the rights of the cultivators are likely to be imperilled." The Act empowered the Commissioner, with the previous sanction of the Lieutenant-Governor, to appoint a manager and to vest in him the entire management of encumbered estates, whenever he thought fit to do so. On publication of the vesting order, all proceedings in the Courts, including processes for the execution for debts, become barred ; the holder of the property is not liable to arrest for debt and the power to alienate any portion of the estate is vested in the manager. The Act has been amended by Act V (B. C.) of 1884 and again by Act III (B. C.) of 1901. By the latter Act the Deputy Commissioner is empowered to file *suo motu* an application for the protection of an estate, and at the same time it was definitely laid down that the holder of an estate must be of political or social importance or, if this is not so, Government must be satisfied that it is desirable in the interest of the tenantry that the estate should be protected. Frequent use has been made of this latter provision and estates of no political or social importance have been taken under management in the interests of the tenants. The recent Settlement operations, however, have placed the tenants in a much stronger position. Their rights have been carefully recorded and, with the spread of education and Christianity, they are better able to protect themselves. The necessity of protecting some of the older estates still remains but it may safely be said that the estates will not be brought as readily under management in the future as in the past.

In 1916 there were thirty-five encumbered estates under the management of Government. Of these the most important are the Armai and the Tamār estates, of which the rent-rolls are Rs. 29,640 and Rs. 21,384 respectively. The proprietors of the Armai estate are of the money-lending caste, and the estate was taken over in the interest of the tenantry. The remaining estates are comparatively small and their total rent-roll is only a little over one lakh, while their debts amount to rather more than 5¼ lakhs. There are two estates under the Court of Wards of which the largest is that of the Thākur of Jariā, with a rent-roll of Rs. 35,000.

Government Estates.

Three of the tenures subordinate to the Chota Nāgpur Estate were confiscated by Government on account of the assistance given by the proprietors to the mutineers in 1857. Like other estates in the district they are resumable on the failure of male heirs. A total rent of Rs. 678 is payable to the Mahārājā.

Barkagarh. The Barkagarh estate was created by Mahārājā Raghunāth Sahi, who gave the villages forming the estate to his brother Ani Sahi for maintenance. Thākur Biswanāth Sahi, the grandson of the original grantee, joined the mutineers and was hanged in the following year, his estate being confiscated under Act XXV of 1857. In 1872 Kapilnāth Sahi, the only son of Thākur Biswanāth Sahi, brought a suit against Government to obtain possession of the estate but was unsuccessful. The estate consists of 113 villages, of which 23 are held in *jāgīr*, *khorposh*, etc., and the remainder are under direct management. Thirty villages which were leased to Mr. Stainforth in 1881 have recently been resumed and brought under direct management.

Patia. The proprietor of the Patia estate was Pānde Ganpat Rai, the hereditary secretary of the Mahārājā. The estate consists of 9½ villages, of which three are in Lohardagā thana, and the remainder scattered over the Gumlā subdivision. The estate was settled by Captain Grey for a period of thirty years in 1881 and the whole of the estate, except for half a village leased out in *thika*, is now under direct management.

Silam. The proprietor of the Silam estate who joined the mutineers was Bhika Rām Rāutiā, whose ancestor had received the village in *jāgīr* from the *jāgīrdār* of Pālkot. It is thus a sub-tenure of a subordinate tenure-holder and rent is payable to the Armai Encumbered Estate, the successor in interest of the *jāgīrdār*.

TENANCY LEGISLATION. From the foundation of the Agency till the passing of Act X of 1859, it does not appear that there was any Code of law in force prescribing a procedure for the disposal of revenue suits or for the realization of revenue. The Courts, however, followed the old summary suit laws (Regulation V of 1800 and VII of 1837). In 1859 the Commissioner submitted a proposal to the Board of Revenue for the introduction of Act X of 1859 throughout the division with some modifications and omissions. The Board questioned the expediency of the proposal, and strongly objected to the proposal for extending the distraint clauses of the Act for the benefit of the landowners. The Act was accordingly not introduced, but the existing procedure was modified in accordance with its spirit, save that appeals continued to lie to the Commissioner, instead of to the Judge and the High Court. Eventually, however, the Commissioner ordered that the procedure laid down in the Act regarding appeals should also be followed, and, by the year 1869, all the provisions of the Act were generally followed, except that the distraint clauses were not applied and that the sections relating to the sale of land were subject to the restriction that no sale could be effected without the permission of the Commissioner. Act X of 1859 was never actually declared to be in force in the district, though the High Court appear to have held so. The correctness of this decision is open to doubt, in view of the provisions of Regulation XIII of 1833, which were in full force when Act X of 1859 was passed, and the Commissioner and the local authorities did not themselves consider that the Act applied to the district.

Act II (B. C.) of 1869.

In 1869 the Chotā Nāgpur Tenures Act [Act II (B. C.) of 1869] was passed, authorizing the appointment of special commissioners for the survey and demarcation of the privileged lands of both the landlords (*mānjhihās*) and the tenants (*bhūinhāri*). The causes which led to the passing of this Act and the survey which was carried out under its provisions are described in detail in Chapter II. Its defect was that it only dealt with one particular kind of tenancy; it left untouched the *Mundāri khuntkātti* villages, on the one hand, and the ordinary raiyati lands, on the other; it made no attempt to deal with the question of praedial dues and services, which had even at that time begun to be a fruitful source of strife between landlords and tenants; it even omitted from the survey one important class of privileged lands, the *sarnās*, or sacred groves, which are to be found in every Mundā or Orāon village. It was soon recognized that a Tenancy Act suited to the peculiar conditions of the district was an administrative necessity, for, though the provisions of Act X of 1859 were generally followed, it was clear that, in many respects, they were unsuitable. The distraint clauses were considered to be inapplicable to the wild aboriginal population, while the clause which practically prohibited the realization of *abwābs* was unduly harsh on the landlords. *Abwābs* were in accordance with the local custom of the district, and, as long as the demands were moderate and reasonable, were paid without objection. The levy of *abwābs* had also been expressly permitted by earlier legislation. The Rāmgarh district was exempted by Regulation IV of 1794, from the operation of the section 54 of Regulation VIII of 1793, on which the clause prohibiting the levy of *abwābs,* in Act X of 1859, was based, and to quote the words of Mr. Oliphant, the Deputy Commissioner, writing in 1875, "it was obviously unfair to force on the country a law which prohibits the levy of all cesses without affording to the zamindārs an opportunity in the first instance of commuting their cesses into rent".

Act I (B. C.) of 1879.

In recognition of the inapplicability of the ordinary tenancy laws to Chota Nāgpur, the Chota Nāgpur Landlord and Tenant Procedure Act (Act I of 1879) was passed. The provisions of Act X of 1859 were generally followed, but the provisions regarding distraint and enhancement of rent were omitted. The restrictions on the sale of landed property which had been observed for many years were legalized by the insertion of a clause prohibiting the sale of all under-tenures for arrears of rent without the permission of the Commissioner, and, finally, landlords were allowed the option of applying for commutation of any conditions or services, to which they were entitled in addition to money rents. The provisions of Act I of 1879 had as little effect in allaying the agrarian discontent or in improving the relations of landlords and tenants, as the proceedings of the special Commissioners appointed under Act II of 1869. Disputes as to praedial dues (*rukumāts*) and praedial services (*beth begāri*) grew more frequent and more violent, and in 1897, after several years of discussion, a Bill was passed by the Bengal Council providing for the voluntary commutation of praedial conditions and services, laying down a procedure for the enhancement of rents, and regulating the registration and resumption of intermediate tenures.

Proposed Amendment of Act I of 1879.

It was also proposed to repeal Act I (B. C.) of 1879 and to extend to Chotā Nāgpur the Bengal Tenancy Act with some modifications. The Bill was, however, referred back by the Government of India for reconsideration, especially of the clauses dealing with registration and resumption, which were opposed by the majority of the persons concerned and the Government of Bengal decided only to proceed with that part of the Bill dealing with the commutation

Act IV (B. C.) of 1897.

of praedial conditions and services. The Commutation Act [Act IV (B. C.) of 1897] was accordingly passed. The question of the extension of the Bengal Tenancy Act to Chotā Nāgpur remained under consideration, but in 1899 the Lieutenant-Governor, Sir John Woodburn, decided that it was inadvisable for two reasons to proceed with a consolidating Bill like the one proposed. In the first place the agitation of the Mundā *sardārs*, which culminated in the Birsa revolt, rendered it extremely undesirable to introduce a contentious measure of such magnitude, and, secondly, it was held that, until a survey and record-of-rights had been prepared, it was impossible to say definitely which provisions of the law were suitable to Chota Nāgpur. Settlement operations were accordingly begun in 1902, and by the end of 1903 sufficient data had been collected by the Settlement Officers to justify the introduction of an amending Act. The chief object of the amending Act V of 1903 was to give finality to the record of rights regarding the incidents of Mundāri *khuntkātti* tenancies. At the same time provision was made for the summary sale of holdings in execution of decrees for rent and a special procedure was prescribed for the recovery of arrears of rent from Mundāri *khuntkāttidārs*. The vexed question of the registration of transfers of, and succession to, tenures, was settled and all tenures were made saleable for arrears of rent.

Act V of 1903.

The Act, as amended in 1903, remained in force till 1908, by which year the Settlement operations were nearly completed. The Chotā Nāgpur Tenancy Act (Act VI of 1908) came into force from November 11th, 1908. It reproduced with certain modifications the provisions of the Commutation Act (Act IV of 1897) and of Act V of 1903. The provisions of the Limitation Act and of certain sections of the Civil Procedure Code were made applicable to all proceedings under the Act, in so far as they were not inconsistent with any of its provisions; the law relating to "settled raiyats" and the procedure for making surveys and records-of-right, with some modifications, were incorporated from the Bengal Tenancy Act. Landlords' privileged lands were defined and provision was made for a final and conclusive record of their rights.

Act VI (B. C.) of 1908.

A topographical survey of the district was made in the sixties by Captain Depree; the boundaries of estates, parganas, and even of the district were not accurately recorded and the map was found to be of little use in the recent cadastral survey. In 1862 a survey was begun of the villages of the Government estates of

Survey and Settlement.

Barkagarh, Patia and Silam and the work appears to have been continued, off and on, for nearly ten years. Between the years 1876-1880 a complete survey and settlement was carried out by Captain Grey. The *bhūinhāri* survey carried out by the special Commissioners appointed under Act II (B. C.) of 1869 was begun in 1869 and was not completed till 1880.

In 1876 the survey of the Chota Nāgpur Estate was taken in hand by a professional party of the Survey Department, but it was found that the estate could not bear the cost of such an elaborate survey, and it was decided to carry out the work by a non-professional party, working under the Manager of the estate. After the survey had been completed in 1885, the settlement of rents and the commutation of all praedial dues and services in the villages in the *khās* possession of the Mahārājā was taken in hand by Mr. Slacke, the Divisional Settlement Officer, and completed in 1888. The total area surveyed, for which a record-of-rights was prepared, amounted to 742 square miles. Rents were settled for all cultivated lands, except *bhuinhāri* and *mānjhihās* lands, which had been dealt with by the *bhuinhāri* Commissioners. The work was not carried out under the authority of any law, or rules having the force of law, but the decisions, especially the rent settlement, were accepted by the proprietor and the great majority of the raiyats. In only three per cent. of the cases did the raiyats refuse to accept *jamābandis* in token of their acceptance of the Settlement Officer's decision. The good effects of this settlement are shown by the fact that in the recent settlement operations the agrarian conditions in these villages presented a striking contrast to the conditions prevailing in neighbouring villages, disputes of all kinds being less numerous and less acute.

The discussions regarding the Tenancy Bill of 1899 showed clearly that it was necessary to prepare a record of local agrarian rights and customs before undertaking any legislation. Such a record had long been recognized by the local authorities as the only measure which was likely to remove some of the chief causes of agrarian discontent. The Birsa revolt brought matters to a head, and in 1902 survey and settlement operations were commenced in the Mundā country in an area, as at first defined, of 1,846 square miles. It was soon found that it was impossible to confine the operations to the Mundā country. The Mundās were scattered over the district, and it was recognized that equally cogent reasons existed for preparing a similar record for the areas occupied by non-Mundāri races. The absence of standards of measurement, the uncertainty of the incidence of rents and the insecurity of tenure all combined to make a record necessary, while such a record was an essential preliminary to any commutation of praedial dues or services.

The operations were finally completed in 1910. Mr. Lister was in charge of the operations from 1902 to 1907 and Mr. Reid for the remainder of the period. The total cost of the operations amounted to rather more than 16¼ lakhs of rupees, of which one-quarter was met from Imperial Revenues and the balance recovered from the landlords and tenants.

CHAPTER XII.

GENERAL ADMINISTRATION.

Administrative staff.

Rānchi, like other districts of the Chotā Nāgpur Division, is a non-regulation or scheduled district, i.e., one to which certain Acts and Regulations in force in other parts of India have not been extended. From a practical point of view the main distinction may be said to be that the executive officers have higher judicial powers than in regulation districts. Thus the Deputy Commissioner had till recently enhanced judicial powers under section 30 of the Code of Criminal Procedure but with a resident Sessions Judge these powers were exercised less frequently than in the outlying districts of Palāmau and Singhbhūm. The Deputy Commissioner and the Deputy Collectors subordinate to him also have powers under the Chotā Nāgpur Tenancy Act [Act VI (B. C.) of 1908] to try rent and other suits which in regulation districts come before the Munsifs and Sub-Judges.

Till 1902 the whole district was administered from the headquarters at Rānchi ; the evils of this system and the reasons which led to the establishment of a subdivision at Gumlā in 1902, at Khunti in 1907 and at Simdegā in 1915 have been detailed in a previous chapter. At the District headquarters the Deputy Commissioner is assisted by a staff of five Deputy Collectors, of whom one is occasionally a Joint Magistrate in the Indian Civil Service, one or two Probationary Deputy Collectors or Sub-Deputy Collectors, and from time to time an Assistant Magistrate. The administration of excise and income-tax is in the hands of a special Excise Deputy Collector, while the management of the Wards and Encumbered Estates is entrusted to a European Manager. The subdivisions are administered either by Joint Magistrates of the Indian Civil

Service or by European Deputy Collectors. At Gumlā the Subdivisional Officer was assisted by a Munsif, who had the powers of a Magistrate of the second class and of a Deputy Collector, and by a Sub-Deputy Collector; while at Khunti the Subdivisional Officer himself exercises civil as well as criminal and revenue powers and is assisted by a Sub-Deputy Collector. Since the opening of the new subdivision of Simdegā, the Subdivisional Officer, both there and at Gumlā, has been given similar powers to those of the Subdivisional Officer at Khunti and is assisted by the same staff.

Other local officers are the Superintendent of Police, the Civil Surgeon who is also Superintendent of the Jail, the Deputy Inspector of Schools, and the District Engineer.

Rānchi is also the headquarters of the Commissioner of the Chotā Nāgpur Division, of the Superintending Engineer in charge of the Western Circle, of the Public Works Department, the Executive Engineer in charge of the Chotā Nāgpur Division, of the Inspector and Assistant Inspector of Schools in the Chotā Nāgpur Division, and of the Inspectress of Schools in Chotā Nāgpur and Orissa.

Revenue. The total revenue of the district under the main heads amounted in 1880-1 to Rs. 41,91,000 and in 1890-1 to Rs. 7,14,000. In 1892 Palāmau was formed into a separate district, and the revenue in 1900-1 fell to Rs. 5,93,000. The ordinary revenue of the district is now over 10 lakhs, Rs. 50,000 being derived from Land Revenue, over one lakh from Cesses, six lakhs from Excise, a lakh and a half from Stamps and three-quarter of a lakh from Income-tax.

Land Revenue. The only permanently-settled estate in the district is that of the Mahārājā of Chotā Nāgpur. The land revenue demand of the district consists of the revenue payable by this estate and of the rents realized from the subordinate estates of Barkagarh, Patiā and Silam which were confiscated after the Mutiny. The land revenue payable by the Chotā Nāgpur Estate amounts to Rs. 15,041, against which is set off the rent due to the estate for the three subordinate tenures in the *khās* possession of Government, leaving a net demand of Rs. 14,364. Of the confiscated estates a small portion is leased out in farm, as *jāgir*, *khorposh* or *debottar* and is classified under the head "Temporarily-Settled Estates". For these estates a rent of Rs. 378 is paid. The greater portion of the estates is under direct management, and the raiyats pay their rent direct to Government. The total demand on account of Land Revenue amounted in 1914-15 to Rs. 50,725.

Excise.

Excise always has been, and always will be the principal source of revenue in the Rānchi District. The Rājā of Chotā Nāgpur appropriated this source of revenue till 1823, when, in spite of his protests that he derived no revenue from it, it was taken away from him and farmed out for the pargana for Rs. 6,500. In 1859 the excise revenue was Rs. 53,750 and by 1871 had risen to Rs. 60,050. In the decade ending in 1901-2 it only fell below three lakhs of rupees in two years of famine, and between the years 1900-1 and 1910-1 it rose from Rs. 2,91,160 to Rs. 5,78,771, the increase being over half a lakh in each of the years 1905, 1906 and 1907. In the year 1914-15 the excise revenue amounted to Rs. 6,39,953, of which 86 per cent., or Rs. 5,52,760, was derived from the sale of country liquor. The manufacture of country liquor was formerly carried on solely in licensed outstills, but in 1908 a central distillery was opened in Rānchi for the supply of liquor to the adjacent thanas. The central distillery now supplies the whole of thanas Rānchi, Ormānjhi, Angara, Silli, Bundu, Sonahatu, the larger portion of Tamār and small portions of Burmu, Karra and Bero ; the area of the tract supplied being 1,468 square miles with a population of 352,711. During the year 1914-15 the total amount of liquor consumed in the forty-five shops supplied from the distillery was 54,719 gallons (London Proof) and the total revenue realised in license fees and duty was Rs. 1,76,616. The contract system will soon be extended to the greater part of the district. It has many advantages over the outstill system ; it enables the excise authorities to exercise a close control over consumption, and is thus peculiarly suitable for a district in which the inhabitants are addicted to excessive drinking. The success of the system is proved by the fact that since the year 1908 the consumption per 100 of population in the area served by the distillery has fallen from 21 gallons to 15 3 gallons, and this in spite of the fact that recent years have been years of marked agricultural prosperity.

In the remainder of the district liquor is supplied from out-stills which are sold annually by auction, and in 1914-15 Rs. 3,76,144 was realized from 85 outstills. The amount of liquor consumed in the outstill area has been roughly calculated at 32 gallons per 100 of population, but this figure is probably too high, as the outstill vendor's methods of distillation are extremely crude and outturn is consequently considerably less than it would be with more efficient plant. *Mahua*, from which the liquor is manufactured, varies in price from annas 6 per maund in the western and inaccessible parts of the district to Re. 1-12-0 per maund in the neighbourhood of Rānchi : the average price being Re. 1-8-0 per maund.

The excise administration of the district presents a difficult problem, and, even though steps are being taken to check consumption, the excise income shows a steady increase. The number of shops has been decreased considerably in recent years, and in 1915, there were 85 shops, or one for every 67 square miles of country and every 12,000 of the population. No shop may now be established within a quarter of a mile of a market or a public road, a measure which checks to some extent the number of visits which cart-men and other travellers pay to an out-still but does little to prevent the raiyat, who has walked ten or fifteen miles to market, from refreshing himself to excess before he turns homeward. The excise authorities have also recently adopted the policy of consulting public opinion as to the situation of shops and out-stills, and this policy will enable them to obtain the advice of the missionaries on this important question. It will, however, be many years before drunkenness decreases to any marked extent, though there can be little doubt that one of the best effects of Missionary teaching has been to stop the vice among the Christian converts.

The high figures for the consumption of country liquor are the more remarkable, when it is remembered that the national drink of the aboriginals is rice-beer (*hānriā* or *pachwai*) and that they are allowed to brew this comparatively harmless liquor for their own consumption. The preparation of this liquor is simple. Rice, or sometimes *gondli* or *maruā*, is the grain used. Four seers of the grain are boiled with a small quantity of water and are spread out to dry. The grain is then rubbed between the hands and mixed with *ranu*, a concoction of wild roots which is sold in the bazar and the preparation of which is confined to a few aboriginals. The ingredients are secret, but apparently include, like the yeast used in the preparation of *sake* in Japan, something which will convert the starch in the grain into sugar as well as the yeast proper which is required for converting the sugar into alcohol. The mixture is put into an earthen vessel of water, the mouth of which is covered with straw. The liquor will be ready for consumption in three days in the hot weather and in a week or ten days in the cold weather. The amount of undiluted liquor obtained in this way is about six seers, which is diluted for drinking to eighteen seers, or about two and half gallons. The aboriginals require *hānriā* for all their social and religious ceremonies. It is in fact used as food and drink, and the privilege of home-brewing checks the temptation to resort to the more harmful country liquor. The tribes who are permitted this concession are :— Mundā, Orāon, Asur, Bhuiyā, Bhumij, Birhor, Nagesiā, Pahāria, Lohār, Khariā, Karwar, Gond, Bedeā, and Korwār. Many of the semi-aboriginal tribes of the district are also addicted to the consumption of this liquor, but the policy has always been to restrict the privilege of home-brewing to the animistic tribes whose religious customs require its preparation and consumption. The non-aboriginals have to obtain a license for brewing *pachwai* or to run the risk of being detected by the excise staff and fined. That they prefer to run the risk is shown by the fact that only one license for home-brewing was issued in 1914. There were also 73 shops for the sale of *pachwai* which produced a revenue of Rs. 7,730.

Drugs. The aboriginal is not addicted to drugs such as opium, *gānja*, or *bhang*, and the receipts from drugs only amounted to Rs. 77,439 in 1914-15. The greater part (Rs. 42,146) was derived from *gānja*. This drug is imported from Rajshahi by licensed wholesale dealers at the rate of about Rs. 100 a maund, sold by them to retail dealers at about Rs. 150 a maund, and by the retail-dealers, who pay the duty of Rs. 13 a seer, to the public at Rs. 30 a seer. The consumption has risen slightly in recent years, but this is probably due to the immigration of labourers for work on the railways, etc. The revenue from opium in 1912-13 was only Rs. 31,880, but in 1913-14 it rose to Rs. 41,486, an abnormal figure due to an increase in the opium consuming population of Rānchi town, and perhaps to smuggling of the drug by Chinamen to Burma and Eastern ports. In 1914-15 it fell to Rs. 35,293. The aboriginal population is not addicted to opium, and *madak* smoking is confined to the inhabitants of Rānchi, Lohardagā, Silli, Bundu and Tamār.

Stamps. The revenue from stamps rose from Rs. 1,12,270 in 1892-3 to Rs. 1,23,956, in 1900-1, and to Rs. 2,06,440 in 1910-11. In 1914-15 the revenue amounted to Rs. 1,66,605 of which Rs. 1,29,835 were obtained from the sale of judicial stamps and Rs. 36,770 from the sale of non-judicial stamps. The income derived from the sale of stamps varies with the amount of litigation. The settlement operations have put a stop to infructuous litigation and hence the income derived from stamps has decreased during the last few years.

Income-tax. In the decade ending 1901-2, during which the minimum assessable income was Rs. 500, the number of persons assessed to income-tax averaged 1,000 and the net collections about Rs. 18,700. When the minimum assessable income was raised in 1903 to Rs. 1,000, the number of assessees fell to 434, while the net collections rose to Rs. 22,987. In 1914-15 the number of assessees was 907 and the collections amounted to Rs. 70,848. This figure, however, gives a false impression of the economic condition of the district, as nearly Rs. 40,000 was realized from the officers of Government temporarily resident in Rānchi. The number of professional men, traders, and merchants assessed to income-tax in this year was 549, of whom 218 were money-lenders, and 166 dealers in food-grains, liquors, piece-goods, etc., and the amount levied was Rs. 27,632. That the district has increased in prosperity since the opening of the railway is shown by the fact that the corresponding figures for 1905-6 were 353 and Rs. 15,634.

Cesses. As in other districts, the road and public works cesses are levied at the rate of one anna in the rupee. The first valuation under Act X of 1871 was made in 1874-7. Three general revaluations under Act IX of 1880 were completed in 1883, 1892, and 1900, and a revaluation of the whole district, on the basis of the Settlement Record, was completed in 1913. In the older revaluations it was a systematic practice of the landlords to file returns showing rents far in excess of what was actually paid or was legally demandable with the object of filing them subsequently in rent suits. The publication of a record-of-rights has stopped this evil practice, and a valuation can now be fairly made on the basis of that record. The greater part of the cess is paid by the Chotā Nāgpur Estate, though recovered not without difficulty from the subordinate tenure-holders. In 1914-15 the total demand was Rs. 1,25,143, of which Rs. 2,088 were derived from mines and jungles and the remainder from land.

Registration.

There are four Registration offices in the district, viz., at Rānchi, opened in 1865, Khunti transferred from Bundu in 1907, Lohardagā 1898 to 1904 and again in 1907, and Gumlā transferred from Lohardagā in 1904. At the headquarters station the District Sub-Registrar deals, as in other districts, with the documents presented there and assists the Deputy Commissioner, who is *ex-officio* District Registrar, in supervising the work of the Sub-Registrars at the outlying offices. In 1908 the total number of registrations was 12,670. On the introduction of the Chotā Nāgpur Tenancy Act of 1908, the number of registrations fell to 8,491 in 1910 and 7,227 in 1911; the reason for this was that the Act prohibited the sale of raiyati holdings and the provision of the Act permitting mortgage under certain conditions for a term of years was not understood by the inhabitants. Since 1911 mortgages have become more common and the raiyats circumvent the provisions of the Act by surrendering their holdings in collusion with their landlords as an indirect way of selling them.

Administration of Justice Criminal Justice.

The Judicial Commissioner of Chotā Nāgpur, whose headquarters are at Rānchi, is Sessions Judge for the district as well for the districts of Palāmau and Hazāribāgh. The Deputy Commissioner had powers under the Criminal Procedure Code to try all cases not punishable with death, but these powers have now been withdrawn. Of the Deputy Magistrates stationed at headquarters four are usually vested with the powers of a first-class Magistrate and the remainder with the powers of a second or third-class Magistrate. The Subdivisional Officers also have first-class powers while the Sub-Deputy Collectors are vested with second-class powers. There are benches of Honorary Magistrates at Rānchi and at Lohardagā which dispose of unimportant cases under the Municipal by-laws and the Police Act, and two Honorary Magistrates at Khunti, one of whom has the powers of a Magistrate of the second-class.

The Judicial Commissioner is the chief Civil Court of the district. He occasionally tries original suits but is occupied mainly with civil appeals. The Subordinate Judge at Rānchi deals with original suits valued at over Rs. 1,000 and hears appeals from the decisions of Munsifs. He also exercises jurisdiction in the districts of Palāmau and Hazāribāgh. A Munsif is also stationed at Rānchi while the Subdivisional Officers of Khunti, Gumlā and Simdegā exercise the powers of a Munsif. Suits under the Chotā Nāgpur Tenancy Act are tried by the Subdivisional Officers or by Deputy Collectors. Civil Justice.

For police purposes the district is divided into 18 thanas and 10 outposts. The latter, which have been found to facilitate the investigation of crime, were, in 1905, declared to be police stations within the meaning of the Criminal Procedure Code. They are not thanas, but for the sake of convenience were treated as thana units for the purposes of the settlement record and also for census purposes. Police.

Recently three new police-stations have been formed in thanas Kolebirā, Kochedegā and Kurdeg, to facilitate the investigation and prevention of crime and to improve the general administration, as it had been found that it was not possible to control these large areas from one centre. The new police-stations are at Jaldega in thana Kolebirā, Thethaitangar in thana Kochedegā, and Bolba in thana Kurdeg.

The sanctioned strength of the regular police force in 1915, was one Superintendent, eight Inspectors, 59 Sub-Inspectors, one Sergeant, 74 Head-Constables and 495 Constables, representing one police office to every 11·1 square mile and to every 2,114 persons. To assist the Superintendent, an Assistant or Deputy Superintendent is usually posted to the district. In addition to the civil police, a Gurkha Company of Military police is stationed at Doranda and consists of two Subadars and Jamadars, twelve Havildars and Naiks, and 97 Sepoys.

The rural police force, intended for watch and ward duties in the villages, consists of 2,457 Chaukidars appointed under the Chotā Nāgpur Rural Police Act (Act I), Bihar and Orissa, of

1914. The total cost of the rural police amounts to Rs. 91,667 and is realized from the inhabitants of the villages. The tax is collected by thirty Tahsildars appointed by the Deputy Commissioner. The Chaukidars are usually Ghāsi Ahir or Lohrā by caste, and occasionally Mundās, Orāons or low caste Muhammadans are employed; their pay varies from Rs. 3 to Rs. 4 a month.

Ghātwāls and Ghātwāli cess.

The history of the police system in the early days of British administration has already been given in Chapter II. The system of zamindāri police proved a failure, and after the passing of the Police Act (Act V of 1861), an organized system of police, paid for and managed by Government, was introduced. The Rājā was thus relieved of a considerable burden, and, though by the terms of his covenant with the British Government, he was bound to make provision for the protection of life and property within his territory, it appears that he was only required to make a small contribution for the upkeep of the new police, and a *ghātwāli* cess was realized from proprietors and holders of tenures which were subject to a condition, express or implied, of protecting lines of roads or passes. The realization of this cess was legalized by the Chotā Nāgpur Rural Police Act [Act V (B. C.) of 1887], which also empowered the Deputy Commissioner to fix the number of, and appoint, road patrols or *ghātwāls* for the protection of such roads and passes. The duties of the *ghātwāls* differ from those of the village chaukidars in that they are exercised not within any village but within any area roughly determined by immemorial custom as a *ghāt*; their chief duties are to patrol the *ghāt*. There are in all 70 *ghātwāls*, ten of whom receive a salary of Rs. 5 a month and the remainder Rs. 3-8. The cess is collected by the Chaukidari Tahsildars and the annual demand is Rs. 4,061. The *ghātwāli* fund is administered by the Superintendent of Police, subject to the control of the Deputy Commissioner, and is applied in the first instance to meeting the pay of the *ghātwāls* and the office establishment, and also for the construction and repairs of the *ghātwāli* bungalows, which have been constructed for the convenience of touring officers on all the principal roads of the district.

Crime.

In the early days of British administration Chotā Nāgpur had an unenviable notoriety as a criminal district and was described by the Collector of Chatrā writing in 1793 " as a receptacle for murderers, thieves and vagabonds and disturbers of the public peace." The establishment of the South-West Frontier Agency in 1834, and of the State constabulary in 1863, caused some improvement in the criminal administration of the district, but apart from crime which was the direct result of the strife between the landlords and tenants, murders, dakāitis, and similar crimes of violence were common, at least in the outlying parts of the district, till the beginning of the present century, and it was not till the opening of subdivisions at Gumlā and Khunti that there was any marked improvement in the administration of criminal justice or in the prevention and detection of crime. The wild nature of the country gives exceptional facilities for the commission of dakāitis and highway robberies and the escape of the culprits, as well as for the concealment of murders. Mr. Reid, who was the first Subdivisional Officer at Gumlā, thus describes the condition of the west of the district :—"There were parts of the area, notably the more remote parts of Kurdeg, Kochedegā and Kolebirā thanas, where the system of British administration could hardly be said to be in force. Murder cases and other very serious offences were usually brought before the courts, but offences of lesser magnitude went unpunished. Even murders were frequently concealed: and I know of one case at least, in which a zamindār was reported to have committed as many as ten and yet has escaped conviction. The control over the police was so ineffective that they were the real rulers of the country and before any reform could be effected, it was found necessary to prosecute or dismiss many of them. The Chaukidāri force was equally corrupt. During the first year after the foundation of the subdivision, the convictions of the chaukidārs, who were the supposed guardians of the peace, for serious offences, such as dakāiti, robbery, theft and trespass, were numerous, the percentage being nearly treble that of any other class of the community. It was therefore necessary to discharge or dismiss large numbers of the worst of them who usually belonged to the Ghāsi and Mahali caste." A recent outbreak of dakāiti in the south-west of the district committed by a branch of the Mundās, known as the Eranga Kols, showed the necessity of exercising an even closer control over these outlying tracts and led to the decision to form a fourth subdivision at Simdegā. The Eranga Kols, though not a criminal tribe, were no doubt encouraged by the facility with which petty crimes escaped notice to commit crimes of a more serious nature and trusted to make good their escape to the jungles of the neighbouring Feudatory States. Generally speaking, the aboriginals of the Rānchi district are not criminal, and the Mundās, Orāons and Khariās are justly proud of their respectability. Before the Settlement operations put a stop to agrarian disputes, cases of trespass and paddy-cutting, often accompanied by violence, were common, but such crimes were committed in defence of real or imaginary rights, and one cannot but feel sympathy with the aboriginal who, failing to obtain any redress in the Courts, took the law into his own hand and reaped the crops of his ancestral holding of which he had, often unjustly, been dispossessed by the zamindār. Cases of murder are still common, but the majority of them are pathetic rather than revolting. In a sudden drunken quarrel the quick-tempered aboriginal uses the axe, which he invariably carries with more violence than discretion. He confesses his crime and is quite ready to undergo the punishment. A more serious class of case is the murder of suspected witches or wizards. Sometimes a whole village combine to beat from their boundaries the old woman who is pointed out by the *sokha* or witch doctor as the cause of disease among men or cattle, and such cases are often never reported to the police, or, if reported, no evidence is forthcoming against the guilty persons. In other cases a man in a frenzy of grief at the loss of his child or wife or cattle, considers that the only way to save himself from further trouble is to destroy the person or persons who have cast the evil eye upon him. The tribes most addicted to theft, petty burglaries, and robberies are the Ghāsis, Mahlis, and Domrās. Cattle-theft is common, and often the thieves themselves or the receivers of the stolen property are detected by the owners of the cattle who visit market after market in their search for the missing property. Cattle-poisoning is also not uncommon and is committed by Chamārs, Lohrās or Ghāsis for the sake of the hides. A method frequently adopted is to shoot the animal with a bamboo-headed arrow, such as is commonly used by graziers for driving cattle, into which has been fixed a poisonous berry, hardened to a sharp point. A small puncture is made in the skin, but the poison rapidly spreads through the veins. The crime is difficult to detect and often the villagers themselves attribute the deaths to the work of a *bhūt* and do not realize that they are caused by human hands.

CHAPTER XIII.

LOCAL SELF-GOVERNMENT.

The District Board.

Outside the two municipal areas of Rānchi and Lohardagā the administration of local affairs, such as the maintenance of roads, bridges, and roadside rest-houses, except those maintained by the Public Works Department, the management of pounds, the establishment and maintenance of schools, either wholly or by means of grants-in-aid, the provision of medical and veterinary relief, and the control of village sanitation, rests with the District Board. There are no Local Boards. The District Board was constituted in 1900 under Act III (B. C.) of 1885 to take the place of the Road Cess Committee, which up to that time had looked after the communications of the district.

The Board consists of nine members, appointed *ex-officio,* including the Deputy Commissioner as Chairman and nine members nominated by Government. The district is too backward for an elective system and this system of nomination secures the appointment of persons representative of all interests and well acquainted with the needs of the district. Of the nominated members, two are tea-planters and one is a lawyer ; the landed interest is represented by the Manager of the Chota Nāgpur Estate, the Manager of the Encumbered Estates and a land-holder, while the heads of the Christian Missions form a most useful element on the Board.

Income.

The income of the District Board in the first year of its existence was Rs. 93,872, of which Rs. 47,679 were derived from Road-Cess, and during the decade 1901-2 to 1910-11 the average income was Rs. 1,36,373. In 1912-13 the income was Rs. 1,31,472, of which Rs. 55,974 were derived for Road-Cess. In 1914-15 the income rose to Rs. 2,85,769, owing to the surrender to the Board of the Public Works Cess (Rs. 39,818) and to special grants received from Government for education and for the improvement of roads and communications. Of the minor items of revenue, receipts from pounds are the largest and amounted to over Rs. 4,000 while about Rs. 1,300 are derived from school fees and Rs. 2,000 from veterinary receipts. The incidence of taxation is very low and amounts only to ten pies per head of population.

Expenditure. The average expenditure during the decade 1901-2 to 1910-11 amounted to Rs. 1,33,750. In 1912-13 it amounted to Rs. 1,37,849, of which Rs. 77,241 were spent on civil works, including Rs. 58,007 on the extension and maintenance of roads. In 1914-15 the total expenditure rose to Rs. 3,16,588, that on Civil Works to Rs. 2,29,511, over Rs. 1,80,000 being spent on roads. Special grants received from Government were devoted to the improvement of the road from Lohardagā to the plateau of Netarhāt in Palāmau via Ghāghrā and Bishunpūr. Apart from the desirability of connecting Rānchi by a good road to this potential hill station, the road from Lohardagā to Ghāghrā and Bishunpūr carries the traffic from the western part of the district to the railway and has become of increasing importance since the extension of the Bengal-Nagpur Railway to Lohardagā was opened.

Next to Civil Works, Education constitutes the heaviest charge on the resources of the Board; the amount expended on it in 1912-13 was Rs. 39,467, Rs. 30,227 being given as grants-in-aid to primary schools. In 1914-15 the expenditure under this head rose to Rs. 61,885, including Rs. 45,763 for aided schools. The increased expenditure was mainly due to a grant of Rs. 15,000 received from Government for raising the stipends of Gurus in primary schools. Seven middle schools are maintained by the Board, at Gumlā, Khunti, Jaria, Thakurgaon, Pālkot, Silli and Tamār, and grants-in-aid are made to two middle schools (at Bundu and Murhu), to 57 upper primary schools, and 719 lower primary schools. Large grants are also given to the three Missions for the maintenance of primary schools, the S. P. G. Mission receiving Rs. 3,420, the Lutheran Mission Rs. 4,860 and the Roman Catholic Mission Rs. 1,668.

The Board in 1914-15 spent Rs. 9,329 on medical relief, maintaining five dispensaries, at Gumlā, Khunti, Silli, Chainpur, and Bundu, giving contributions to the Government hospitals at Rānchi and Lohardagā and grants to the hospitals of the S. P. G. Mission at Itki and Murhu. The question of village sanitation also receives attention and, though rapid progress cannot be made owing to the limited resources of the Board, steps are taken to improve the water-supply by the construction of wells in the larger villages and bazars and by cleansing private wells and tanks. Since 1912 a sanitary inspector has been employed to supervise this work.

A veterinary dispensary has been opened at Rānchi, with a shoeing forge attached to it, and a veterinary assistant and a farrier have been entertained since 1902. There are also two itinerant veterinary assistants, in charge of the Gumlā and Khunti subdivisions. Rinderpest and hæmorrhagic septicæmia cause great mortality among cattle in the district, and the duty of these officers is to instruct the inhabitants in preventive measures and to persuade them to have their cattle inoculated in the event of outbreaks of infectious diseases.

Municipalities.

There are only two Municipalities in the district. The Rānchi Municipality, which is the largest in Chota Nāgpur, was constituted in 1869, and the Lohardagā Municipality in 1888. Municipal administration is still in an elementary stage, but there are hopeful signs of a more corporate activity. In the case of a petty rural Municipality like Lohardagā it is no easy matter to instil life and vigour into the proceedings of the Commissioners. An account of both towns will be found in the Gazetteer.

Rānchi.

Rānchi has a Municipal Board of nineteen Commissioners, including the Chairman. Of these three, the Deputy Commissioner, the Civil Surgeon, and the District Superintendent of Police, are members *ex-officio*, twelve are elected triennially by the ratepayers, and four are nominated by Government. Thirteen members are Indians, ten being Hindus, two Muhammadans, and one a Christian, and of these all are lawyers, with the exception of a schoolmaster, a doctor, and a retired Government officer.

The Municipal area is about 6 square miles, but the Commissioners are taking steps to extend the boundaries, so as to be in a position to control the future development of the town and to include the suburb which is rapidly growing to the north-east of the town by Morābādi hill. The population of the town according to the last census was 33,069, but since Rānchi has become the temporary headquarters of Government, has risen considerably and is now probably not far short of 38,000. Not only have a large number of Government officers taken up their residence within municipal limits but the increased trade and prosperity of the town has caused a corresponding increase in population. The number of rate-payers in 1914-1915 was 4,984, or 15·1 per cent. of the population and the incidence of taxation per head was Re. 1-8-5. The average annual income of the Municipality during the decade ending 1901-2 was Rs. 16,955 and the expenditure Rs. 20,998; during the following decade they were Rs. 55,667 and Rs. 49,157, respectively. In the three succeeding years the income has shown a marked increase and rose to Rs. 1,02,726 in 1912-13, Rs. 1,01,709 in 1913-14, and Rs. 1,21,204 in 1914-15. The chief source of income, apart from grants and loans from Government, is a tax on houses and arable lands, assessed at 7½ per cent. on their annual value, which in 1914-15 brought in Rs. 25,604, while a conservancy tax levied on a sliding scale on the annual value of holdings brought in Rs. 21,300 and the fees from markets and slaughter-houses Rs. 13,155. During the past years the Municipality has received liberal assistance from Government, the grants amounting to Rs. 43,905 in the year 1912-13, to Rs. 37,681 in 1913-14, and to Rs. 51,271 in 1914-15. The expenditure in 1914-15 amounted to Rs. 1,20,581, of this amount 24·7 per cent. was spent on conservancy, 29·2 per cent. on the maintenance of roads, and 16·4 per cent. on medical relief. About 100 miles of roads are maintained by the Municipality, of which 15 miles are metalled, 60 miles gravelled, and the remainder unmetalled.

Rānchi, from its position as the headquarters of the division and its reputation as a health resort, has always been of considerable importance, and its importance has been enhanced by the temporary establishment of the seat of Government. The assistance given by Government has enabled the Commissioners to carry out many much needed reforms. The staff has been increased and the conservancy arrangements, which were formerly inadequate, have been improved with the aid of the special grants given in 1912-13 and subsequent years. The roads have received more attention and the lighting of the streets is much better than it was a few years ago. A daily market, to supply the needs of the well-to-do inhabitants, has been instituted, the cost of the building being met by a loan of Rs. 15,000. Though the last few years show a record of steady progress, much remains to be done, but the Municipality, like others in the province, is hampered by lack of funds from taking in hand any large projects. A drainage scheme has been under consideration for some time past, but without liberal assistance from Government the Municipality cannot hope to meet the cost of over two lakhs of rupees. The natural drainage of the town is good, and it is only in the more congested portions that a system of artificial drainage is needed. An even more ambitious scheme is the supply of good drinking water, either by damming the Subarnarekhā or Potpoto rivers or by constructing a reservoir in the highlands to the west of the town. But this scheme involves an expenditure of more than seven lakhs of rupees, and it will be many years before funds are available for carrying it into effect.

Lohardagā. The Lohardagā Municipality is administered by a Board, consisting of ten members nominated by Government. The area included in the Municipality is only 2·5 square miles and the rate-payers number 947, or 13·9 per cent. of the total population. The total income in 1914-15 was Rs. 6,497. This income is chiefly derived from a tax on persons, levied at one per cent. on the income of the assessees, and in 1914-15 Rs. 2,643 was obtained from this source. Other items of revenue are rent of pounds (Rs. 415), and rent of sarais (Rs. 252). The incidence of rates and taxes, which is 7½ annas per head of population, is the lowest in Chotā Nāgpur. In 1914-15 Rs. 1,080 were spent on conservancy, Rs. 1,193 on roads, these being the two chief items of expenditure, apart from the construction of a hospital with the aid of a grant from Government. The Board maintains one Upper Primary School for boys and one Lower Primary School for girls and grants are given to two Lower Primary Schools for boys and to a local *maktab*.

CHAPTER XIV.

EDUCATION.

Progress of Education.

The progress of education in Rānchi district during the last forty years has been remarkable and the credit for it must be given to the Christian Missions. At the time of the British occupation, and during the sixty years that intervened between that and the Kol insurrection, there were hardly any literate persons in the district. After the establishment of the Agency, in 1834, a school was founded at Rānchi, but even in 1857 it was still the only Government institution in the district and contained only 67 pupils. During the next decade some progress was made, but in 1871-2 there were only 22 schools in the district (including Palāmau), with 986 pupils, and a few indigenous *pathsals* and *maktabs*. From 1871 to 1881 progress was more rapid and was due largely to the expansion of the Lutheran Mission during this period, and partly to Sir George Campbell's scheme, introduced in 1872, under which grants-in-aid could be given to schools under private management. The effect of this scheme was at once apparent, and in 1872-3 there were 178 (Government and aided schools, with 4,553 pupils, and 57 unaided schools, attended by 580 pupils. Since that date there has been a steady increase in the number of schools. Between 1892 and 1902 the number of schools rose from 492 to 796, and the number of pupils from 12,569 to 20,503. In 1915 there were over 1,300 schools and nearly 40,000 pupils, the number of boys under instruction being 34,693 or 34 per cent. of the male population of school-going age. With the increase in the number of schools and pupils, there has been a corresponding increase in the number of literate persons, in 1881 only 30 males in every 1,000 were literate and in 1891 only 36, but during the last twenty years, in which the number of Christians has risen by over 100,000, the number of literate males has risen to 57 per mille.

In spite of this marked progress, Rānchi is still more backward in education than other districts of the province, except Palāmau, Angul and Singhbhūm. The conditions of the district are such as to render the diffusion of education difficult. The villages are few and far between, the inhabitants are poor and indifferent to the benefits of education, and it is only in those parts in which there is a large proportion of Christians in the population that the number of literates is at all large. Among the aboriginals, who still adhere to their animistic religion, only 4,385 persons were recorded as literate in 1911 out of a total population of 607,820, or 13 per mille of the male and 2 per mille of the female population, but out of the Christian population of 177,473, 10,436 were literate, or 93 per mille among men and 25 per mille among women. The progress of education among the Christian inhabitants of the district has had the effect of stirring up the Hindus and Muhammadans to improve their condition. Among Hindus 83, and among the Muhammadans 146 per mille of the men are literate, a higher proportion than is found in the district of North Bihār.

Secondary Education.

There is no college in the district, but there are four flourishing High English Schools, with more than 1,500 boys on their rolls. The Rānchi Zila School, maintained by Government, is under the charge of a European Head-master of the Indian Educational Service, and is rapidly growing in size and popularity. New school buildings, including hostels for the various classes of pupils, have recently been constructed on a site in the compound of the house formerly occupied by the Commissioner of the Division. The other three High Schools are maintained by the three Missions, who are assisted by annual grants from Government and have also received recently special grants to enable them to erect new school buildings and boarding-houses. They are the Lutheran Mission School, St. Paul's High School maintained by the S. P. G. Mission and St. John's High School maintained by the Roman Catholic Mission.

There are thirteen Middle English Schools, of which three (at Gumlā, Khunti, and Jari?) are maintained, and one (at

Bundu), is aided, by the District Board; one is aided by the Rānchi Municipality; and five are aided by Government. Three of the latter, as well as three which are unaided, are under the management of one or other of the Missions.

Primary Education.

There are five Middle Vernacular Schools in the district, of which one is attached to the Rānchi Training School and is maintained by Government, and the remainder are maintained and managed by the District Board. The Missions have no Middle Vernacular Schools. The schools, which are but little superior to primary schools, are declining in popularity, as parents of all classes prefer an English education for the children.

Primary Schools are the principal agency for diffusing education among the mass of the population, and the rapid strides which education is making may be judged by the fact that during the past seven years the number of primary schools has risen from 788 to 1,284, and the number of pupils from 18,256 to 34,289. Upper Primary Schools generally have satisfactory accommodation, but the Lower Primary school is usually found in a wretched hut, or in the verandah of the house of the leading villager.

Training Schools.

At Rānchi there is a first-grade training school for vernacular teachers in Secondary Schools, with 60 pupils on its rolls. The school is maintained by Government, and is accommodated in the buildings formerly occupied by the Zila School. There are four schools for the training of teachers in Pimary Schools with about 60 pupils, one of which prepares teachers to teach up to the Upper Primary stage and the remainder up to the Lower Primary stage. Two of these were formerly reserved for Mundās and Orāons, but, owing to the inferior qualifications both of the pundits and the pupils did not prove a success. They have now been thrown open to all castes, and aboriginal teachers, both Christian and non-Christian, are trained in the schools which have for some years been efficiently maintained by the three Missions. The Missions receive a grant-in-aid from Government, on condition that 24 gurus are trained each year, 12 of whom are nominated by the Deputy Inspector of Schools with a view to their subsequent employment in Government or Board Schools. The S. P. G. Mission and the Lutheran Mission each maintain a training school for mistresses. The schools contain about 30 pupils and are aided from Provincial funds. The Roman Catholic Mission also has a female Training School on a smaller scale which is at present unaided.

Technical and Industrial Schools.

The Rānchi Industrial School was started with the balance of the assets of the Chutiā Fair fund, the object being to give a training in handicrafts to aboriginal youths. It is now maintained by Government, and has been enlarged by the opening of classes for sub-overseers and for motor mechanics. In 1915 there were 181 students in the sub-overseer classes, 11 in the motor mechanics class, and 87 pupils in the artisan classes. A hostel is attached to the school, and considerable improvement has been made during the last few years in the plant and machinery. In an Industrial School at Bundu, aided by the District Board, blacksmiths' and carpenters' work used to be taught to some twenty boys, but the school has not proved a success and has now been closed. A more promising school has lately been started by the S. P. G. Mission at Murhu. The Lace Schools maintained by the three Missions, and the Blind School maintained by the Anglican Mission are described in the chapter on Missions.

Since the influx of Secretariat clerks into Rānchi, a commercial school has been opened, at which candidates for employment under Government can get instruction in Typewriting and Shorthand. Only 17 pupils were under instruction in 1915.

Female Education.

Female Education in Rānchi has made greater progress than in many districts of the province, as the Missions maintain a large number of schools, many of which are efficiently managed by Europeans. The S. P. G. Mission maintains a Middle English School for girls at Rānchi, which has 16 girls in the secondary classes and 271 girls in the primary classes. The school receives a monthly grant of Rs. 60 from provincial revenues, and Rs. 40 for the Kindergarten school. There are in all 85 primary schools for girls, with 3,411 pupils on their rolls, the majority of which are privately managed, but receive aid from public funds. Of these 42 are under the management of the Missions. The success of the Missionaries in spreading education among the women and girls belonging to their congregations is shown by the fact that 25 per mille of the female Christian population is literate, whereas among the Hindus, Muhammadans, and Animists, the proportions are only 5, 11, and 2, respectively.

Special Schoos.

Besides these schools there are 37 *Madrassas* and *Maktabs*, 28 of which are aided, for the special education of Muhammadans. The principle is the Seraj-ul-Islam Madrassa at Rānchi, recognized as an Urdu Upper Primary School. There is also a Sanskrit *Tol* at Rānchi, which is aided by Government and the Municipality.

Expenditure.

The total expenditure on education in the year 1914-15, including inspection and miscellaneous charges, was Rs. 4,60,912, of which Rs. 1,08,973 were met from Provincial funds, Rs. 67,848 from District Board funds, Rs. 5,696 from Municipal funds, and Rs. 2,78,385 from fees and private sources.

Inspection.

The Inspector of Schools in the Chotā Nāgpur Division has his headquarters at Rānchi, but the work of inspecting and superintending the schools in the district mainly falls on the Deputy Inspector, assisted by eight Sub-Inspectors, two Assistant Sub-Inspectors and two inspecting Pandits.

Newspapers.

The only newspapers in the district are the *Ghar Bandhu* which is published by the Lutheran Mission and the *Rānchi Church Messenger* published by the English Mission. Both these papers deal principally with topics of missionary interest.

CHAPTER XV.

MISSIONS.

Progress of Christianity.

The rise and progress of Christianity among the aboriginals of the district is an outstanding feature of the history of the last half century. Work amongst aboriginals has always been a favourite field for missionary enterprise, and in Rānchi the conditions were exceptionally favourable. The population was backward, uncivilized, and illiterate; agrarian strife was rife, and the spread of Christianity has gone hand in hand with the efforts of the aboriginals to resist the oppression of the landlords and to assert, and secure recognition for, their claims to the lands on which they were the first settlers. In the struggle against the landlords it was the Missionary who could give the raiyat the greatest assistance.

A well-known Roman Catholic Missionary writes as follows regarding inducements to conversion :—" As a general rule religious motives are out of the question. They want protection against zamindari and police extortions and assistance in the endless litigation forced on them by zamindars. As a consequence—

(*a*) most of the converts came over (after panchāyats) in whole villages or in groups of villages ;

(*b*) a certain number of isolated families came over, either for help against zamindars or police extortion, or against the rest of their co-villagers who persecuted them because they were pointed out by the *Sokhās* as wizards or witches ;

(*c*) Personally I know of some cases where individuals came over from religious motives. But these cases are rare."*

* " Census of India, 1911", Volume I, Part I, page 128.

In numbers the Christians have increased from 1,227 in 1860 to 11,108 in 1868, 36,265 in 1881, and 75,693, 124,958 and 177,473 at the subsequent censuses; but apart from this remarkable increase in the number of converts the spread of Christianity has exercised a profound influence on the lives, customs and habits of thought of the whole population, particularly in developing a manly independence of character. To the Christian Missionaries must be given the credit for freeing the cultivator from the oppression of the landlord; they have now taken up the work of freeing him from the clutches of the money-lender, and the spread of the Co-operative movement among the Christian converts promises to effect an economic revolution in the district.

Mission work in Chota Nāgpur owes its origin to Johannes Gossner, a scholarly Bavarian priest, who, on being excommunicated from the Church of Rome on account of his liberal tendencies, joined the Evangelical Lutheran Church and devoted the latter part of his life to founding Missions in all quarters of the globe. In 1844 he sent out four young missionaries, E. Schatz, F. Batsch, A. Brandt and H. Janke, to Calcutta with no definite instructions as to the region in which they should take up their work. While waiting in Calcutta they were attracted by the appearance of some Kols from the Rānchi plateau and, after making further enquiries, decided to start work in this district. Like other pioneers of mission work, their first efforts met with little success. The Kols received their preaching with animosity and even stoned them from their villages, and for five years they continued preaching without making a single convert. At last, in 1850, four Orāons came to the Mission House and asked to see the man "Jesus" of whom they had read in a tract. No explanation of the missionaries would satisfy them that Jesus was not a living person, and they left the house vociferating and abusing the missionaries. Some time later, they returned, professed their readiness to join the Church, and thus became the first converts of the mission. During the next few years the number of converts increased rapidly, so that by 1857 there were no less than seven hundred baptized Christians. Soon after their arrival the German Pastors had begun the erection of a church in Rānchi and, labouring largely with their own hands, completed in 1855 Christ Church, the first Christian Church in Chotā Nāgpur. Foundation of Gossner's Mission.

Mutiny of 1857.

The Mutiny of the Rāmgarh Battalion in July 1857 seemed to shatter the hopes of spreading Christianity. The missionaries themselves were compelled to flee to Calcutta, the converts and enquirers were scattered among the villages and exposed to the attacks not only of the mutineers but also of the zamindārs who, even before the outbreak, had endeavoured to stop the spread of the movement. A wholesale spoliation of the property of the Christians occurred; many died of starvation in the jungles, and some were only saved by their non-Christian neighbours. The missionaries, however, took the first opportunity of returning to Rānchi and arrived with the troops in October 1857 to find their bungalows looted and damaged, the Christian village of Prabhusharan levelled to the ground, the windows of the Church broken, the organ destroyed, and the bells removed.

Progress, 1857—1867.

But the Mutiny only caused a temporary set-back to the progress of Mission work, and in the next ten years a remarkable advance was made. At the time of the Mutiny the number of converts was only a little over seven hundred. At the end of 1860 it had risen to fourteen hundred, and seven years later there were no less than ten thousand converts. There was at this time, according to Colonel Dalton, a widespread feeling among the Kols that it was their destiny to become Christians. Enquirers no longer came by twos or threes, but whole families, and in some cases whole villages, applied eagerly for baptism. On one day in November 1864 no less than six hundred men, women and children presented themselves. This rapid increase in numbers rendered the work of organization imperative. The small body of missionaries at Rānchi could obviously not keep in touch with the large body of Native Christians, living, as some of them did in villages fifty or sixty miles distant. Elders were therefore appointed in each village, or group of villages, in which there were a large number of converts. The elder received no salary but was taught to regard his position as one of great honour, and his duties consisted in assembling the converts for Sunday service and instructing them in the Bible and Catechism. In addition to these stationary elders there was a body of catechists constantly going backwards and forwards for purposes of instruction and exhortation.

During this period of progress the Mission was sadly hampered by lack of funds, and branches which had been opened at Lohardagā, Gobindpur, and elsewhere, had to be abandoned. The Mission was no longer under the fostering care of Pastor Gossner, but was supported and managed by the central committee, or Curatorium, of the Evangelical Mission Society of Berlin, founded shortly before Gossner's death in 1858. An appeal made by Bishop Cotton, the Metropolitan of India, who visited Ranchi in 1864 and was much impressed with the work of the Mission, had little effect in stirring up to the central society in Germany to give the financial assistance needed but resulted in some funds being collected in Calcutta.

Division of the Lutheran Mission.

A few years later the Curatorium, in response to an urgent appeal for more men, sent out several younger men who had educational qualifications at the Universities denied to the older missionaries. Their arrival in 1868 led to a split in the Lutheran Mission and to the founding of the Anglican Mission in Rānchi. Shortly after their arrival the young missionaries sent letters to Berlin in which grave insinuations were made against the older missionaries, charges of irregularity in their accounts, of neglect of Mission duties, even of misappropriation of Mission funds. So serious were these charges that the Curatorium sent out their Secretary, the Rev. Mr. Ansorge, to enquire into them. A conference was held at Rānchi in November 1868 in which two leading Calcutta merchants, one an Englishman and the other a German, were present as assessors. The assessors found the charges "frivolous and unfounded" and sympathized entirely with the older missionaries, but Mr. Ansorge's sympathies were with the younger men. Under the authority given him by the Curatorium, he endeavoured to create a "new organization" which practically deprived the elder missionaries of the position they had held for twenty-four years and placed them as a minority in the hands of the younger men, who had brought such serious and, in their opinion, unproved charges against them. Rather than join this constitution, the older missionaries withdrew and sent an appeal to the Bishop of Calcutta (Bishop Milman) for assistance. For some time Bishop Milman declined to interfere, but when all hope that the dispute might be settled from within vanished on receipt of a letter from the Curatorium upholding Mr.

Ansorge's decision, dismissing the missionaries and denouncing them as traitors and seceders, he decided to visit the Mission and endeavour to restore peace and harmony. On his arrival in Rānchi over six thousand converts came to him with a petition to be received into the English Church, and were supported by the European inhabitants of the town. The Bishop, after he had obtained a promise of support from the Calcutta Diocesan Committee of the Society for the Propagation of the Gospel, decided to accede to their request, and in April 1869 ordained into the English Church the German pastors, F. Batsch, H. Batsch and F. Bohn, and a Rājput Catechist, Wilhelm Luther Dāud Singh, and admitted by confirmation a large and representative body of native converts.

From that time the Anglican and the Lutheran Missions have continued working side by side. "Such a division", says the Report of the Anglican Mission for 1869-70, "necessarily involved, especially at first, much that is to be regretted, but already we see with thankfulness that very much good is resulting from what some have imagined to be an unmixed evil." The good that resulted from the division is exemplified by the history of the next forty years. Both Missions have made great progress and there has been keen but generous rivalry between the members of the two churches.

The Lutheran Mission, Progress, 1870–1880.

Of the two, the Lutheran Mission has throughout this period been better staffed in respect of numbers and has made the greater progress. In 1872 the working staff of the Mission consisted of six ordained, and seven lay, European missionaries, two native teachers, 50 catechists, 25 teachers, and 195 *prachāraks*, or village elders, while the total number of Christians belonging to the Mission was 16,742. The congregation was soon found to be too numerous and too scattered for effective supervision from Ranchi. Accordingly out-stations were added at Burju (1869), Gobindpur (1870), Lohardagā and Takarmā (1873). Burju, or Patrasburj as it was first called, is in the centre of the Mundā country and was founded by a Russian nobleman, who made over 3,000 roubles for the purpose, on condition that the new station should be called after St. Petersburg. Lohardagā was conveniently situated for spreading the work in the north-west of the district, and Takarmā, in the south of Basiā thana, is at the centre where the three tribes of Mundā, Orāon and Khariā meet and was therefore particularly suited for spreading the work in the south and south-west of the district. The educational work was also well organized; at the headquarters in Rānchi a theological seminary or training class for pastors and teachers was established in 1867, and by 1873 contained thirteen pupils who received instruction in sacred and profane subjects. A boarding school for boys contained 110 pupils, and that for girls 50 pupils. The efficiency of the teaching may be estimated from the fact that three European missionaries assisted by two *pandits* and six native teachers devoted their whole time to the management of the seminary and the school.

During the eighties two causes contributed to make the development of the Mission less rapid. The nationalist Sardārs, whose exaggerated claims were discountenanced by the missionaries, set up a bitter opposition and endeavoured to seduce the converts and enquirers from their allegiance. During this decade also the Roman Catholic Mission was established in the district and carried out the work of proselytization with characteristic energy and enthusiasm. The new Mission, which devoted as much attention to the temporal as to the spiritual welfare of their converts, not only won over many who would otherwise have joined the Lutheran Church but also many members of that Church, but the great campaign of Rev. Father Lievens, S. J., among the Orāons (in 1893), paved the way for a marked expansion of Lutheran missionary work, especially in the west of the district, during the closing years of the 19th and the opening years of the 20th century. New stations were opened at Chainpur, in Barwe, in 1892, at Khutitoli, in Biru, and at Gumlā in 1895, at Kinkel in Kurdeg thana in 1899, at Tamār in 1901 and at Koronjo in 1903. Since that date the Mission has endeavoured to spread its work among the inhabitants of Jashpur State and though not permitted to build churches or chapels within the State has established stations at Kondra and Kinkel on its borders and has won over a large number of converts. In 1880 the Mission had 31,253 Christians, with a staff of seventeen missionaries, seven ordained native pastors and 111 catechists. By 1890 the number of Christians in the division had risen to over 35,000; by 1901 the number had nearly doubled, and at the census of 1911 over 75,000 persons in the district of Rānchi alone were recorded as members of the Lutheran Church. This figure includes a certain number of persons not admitted by the missionaries

1880—1913.

themselves to belong to their church, and more accurate statistics compiled by the Mission for the year 1913 show that in that year there were 96,543 Christians, of whom rather more than 73,000 were attached to churches in the Rānchi district. The European staff consisted of twenty-one ordained missionaries, five unordained missionaries, and three deaconesses, and the Indian staff of 31 pastors and 322 catechists. Of the Christians over 37,000 are Mundās, over 30,000 Orāons and over 6,000 Khariās.

The outbreak of war between England and Germany in 1914 rendered it necessary for Government to take measures against all hostile aliens, including those engaged on missionary work. Of the missionaries in Rānchi district, those of military age were interned, while the older men and women and children were repatriated to Germany. In spite of the removal of the missionaries, the Mission, thanks to its excellent organization, still continues its work, the pastoral work being left entirely to the Indian pastors, while the educational work is supervised by members of the Anglican Mission.

Schools. Of the schools the most important is that at Rānchi, which originally taught up to the Primary Standard, was raised to the Middle Vernacular Standard in 1884, and to the Matriculation Standard in 1895. The substantial and spacious building in which the school is held was built forty-three years ago, a solid testimony to the wise forethought of those pioneers of education. The majority of the pupils, who number over 300, are boarders, and a new boarding-house has been constructed with the assistance of a grant from Government. The school is very efficiently managed, and the late Mr. Cunningham, Inspector of Schools in the Chotā Nāgpur Division, wrote of it a few years ago :—"In every really essential respect I am satisfied that the school may serve as an excellent 'model' school to which others may with advantage aspire. I am impressed with the school as a masterpiece of educational organization and only those who have attempted such organization in India can appreciate what that means." Apart from the High School and the Girls' School at Rānchi, there are 32 Primary boarding schools at the out-stations and native pastorates, with 2,400 pupils of both sexes, and 223 village schools with nearly 4,009 pupils, of whom 900 are non-Christians.

Medical work has also not been neglected. There is a dispensary at Rānchi, and at Lohardagā a small Leper Asylum and Home for Incurables. Hospitals.

An account of the Lutheran Mission would be incomplete without some mention of Rev. Dr. Nottrott, to whose indefatigable exertions and wise guidance the Mission largely owes its success among the tribes of Chotā Nāgpur. He arrived in Rānchi in 1867 and retired only in 1913. In spite of the arduous work devolving on him as the head of a large community, Dr. Nottrott also devoted his time to translating the Scripture into Mundāri. His translation of the New Testament was published, many years ago, by the Bible and Tract Society and his translation of the Old Testament was completed shortly before his retirement.

The S. P. G. Mission.

If the Lutheran Mission owes its success largely to Dr. Nottrott, the Anglican Mission is equally indebted to the Rev. J. C. Whitley, the first Bishop of Chotā Nāgpur. Shortly after the pioneer pastors of the Lutheran Mission had been received into the English Church, Mr. Whitley, who had worked for seven years in the Punjab, was sent to Rānchi from Kurnal, to superintend the work of the new Mission. His first work was to organize the work among the six thousand Christians who had come over. The three hundred villages, in which all or some of the inhabitants were Christians, were divided up into thirty-five circles; the old system of village elders remained as before, and in each circle a catechist or reader was appointed, on a small salary, to hold services and instruct the young in the Bible and Catechism. Owing to the small staff the missionaries were only able to visit the circles occasionally. During this early period one great lack was the want of chapels and schools in the villages. This defect was soon removed, and by 1870 enough money had been collected, chiefly by the European ladies of Rānchi, to build small chapels, rough mud buildings. with red-tiled roofs, in each of the central villages of the circles. Another need was a central church at Rānchi. The service of ordination and confirmation, held by Bishop Milman in 1869, was performed in a primitive mud-walled building. When he returned in the beginning of 1873, there was a fine stately brick church capable of holding fully twelve hundred persons. The church was designed by General Rowlatt, then Judicial Commissioner of Chotā Nāgpur, and the foundation-stone was laid on September 1st, 1870, by General Dalton. Of the total cost of the building, Rs. 26,000, Rs. 7,000 was raised in Rānchi itself, General Dalton contributing over Rs. 3,000, Rs. 3,600 represented a grant from the Government of India and the balance grants from the Society for the Propagation of the Gospel and Society for the Propagation of Christian Knowledge. Bishop Milman's visit to Rānchi in 1873 is noteworthy not only for the consecration of the new church but also for the ordination of the first five Indian clergy of Chotā Nāgpur. These five deacons were placed in charge of five districts, with headquarters at Maranghada, Murhu, Tapkara, Rāmtolia and Itki. Their salary, at first only Rs. 15 a month, was met partly by the offerings of their congregations and partly by the Native Pastorate Endowment Fund of Calcutta, no contribution being received from the ordinary Mission funds. The progress of the Mission during the first ten years of its existence may be judged by the following facts. The number of Christians had risen from 5,773 in 1870 to 10,679 in 1880; the number of communicants had quadrupled and, though the number of European missionaries had not increased, there were no less than eleven Indian clergymen. In the next decade the progress of the Anglican Mission was hampered by the same causes that affected the Lutheran Mission the Sardāri agitation and the rise of the Roman Catholic Mission. Still there was some progress; the number of Christians rose to 12,519 in 1890, while the number of pupils rose from 865 to 1,209. Churches were built at Kachabari and Murhu, the former in memory of the Rev. Mr. Vallings, the latter out of a legacy left by General Dalton.

Bishopric of Chota Nāgpur.

But the most noteworthy event of this period was the foundation of the Bishopric of Chotā Nāgpur. In the year 1885, a petition was sent to the Bishop of Calcutta signed by all the priests and deacons of the Mission, praying for the appointment of a Bishop for Chotā Nāgpur. Bishop Johnston favoured the scheme, but legal difficulties stood in the way, as the diocese of Calcutta had been created by Act of Parliament in 1814, and it was only by a similar Act that a new bishopric could be created. The problem was at last solved by the appointment of a kind of suffragan bishop, "on the primitive foundation of consensual compact and canonical obedience".

An endowment of Rs. 13,500 was raised by the Missionary Societies in England, and in March 1890 the Rev. Mr. Whitley was consecrated to be the first Bishop of Chotā Nāgpur. Finding the staff of the Mission insufficient for the work they were called upon to perform, Bishop Whitley, in 1902, invited the Dublin University Mission, which had been established at Hāzaribāgh since 1892, to undertake the educational, medical and evangelistic work at Rānchi, but since 1908, owing to paucity of recruits, the Dublin Mission has been forced to confine its work mainly to the former district.

Present-day Staff.

In 1904 Bishop Whitley died, and was succeeded by the Rev. Foss Westcott, under whose able and energetic guidance the Mission has continued its progress.

The staff now consists of seven European and seventeen Indian clergymen, assisted by 94 Readers and *Prachāraks,* with a congregation of over 15,000 persons. At Rānchi and the two out-stations of Itki and Murhu, which are in charge of European clergymen, there is a staff of nine ladies who render valuable assistance in the medical and educational work. In addition to this staff, some members of the Mission have been engaged, since the removal of the Lutheran missionaries, inthe educational work of that Mission.

Schools.

Of the educational institutions, the most important is the St. Paul's High School at Rānchi. The numbers are rising rapidly and there are now 322 boys in the senior school, an increase of 171 boys in five years, and 161 in the junior school. Of these 139 are non-Christians, but all alike receive religious instruction daily. One hundred and ninety-three boys from this school and others connected with the Mission are boarders, and a spacious new hostel has recently been opened, while the construction of new buildings for the school itself has been taken in hand. A Training School for masters provides teachers for the numerous village schools, and its efficiency has been recognized by Government who send for training a certain number of teachers, destined for Government and District Board Schools. Female education has not been neglected; the girls' school at Rānchi, under the able management of a European Lady missionary, has nearly 300 pupils on its rolls, of whom 110 are boarders. A Training School for mistresses was opened in 1909 and a Lace School in 1908. At Chutiā near Rānchi there are flourishing schools for boys and girls, the majority of the pupils being Hindus or Muhammadans, and at Dorunda schools for the children of the Bengali clerks of the Secretariat have recently been opened. At Murhu, in the Mundā country, there is a boys' Middle English School with over 150 pupils, of whom more than 100 are boarders, and a girls' school with 113 children, of whom 82 are boarders. In all, the Mission maintains in the district 28 boys' schools, 11 girls' schools, and 46 mixed schools, with 3,266 pupils. The Blind School at Rānchi is an institution almost unique of its kind in India. It was started in 1895, and blind men are trained in industrial work in cane and bamboo, and blind women in mat-making. Reading and writing are also taught on the Braille system.

Hospitals. The medical work of the English Mission is important and its ministrations are extended to Christians and non-Christians alike. Details of the hospitals maintained by the Mission have been given in Chapter IV. The good work done at Mission hospitals may be judged from the following extract from the annual report:—"Among the patients fifteen cataract operations have been done and a considerable number of corneal ulcers treated. There has been a marked absence of serious cases requiring immediate operations, the three chief ones being two Muhammadans, one with a liver abscess and one with an empyæma and a small Mundā boy badly gored in the stomach by a buffalo, all three of whom made complete recoveries. A fair number of operations which, though small and unimportant in themselves, will add greatly to the future usefulness and comfort of the patients have been done, such, for instance, as the freeing of joints and limbs bound by contracting scar tissues and adhesions, operations for entropia and ectropia, removal of cysts, etc. Chloroform has been given 34 times for operations and about a dozen times for examination purposes, dressings and movings of joints. Local anæsthesias, apart from cataract operations, have been given about twenty times. One high amputation of the arm has been done. The medical work as distinct from the surgical in a hospital like Murhu is, on the whole, rather disappointing as it is almost impossible to keep patients under treatment when once they begin to improve."

Though the success of the Lutheran and Anglican Mission is remarkable, even more remarkable is the story of the rise and development of the Roman Catholic Mission. An idea of the rapid expansion of the Mission may be gathered from the following figures :— Roman Catholic Mission.

The number of Catholic converts rose from 15,000 in the year 1887 to 39,567 in 1897, of whom 22,728 were baptized converts and 16,839 neophytes. By 1900 the number had swelled to 71,270, and by 1909 the Roman Catholic Mission in Chotā Nāgpur counted as many as 147,366 converts, including 72,943 neophytes, of whom over 91,000 belonged to the district of Rānchi. In the census of 1911 over 77,000 persons in the district of Rānchi were recorded as Christians of the Roman Church, but the figures compiled by the Ecclesiastical authorities in their own census show that the total number of Christians is 107,187, of whom 70,668 were baptized Catholics and 36,519 Catechumens. The Catholic Mission centres in the district are now sixteen in number and are located at Rānchi (established in 1887), Sarwadā (1882), Torpa (1885), Mandar (1893), Nawātoli (1890), Karrā (1888), Khunti (1891), Tongo (1891), Katkahi (1892), Rengāri (1901), Soso (1901), Kurdeg (1903), Sāmtoli (1903), Nawādih (1907), Majhatoli (1907) and at Dighia (first established in 1866, then abandoned and re-established in 1913). Each of these stations is a flourishing centre of religious, educational and social work. In spite of the difficulty of obtaining efficient workmen in the out-of-the-way parts of the district the missionaries have succeeded in building handsome brick churches in each station, many of which are fine specimens of ecclesiastical architecture and copies of the picturesque churches of Flanders, Brittany and Belgium, from which most of the Fathers come. Large spacious schools have also been built, and a traveller who arrives at one of these stations in the jungles must be filled with admiration at the work. Statistics.

The Roman Mission, as it is popularly termed, is a part of the Archdiocese of Calcutta, formerly known as the Vicariate Apostolic of Western Bengal. The Vicariate was established in 1834, but in 1886 was raised to the status of an Archbishopric. When the English Jesuits left Bengal, the Mission was entrusted in 1859 by Pope Pius IX to the Belgian Jesuits. For a time their activity was confined to educational work in Calcutta and to missionary work in the immediate neighbourhood. In 1869 History.

the Rev. Father Stockman was sent by the Vicar Apostolic to Chaibassa, to try and establish a Mission among the aborigines, and extended the work to Rānchi, in 1874, by establishing a station in the jungle at Burudih near Kochang. In 1876 the Rev. Father DeCock, who had been sent to Dorundā to look after the Madrasi sepoys, opened a Mission there. In 1881 another station was opened at Sarwada. In 1886 the Dorundā Mission was transferred to Rānchi. The real founder of the Roman Catholic Mission in the district of Rānchi is, however, the Rev. Father C. Lievens, S. J., whose marvellous work won for him the title of "the Apostle of the Orāons". Arriving in 1885 he stayed for a few months at Jamgain and in the same year established a station at Torpā, where he speedily acquired a wonderful influence in the west of the Mundā country. In 1886—88 the Roman Mission stood forth as the champions of the raiyats against the oppression of alien landholders, and in that short period not only won over many non-Christians to their church but caused some 5,000 converts to desert the Protestant Missions, in the hope of obtaining greater and more efficacious help in their law suits against the zamindārs. But it was in the Orāon country in the west of the district, which was as yet untouched by missionary work and in which the antagonism of raiyats and landlords owing to the exaction of unlimited *beth begāri* was acute, that Father Lievens met with the greatest success. Here whole villages became Christian, new stations were established, generally in the neighbourhood of police-stations, and Father Lievens, when he became Director of the Catholic Mission in Lohardagā, received into the Church in Parganas Khukra, Panāri, Nawagarh, Barwe, Biru, and Chechāri (Palamāu) no less than 40,000 aboriginals, mostly Orāons. His health broke down and he died at Louvain in 1893. He had, however, laid a solid foundation for future work, and the success of the Mission, which is far the best equipped both in men and money of all the missions, has continued unbroken.

Staff. The staff of the Mission now consists of more than fifty European priests, over five hundred catechists and more than three hundred schoolmasters.

The out-stations are grouped into four circles under local superiors at Rānchi, Khunti, Tongo, and Rengāri, and at each station there is a staff of two or three priests, while at the larger stations there are convents of European Nuns who superintend the secular and religious instruction of the girls and women.

Schools.

Great importance is attached by the missionaries to the educational side of their work, as they realize that the best hope of progress of religious work lies in establishing an influence over the boys and girls. Apart from the High School at Rānchi, the Catholic Mission has no less than 230 Boys' Schools in Chotā Nāgpur with over 6,800 pupils, of whom 1,326 are boarders. Of these schools, the majority of which are in the Rānchi district, twelve are Upper Primary Boarding Schools, four Lower Primary Boarding Schools, and the remainder village day-schools. The Central School at Rānchi was started in 1887 as a Lower Primary School to impart elementary instruction to the children of Catholic converts in the town and neighbouring villages. It was soon necessary to admit to the school-boys from the stations in the interior of the district, with a view to training them for the posts of catechists and schoolmasters. In 1903 the school was raised to the Middle English standard, and in 1905 to the High English standard. The school was at first a boarding school for Christian boys, but since 1904 non-Christian boys are admitted as day-scholars. At present the number of boarders, mostly Mundās and Orāons, is over 270, and the number of day boys 192, of whom 143 are Hindus and 40 Muhammadans. The increase in the number of pupils made it necessary to erect a new class building. This building, having a frontage of 330 feet, was completed in 1914. Its 17 class-rooms and three large halls can accommodate 500 pupils. The plans were prepared by a Calcutta architect and the actual work of building undertaken by one of the lay-brothers of the Mission, at a cost of Rs. 78,000, Rs. 36,000 being contributed by Government. A new hostel has also been constructed, to accommodate 300 boarders, allowing to each boarder the floor space required by Government regulations. Apart from the actual school work the boys are expected to do some manual work, and an interesting feature in the training of the boys is the performance of dramatic plays on the lines of the mystery plays of the Middle Ages.

To obtain better masters for their numerous schools, the Roman Catholic Mission have opened a Training School, exclusively reserved for aboriginals. The school has been recognized by the Education Department, and, together with its own candidates, trains a certain number of Government nominees.

A more ambitous institution is the Apostolic School of the Mission which was started in 1903 for training for the priesthood such of the more intelligent of the boys as feel spontaneously called to it. As long as the school was in the experimental stage, the students after completing a six years' classical course in Rānchi, were sent to the Papal Seminary in Ceylon for a further seven years' course in Philosophy and Theology. When, however, the success of the school seemed assured, the authorities decided to build, in the Mission ground at Rānchi, a seminary for the teaching of Philosophy and Theology. The building is expected to be ready by the beginning of 1916. As before, the whole course will remain spread over a space of thirteen years. There are at present 27 students in the section of Philosophy and Theology. The first Orāon Priest was ordained in Rānchi on October 25th, 1914.

The Girls' School at Rānchi is typical of the Girls' Schools at the other centres of Khunti, Rengāri, and Tongo. It was started in 1890 by an Irish congregation of Nuns, known as the Lorettine Nuns, and in 1903 was taken charge of by the Ursuline Nuns. The school is divided into two departments. The first department is conducted in accordance with Government regulations, and the girls, who number nearly six hundred, receive instruction up to the Upper Primary standard. The second department contains girls who only attend for three or four months in the year, principally during the cold weather, when they are not required to help their parents in the fields, and receive only elementary and religious instruction. The number of girls in this division varies considerably but they may be taken at an average of 1,500 per annum. All the girls in these departments are aboriginals and free boarders.

Another interesting institution under the charge of the Ursuline Nuns is the Lace School which was started in 1905. More than a hundred aboriginal women daily attend the school. Most of them are married women and are paid at a fixed rate for every yard of lace. The lace is of excellent quality and commands a good market in Calcutta and England.

Industrial school.

The Jesuit missionaries have also paid great attention to the industrial development of the people. Agriculture is practically the sole occupation of the aborigines, and as a raiyat's holding barely yields sufficient produce for the consumption of himself and his family, and as he is also notoriously improvident, he is in a state of habitual indebtedness. To ameliorate the condition of the Christians, an Industrial school was opened at Rānchi in 1894 for training carpenters and masons but was discontinued a few years later, and a more ambitious school started at Khunti. This school consisted of four departments, viz., the weaving and dyeing departments, the carpentry department, the iron-work department and the silk-worm-rearing department. The Mundās have a strong prejudice against weaving, which is done in a Mundā village by the low caste of Pāns, and a Mundā who weaves his own cloth loses his caste. An attempt was made to get rid of this custom by the introduction of Japanese looms which are worked with the feet, but unfortunately the prejudice against the work of weaving could never be entirely overcome. The young men, who, after completing their course of training in Khunti, had returned to their villages, one after another gave way before the prejudice and gave up the work. It had never been the aim to found a factory or weaving establishment but only a school where boys could learn a trade which they could practise in their homes. The costly experiments did not seem to help towards the attainment of this object, and ultimately the school was discontinued, and the looms sold off.

Another industrial experiment was tried at Rānchi. In 1908 Rev. Father Hoffmann conceived the idea that it might be possible to interest the aborigines in a scheme of Industrial Co-operation. A tile factory was opened on a plot of ground lent by the Mission; the required capital being also advanced by the Mission. The idea was that the aborigines might slowly pay back the capital and thus become the proprietors of an independent and promising industrial concern. From the very beginning the tile factory was meant as an experiment in the Industrial Co-operation, and an experiment it has remained. Hence though the Roman Mission tiles, as they are called, have been in great demand, the factory has never been a commercial success, and will soon be closed down altogether.

Co-operative Societies.

As measures for improving the material condition of the people, these industrial enterprises are overshadowed by the Chotā Nāgpur Catholic Co-operative Society started by Rev. Father Hoffmann a few years ago. A detailed account of this society is given in another Chapter. A quotation from the Government Report on the working of Co-operative Societies for 1909-10 will suffice to show the aims and prospects of this movement :—" The problem is how to give the aboriginal tribes the full advantages of co-operation, in order to prevent their future exploitation by their more advanced and pushful neighbours and to enable them to hold their own in the economic struggle. Father Hoffmann's society offers a practical solution of the problem. The scheme cannot fail of ultimate success, and it is bound sooner or later to effect an economic revolution in Chotā Nāgpur. "

CHAPTER XVI.

GAZETTEER.

Barwe, the most western pargana of the district, comprises the whole of thana Chainpur (Bhitar Barwe) and part of thana Bishunpur (Bahar Barwe). The plain of Bhitar Barwe is shut off from the rest of the district by a long range of hills and is drained by the Sānkh. The Barwe estate was formerly subject to the Rājā of Surguja, and Brāhman tradition gives the following story of its origin. A Brāhman of Benares, who was on a visit to the Rājā of Sūrguja, mistook a Chamār bearer who was seated near the *gadi*, dressed in the cast-off clothes of his master, and addressed him as " Mahārāja Sahib ". Finding out his mistake, the Brāhman begged the Mahārājā not to let him fall under the imputation of having told a lie, and the latter thereupon conferred upon the bearer the title of " Rājā " and gave him the estate of Barwe. The Estate finally became subject to the Rājā of Chotā Nāgpur in 1801. Some years previous to this, the Rājā of Sūrguja overran the pargana and the Rājā of Barwe, receiving no help from the Rājā of Choṭā Nāgpur, submitted to him. Later, the Rāja of Chotā Nāgpur, who was assisted by the British troops, induced the Rājā of Barwe, on promise of personal safety, to submit and place himself in his hands. The promise, however, was broken, and the officers of the Rājā of Chotā Nāgpur put the Rājā of Barwe to death near Pālkot. The present family hold the estate under a *patta* granted by Mahārājā Jagannāth Sahi Deo, and the estate was recorded in the Settlement records as a tenure resumable on the failure of male heirs. The estate, however, is claimed by the Mahārājā as a life-grant, and the case is still before the Courts.

Barwe is a great stronghold of the Orāons, many of whom have become converts to Christianity. The Lutheran Mission has a station at Chainpur, and the Roman Catholic Mission stations at Tongo, Katkahi and Nawādih. The total population of Chainpur thana is 54,404, of whom over 29,000 are Christians.

Chainpur is connected with the subdivisional headquarters at Gumlā by two unmetalled roads; one, running in an easterly direction, crosses the hills by the Kurumgarh-Jori *ghāt* and joins the Lohardagā-Gumlā road at Toto; the other runs due south to Raidih and there joins the Lohardagā-Sambalpur road. The distance from Chainpur to Gumla by the former route is about 28 miles and by the latter about 31 miles. There are *ghātwāli* bungalows at Chainpur, Kurumgarh, Jori, Toto and Raidih. The road connecting Netarhāt, on the borders of Palāmau district, with Ghaghrā and the Lohardagā-Gumlā road passes through the centre of Bahar Barwe; it is 25 miles in length and is gravelled and with one exception bridged throughout There is a *ghātwāli* bungalow at Adar, six miles from Ghaghrā.

Biru Pargana, in the south-west of the district, comprises the whole of thānas Kochedega and Kurdeg and some villages of thāna Kolebira. Khariās and Orāons form the bulk of the population. The estate belongs to Bahera Hukm Singh, who is locally known as "Rājā". The family claim descent from Hitambar Deo, the son of a Mahārāja of Puri, who removed to Sambalpur, where he received a grant of some villages. His son, Hari Deo, in pursuance of divine direction, left Sambalpur in 1557 and went to Bijadih in pargana Kesalpur, which was then included in the dominions of the Rājā of Chotā Nāgpur. In return for a gift of a diamond the Chief gave him the pargana as *jāgir* and recognized him as Rāja. Later, Rājā Bhim Singh assisted Rājā Durjan Sal against the Muhammadans and was taken prisoner with him to Delhi. Durjan Sal gained his release by his skill in testing diamonds and is said to have been assisted in this by Bhim Singh, to whom, out of gratitude, he gave the whole of pargana Biru, in addition to that of Kesalpur. A successor of Bhim Singh incurred the displeasure of the Mahārājā by his failure to embank the Sānkh, and was deprived of the title of Rājā, that of Bahera being substituted, and made to pay a rental of Sikka

Rs. 375. The Zamindār is still locally known as Rājā, but the title is not recognized by Government. The estate is now under the management of the Encumbered Estates Department. Over 40 per cent. of the total population of thanas Kochedegā and Kurdeg are Christians, mostly Khariās and Orāons. The Roman Catholic Mission has stations at Rengāri, Kurdeg and Sāmtoli and the Lutheran Mission at Khuntitoli, Koranjo and Kinkel. Buildings for the headquarters of the subdivision have been recently erected at Simdegā, an important market, ten miles south-west of Biru.

Bundu, the only town in the Khunti subdivision, is situated about 18 miles from Khunti and 27 miles south-east of Ranchi, in 23° 10′ N. and 85° 36′ E. The population increased from 5,496 in 1901 to 6,950 in 1911, of whom 5,256 were Hindus, 114 Jains, 372 Musalmans and 1,385 Animists. The town contains a police-station, District Board Dispensary, Middle English School, and Guru Training School. It is important as the centre of the lac industry and contains several factories for the conversion of lac into shellac. Owing to the fall in prices, the number of the factories has decreased considerably in recent years and there are now only 18 as against 37 a few years ago. Situated below the tableland, Bundu is hot, and, owing to the effluent of the lac factories, is unhealthy. A Union Committee has recently been appointed to look after the sanitation of the village. The Bundu pargana, one of the five parganas, is now in possession of Rājā Srinath Rai of Dacca, who purchased it in 1909 in execution of a Civil Court decree for money lent to the local Rājā.

Chokāhatu, a village in thana Sonahatu, pargana Baranda, is famous for its large burial ground, the largest in the Munda country. The burial-ground covers over seven acres in area and contains more than 7,000 *sasāndiris* or sepulchral stones. According to Mundā custom, only the *bhuinhārs*, or descendants of the original settlers of the village, are buried in the *sasān*, and it is somewhat curious to find such a large burial ground attached to one small group of villages. It has been conjectured that in the *lutur desam*, or low country of the Five Parganas, the Mundās followed a different custom from those of the central plateau and allowed all settlers in the village the privilege of burial in the *sasan*. There is little proof in support of this conjecture, and it is more probable that the burial ground at Chokāhatu dates back to the time when the Mundās retired westwards from Mānbhum. The Bhumij of that district have one *sasān* for each *taraf* or group of twelve to seventeen villages, a *taraf* being the area allotted to a *kili*, or sept, and burial grounds nearly as large as that at Chokāhatu are to be found in the Bhumij country. The Bhumij are probably ethnologically identical with the Mundās, but among the Mundās *kilis* are now scattered and are not, as among the Bhumij, confined more or less to one area. It is possible, therefore, that Chokāhatu was a *kili sasān* of the Mundās who settled in this part of the country, being driven there either by pressure of population in their settlements in Mānbhum, or, less probably, by the incursions of the Kurmi Mahatos. From Chokāhatu they spread westward into the jungles of Tāmar, Sonpur and Bundu and lost touch with their original settlements.

Chutia, a straggling village on the eastern outskirts of Rānchi and within the Municipal limits. The village was one of the earliest residences of the Nāgbansi family of the Rājās of Chotā Nāgpur and is said to have been selected for the capital by Rājā Partab Rai, the fourth in descent from Rājā Phani Mukut; it gives its name to the country, which, though now spelt Chotā Nāgpur, is found in old records as Chuttiah, or Chutea, Nāgpur. It contains an old temple, standing in a small square enclosure, with four flanking bastions and a well in the centre, which is approached by a sloping covered stone passage. An inscription on the northern wall of the temple shows that it was constructed by Hari Brahmachāri, the *guru* of the Rājā, in Sambat 1742 (1684 A. D.) during the reign of Rājā, Raghu Nāth, the fiftieth in descent from Rājā Phani Makut. At the time of the Mundā rising under Birsā, the temple was entered and desecrated by Birsā and some of his followers.

Chutiā was formerly the site of a large annual fair. The fair was established in 1851 by Mr. Crawford, Agent to the Governor General, at Silli, but, Silli not providing sufficient shelter for the persons attending the fair, it was removed in 1855 to Chutiā, where there were large mango groves and a plentiful supply of water. The object of the fair was to establish an attractive centre for the general encouragement of trade, to improve the social relations between the different Chiefs, and to bring them into friendly communication with the European officers. For some years these objects were attained, but, with the rise of permanent shops in Rānchi and elsewhere, the fair gradually declined as a meeting for purposes of trade. It continued for some years as a social gathering and the athletic sports and games, such as cock-fighting, ram-fighting and push-push races, attracted a large concourse of Europeans and Indians. It was discontinued in 1874, and the funds in hand were diverted to other objects, such as the establishment of the Rānchi Industrial School. In 1907 the District Board held its first agricultural and horticultural exhibition on the site of the old fair, and this exhibition is yearly growing in popularity.

Doisa, or **Doisa Nagar** in the Fiscal Division of the same name and in Sisai thana, about 40 miles south-west of Rānchi, is the site of a ruined palace of the Rājās of Chotā Nāgpur, which is the chief object of archæological interest in the district. The palace, which is known as the *Nauratan*, was built of brick and was five-storied, each story containing nine rooms. An object of interest is the treasure-house, full of quaint niches and corners, in which the children of the family, and also, it is said, the Rājā and Rāni, used to play at hide-and-seek. Round the palace are numerous temples, one of which contains curious underground chambers, said to have been used either as dungeons, or as hiding-places in times of trouble. The temples and buildings are of carved granite, but the carvings are not of any great artistic merit and consist of conventionally designed friezes in slight relief and representations of birds, animals, elephants and horsemen. An inscription on the front door of the temple of Jagannāth shows that the temple was built in Sambat 1739 or A. D. 1683, by Hari Nāth, who also built the temple at Chutiā. Another inscription on the temple of Kapilnāth, i.e., Srikrishna, bears the date 1767 Sambat or 1711 A. D. A picturesque little temple known as the Dhobi Math was probably built at a later date.

Tradition gives the following account of the building of the palace: Rājā Durjan Sal, after he had been defeated and taken prisoner to Delhi, was confined in the fort of Gwalior, but owing to his skill in distinguishing a real from a false diamond was released and restored to his former position. Durjan Sal secured the release of some other Rājās who were also in confinement, and, some years later, they came to Jhārkand to pay their respects to their liberator, and were surprised to find him living in an insignificant house at Khukhrā. Accordingly, on their return, they sent down architects and masons, marble slabs and other materials, for the construction of a palace befitting his dignity. The legend goes on to say that the Rājā, after living there for a few years, was told by a Brāhman that it was unlucky, and accordingly went and lived at Pālkot, selecting that spot on account of the perennial stream issuing from the rocky hill side.

The tradition does not agree with the date given in the inscriptions, but there is no doubt that the Rājās frequently changed their place of residence. Chutiā, Khukhrā, Doisā, Pālkot, Bharno, all claim the honour of having at one time or another formed the seats of the Rāj family, now established at Rātu. Doisā, however, is the only village in which buildings of any importance were erected.

Doranda, a village two miles south of Rānchi and separated from it by a small tributary of the Subarnarekhā, was formerly a military cantonment. Soon after the establishment of the South-West Frontier Agency in 1834, the headquarters of the Rāmgarh Battalion, which had been raised at Chatrā in 1778, were transferred to Dorandā, so as to be near the civil headquarters at Kishanpur. The Rāmgarh Battalion consisted of light infantry, irregular cavalry and artillery. In 1857 the infantry joined the mutineers of the 8th Native Infantry, who were stationed at Hazāribāgh, and, after doing considerable damage to public and private property in Rānchi, Dorandā and the neighbourhood, were defeated near Chatrā. After the mutiny, it was proposed to make Dorandā a cavalry station but the buildings constructed were never used for this purpose and were subsequently sold for a Lac Factory. The troops stationed here consisted of a wing of a native infantry regiment, and were removed in 1905. The barracks and buildings occupied by the troops were utilized for a Police College and Police Training School, and a new college, a spacious red-brick building, was built in 1910. On the formation of the province of Bihar and Orissa and the selection of Rānchi as the temporary headquarters of the Local Government, the Police College and Training School were removed to Hazāribāgh; the college buildings were converted into the Secretariat, and the old lac factory, which had been re-acquired by Government for the Survey Department in 1905, into offices for the Accountant-General and the Heads of departments. Lines of temporary houses for the accommodation of both officers and subordinates were erected at Dorandā and Hinu. The area formerly included in the cantonment is administered by a Committee, appointed and financed by Government.

The main objects of interest in Dorandā, apart from the Secretariat and the staff quarters, are the picturesque tank and the European military cemetery on its bank. There is a large parade-ground, and a maidān, round which a short golf course has been laid out.

Gumla, the head-quarters village of the thana and subdivision of the same name, is situated in 23°2°N. and 84°33°E., about 59 miles west of Rānchi and 32 miles south of Lohardagā. The village is a flourishing trade centre and an important cattle market: the name, in fact, is said to be derived from *gau* (cow) and *melā* (market). The subdivisional buildings consist of courts and offices for the Subdivisional Officer, the Deputy Collector, and the Sub-Deputy Collector; the office of the Sub-Registrar and the Jail. There is also a Dispensary, maintained by the District Board, a Middle English School, and a Guru Training School. The landlord of Pargana Panāri, in which Gumlā is situated, is a Rautiā by caste, who received his estate as *jāgīr* from the Rājā of Chotā Nāgpur. He is known by the title of "Barāik". The Lutheran Mission has a station about a mile from the bazar, and there is a station of the Roman Catholic Mission at Soso about three miles away.

Gumla Subdivision contains an area of 2,057 square miles. When first started, it comprised the whole of the west and south-west of the district, but since 1915 the southwestern thanas have been formed into the Simdega Sub-division. With the exception of thanas Sisai and Basiā and the eastern portion of thānas Ghaghrā and Gumlā, which form part of the undulating central plateau, the country is mountainous and covered with jungle. Thana Bishunpur in the north-west contains the lofty hills (including Sīru hill, 3,604 feet above sea-level), which rise to the west of Lohardagā, and the *pāts* which form such a distinctive feature of this boundary of the district. Thāna Chainpur which corresponds to pargana Barwe consists mainly of the broad valley of the Sānkh, which a quarter of a century ago was covered with jungle but is now almost entirely under cultivation. The greater part of Rāidih and Pālkot thānas consists of jungle-covered hills, which form a barrier, cutting off Gumlā and Chainpur from Kochedegā and Kurdeg in the south. Of the southern thanas, Kurdeg, Kochedegā, Kolebirā and Bano, which border on the Tributary State of Gāngpur and now form the Simdegā subdivision, nearly half of the total area is covered with jungle, intersected with ranges of hills. The only open country in the south of the district is the valley of the Sānkh which flows in a southerly and south-easterly direction through Kochedegā and Kurdeg. The population is very scattered; there are no towns, and the villages, which number 1,396, consist of small *tolas*, often containing not more than five or six houses each. In the whole subdivision the density of the population is only 146 to the square mile, and is highest in thanas Gumlā (224), Sisai (219), Basiā (201) and lowest in thanas Bishunpur (77), Kolebirā (115), Kurdeg (116), Pālkot (120), and Chainpur (134). In the north and west of the subdivision Orāons are the predominant tribe, while Mundās are numerous in Basiā and Bano in the south-east, and Khariās form the greater part of the population of Biru in the south and south-west. Of the total population of 511,711, more than half (225,363) are classified as animists. Christianity has made rapid strides during recent years, especially among the Orāons, and the total number of Christians in the subdivision is over 100,000. In Chainpur thana more than half the population is Christian, and in Kochedegā thana nearly 40 per cent.

Communications throughout the subdivision are bad, though they have been considerably improved of recent years. From Gumlā to Rānchi (59 miles) there is a gravelled road, which is bridged throughout, with the exception of the South Koel. The Koel is easily fordable in the cold and hot weather, but in the rains is frequently impassable even for the primitive *donga*. The opening of the Rānchi-Lohardagā branch of the Bengal-

Nagpur Railway has done much to bring the northern part of the subdivision into touch with the outside world, and as soon as the Gumlā-Lohardagā road (32 miles) is bridged throughout, a work which is being taken in hand, the journey from Gumlā to Rānchi will be easy at all seasons of the year. Chainpur is connected with Gumlā by two unmetalled roads, one passing through Rāidih and the other coming direct over the hills via Jori Ghāt. The south of the district is linked up with Rānchi by an unmetalled road which passes through Kochedegā, Biru, Kolebirā, Basiā, and thence either via Khunti or via Jariā and Lodhmā. There is also an unmetalled road from Gumlā to Pālkot and Basiā.

The subdivision was opened in 1902, and is in charge of a member of the Indian or Provincial Civil Service who is assisted by a Sub-Deputy Collector, and disposes of all civil, criminal and revenue work.

Jagarnathpur, a village in the Barkagarh estate, six miles south-west of Rānchi, contains the largest temple in the district. It stands on a high rocky hill commanding an extensive view of the surrounding plateau, and is built on a plan roughly resembling the Puri temple. The temple was built in Sambat 1748 or 1691 A. D., by Thākur Aini Sahi, a *khorposhdār* of the Nāgbansi family, and the village was granted to the god as *debottar.* The whole of the Barkagarh estate was forfeited to Government owing to the assistance given by the proprietor to the mutineers in 1857, and the appointment and dismissal of the priest now rests with the Deputy Commissioner. The Rath Jātra, or Car festival, which is held here, attracts many thousands from all parts of the district. The image of the god is dragged in a cumbrous wooden Car, decorated with flowers and tinsel, from the main temple to a smaller temple on a rocky spur some two or three hundred yards away, and remains there for seven days till the Ultā Rāth. The festival is also a fair, and dealers in clothes, ornaments, and goods of all kinds, congregate at the foot of the hill.

Khunti, the headquarters of the subdivision and thana of that name, is a village 23 miles south of Rānchi on the Rānchi-Chaibassa road. The combined subdivisional court and munsifi, which was completed in 1908, is situated on rising ground about a mile and a half south of the village. In addition to these buildings, there are a **Sub-jail**, Sub-registry office, and a District Board dispensary, with in-patient and out-patient wards. In the main village are the police-station, Middle English School and Inspection bungalow. The population, of which only a small proportion are Mundās, has increased considerably since the opening of the subdivision in 1905. A bi-weekly market is held in the village.

Khunti is also the headquarters of the Mundā section of the Roman Catholic Mission. There is also a Convent in charge of four European sisters, in which lace manufacture is taught to Mundā girls and women.

Khunti Subdivision contains the south-eastern portion of the district, lying between 22° 38′ and 23° 18′ N. and between 84° 56′ and 85° 54′ E., with an area of 1,545 square miles. The subdivision contains the south-eastern portion of the central plateau and the low-lying country of the Five Parganas; the country is for the most part undulating, the only hills being those which fringe the west and south of the Five Parganas. The tributaries of the Subarnarekhā, of which the most important are the Kānchi and the Karkari, drain Khunti, Bundu, Sonahatu and Tamar thanas; the Kāro forms a portion of the western boundary of the subdivision and then flows through the centre of Torpā thāna and unites with the Koel in Singhbhūm district. The principal roads in the subdivision are the Rānchi-Chaibassa road, which passes through Khunti, and the Khunti-Kamdāra road, passing through Torpā. From Bundu roads run to Silli via Rahe, and to Jhaldā in the Mānbhūm district, via Sonahatu. Except for the Rānchi-Chaibassa road, which is metalled and bridged throughout, the roads are all unmetalled, with only temporary culverts.

The population of the subdivision has risen from 300,205 in 1901 to 349,633 in 1911, the density being 226 persons to the square mile. Of the total population nearly 39,000 are Christians and 139,000 Animists. The Khunti subdivision was opened in 1905, to provide for the better administration of that portion of the district in which the Mundās predominate; it includes the following thanas:—Khunti, Karra, Torpa, Tamār, Bundu and Sonahatu. The Subdivisional Officer, in addition to his magisterial powers, has the powers of a Munsif, and is assisted by a Sub-Deputy Collector.

Lohardagā, a town in the sadr subdivision, 47 miles west of Rānchi was, till 1843, the headquarters of the district to which it gave its name. It is the most important market in the north-west of the district, and its importance has been enhanced by the opening of the Rānchi-Lohardagā branch of the Bengal-Nagpur Railway in 1913. Much timber passes through Lohardagā from the forests on the north-west border of the district, and also rice and oil-seeds from Barwe and the Feudatory States of Jashpur and Surguja. The population has decreased during the last twenty years from 7,110 in 1891 to 6,773 in 1911. Of the total population nearly five-sixths are Hindus or Muhammadans. The town was formed into a Municipality in 1888 and a detailed account of the municipal administration will be found in the Chapter on Local Self-Government. There is a bench of Honorary Magistrates, who dispose of municipal cases, and a sub-registry office.

The Lutheran Mission station at Lohardagā was one of the first to be founded outside Rānchi. Attached to it is a small Leper Asylum and Home for Incurables.

Lohardagā is connected with Rānchi both by the railway and by a good metalled road which passes through Kuru and Māndar. The road to Gumlā (32 miles) is being metalled, and bridges are being constructed over the numerous rivers.

It was at one time intended to made Lohardagā the headquarters of a subdivision, but this project has been dropped.

Murhu, a village 28 miles south of Rānchi on the Rānchi-Chaibassa road, is the headquarters of the S. P. G. Mission in the Mundā country. The handsome church was built out of a legacy of £500 from General Dalton. It holds 600 people and was opened in 1887. The Mission also maintains a dispensary which was established in 1905, with fourteen beds for in-patients, and does excellent work both among Christians and non-Christians. There are also schools for both boys and girls, with boarding houses attached. A bazar instituted by the Mission is held on Monday and Thursday and is a large centre for the sale of lac, salt and jungle products from Porāhāt.

Nāgpheni, a small village in Sisai thāna, picturesquely situated above some rocky falls of the Koel. On a hill near the village many roughly carved stones lie scattered about, one of which bears the date 1761 Sambat (1705 A. D.). It is said that one of the Rājās intended to erect a palace on the site, but died before the work was completed. On a tomb in the village is a rude carving said to represent the Rāja, his seven Rānis, and his dog. The name Nāgpheni means the cobra's hood, and owes its origin to a stone, somewhat of the shape of a cobra's hood, which is visible on the hill side.

Pālkot, a large village and bazar in the thāna of the same name, is situated in 22° 52′ N. and 84° 39′ E. It was formerly the residence of the Mahārājā of Chotā Nāgpur. Doisā having been declared to be ill-omened, the Mahārājā selected Pālkot because of the cool and fresh spring of clear water which issues from the hill, and built himself a cell so that "he could drink and perform his devotions with the aid of the water, pure and uncontaminated by his subjects who lived in the town below". The family, according to its own records, established itself here about 1667 A. D., but more probably in the first half of the 18th century. The extensive buildings of the palace, which is built on the side of the hill, are devoid of architectural interest. The village contains numerous tanks and gardens, one of which is known as the *sati bagicha*, in memory of a lady of the Chief's household who became *sati* on the site of it. Owing to dissensions with his nephew, Bara Lāl Upendra Nath Sahi Deo, Mahārājā Jagannāth Sahi forsook Pālkot for Bharno in 1867. The present owner is Bara Lāl Nawāl Kishore Nāth Sahi Deo, the grandson of Upendra Nāth Sahi Deo. He contested the right of the present Mahārājā to the *gadi* but failed in the appellate courts. The name Pālkot is said to be derived from an Orāon word *pāl*, a tooth, or a Mundāri word *pahal*, a ploughshare, and to owe its origin to a curious natural pillar which stands about a mile to the north of the village.

The Pats have already been noticed in Chapter I. Captain Depree, who conducted the Topographical Survey in 1868, thus described them : " In the north-west corner, and along the boundary of Jashpur, are to be seen the peculiar hill features called *pāts*. These hills extend westward into Sarguja and Jashpur. They are of a nearly uniform height, 3,600 feet above the sea. Looking at them from a distance, their summit is as level and uniform as that of a masonry wall, and they form as perfect an horizon as the sea itself. On a near inspection, however, they are found to consist of rocky spurs of various heights, with deep alleys and many precipitous ravines radiating from the central mass. The ascent of these *pāts* is steep. The path winds amongst boulders of rock, or up earthy slopes covered with forest, until 20 or 30 feet from the summit is reached; here a precipitous rock, the edge of a horizontal stratum, bars progress except through some fissure, not seen at first view. This horizontal stratum of trap rock forms a true contour or level line, being visible like a collar on every side of the *pāt*. It in fact gives the *pāt* its form, were it not that it continued to resist the action of rainfall, these *pāts* would long ago have had their upper soil washed away, and would have put on the form of peaks or ridges common to ordinary hills. On the summits there is generally a small depth of soil overlying the rock, consequently very little can be cultivated; forest trees, however, grow, and the slopes of the *pāts* generally bear heavy timber. It is probable that the *pāts* at an early period were one continuous mass, forming a plateau."

Ranchi, the administrative headquarters of the district and of the Chotā Nāgpur Division and, since 1912, the temporary headquarters of the Government of Bihar and Orissa, is situated in 23° 23′ N. and 85° 23′ E., on the central plateau, at a height of 2,128 feet above the sea level. Rānchi is a long straggling town with traces in the scattered way the houses lie of the separate villages of which it is composed. The history of the development of Rānchi into a town reflects the history of the British administration. On the creation of the South-West Frontier Agency in 1834, the first Agent, Captain Wilkinson, selected the hamlet of Kishanpur as his headquarters, his court being on the site now occupied by the office of the Executive Engineer. To avoid confusion with other places of the same name, the station was, a few years later, designated Rānchi, from a small village now called Purāna Rānchi. Captain Wilkinson built the house, which was, till recently, occupied by the Commissioner, on a site leased from the *jāgīrdār* of the village Chadri, and excavated the Wilkinson, or Bhutaha, tank with jail labour. Lieutenant-Colonel Ousely (1839 to 1848) extended the compound of the house erected by his predecessor to include a coffee garden and the Rānchi hill, and excavated the Sahib Bāndh, or Rānchi Lake, a splendid piece of water, some fifty acres in extent, fringed by trees, with picturesque islands in the midst, and a pillared bathing ghat and two small temples on one side. On the summit of the pyramid-shaped Rānchi hill, he erected a summer house, as a place of rest during his morning walks. This structure, though surmounted with a cross, has been annexed by the inhabitants of Rānchi as a Mahādeo asthān and is a place of worship for both Hindus and Animists. In 1843 the headquarters of the Principal Assistant to the Agent were transferred to Rānchi from Lohardagā, and the first Assistant, Captain R. Ousely (1842 to 1849) acquired from the Mahārājā a site in Chadri with a circumference of nearly three miles, and set about building an imposing residence. To carry out this work, he embezzled Rs. 12,000 from the Government treasury, and, on the crime being detected, his brother, the Agent, committed suicide and he himself went mad, but was subsequently extradited from England and tried by court martial. The house which he built was taken over by Government and now forms the Court of the Commissioner and the Judicial Commissioner, and the extent of the compound can be appreciated by the remains of the two gates which still are to be seen, one on the west side of the Deputy Commissioner's office, and the other about a quarter of a mile south of the jail. Of the other old houses in Rānchi, the principal are that till recently occupied by the Judicial Commissioner, which was built by Captain Hannyington, the first Deputy Commissioner of Chotā Nāgpur (1850 to 1856), and that of the Deputy Commissioner, built by Captain Birch who was Deputy Commissioner in 1862. The bungalow to the north of the office of the Deputy Commissioner was built by Mr. Stainforth, a Civilian, who retired to Rānchi and played a remarkable part in the economic development of the district, by starting tea cultivation at Hotwar in 1862, and by giving considerable impetus to the lac industry by the establishment of a lac factory at Doranda. The present office of the Deputy Commissioner, a long low red-brick building, was built in 1882, and since that date numerous other offices have been erected in its neighbourhood, while houses for Government officers have been built on the open high ground to the north. The selection of Rānchi as the temporary headquarters of the Government of Bihar and Orissa made it necessary to build houses for the Lieutenant-Governor and the officers of Government. A Government House was erected in the compound of the Judicial Commissioner's house and, though a temporary structure, contains a fine Darbar Hall.

The other buildings of importance in Rānchi are those of the Missions. The Lutheran Mission occupies a fine site in the centre of the town, and a cross in the compound marks the spot where the first missionaries pitched their tents in 1845. Six years later the foundation-stone of the first Christian Church in Chotā Nāgpur was laid, and the substantial Gothic edifice of Christ Church which was built by the pioneers of the German Mission, mainly with their own hands, was consecrated in 1855. On the mutiny of the Rāmgarh infantry and the disaffected zamindārs of the district, the Mission compound was pillaged and guns brought to bear against the church. A shot, fired by the mutineers, is still visible in the tower, half embedded in the stonework.

In the compound of the English Mission stands the stately brick church known as St. Paul's Cathedral. The church was designed by General Rowlatt, the Judicial Commissioner, and consists of a lofty nave, the roof of which is supported on strong stone pillars, connected by Gothic arches, and two side aisles. The Chancel is separated from the nave by a high arch and terminates in a capacious apse. At the west end is a tall well-proportioned spire, which is a conspicuous landmark from many miles around. The cost of the church (Rs. 26,000) was met mainly by public subscriptions; the European inhabitants of Rānchi collecting Rs. 7,000, to which Colonel Dalton, the Commissioner, contributed over Rs. 3,000. The foundation-stone was laid by Colonel Dalton in September 1870 and the building was consecrated in March 1873.

The Roman Catholic Mission, which settled in Rānchi in 1887, has acquired a large site on the Purūlia Road. The Catholic Church, with its two steeples 107 feet high, is a large and conspicuous building. It was begun in 1906 and completed in 1909. The plans were prepared, and the work of erection supervised, by one of the lay-brothers of the Mission. All the skilled workmen employed on the building were aborigines trained by the Brother himself. The church is in the simple but effective Roman style. It is 206 feet long and 76 feet broad. The body of the church 125 feet long, with its central nave, 40 feet broad, and two side aisles, each 15 feet broad, can accommodate a large native congregation, while the spacious sanctuary lends itself well to the solemn ceremonies of the Catholic Church. Besides the church and Manresa House, the residence of the Jesuit Fathers, there is a Convent. Handsome and spacious buildings have also been recently erected for the High School.

Besides these buildings there are the Hospital, the new Zila School, the Training School for teachers, and the Jail. Five miles north of Rānchi, a large central Lunatic Asylum for Europeans from Northern India is nearing completion, while the construction of an Asylum for Indians from the provinces of Bengal and Bihar and Orissa has been sanctioned.

Rānchi, though not a commercial or manufacturing centre, is a large trading centre both for the district and the Feudatory States to the west. Rice, oil-seeds, and timber are exported in large quantities and cloth, salt, oil and manufactured articles are imported. The opening of the railway has increased the trade of Rānchi and has also made the town a favourite health resort for Indian gentlemen from Calcutta and elsewhere. The population has risen by more than 20,000 in the last forty years, from 12,086 in 1871 to 32,994 in 1911, and since that year it has risen still further by the influx of officers, clerks, and menials employed in the Secretariat, and by a corresponding increase in the number of traders and merchants. The population, as might be expected, is for the most part alien, and of the total population over 17,000 are Hindus and over 7,500 Muhammadans. The Christian population numbers 5,312, of which a large proportion are the pupils of the Mission Schools. Non-Christian aboriginals number only 2,156 and are either servants, or the descendants of the original inhabitants of the villages of which the town is composed.

The soil is clay mixed with gravel and sand. The climate is extremely healthy and pleasant, the mean temperature varying from 62° in December to 88° only in May and, though the rainfall is considerable (58 inches), the natural drainage of the town is so good that even after the heaviest storm the rain is soon carried away. The atmosphere is consequently very dry.

The town is well served with metalled roads, lined with avenues of shady trees. The Rānchi-Chaibassa road passes through the main bazar, and the Rānchi-Hazāribāgh and the Rānchi-Pūruliā roads branch off to the east from the centre of the town.

Rānchi was constituted a Municipality in 1869, and an account of the Municipal administration is given in the chapter on Local Self-Government.

Rānchi is the headquarters of the Chotā Nāgpur Light Horse, which is attached to the Presidency Brigade of the Lucknow Division. The regiment, formerly known as the Chotā Nāgpur Mounted Rifles, was formed by Mr. Grimley, the Commissioner, in 1885, and now consists of four squadrons and two infantry companies. No. 1 troop of "A" Squadron is composed of volunteers from the Rānchi district.

Ranchi or **Sadr Subdivision**, lies between 22° 21′ and 23° 43′ N. and 84° 0′ E. and 85° 54′ E. and comprises the whole of the north of the district, with an area of 2,054 square miles and a population of 526,172. It contains the following thānas :—Lohardagā, Kuru, Burmu, Māndar, Bero, Lāpung, Rānchi, Ormānjhi, Angara, and Silli. The subdivision consists of the undulating country of the central plateau, the hills which fringe the north and north-west of the district, and the lower plateau on the east. Of the total area, 1,121 square miles are under cultivation, and 620 square miles only under jungle, while the percentage of rice lands to the total area (22) is considerably higher than in the Gumlā Subdivision (13), or in the Khunti Subdivision (19). The population consequently, is considerably more dense than in the other two subdivisions and averages 256 to the square mile. Apart from Rānchi, Lohardagā is the only town. The chief village bazars are at Silli and Jonha on the Rānchi-Purulia line and at Nagri ten miles west of Rānchi.

The Orāons, who occupy the centre and west of the Subdivision are most numerous in Lohardagā, Māndar, and Rānchi thanas ; the Mundās are numerous in the south and east, and Kurmis form a large proportion of the population of Silli thana. A large percentage of the Orāon population has become Christian. Apart from the central Mission stations at Rānchi, there are stations of the Roman Catholic Mission at Māndar, and Dighiā, of the Lutheran Mission at Lohardagā, and of the S. P. G. Mission at Itki in Bero thana.

Communications in the sadr subdivision are good, as the main roads (Rānchi-Purūlia, Rānchi-Hazāribāgh, Rānchi-Chaibassa, and Rānchi-Lohardagā) pass through it.

Simdega, a village in thana Kochedegā and pargana Biru, is the headquarters of the subdivision of that name, opened in 1915. An account of the subdivision is included in the account of the Gumlā subdivision.

Sonapet, a valley about seven miles long by six miles wide lying in the extreme south-east of Khunti Subdivision, 28 miles south of Tamār. This area, which is almost entirely surrounded by the Dalmā trap, has long been known to contain gold, but from the recent investigations of experts it appears very doubtful whether its extraction, either from the alluvium or from any of the quartz veins, can ever prove remunerative. Companies have been formed at various times to extract the gold, but have met with no success and their derelict buildings are still to be seen in the valley. Women still wash for gold in the alluvial sand of the Sonā *nadi* and, if they are lucky, extract gold worth from one to two annas a day. It is said that, before proceeding to work, they divest themselves of all their clothes in the hope that the god, seeing their destitute condition, may take pity on them and help them to secure the precious metal. Three miles from Sonāpet there is a small factory for burning out soap-stone for the Calcutta market.

Sutiambe, a village of 15 inhabitants close to Pithauria, about 10 miles north of Rānchi. It is believed to be the original home of the Nāgbansi Rājās of Chotā Nāgpur. At the Ind festival held annually in *Bhado* at places which are, or have been the headquarters of a Rājā, two giant umbrellas attached to a pole 40 feet long are erected in commemoration of the Nāgbansi Chiefs. At Sutiambe, however, the first umbrella is raised in honour of Madra, the reputed Mundāri foster-father of the first Nāgbansi Rājā, whose descendants are still the Bhuinhārs of the village and enjoy considerable local influence, which they sustain by performing the festivals in commemoration of their former power.

The following legend of the origin of the Nāgbansis is widely known in the district and is given in the "Kursināma" of the Chotā Nāgpur Rājā, submitted in 1794 to the Governor General by Mahārājā Dhirip Nāth Sahi. "In the Pauranik era when Rājā Janmejaya was seeking to destroy the whole race of serpents, by the celebration of Sarpa-yajna, because one had killed his father, one, by name Pundarika Nāg, escaped and, assuming human form, married Parvati, the daughter of a Brāhman of Benares. Pundarika, however, was unable to get rid of his serpent's tongue which not long after attracted the notice of his wife. Parvati became inquisitive about it, and, to divert her mind, Pundarika took her on a pilgrimage to the great temple of Jagarnath at Puri. On their way back they passed through Jhārkand and on their arrival at a jungle near Sutiambe hill Parvati was found to be in the throes of child-birth. She once more questioned the Nāg about his serpent's tongue and he revealed his identity and disappeared in his proper form into a tank close by. Parvati, stricken with grief, gave birth to a son and immediately afterwards created a funeral pyre and immolated herself as a *Sati*. Pundarika, attracted by the child's cries, rose out of the water and protected the child from the sun's rays by spreading his hood over him. Just at this time arrived a Sakaldwipi Brāhman carrying an idol of Surya-devata, the sun-god, and, placing his idol by the pool, went to quench his thirst, but on his return he found he could not raise the image from the ground. Looking round for some explanation of this, he caught sight of the child protected by the cobra. The snake revealed himself to the Brāhman as Pundarika Nāg and prophesied that the child, who was to be named Phani Mukut Rai, was destined to be the Rājā of the country, that the Brāhman was to be his priest and the sun-god his tutelary deity. The Nāg then disappeared and the Brāhman, taking charge of the boy, delivered him over to Madra Mundā, the Rājā or Mānki of the *patti* in which Sutiambe was situated. Madra brought up the boy with his own son and, when both were grown up, he called an assembly of all the Mānkis and Parha Rājās to decide which of the two should be their Chief. Various tests were carried out to decide which was the best. The Mundā boy showed himself slovenly in his dress, undiscriminating in his choice of food and unable to ride a horse and the assembly unanimously decided that Phani Mukut Rai should be Rājā. Phani Mukut invited Brāhmans and other Hindu castes to his palace but as he was reputed to be the son of a Mundā, he had great difficulty in obtaining the daughter of a Rājput as his wife. A marriage was at last arranged with the daughter of the Sikharbhum Panchete Rājā after Pundarika Nag had himself appeared to convince the Rājā's priest of the purity of his son's lineage."

The story given in the Kursināma agrees generally with the legends of the Mundās and Orāons, but also contains many interpolations of a later date. Thus the account contains an explanation of the origin of Brāhman priests of the Mahārājā's family and also seeks to show that Phani Mukut was Rājā not only of the central pargana of Nāgpur but also of the adjacent countries of Rāmgarh, the Five Parganas and Barwe, of which the possession was then disputed. Though the chronicle fixes the date of this event as Sambat 121, or 64 A.D., Phani Mukut is said to have visited the court of the Emperor Akbar at Delhi! According to the genealogical tree of the family, the present Mahārājā is the 61st in descent from Phani Mukut and, allowing an average of 25 years for the reign of each Rājā, the reign of the first Rājā would be fixed as at the end of the 4th century A. D.

Sutiambe is said to have been the seat of the family for four generations, the fourth Rājā, Partab Rai, removing to Chutiā, but the traces of an ancient palace appear to indicate a longer period of occupation.

Sutiambe and Pithauria were, till the settlement of 1894, one village. Pithauria must at one time have been an important market as it was on the main road between Hazāribāgh and Rānchi but it is now of little importance. The pargana was formerly in possession of a Bhogtā family but was resumed in 1884 by the Mahārājā on the failure of male heirs. The Parganāit Jagatpāl Singh rendered assistance to the British at the time of the Mutiny by defending the *ghāt* against the mutinous troops who were advancing from Hazāribāgh, and thus diverting them from their march on Rānchi.

Tamar, a village and extensive thana and pargana in the south-west of the district. Pargana Tamār is one of the Five Parganas and is owned by Tikāit Upendra Nāth Sahi Deo, locally known as Rājā. The family which is very old, is Mundā in origin, but like many others in the district has become Hinduized and now claims to be Rājput. The estate was formerly practically independent and paid some tribute to the Feudatory State of Māyurbhanj in Orissa.

Tilmi, a village in pargana Sonpur and thana Karra of the Khunti subdivision, contains the remains of a fortress of the Nāgbansi Thākurs. On the mouth of a stone well, within the *enceinte* of the fort, is a Sanskrit inscription, written in the Devnagri character, to the effect that the well was dedicated in Sambat 1794 (A. D. 1737) by one of the Thakurs, named Akbar "for the attainment of the four *vargas* or beatitudes". The adoption of the Muhammadan name, Akbār, by the Nāgbansi Hindu is curious but not unprecedented.

B. & O. G. P. (P. A. & E.) No. 156—453—27-2-1917—W.D.

INDEX.

A

	Page.
Aboriginal tribes	62
Administrative staff ...	203
Agariā language	60
Agriculture	111, 120
Persons engaged in— ...	169
Agricultural Association ...	120
Akhrā	58
Ancestor worship	92, 95
Animism	90
Asurs	20, 80
Asur legend	20, 93
Asurī language	60
Asylums	107

B

Barwe	241, 242
Barwe Estate, origin of— ...	189
Begāri	153, 154
Bengal-Nagpur Railway ...	180, 181
Beth Kheta lands...	147, 148
Bhadoi crops	115
Bhogtās	84
Bhuinhāri lands, register of—	44, 45
Bhuinhāri tenancies ...	147, 148
Bhuiyās	85, 86
Binjhiās	84, 85
Birhors	81
Birsa Mundā	49
Rising of—	50, 51
Birsaites	90, 91
Birth rate	102
Biru	242
Bongās	93, 94
Brit tenures	190, 191
Bundu	243

C

Camac, Captain	28
Cattle	118, 120
Census	55
Cesses	207-8
Chainpur	242
Chatra	29, 42
Chattisā holdings ...	149
Chik Barāiks	89
Chokāhatu	243, 244
Cholera	104
Chotā Nāgpur, Bishopric of—	232
Name of—	2
Chotā Nāgpur Estate, history of—	183—188
Chotā Nāgpur Light Horse ...	257
Church of England Mission, *vide* S. P. G. Mission	
Chutia	244, 245
Civil Justice	209
Climate	16—19
Communications	175—182
Co-operative Societies ...	164—166
Co-operative Store ...	167
Crime	210—213
Criminal Justice	208

	Page.
Cotton	116
Cultivation, methods of— ...	114, 115
Cultivating tenancies ...	148, 149
D	
Dalmā	9
Dalton, Colonel	42, 43
Dāsomghāgh	7
Death rate	103
Deforestation, causes of— ...	124, 126
Effects of—	126, 127
District Board	214—216
Dhāngrāi	159
Dhārwār rocks	8, 9
Dhūmkūria	75
Divorce	71
Doisā	245, 246
Don land	111, 112
Dorandā	246, 247
Dripnāth Sahi, Rājā ...	28
Durjan Sāl, Rājā	26, 245
Dysentery	105
E	
Education	219-223
In Lutheran Mission ...	230
In Roman Catholic Mission	237
In S. P. G. Mission ...	233
Emigration	56
Encumbered Estates Act ...	194
Excise	201—206
Excise duties	187
Exorcism	97, 98
Exports	181, 182
Famine, *vide* Chapter VII.	
F	
Fauna	11—15
Festivals	99—101
Fever	103—104
Five Parganas	189
Forests ...	10, 11, 121—133
G	
Ganpat Rai	42
Geology	8—10
Ghāsis	87
Ghatwāls	210, 211
Gold	171
Gonds	86
Gorāits	87
Gossner's Mission, *vide* Lutheran Mission.	
Government Estates ...	195, 196
Gumlā	247
Sub-division	247, 249
H	
Hindus	61
Hospitals	107, 108
Houses, description of— ...	58
Hundrughāgh	7
I	
Ibrāhim Khān	26
Ichādāg	178
Imports	181, 182
Income-tax	207
Industries	170—172
Industrial population ...	170
Infirmities	106
Irrigation	113

	Page.
J	
Jagarnāthpur	249
Jāgīrs	189, 191
Jhārkhand	1, 25, 121
Jhorās	86
K	
Kānchi river	6
Kārkari river	6
Khariās	77-80
Language of—	61
Khaiwari languages ...	60
Khorposh tenures ...	...
Khukra, Chief of— ...	...
Khunti	...
Khunti Subdivision ...	...
Khuntkātti tenancies ...	...
Kili	...
Kokrāh	...
Koel, South	..
Koel, North	...
Koel insurrection	...
Korkar	...
Korwās	...
Korwā language	...
Kūrūkh language	...
L	
Lac	118, 170—171
Land measurement ...	155, 156
Land Revenue	203
Languages	59, 60
Leprosy	106
Lievens, Reverend Father ...	48, 236

	Page
Lohārs	88
Lohardagā	218, 251
Loknāth Sahi	44
Lunatic Asylums ...	107
Lutheran Mission	39, 40, 225-231
M	
Mahlis	88
Māhto	75, 76
Mānjhihās land	192, 139
Mānki ...	23, 66, 143, 144
Mankipatti	67
Marang buru	5
Markets	172
Measures	173, 174
Military Collectorship of Ramgarh	29
Missions ...	39, 40, 44, 224—240
Muhammadan castes ...	61, 62
Muhammadan rule ...	25—27
Mundā ...	23, 62, 143, 144
Mundās ...	21, 24, 62-71, 91—95
Mundāri language ...	60
Municipalities	216-218
Murhu	251
Mutiny	40—43
N	
Nāgbansi family, tradition of—	24
Nāgesiās	82
Nāgpheni	251
Nāgpur name	2
Nāgpuriā language	59
Netarhāt	180
Newspapers	223

O

	PAGE
Orāons ...	21, 22, 72—77
Religion of— ...	95-101
Opium	206, 207

P

Pachwāi	205, 206
Pāhān ...	23, 65, 75, 76
Pālkot	252
Panchāyat ...	66, 67, 76, 77, 79
Pāns	89
Parha	23, 66 ,73
Pasridār	159
Pāts	252, 253
Patti	23, 66
Police	209
Police, Rural	209
Population ...	55
Density and growth of— ...	55
Post Offices	182
Praedial condition ...	150
Prices	160
Push-push	176

R

Rabies	106
Railways	180-182
Rainfall	18, 19, 113
Rājādera	3, 6
Rājhās land	149
Rakumāts	151,.153
Rāmgarh Battalion ...	40
Rāmgarh district ...	29
Rānchi town ...	216, 217, 253-257
Rānchi subdivision ...	257

	PAGE
Rautiās	82—84
Reafforestation	132
Registration	208
Rents	155-157
Incidence of—... ...	157
Produce	157
Revenue	203
Collection of— ...	186
History of—	184, 186
Rice, cultivation of— ...	114, 145
Price of—	160
Roman Catholic Mission ...	48, 235—240

S

Sadnighāgh	7
Sagar	177
Sāl	10
Sale of holdings, restriction on—	162
Sāmbar	14
Sankh river	6
Sardārs, agitation of— ...	46-47
Surnā	58
Saru Pahār	5
Schools	219-223
Mission	230, 233—237
Semi-Aboriginal castes	62
Service tenures ...	189
Incidents of	191
Settlement operations ...	201
Silk	118
Simdegā	258
Subdivision	258, 54
Small-pox	105
Soil	113
Sonāpet	258
South-west Frontier Agency,	36
Abolition of	39
S. P. G. Mission... ...	231-434
Stamp revenue	207
Subarnarekhā river ...	5, 6

	Page
Sugarcane	116
Survey	199-201
Sutiambe	258-260
T	
Tamār	260
Tāṅr land	112
Tea	117
Temperature	17
Tenancy legislation ...	196, 199
Tenures	188, 192
Thanas, establishment of— ...	31, 209
Tilmi	261
Tobacoo	116
Trade, centres of— ...	172
Trees, fruit	117, 10—11
Tuberculous diseases ...	105
Turis	81
U	
Ungulata	14
Union Committees ...	110
V	
Vaccination	109
Vegetables	116, 117
Vehicles	176
Veterinary Dispensary ...	120
Village, description of— ..	57, 58
Vital statistics	102, 103
W	
Wages	158, 159
Weaving	171
Weights and measures ...	173
Wilkinson, Captain ...	34, 35
Witchcraft	97, 99
Z	
Zamindari Police ...	37, 38

DISTRICT GAZETTEERS OF INDIA {IN 245 BINDINGS}

ASSAM DISTRICT GAZETTEERS

11 VOLUMES

ISBN: 9788121286053 (HB Set)
Price: 13000/

BENGAL DISTRICT GAZETTEERS

52 VOLUMES

ISBN: 9789362084484 (HB Set)
Price: 50000/

GAZETTEER OF THE BOMBAY PRESIDENCY

27 VOLUMES (IN 35 BINDINGS)

ISBN: 9788121285612 HB Set
Price: 125000/

CENTRAL PROVINCES DISTRICT GAZETTEERS

30 VOLUMES (IN 33 BINDINGS)

ISBN: 9789362085139 (HB Set)
Price: 47000/

MADRAS DISTRICT GAZETTEERS

23 VOLUMES (IN 25 BINDINGS)

ISBN: 9789362081605 (HB Set)
Price: 47000/

PUNJAB DISTRICT GAZETTEERS

36 VOLUMES (IN 37 BINDINGS)

ISBN: 9789362082480 (HB Set)
Price: 65000/

RAJPUTANA DISTRICT GAZETTEERS

3 VOLUMES

ISBN: 9789362084347 (HB Set)
Price: 9000/

District Gazetteers of India
{In 245 Bindings}
(Rs. 530000/- Hardcover)
(Rs. 370000/- Softcover)
Crown Size

UNITED PROVINCES OF AGRA AND OUDH DISTRICT GAZETTEERS

49 VOLUMES

ISBN: 9789362083111 (HB Set)
Price: 118680/